CW00417791

1 MONTH OF
FREE
READING

at

www.ForgottenBooks.com

By purchasing this book you are eligible for one month membership to ForgottenBooks.com, giving you unlimited access to our entire collection of over 1,000,000 titles via our web site and mobile apps.

To claim your free month visit:
www.forgottenbooks.com/free105069

ISBN 978-1-5282-7510-1
PIBN 10105069

LAWS OF MEXICO

OFFICIALLY AUTHORIZED BY THE MEXICAN GOVERNMENT

CONTAINING THE FEDERAL CONSTITUTION, WITH ALL
AMENDMENTS, AND A THOROUGH ABRIDGMENT OF
ALL THE CODES AND SPECIAL LAWS OF IMPORT-
ANCE TO FOREIGNERS CONCERNED WITH BUSI-
NESS IN THE REPUBLIC. ALL ACCURATELY
TRANSLATED INTO ENGLISH. AN EXTEN-
SIVE COLLECTION OF FORMS BOTH IN
SPANISH AND ENGLISH. A MINUTE
INDEX OF ALL MATTER CON-
TAINED IN THE TEXT

BY

JOSEPH WHELESS

OF THE ST. LOUIS, MISSOURI, BAR

Member of the St. Louis, the Missouri and the American Bar Associations; Counsel of
the Consulate of Italy in St. Louis; Associate Editor of the Bulletin of the Com-
parative Law Bureau of the American Bar Association, and one of the Revisors
of the Government Translations of the Spanish Codes for Cuba and the
Philippines; Member of the American Society of International Law;
Correspondent of the Instituto Ibero-Americano de Derecho
Positivo Comparado, of Madrid, Spain

OFFICES IN ST. LOUIS AND THE CITY OF MEXICO, D. F.
(MEXICO) 2A SAN JUAN DE LETRÁN, No. 29
ST. LOUIS, MO., SUITE 907 CARLETON BLDG.

VOL. 2

ST. LOUIS
THE F. H. THOMAS LAW BOOK CO.
1910

BOOK XII.
FOREIGNERS, NATURALIZATION AND COLONIZATION.

TITLE I.

LAW OF FOREIGNERS AND NATURALIZATION.

(Ley de Extranjería y Naturalización, de 28 Mayo, 1886.)

CHAPTER 1.

MEXICANS AND FOREIGNERS.

Art. 822. Mexicans — Who Are.
    823. Foreigners — Who Are.
    824. Diplomatic and Seaborn Persons — Corporations.

Art. 822. Mexicans — Who Are.— Mexicans are: 1, Those born within the national territory of Mexican father either by birth or naturalization; 2, those born within such territory, of a Mexican mother and of a father not legally known according to law or born of parents unknown or of unknown nationality; 3, those born without the Republic of a Mexican father who has not lost his nationality; if lost, his children will be regarded as foreigners, but they may adopt Mexican nationality within one year after they become 21 years of age, upon making the requisite declaration before the Mexican diplomatic or consular agent, if they reside out of the country, or before the Department of Foreign Affairs, if they reside in it. If such children reside in the country, and upon becoming of age accept any public employment, or

51424

serve in the army, navy or national guard, they will be considered by such acts as Mexicans without necessity of other formalities; 4, those born without the Republic, of a Mexican mother, if the father is unknown, and the mother has not lost her nationality according to law; if the mother has become naturalized in a foreign country her children will be foreigners; but they may become Mexicans upon the terms and conditions stated in clause 3; 5, those Mexicans who, having lost their nationality according to this law, recover it by complying with its requirements, as the case may be; 6, the foreign woman who shall marry a Mexican, such Mexican nationality being retained even during her widowhood; 7, those born out of the Republic, who, residing within it in 1821, swore to the Act of Independence, have continued to reside in the country and have not changed their nationality; 8, those Mexicans, who, residing in the territories ceded to the United States by the Treaties of 2 February, 1848, and 30 November, 1853, complied with the conditions required by said Treaties in order to preserve their Mexican nationality; likewise those Mexicans who continue to reside within the territory belonging to Guatemala, and those citizens of that Republic who remain in those belonging to Mexico, according to the Treaty of 27 September, 1882, provided such citizens comply with the terms of **Art.** 5 of said Treaty; 9, foreigners who become naturalized according to the present law; 10, foreigners who acquire real estate in the Republic, provided they do not declare their intention of preserving their nationality; at the time of making the acquisition, the foreigner must declare to the Notary or Judge acting as Notary, whether he desires or not to obtain the Mexican nationality conferred by Sec. III of **Art.** 30 of the Constitution, the foreigner's declaration on this point being stated in the deed; if he chooses Mexican nationality, or omits to make any declaration on the subject, he may apply to the Department of Foreign Relations within one year, in order to comply with the requirements of **Art.** 828, and be held as a Mexican; [1] 11, foreigners who have children born in the Republic, provided they do not prefer to retain their foreign nationality; at the time of making the registry of the birth, the father shall declare before the Judge of the Civil Register his intention on this subject, which shall be entered on the record; and if he chooses Mexican nationality, or omits to make any declaration on the subject, he may apply within one year to the Foreign Department, in order to comply with the requirements of Art. 828, and be held as a Mexican; 12, foreigners who shall officially serve the Mexican government, or who accept from it titles or public functions, provided that within a year from any of these things they apply· to the Foreign Department for the purposes stated in Section 11, *supra*. (Art. 1.)

Art. 823. Foreigners — Who Are.— Foreigners are: 1, Those born without the national territory, who are subject of foreign governments and have not become naturalized in Mexico; 2, the children of a foreign father, or of a foreign mother, or of a foreign mother and unknown father, born within the national territory, until they shall reach the age at which, according to the law of the nationality of the father or of the mother, respectively, they would attain their majority; if within one year from attaining their majority, they shall not have declared before the political authority of the place of their residence that they retain the nationality of their parents, they shall be considered as Mexicans; 3, those who absent themselves from the country without license or commission from the government, or on account of studies, public interests or business, and who remain away ten years without asking license to prolong their absence, which licenses shall not exceed five years each time applied for, and good cause having to be shown to obtain

[1] This Sec., 10, and the next, 11, are in evident conflict with the constitutional precept referred to, which in terms imposes Mexican citizenship on the foreign persons indicated, *ipso facto* upon failure to make the declaration of retaining their previous nationality.

remaining foreigners even during widowhood; but if the marriage be dissolved, she may recover her nationality by establishing residence in the Republic and making declaration before the Judge of the civil status, at her place of residence, of her desire to recover her nationality; the Mexican woman who does not acquire the nationality of her husband by marriage, according to the laws of his country, retains her own; the change of the husband's nationality, after marriage, involves the change of that of his wife and minor children subject to the *patria potestad,* if they reside in the country wherein he becomes naturalized, except when the woman does not acquire her husband's nationality, as just above stated; 5, Mexicans who become naturalized in other countries; 6, those who enter any department of service of a foreign government without the license of Congress; 7, those who accept foreign titles, decorations and employment, except literary, scientific and humanitarian titles, without leave of Congress.[2] (Art. 2.)

Art. 824. Diplomatic and Seaborn Persons — Corporations. — National ships of every class are declared to be part of the national territory, and persons born on board of them are to be considered as born within the Republic. The children of diplomatic representatives and attachés, born abroad, are always Mexicans, upon the principle of extraterritoriality. The nationality of moral persons or corporations is governed by the laws creating them, so that those organized under Mexican law are Mexicans, provided they have their legal domicile in the country. Foreign " moral persons " or corporations enjoy in Mexico the rights granted to them by the laws of the country in which they are created, so long as these are not contrary to the Mexican laws. (Arts. 3–5.)

[2] See Const., Art. 34.

CHAPTER 2.

EXPATRIATION.

Art. 825. Right — Incidents.

Art. 825. Right — Incidents.— The Mexican Republic recognizes the right of expatriation as natural and inherent in all men and as necessary to the enjoyment of personal liberty, and therefore permits its inhabitants to exercise that right and leave the country and establish themselves in foreign countries, and also protects the right of foreigners of all nationalities to come and establish themselves within its jurisdiction, and to be received and naturalized according to the law.

But expatriation and naturalization in a foreign country do not exempt criminals from extradition and from the trial and punishment to which they are subject according to treaties, international practices and the laws of the country. Naturalized Mexican citizens, although in a foreign country, have the right to the same protection from the Mexican government, both in their persons and property, as citizens by birth; but should they return to the country of their birth they shall be liable to any responsibilities which they may have incurred, according to the laws of such country, before their naturalization. The Mexican government will protect its citizens in foreign lands by all means authorized by international law short of acts of hostility; but if diplomatic means are not sufficient, or the wrongs to Mexican nationality are so grave as to demand more severe measures, the President will lay the whole record before the Congress for its action.

The naturalization of a foreigner becomes ineffective by his residence in his native country for two years, unless in the discharge of some official commission of the Mexican Government, or with its permission. (Arts. 6–10.)

CHAPTER 3.

NATURALIZATION.

Art. 826. Who May Become — Application.— Any foreigner who complies with the requirements of the law may become naturalized in Mexico. At least six months before applying for naturalization, he must present to the Municipal Council (*Ayuntamiento*) of his place of residence, a written petition declaring his wish to become a Mexican citizen and to renounce his nationality; the original of this petition will be filed, and a certified copy issued to him. After the expiration of the six months, and when the foreigner shall have completed two years of residence in the Republic, he may petition the Federal Government to grant him a certificate of naturalization; absence in a foreign country with the permission of the Government for not more than six months during the two years, does not interrupt the residence required by law. The applicant must first appear before the Judge of the District in whose jurisdiction he is and offer to make proof of the following facts: 1, That according to the laws of his native country he is in the full enjoyment of civil rights by reason of being of legal age; 2, that he has resided for at least two years in the Republic and been of good conduct; 3, that he has a trade, business or **profession**, or income by which to live. To this petition presented to the District Judge, shall be attached the certified copy of the original petition above mentioned, together with an express renouncement of all submission, obedience and **fidelity** to every foreign government, and especially to that to which the applicant has been subject; of all protection foreign to that of the laws and authorities of Mexico, and of all rights which treaties or international law grant to foreigners. (Arts. 11–14, 20.)

Art. 827. Procedure on Application.[3]— The District Judge, upon the ratification by the applicant of his petition, shall order the hearing of witnesses upon the points proposed, with the assistance of the *Promotor Fiscal,* and he may ask the *Ayuntamiento* for a report on the original application, and hear any other proofs offered, and take the opinion of the *Promotor Fiscal.* If the decision of the Judge is favorable to the applicant, he will remit the original record to the Department of Foreign Relations, that it may issue the certificate of naturalization, if in its judgment proper; and the applicant shall present to the Department, through the District Judge, a petition requesting the certificate of naturalization, ratifying his renouncement of his nationality, and affirming his adhesion, obedience and submission to the laws and authorities of the Republic. (Arts. 15–16.)

Art. 828. Special Naturalization.— Foreigners who have served in the national merchant marine may become naturalized after one year's service, making their application to the District Judge of any port at which the ship may touch, and their declaration before the *Ayuntamiento* of such port. The formalities prescribed to the two preceding Articles do not apply to the naturalization of those classes of persons mentioned in clauses 3, 4 and 6 of Art. 822 and in clauses 2 and 4 of Art. 823, who become naturalized by force of law, or who have the right to choose Mexican citizenship, who are held to be naturalized to all legal intents upon the simple compliance with the requirements prescribed in regard thereto. Those foreigners who come within the terms

---

[3] Suits concerning naturalization and the rights of citizenship are governed by the new Federal Code of Civil Procedure, Arts. 643–648.

34

of clauses 10, 11 and 12 of **Art.** 822, must apply to the Department of Foreign Relations for their certificates of naturalization within the terms therein fixed, accompanying their application by the document which proves their acquisition of real estate, the birth of children in Mexico, or their acceptance of a public employment, as the case may be, together with the renouncement of nationality and oath of allegiance as required in ordinary cases.   (Arts. 17–19.)

Art. 829.   Naturalization — Effects and Incidents.— Certificates of naturalization will be issued gratis, without costs of any kind.   The act of naturalization being strictly personal, the applicant can only appear by attorney with special and sufficient power for this act, which shall contain the renouncement and oath of allegiance which must be made by the applicant personally as required by the law, but in no case can the actual residence of the applicant in the country be dispensed with.   The status of native or foreigner cannot be transferred to third persons, so that a native cannot enjoy the rights of a foreigner, nor the latter those of the former, because of one or the other status.   The change of nationality produces no retroactive effects; and the acquisition or rehabilitation of the rights of a Mexican takes effect only from the day after all the formalities required by law have been fully complied with.   Certificates of naturalization will not be issued to citizens of any country with which Mexico may be at war, nor to those suspected or convicted in other countries as pirates, slave-traders, incendiaries, counterfeiters, assassins, kidnappers and thieves.   Every naturalization obtained fraudulently and in violation of **law** shall be totally null and void.   (Arts. 19, 21–26.)

Art. 830.   Colonists — Status.— Colonists who come to the country by virtue of contracts with the Government, and whose expenses of travel and establishment are paid by it, **are** regarded as Mexicans.   Their declaration of intention ·

to renounce their original nationality and to adopt the Mexican, shall be set forth in their contract of joining the enterprise, and upon the establishment of the colony, the renouncement and oath of allegience required by law shall be taken before the proper authority, and remitted to the Ministry of Relations for the issuance of the certificate of naturalization to the interested party. Colonists coming to the country on their own account, or that of private enterprises not subsidized by the government, as well as all classes of immigrants, may become naturalized according to the law, which is also applicable to existing colonists so far as it may not conflict with acquired rights. (Arts. 27–28.)

Art. 831. Effects of Naturalization.— The naturalized foreigner shall become a Mexican citizen as soon as he meets the conditions required by Art. 34 of the Constitution, sharing fully all the rights and obligations of Mexicans, except that of holding office or employments which according to the laws require nationality by birth, unless he was born in Mexico and his naturalization effected in conformity with clause 2 of Art. 823. (Art. 29.)

CHAPTER 4.

RIGHTS AND OBLIGATIONS OF FOREIGNERS.

Art. 832. Civil and Property Rights.
    833. Residence —·Subjection to Law.
    834. Political Disabilities — Expulsion.
    835. Matriculation — Certificates of Nationality.

Art. 832. Civil and Property Rights.— Foreigners in Mexico enjoy the same civil rights as Mexicans, and the guaranties secured by Section I, Title I, of the Constitution, saving the right of the Government to expel pernicious foreigners.[4] It is not necessary that foreigners reside in Mexico

---

[4] See Constitution, Art. 11.

in order to acquire public lands, real estate and ships, but they are subject to the restrictions imposed on them by law, and every lease of real estate made to a foreigner for a term exceeding ten years will be regarded as a sale. The Federal law only can modify and restrict the civil rights enjoyed by foreigners, upon the principle of international comity, in such way that they shall be subject in Mexico to the same disabilities as may be imposed by the laws of their country upon Mexicans residing therein; therefore the provisions of the Civil and Civil Procedure Codes of the Federal District upon this subject shall have the character of Federal laws and be obligatory throughout the country. (Arts. 30–32.)

Art. 833. Residence — Subjection to Law.— Foreigners may reside in Mexico without losing their nationality, the acquisition, change and loss of domicile being governed by the Mexican laws. Should the individual guaranties be suspended as provided in Art. 29 of the Constitution, foreigners are subject the same as Mexicans to the terms of the law declaring the suspension, except as may be provided by treaty. Foreigners are bound to contribute to public expenses as provided by law, and to obey and respect the institutions, laws and authorities of the country, and to submit to the decisions and judgments of the courts, without attempting other recourses than are by the laws granted to Mexicans; they can only appeal to diplomatic intervention in the event of denial or willful delay in the administration of justice, after vainly exhausting the ordinary recourses created by law, and in the manner sanctioned by international law. (Arts. 33–35.)

Art. 834. Political Disabilities [5] — Expulsion.— Foreigners are not entitled to the political rights of Mexican citizens,

5 See, generally, as to rights of foreigners under the Constitution, Arts. 8, 9, 11, 15, 30–38.

can neither vote nor be voted for or hold any public office, nor belong to the army, navy or national guard, nor assemble to discuss the political affairs of the country, nor exercise the right of petition in political matters, except they be naturalized as hereinbefore provided. They are exempt from military service, but domiciled foreigners must render police service when required for the safety of property and the preservation of order in the place in which they reside. Foreigners taking part in the civil dissensions of the country may be expelled from its territory as pernicious, but are subject to the laws for any crimes they may commit against the Republic, and during a state of war their rights and obligations may be regulated by international law and treaties; this law does not confer on foreigners any rights denied them by international law, treaties or existing legislation. (Arts. 36–38, 40.)

Art. 835. Matriculation — Certificates of Nationality.— The matriculation of foreigners is abolished. Only the Department of Foreign Relations can issue certificates of foreign nationality to foreigners requesting them, which certificates constitute presumption of foreign citizenship, but do not exclude proof to the contrary; such proof must be made before competent tribunals and in the manner prescribed by law or treaty.[6]   (Art. 39.)

[6] See note to Art. 827.

TITLE II.

COLONIZATION.

(Ley de Colonizacion, de 15 de Diciembre de 1883.)

CHAPTER 1.

SURVEY OF LANDS.

Art. 836. Survey and Sale of Lands.

Art. 836. Survey and Sale of Lands.— For the purpose of obtaining lands necessary for the establishment of colonists, the Executive will order the survey, mensuration, subdivision and appraisement of the public lands in the Republic, appointing such commissions of engineers for the purpose as he may deem necessary and determining the system of the operations to be followed. The tracts laid out are not to exceed twenty-five hundred hectares, which is the largest amount which can be sold to one person, of lawful age and capable to contract.

Such lands shall be granted to foreign immigrants and to the inhabitants of the Republic who wish to settle on them as colonists, on the following conditions:

1, By sale, at the appraised value made by the engineers and approved by the Department of Fomento, on installments payable in ten years, beginning after the second year after the colonist is established; 2, by sale for cash, or on less time than above provided; 3, gratuitously, if so solicited by the colonist, but in such cases the tract cannot exceed one hundred hectares, and title cannot be obtained until the colonist proves that he has remained in possession of the land, and has cultivated at least one-tenth of it, for five consecutive years.

The Executive will determine what lands should be colonized at once, and will publish plans of the same and the prices at which they will be sold,[1] selling only alternate tracts, and reserving the remainder to be sold on the conditions herein prescribed, when solicited or when directed to be sold by the Executive, who may mortgage them for the purpose of obtaining funds which, together with the proceeds of sales of the lands, will be devoted exclusively to the purposes of colonization. (Arts. 1–4.)

CHAPTER 2.

COLONISTS.[2]

Art. 837. Requirements — Certificates.
838. Privileges and Exemptions.
839. Duties of Colonists — Loss of Rights.
840. Other Grants and Aids to Colonists.

Art. 837. Requirements — Certificates.— To be considered a colonist and enjoy the privileges granted by this law, foreign immigrants must bring a certificate of the consular or immigration agent, issued at the instance of the immigrant himself, or of a Company or concern authorized by the Executive to bring colonists to the Republic. If the soliecitant resides in Mexico, he must apply to the Department of Fomento or to the agents authorized by it to admit colonists, in the several colonies established in the Republic. All solicitants must present certificates from the respective authorities showing their good character and their occupation prior to the application. (Arts. 5–6.)

Art. 838. Privileges and Exemptions.— Colonists locating in Mexico shall enjoy for ten years from the date of their settling the following exemptions: 1, Exemption from military service; 2, exemption from all kinds of taxes except municipal; 3, exemption from import and internal duties

---

[1] See Tariff of Prices for Sale of Public Lands, Art. 872.
[2] See Art. 830.

on provisions, where there are none, on farm implements, tools, machines, chattels, building materials, furniture for use, and breeding or blooded animals, intended for the colouies; 4, personal and untransmissible exemption from export duties on the products which they raise; 5, rewards for notable works and premiums and special protection for the introduction of any new cultivation or industry; 6, exemption from fees for the legalization of signatures and issuance of passports by consular agents, to persons coming to Mexico as colonists under contract between the Government and any company. The Department of Fomento will determine the amount and kinds of articles which may be brought in free of duties in each case; [3] and the Department of Hacienda will make regulations in regard to the manner of bringing them in, so as to prevent frauds and contraband, but without hindering the prompt dispatch of the articles.[4] Colonists settling on treeless lands, who plant at least one-tenth of the tract with trees in a number proportionate to its area, more than two years before the expiration of the term of exemptions, shall be entitled to one additional year of exemption from taxes on the whole tract for each tenth part thereof which they devote to the cultivation of forests. (Arts. 7-9.)

Art. 839. Duties of Colonists — Loss of Rights.— Colonies must be established under a municipal form of government, subject in regard to the election of their officers and the laying of taxes to the general laws of the Republic and of the State in which they are located; but the Department of Fomento may appoint agents in the colonies in order to better direct their works and to enforce the payment of any amounts due to the Government. The colonists are bound to comply with their contracts with the Federal Government, or with private persons or companies who brought and established them in the country.

[3] See Free List, Art. 845.
[4] See Arts. 846-847.

Every foreign colonist must make a declaration in the act of settlement, before the federal colonization agent or the proper notary or judge, of whether he intends to retain his nationality or wishes to acquire Mexican nationality as conferred by Art. 30 of the Constitution; colonists have all the rights and obligations granted or imposed by the Constitution on Mexicans and foreigners, as the case may be, and are entitled to all the temporary exemptions granted by this law, but in all questions arising from any cause they are subject to the decisions of the Mexican tribunals, to the entire exclusion of foreign intervention.

Colonists who abandon the lands sold to them for more than one year, 'and before paying for them, without good cause proven, lose all rights to said lands and to all amounts paid; where the land was donated gratis as above provided, they lose the land by abandoning or failing to cultivate it for six months without just cause. (Arts. 10–14.)

Art. 840. Other Grants and Aids to Colonists.— In places designated by the Government for new towns, a lot of land will be granted free to Mexican or foreign colonists who wish to locate therein as founders; but they will not acquire title to such lot, but will lose all rights to it, if they do not prove the erection of a residence thereon within two years after their establishment; such grants will be of alternate lots. Mexicans residing abroad who wish to settle in the uninhabited places along the frontiers of the Republic, are entitled to a free grant of not to exceed two hundred hectares, on the conditions above prescribed, and to the exemptions herein granted, for fifteen years.

The Executive may aid colonists or immigrants, in proper cases and within the amount allowed by the appropriation laws for the purpose, by payment of the costs of transportation for themselves and their equipage by sea and into the interior as far as the railroads extend, with gratuitous maintenance for fifteen days, in the places which he may determine, and with tools, seeds, building materials and animals for work and breeding, the amount of such advances to be repaid in the same way as the price of the land. (Arts. 15–17.)

CHAPTER 3.

COLONIZATION COMPANIES.

Art. 841. Survey of Lands — Conditions and Terms.
   842. Contracts for Colonization — Conditions.

Art. 841. Survey of Lands — Conditions and Terms.— The Executive may authorize Companies to open up public lands (*terrenos baldíos*), upon condition of making their measurement, survey, subdivision into lots, appraisement and description, and to transport and settle colonists upon said lands; to obtain such authorization the companies must designate the lands which they wish to open up, with their approximate area and the number of colonists they will settle on them in a given time; such authorization becomes ineffective and not subject to extension, unless the operations thereunder are begun within the unextendable term of three months.

The proceedings for the survey will be authorized by the District Judge within whose jurisdiction the land lies, and when concluded, if there is no *opositor,* the records will be delivered to the company to be presented to the Department of Fomento, together with the Executive authorization above referred to; but if there is opposition, the proper suit will be proceeded with, a representative of the Treasury Department being a party thereto. As compensation for the works done, the Executive may grant the companies not to exceed one-third of the land or its value, but on condition that they cannot transfer the same to foreigners not authorized to acquire them, nor in greater parcels than twenty-five hundred hectares, under penalty of forfeiture to the Government of the lands conveyed in contravention to these restrictions.[5] The lands surveyed by the companies, except the part so granted to them in compensation, will be granted to the colonists or reserved, on the terms and conditions prescribed in Art. 836 above. (Arts. 18–23.)

Art. 842. Contracts for Colonization — Conditions.— The Executive may enter into contracts with companies or concerns for the introduction and settlement in the country of foreign colonists and immigrants, on the following conditions: 1, The companies must fix a specific time within which they will bring in a certain number of colonists; 2, the colonists or'immigrants must comply with the requirements of Art. 776 above; 3, the terms of all contracts made between the companies and the colonists must conform to the provisions of this law and be submitted for approval to the Department of Fomento; 4, the companies must guarantee to the satisfaction of the Executive the performance of the terms of their contracts, in which the grounds of forfeiture and fines must be set out.

Companies making such contracts with the Executive shall enjoy for a term not to exceed twenty years the following franchises and exemptions: 1, Sale at long time and low price of public lands for the sole purpose of colonization; 2, exemption from all taxes except stamp tax on the capital invested in the enterprise; 3, exemption from port duties, except those laid for improvements in said ports, on ships bringing in on behalf of the companies at least ten families of colonists; 4, exemption from import duties on tools, machines, construction material, and draft or breeding animals intended exclusively for an agricultural, mining or industrial colony authorized by the Executive;[6] 5, bounty for each

[5] This prohibition on sale is repealed by Art. 8 of the Land Law of 26 March, 1904, herein contained in Art. 849.

[6] Such exemption is subject to the provisions of the Regulations of 17 July, 1889. See Arts. 845–847.

family established, and a less bounty for each family dis-
embarked, and a bounty for each Mexican family established in a colony of foreigners; 6, transportation of the
colonists at the Government's expense on the subsidized
steamship and railway lines.

Foreign colonization companies will be considered always
as Mexican, and must have a domicile in some city of the
Republic, in addition to such as they may have elsewhere,
and are obliged to have in Mexico a part of their Board of
Directors and one or more attorneys-in-fact amply empowered
to negotiate with the Executive. All questions arising between the Government and the companies shall be decided
by the Mexican tribunals, according to the laws, without any
interference therein by foreign diplomatic representatives.
(Arts. 24–27.)

CHAPTER 4.

MISCELLANEOUS PROVISIONS.

Art. 843. Private Enterprises — Conditions.
    844. Colonization of Islands.

Art. 843. Private Enterprises — Conditions.— Private persons may set aside all or a part of their own lands for colonization by at least ten families of foreign immigrants, who
shall have the same franchises and exemptions as those established by the Government, provided they subject themselves
to the conditions fixed by the Executive to insure the success
of the colony, one of which conditions shall always be that
each colonist is to acquire by purchase or grant a lot of land
for cultivation; the Executive may also provide foreign
colonists to such individuals, stipulating with them the conditions on which they are to be settled, and may aid them
with the costs of transportation of the colonists. The Execu-

tive is authorized to acquire private lands by purchase or grant, where deemed advisable, in order to establish colonies thereon, subject to the appropriations made for such purpose by the law. (**A**rts. 28, 30.)

Art. **844.** **Colonization of Islands.**— The Executive may colonize the islands in both seas under the provisions of this law, reserving to the Government an area of fifty hectares on each island for public uses; if the island is too small to allow of such arrangement, no lands on it will be sold, but they may be leased for short terms. In all colonies established on islands there must always be a number of Mexican families not less than one-half the total number of colonizing families. (Art. 29.)

CHAPTER 5.

REGULATIONS IN REGARD TO COLONIZATION.

(*Reglamento de* 17 *Julio de* 1889, *sobre Franquicias concedidas á los Colonos por la Ley de* 15 *Diciembre de* 1883.)

Art. 845. Imports Exempt from Duty.
　846. Free Importation — How Secured.
　847. Duties of Agents — Frauds.

Art. 845. **Imports Exempt from Duty.**— Pursuant to the provisions of the Law of 15 December, 1883, the following articles for the use of colonists and recognized Companies, are free of duty:

FOOD STUFFS.

Oil, garlic, dry peas, rice, oats, common and refined sugar, coffee of all classes, salted and smoked meats, hams, barley, onions, beans, fruits and fresh vegetables, ordinary crackers, chick peas, wheat flour and that of cereals of all classes, con-

densed milk, lentils, corn, lard, butter, ground mustard, pota-
toes, pastries, pepper, common or table salt, tea of all classes,
vinegar in earthen, glass or wooden receptacles.

STONE AND EARTH.

Clay piping, bricks other than refractory, paving flags and
slate tiles of all classes and dimensions worked on one face
only, except those of marble or alabaster, grinding or whet
stones, plain glass for windows and doors, sulphate of lime.

WAGON MATERIAL.

Wheel-barrows or hand carts of all classes; carts and wagons
of all classes and sizes; iron and steel axles and separate
wheels for the same.

LEATHER GOODS.

Common harnesses for carts and wagons.

DRUGS, starch.

IRON, STEEL AND OTHER METALS.

Woven wire for fences; hooks and door-latches; iron and
brass hinges of all classes; iron, steel or brass key-hole
plates, without plating or gilding; iron, steel, brass, copper
or bronze locks of all classes; nails, brads, tacks, screws,
bolts and nuts, and rivets of iron or zinc; channel iron and
sheet iron for roofs; bellows for chimneys; tools and iron,
brass, steel or wooden implements, or composed of these materials, as well as stakes and handles for tools; iron ovens for
cooking and stoves with the corresponding iron pipes; iron
shoes for animals; wind-mills, of iron or wood, or of both materials, for drawing water from wells; iron beams for the construction of houses; corrugated zinc for roofs; machinery and
accessories.

MISCELLANEOUS ARTICLES.

Geldings; brooms; ordinary lumber; hair for plastering; doors and windows of wood, and of wood and glass; tents and tent-poles.

The colonists may also bring in free of duty, once for all, their new or used furniture and household stuff, if of ordinary quality according to the condition of the colonist; the Department of Fomento will determine what colonies shall have the right to bring in provisions free of duty for such time and on such conditions as may be deemed proper, as provided in the law. (Arts. 1–3.)

Art. 846. Free Importation — How Secured.— Free importations under these Regulations or under the General Customs Tariff, may be made by recognized colonists directly or through the agencies of the colonization companies, or through commission agents, under the following conditions: The colonists or their agents must apply to the proper agent of the Department of Fomento, requesting the importation of the articles which they need, which are free under the regulations or tariff, with a list in duplicate, detailing clearly the kind and quality of effects which they wish; if this list is approved by the Agent, he will endorse his authorization on it, and forward one copy to the customs house through which the importation is to be made, keeping the other copy in his files, and sending another to the Department of Fomento, and will issue a certificate to the applicant as his voucher; if there is no Agent, the Department may authorize some federal employé to act as such. Such importations must come in a consular invoice containing no other goods which are subject to duty; when the importation is made, the Agent or the colonists will make out the petitions required by the tariff law for forwarding the articles, which will be presented to the customs house, and if found to correspond with the document authorized by the Agent of Fomento, the goods will be delivered, but if there is any difference, **the** provisions of Art. 388 of the tariff law on the subject will **be** followed. (Arts. 4–7.)

Art. 847. Duties of Agents — Frauds.— The colonization agents must give notice in advance to the agents of Fomento of the expected arrival of colonists at the places where they are to enter the country, so that the customs houses may **be** notified, in order that no difficulty may be had in regard to the forwarding of the effects when they arrive; the names of the colonists must be stated in said notices. The **Agents** of Fomento must not permit colonists to bring in **more** goods than is strictly necessary; should any colonists or their agents abuse the concession made them by selling or trading in the goods admitted free of duty, the Agent of Fomento or **A**dministrator of Customs will at once notify the District Judge, who will investigate the matter and if a crime has been committed, will proceed to punish it according to the law. Details of duties of the **A**gents of Fomento and their records are omitted. (Arts. 8–13.)

BOOK XIII.
LAND AND WATER LAWS OF MEXICO.

TITLE I.

- LAND 'LAWS AND AMENDMENTS.[1]

(*Ley sobre Ocupación y Enajenación de Terrenos Baldíos de los Estados Unidos Mexicanos, de 26 Marzo, 1894.*)

CHAPTER 1.

PUBLIC LANDS AND GENERAL RULES FOR THEIR OCCUPATION
AND ALIENATION.

'Art. 848. Classification — Definitions.
    849. Lands Subject to Acquisition.
    850. Lands Exempt from Acquisition.
    851. Leases and Contracts.
    852. Effects of Grant.

Art. 848. Classification [2]— Definitions.— All lands of public ownership affected by this Law are divided into four classes: 1, *Baldíos;* 2, *Demasías;* 3, *Excedencias;* 4, *Terrenos nacionles,* or national lands. *Baldíos* are all public lands which have not been devoted to public uses by the proper legal authority nor granted upon onerous or lucrative title to indi-

---

[1] The Regulations of this Public Lands Law bear date 5 June, 1894; owing to their great length, and to the fact that the Lands Law is pending extensive amendments, as indicated in Art. 867, the Regulations are herein omitted.

[2] See Art. 867, frac. I. amending this Classification.

35

viduals or corporations. *Demasías* are lands held by private persons under original grants, but in excess of the extension called for by the patents, provided that such excess is within the boundaries called for in the patent. 3. *Excedencias* are lands held by private persons for twenty years or more, outside of but lying alongside the boundaries of their original grants. 4. National lands are those *baldíos* which have been officially selected, surveyed and measured, but have not been legally granted, also *baldíos* which have been denounced by private persons but abandoned after survey and measure. (Arts. 1–5.)

Art. 849. Lands Subject to Acquisition.— Every inhabitant of the Republic, of legal age and capacity to contract, may denounce *baldíos, demasías* and *excedencias,* as herein provided, in any part of the Republic and in any amount, except native and naturalized citizens of the countries bordering on the Republic, who by no kind of title may acquire *baldíos* in the border States. The privileges herein granted do not remove the limitations imposed by existing laws upon the acquisiton by foreigners of real property in the Republic. Former requirements upon holders of *baldíos* to keep them settled, demarked and cultivated, and those forbidding surveying companies to sell lands held by them except in certain instances, are abolished, together with all penalties and forfeitures.[3] *Baldíos, demasías* and *excedencias* can only be acquired by denouncement and in the manner herein provided, and at prices fixed by the Executive, and all those held for twenty years or more by private persons without original grant, but under conveyances of title emanating from private persons or public authority not authorized to grant *baldíos,* may be acquired in the same manner or by arrangements made directly with the Department of Fomento as herein provided. National lands can only be disposed of by said Department at

---

[3] The prohibition here repealed is that of Art. 21 of the Colonization Law of 15 December, 1883, herein contained in Art. 841.

the prices and on the terms fixed in each case in view of the quality, location and use of the lands, which prices can never be less than the current tariff prices for *baldíos,* and lands can never be granted gratuitously except for public uses, rewards for services or otherwise as expressly provided by law. The tariff of prices for *baldíos* in each State and Territory will be fixed each year by a decree of the Executive published in January, and in force during the fiscal year;[4] of the price received for lands sold two-thirds will be paid into the Federal Treasury and one-third into that of the State where the land lies, but neither can refuse to accept their own evidences of public debt which may be tendered them in payment by the purchaser; the entire price of lands located in the Federal District and Territories goes into the Federal Treasury. (Arts. 6–13.)

Art. 850. Lands Exempt from Acquisition.— Neither by grant nor prescription can title be acquired to the following, the dominion of which shall remain always in the Federation: **1,** The sea shore; 2, the maritime zone extending twenty meters from the highest tide mark and along the coasts of mainland and islands; 3, a zone of ten meters on both banks of navigable and of five meters on floatable rivers; 4, lands on which monumental ruins are found, with such extension as is deemed necessary to preserve them. *Baldíos* on islands in both oceans may be acquired the same as on the mainland, but in addition to the maritime zone a tract of at least fifty hectares will be reserved for settlement and other public uses, but if the island is not so large it will all be reserved; islands in navigable rivers, lakes and inlets cannot be acquired except after expert examination and reports from the chief political authority of the State, District or Territory showing that there is no objection to the alienation; inlets, lagoons and ponds which are not and cannot become navigable, and marshes, may be acquired upon like

----

[4] See Tariff of Prices, Art. 872.

conditions together with the report of the proper naval authority; lands wanted for salt-pits may also be acquired as herein provided, but the Fomento may have them specially appraised and sell them at higher than tariff prices if deemed advisable. (Arts. 14–17.)

Art. 851. Leases and Contracts.— The Department of Fomento may enter into leases or other contracts for the exploitation of *baldíos* while they are not taken up, as well as make regulations for the exploitation of woods, resins or other products of such lands and providing penalties for their infringement, besides the penalties prescribed by law for entering or exploiting *baldíos* without permission. Such leases may provide that the lessee may acquire the lands preferentially (by the *derecho del tanto*) when another person denounces them, if he makes use of the right within one month, and reimburses the denouncer for the costs of denouncement, measure and survey of the land. Such contracts cannot prevent the granting of the lands and they must be delivered to the denouncer within six months from the issuance of his title; all permits granted will also cease upon the land being granted, and the licensee can only recover the part of the consideration paid proportioned to the unexpired time. (Arts. 18–19.)

Art. 852. Effects of Grant.— The adjudication or grant of public lands under the proceedings herein established, vests the title of the land in the grantee as against the Nation and private persons who have acquiesced in it or who having made opposition have been judicially defeated; but as against third persons who have not been heard, the ownership is only acquired by prescription or other legal title.

The Executive may temporarily reserve such *baldíos* as he may deem advisable for the conservation or planting of woods, Indian reservations, or colonization, as provided by law. (Arts. 20–21.)

CHAPTER 2.

MANNER OF ACQUIRING PUBLIC LANDS.

Art. 853. Land Agents — Denouncements.— For the purpose of disposing of public lands the Department of Fomento will establish the Agencies with one or more Agents and deputies for each, in the several States, Territories and Federal District, particularly defining the districts in which they are to act; they will receive no salary but will collect fees in accordance with the tariff to be issued by the Department. An applicant (*denunciante*) for public lands must present to the Agent in the district where the land lies, a written denouncement, in duplicate, in which the location of the land and its boundaries must be accurately described. Upon presentation of the denouncement, the Agent will register it in a special book, and will record the day and hour of its filing in the book and on the denouncement and its duplicate, returning the latter to the applicant as an evidence of his rights; within fifteen days afterwards the Agent will ascertain whether the land denounced has been surveyed or is reserved for any purpose, and if not, he will admit the denouncement and proceed with it as provided in the administrative regulations; the Agent will not proceed with denouncements presented in regard to lands already patented or denounced, but will record them, and his decision is subject to review by the Department as provided in the regulations. (Arts. 22–26.)

Art. 854. Proceedings Under Denouncements.— Every de-

nouncement of public lands must be published in the office of
the Agency and in the official newspaper of the State, District or Territory where the land lies, for the time and in the
form prescribed by the regulations; the applicant must pay
all the expenses of publication, and of the measurement and
survey of the land, which must be made in every case, upon
notice to the adjoining owners, by a qualified expert appointed by the applicant with the approval of the Agent.   If
the *baldío* denounced is surrounded entirely by lands not
baldío, it may retain whatever shape it has; but if not so
bounded, the new sides laid out must be straight and the
angles as nearly right angles as possible; if entirely surrounded by other *baldíos,* its figure must be a square.
Where the *baldío* denounced adjoins lands not *baldío,* the line
of the latter will be taken as the line of the land denounced,
or a clear distance of not less than one kilometer will be left
between them both, as the applicant may prefer.   When the
survey is finished, a plan of the land made, and the terms
fixed by the regulations passed without any oppositor presenting himself, the Agent will make copies of the record and
plan, and forward them to the Department of Fomento,
through the medium of the Governor of the State, who will
make such report on it as he deems proper; the Department
of Fomento, upon examination of the record and plan and
after finding that all requirements have been complied with,
will adjudicate the land to the applicant, and will notify
him to pay the price of the land so that the proper patent
of title may be made to him, such notice being given through
the Agent before whom the denouncement was made, if the
denunciant does not reside or has no representative at the
Capital.   The price to be paid will be that fixed by the tariff
then in force, and must be paid within two months after
the adjudication, whereupon on presentation of the vouchers
of payment the patent or title will be executed and delivered;
if payment is not so made the applicant loses his rights and
the land will be incorporated among the national lands; it

may also be declared national land and the adjudication to the denunciant refused by the Department if desired to be reserved or for other public use, upon refunding to the denunciant all expenses incurred in the denunciation; adjudication may also be refused of lands denounced along a water course where the grant would cut off access of adjoining owners to the water, and lands along a water course should be laid out so far as possible so that all may have access to the water. (Arts. 27–32, 36.)

Art. 855. Oppositions — Judicial Proceedings.— If opposition is presented affecting the whole of the land denounced, formulated in such way that a determined area cannot be specified, the Agent will at once suspend the proceedings; but if the opposition relates only to a clearly specified part of the land, the proceedings will continue as to the part not embraced in the opposition, and the proper judicial procedure will be begun as to the part affected, before the District Court of the State, District or Territory where, the land is situated; such suit will be conducted in accordance with the procedure in summary suits in federal matters,[5] the Fiscal Promoter appearing as representative of the public *Hacienda,* and judgment in the second instance shall be final. Such final judgment will award the costs of the suit, and a certified copy will be forwarded to the Land Agent to be added to the administrative record; if entirely adverse to the denunciant, the denouncement will be dismissed so far as it affects the rights of the oppositor; if adverse to the latter, the denouncement will proceed as if no opposition had been made. The proceedings under a denouncement can only be suspended or the time extended, in case of an opposition and not otherwise; when the time is expired, the Agent must forward a certified copy of the record to the Department of Fomento so that it may declare the denouncement abandoned or impose any penalty incurred by

[5] See Federal Code of Civil Procedure, of 1908, Arts. 590–598.

the Agent; an applicant who has been declared in default cannot again denounce the same land within one year after his first denouncement was declared abandoned. (Arts. 33– 35, 37.)

Art. 856. Special Proceedings with Department.— *Excedencias* and *demasías* of a property, as well as *baldíos* improperly held by private persons as hereinbefore specified, may be acquired by denouncement as above provided, or by direct application to the Department of Fomento, which is authorized to enter into any arrangement or settlement which it deems to the interest of the Nation, either declaring that there are no *baldíos, excedencias* or *demasías* within the limits of a property or by adjudicating to the owner any which there may be; but no such arrangement can be made, until: Plans of the land have been made by a titled expert as required by the regulations and approved by the Department, and positive proof is made that every adjoining owner approves the boundaries shown by the plan, or that, if any objection was made, it has been settled by a final judgment; such proof may be made by *escritura pública* duly executed or by appearance before a judge of first instance or the Land Agent in the district where the land lies; the original grants or later deeds of conveyance in legal form must also be presented to the Department, together with the latest conveyance of title, duly recorded in the Register of Property of the place wherein the land lies, and the original or a certified copy of the report rendered to the proper District Court evidencing the possession of the land or of the *excedencias* or *demasías* during the time required by this law. Upon compliance with these requirements, the Department may declare that no *baldíos* exist within the limits of the property, or may adjudicate any such *baldíos, excedencias* or *demasías* to its owner, upon payment of the price fixed in the tariff in force when the application was made, less the rebates allowed by Art. 857 to persons in possession.

National lands may be sold by the Department, for cash or on time, and at prices to be agreed upon, but not less than the tariff rates at the time of sale; if sold on time the title will not be issued until the price is entirely paid. (Arts. 38–41.)

Art. 857. Rebates to Possessors — Preëmption.— A rebate of sixty-six per cent. of the tariff price will be made to those in possession of *demasías;* of fifty per cent. to those in possession of *excedencias* and of *baldíos* under color of title for more than twenty years; and of thirty-three per cent. to those in possession of *baldíos* under color of title for more than ten but less than twenty years. The possessor shall also have the right to be preferred in case such lands are denounced by third persons, provided he exercises the preëmption before the record is forwarded by the Agent to the Department and repays the denunciant all expenses incurred in the denouncement. (Arts. 42–43.)

Art. 858. Prescription of Baldíos.— Former laws prohibiting prescription of *Baldíos* are repealed, and henceforth any person not forbidden by law, may acquire by prescription not more than five thousand hectares of *baldío* lands under the terms of the Federal Civil Code.[6] (Art. 44.)

CHAPTER 3.

GRAND REGISTER OF PROPERTY.

Art. 859. Establishment — Public.
860. Effects of Registration.
861. Registration — How Made.
862. Changes of Ownership — Subdivision.
863. Tax on Registration.

Art. 859. Establishment — Public.— There is established the Grand Register of Property of the Republic,[7] which shall

[6] See Arts. 284–292.
[7] See Art. 867, frac. XII.

be in charge of an Office of the Department of Fomento, and in which shall be recorded with such requisites and formalities as prescribed by this law and the regulations, the original titles of *baldíos* and national lands and those issued by virtue of arrangements made or hereafter made with the Department of Fomento; the Register shall be public and anyone may examine it and secure certified copies of the entries and plans recorded in it. The Keeper of the Grand Register will give a bond of not less than $10,000 for damages which may be caused to the public *Hacienda* or to private persons by fraud or omissions in the inscriptions which he makes, but he shall have the right to make objections to the decisions by which inscriptions are ordered made, and his liability shall only cease where in spite of them the order is repeated. (Arts. 45–46, 62.)

Art. 860. Effects of Registration.— Inscription in the Grand Register is entirely voluntary for the owners and possessors of lands, who lose none of their rights by failure to make such inscription, but they can enjoy none of the privileges granted to registered properties. Every property so registered will be considered by the Federal Government as perfect, irrevocable and exempt from every kind of revision, the simple certificate of registration being conclusive on all government authorities and agencies, which cannot at any time require the production of the original titles, or subject them to any kind of inquisition or revision, nor is the area of the land inscribed subject to any rectification. Property so protected cannot be denounced, and any denouncement will be declared ineffective upon presentation of the certificate of registration, such declaration being however subject to review by the Department of Fomento as hereinbefore provided; in respect of adjoining owners the certificate has the same legal effect as a valid and perfect title so long as the inscription is not declared void or modified by a final judgment obtained by such adjoining owner. The validity of an inscription cannot be questioned by anyone who himself or through those under whom he claims, had consented to the boundaries fixed in the plan presented for registration, or who, having made opposition before registration, has been defeated by a final judgment; but the boundaries of such properties are subject to be identified in proper cases by the government agents or by private persons interested therein. (Arts. 47–52.)

Art. 861. Registration — How Made.— No registration of lands or property can be made except upon express authority from the Department of Fomento, which must be filed with the plan of the property. Every inscription shall contain: 1, The name 'of the applicant; 2, the name by which the estate or land is known or which is given to it by the owner; 3, the location of the land, stating at least the State, District, Cantón and Municipality; 4, the boundaries on all sides, with reference as far as possible to fixed points of easy identification or to solid and permanent artificial landmarks; 5, the date and abstract of all the original titles of ownership which serve as the foundation of the inscription; 6, date and abstract of the last deed of conveyance of title executed in favor of the applicant for registration; 7, literal copy of the decision of the Department of Fomento ordering the inscription; 8, such other data as the regulations may require.

The Department of Fomento cannot order the registration of a property until the following requirements are complied with: 1, Declaration by the Department that all interests of the government in respect to the land in question are satisfied; 2, presentation of the last conveyance in favor of the applicant, duly registered in the district where the land lies; 3, presentation of a plan of the land as required by the regulations; 4, proof of the consent of adjoining owners to the boundaries established in the plan, or of final judgment against their opposition, in the form hereinbefore provided. Each inscription must embrace only one estate or property, and cannot include several separate tracts, although belonging to the same owner.   (**Arts.** 53–56.)

Art. 862. Changes of Ownership — Subdivision.— The certificate of registration is effective although the property passes to other owners; but the latter may present to the Grand Register a public instrument, duly registered in the district where the land lies, proving their lawful succession in title, and have the certificate changed to their name.   Where a registered tract of land or property is divided, the fact will be noted on the original entry and plan, and a new inscription will be opened for each part which has passed to the new owner, and a plan of such part must be presented and filed.   Except by transfer and subdivision, an inscription can only be altered or cancelled by virtue of a final judgment of a competent federal judge or tribunal of the place where the land is located decreeing that the inscription is void or should be modified; the only legal cause for such decree is proof that the inscription was procured by error, deceit or fraud or without complying with the requirements of the law; the Fiscal Promotor shall always be a party and be heard in such suits.   The Department of Fomento must notify the Land Agents of all inscriptions of lands within their respective districts so that no denouncement of any part of the same will be allowed.   (Arts. 57–60.)

Art. 863. Tax on Registration.— Inscription in the Grand Register of Property is subject to a tax payable in stamps, which must be affixed to the book in which each inscription is made, according to the following tariff: Tracts of less than 10,000 hectares, at the rate of one cent per hectare, but such tax cannot be less than $2; between 10,000 and 50,000 hectares, one cent per hectare on the first 10,000, and one-half cent per hectare on the excess; for tracts of more than 50,-000 hectares the above rates will be paid on the first 50,000, and one-fourth cent per hectare on all the excess; the foregoing taxes will be paid but once, but additional rates payable also in stamps, may be established by the Department, for certified copies of inscriptions, and for the entries made on them in cases of change of owner or division of property. (Art. 61.)

CHAPTER 4.

GENERAL PROVISIONS.

Art. 864. Prior Titles — Validity.
    865. Surveyors — Denouncements.
    866. Corporations — Town Lands and Commons.

Art. 864. Prior Titles — Validity.— All titles issued by competent authority, according to the laws, and especially those issued since the law of 20 June, 1863,[8] went into effect, are declared exempt from all revision and composition, and are expressly confirmed and ratified so far as the interests of the public Treasury are concerned, and the same cannot hereafter be nullified or modified except for error or fraud established by final judgment of the competent tribunals of the Federation; but said titles only protect the lands within the superficial area to which they refer, and the boundaries therein established, and cannot be extended to any others. Likewise and on the same terms are confirmed and ratified all grants made by the Department of Fomento by way of compositions, and the declarations of said Department to the effect that specified properties do not embrace public lands. Every original title to *terrenos baldíos,* issued by competent authority and in conformity with the requisites of the laws in force at the time the same was issued, is valid and binding, and does not require any revision, ratification or confirmation of any kind, provided said title conforms

---

[8] The law of 20 June, 1863, governed the matter of *baldíos* and public lands up to the date when the present law of 26 March, 1894, was enacted.

with the superficial area and boundaries therein fixed for the land, or that any defects therein have been cured by composition with the competent authority; but lands inscribed in the Grand Register of Property are not affected by this requirement, their owners only being required to permit the identification of their boundaries as provided in Art. 860. All contracts and arrangements made in regard to public lands by officials not authorized by law to make them are entirely void and do not in any way affect the public Treasury. (Arts. 63–65, 71.)

Art. 865. Surveyors — Denouncements. — Surveyors engaged in the survey of public lands are civilly liable to the Treasury Department for all damages caused by their negligence or want of skill in the discharge of their office, besides the penalties to which they are liable for deceit or fraud according to the penal laws. No one can oppose the survey or mensuration of land or the performance of any other act ordered by competent authority necessary to ascertain the truth or legality of a denouncement, but if the land is adjudged not to be *baldio* in whole or part, the owner is entitled to indemnity for all damages caused by the denouncement, besides the criminal action which lies according to law; the foregoing rule does not alter the provisions of **Art.** 860 in regard to lands inscribed in the Grand Register. The mere denouncement of public land does not carry the right to take possession of it, which is only conferred by the issuance of the proper title in accordance with the requirements of this law. (Arts. 66, 72–73.)

Art. 866. Corporations — Town Lands and Commons. — Civil communities and corporations are prohibited from and incapable of holding real estate. The State governments, aided by the Federal authorities, will continue to lay out, subdivide and adjudicate among the inhabitants of the towns the lands which form the commons (*ejidos*) and the surplus of the town lands (*fundo legal*) ; the details of this procedure are omitted, as of no general concern. The Department of Fomento will issue Regulations for the exploitation of forests and public lands (*baldíos*) temporarily reserved.[9] (Arts. 67–70.)

TITLE II.

AMENDMENTS TO LAND LAWS.

CHAPTER 1.

BASES FOR REFORMATION OF LAW.

(Law of 30 December, 1902, as Amended by Decree of 26 December, 1905.)

Art. 867. Nature and Extent of Proposed Amendment.

Art. 867. Nature and Extent of Amendment.— The Federal Executive is authorized to reform the existing legislation in regard to public lands (*terrenos baldíos*), in accordance with the following Bases:

I. The classification made by the law of 26 March, 1894, into *baldíos, nacionales, demasías* and *excedencias,* is repealed, and only one class called *baldíos,* as established in Base III, and as defined in said Law, *ante,* Art. 848, will be recognized; but the lands embraced in the original title will be considered protected by it, although the identity of the boundaries and of the lands within the boundaries indicated in said title is not strictly preserved, and although they embrace an area greater than the title calls for. (Amendment of 26 December, 1905.)

II. In a separate Article there shall be enumerated the lands which are considered as taken out of the ownership (*salidos del dominio*) of the Nation, and which cannot be sold as *baldíos,* including therein lands of whatever extent

---

[9] The Regulations for the exploitation of forests, *baldíos* and national lands, are of date 1 October, 1894.

which have been possessed by private persons within the terms of the Civil Code regarding prescription, as well as those which have been simply occupied for thirty years or more by herds, cultivation or construction, and inclosed by fence, ditch or artificial monuments.

III. All *baldíos,* whether or not comprised within the boundaries indicated in any title, shall be divided, in respect of the requisites necessary to their acquisition, into surveyed and unsurveyed; the former may be sold directly by the Department of Fomento, at prices fixed by it, but not less than the tariff of unsurveyed *baldíos,* and on such terms as the Department may determine in each case; the latter can only be acquired by denouncement or composition made before the officials, and with the requisites, prescribed by law.

IV. The Executive is authorized to cause all public lands (*baldíos*) to be surveyed by official commissions; all laws and regulations authorizing the surveying of such lands by private surveying companies shall be expressly repealed for the future, and subsidies and other obligations payable in such lands shall be prohibited.

V. The Executive is also authorized to issue the proper titles of ownership to the possessors and occupants of surveyed lands in the cases specified in Base II, upon their request and payment of the costs incurred by the Government in making the survey, in proportion to the area solicited.

VI. Possessors and occupants of such lands who are not within any of the cases mentioned in Base II, shall have the right to be preferred in the purchase of the lands which they are possessing or occupying, provided they exercise the right before the lands are granted to another applicant.

VII. Occupants and possessors of unsurveyed lands coming under the terms of the preceding Base, shall have the same right when the land is denounced by another person, provided they exercise the right before the grant is made to the denunciant and pay the costs which he has incurred in the denouncement.

VIII. The provisions of the present law in respect to the validity and force of titles issued by competent authority, and that they shall not be revisable by the Executive except after judgment of the competent Tribunals of the Federation, shall be continued in force, being amplified by the provision that the *baldios* comprised within the boundaries stated in the title shall not be subject to denouncement where they have been possessed for the length of time necessary under the Civil Code for their prescription, in which case such lands will be considered as withdrawn from the national domain.

IX. The Department of Fomento is empowed to declare, on the petition' of any interested party, that any lands are withdrawn from the public domain which are shown to be protected by a title of ownership issued by an authority thereto empowered by the law; such declaration to be made upon presentation of the said title and of the plan and expert report in regard to the land, with the requisites prescribed by the regulations, and from which title and report it appears that the entire tract is covered by the title. Such declaration shall be limited to the fact that the land is withdrawn from the public domain, without reference in respect to the person of the possessor or owner nor to the titles under which he holds.

X. The Department of Fomento is also empowered to declare a *baldío* as withdrawn from the public domain, in favor of a person acquiring it by prescription, provided that upon presentation of the plan and report as above required, it is proven to be in compliance with the conditions of Base II, by means of an *information ad-perpetuam,* or by a final judgment rendered by the Tribunals of the Federation, declaring that the fact of prescription has been proven by the applicant; the law will determine before what authority or offiee such information shall be taken and the requisites of the same. (**A**mendment of 26 December, 1905.)

XI. The Department of Fomento will make up a register

tified copies of the plans and declarations may be issued to any person requesting the same.

XII. The Institution of the Grand Register of Property of the Republic, established by the Law of 26 March, 1894, shall be substantially preserved, but the Department of Fomento is authorized to reorganize the administrative details of the registry, and to bring together under the same organization, said Registry and the other offices, commissions and dependencies regarding the lands and waters of the entire Republic. (Amendment of 26 December, 1905.)

XIII. Unsurveyed *baldíos* which are not possessed or occupied as provided in Base II, may be acquired by denouncement. The proceedings relative to the measurement and survey of the lands denounced will be conducted by the administrative Agents of the Department so long as no opposition is presented to the denouncement, in which event and straightway the proceedings will be transferred to the Judge of the District in whose jurisdiction the land lies.

XIV. Of the proceeds of sale of *baldíos,* surveyed or unsurveyed, one-third shall belong to the State in which they are located, and two-thirds to the Federation.

XV. The Federal Executive may order the temporary reservation of *baldíos* the sale of which is not deemed presently advisable because the same are needed for some public ?, or for colonies, or other public interests, and may temorarily or permanently reserve lands intended for forests.

CHAPTER 2.

SUSPENSION OF DENOUNCEMENTS AND SALES.

(Decree of 18 December, 1909.)

Art. 868. Certain Provisions Suspended.— Pending the reformation of the legislation in regard to public lands (*terrenos baldíos*), in accordance with the bases of the Decree of 30 December, 1902, the provisions of the Law of 26 March, 1894, now in force, so far as concerns the denouncement of *terrenos baldíos,* are suspended; wherefore, the Agencies of the Department of Fomento will not hereafter admit any denouncements of such lands, but will proceed with and finish all denouncements previously made in accordance with said law up to this date. The power granted by the laws to the Executive to sell national lands is suspended until the surveys previously made have been rectified by official commissions. Contracts or promises of sale of *baldíos* and national lands, made under the laws of 15 December, 1883, and 26 March, 1894, will be declared terminated upon the expiration of the periods therein stipulated, and no such contract can be revalidated nor its time extended. (**Arts.** 1–2, 4.)

Art. 869. Contracts of Lease — Terms.— The Department of Fomento may enter into contracts of lease for the exploitation of *baldíos* and national lands, subject to the following bases: 1, The term of lease cannot exceed ten years; 2, the price of lease can in no case be less than five per cent. of the annual value of the land; for such purpose, the *baldíos* will be taken at the valuation assigned to them by the tariff for the current fiscal year, and national lands at the same prices, plus fifty per cent.; 3, the contracts of lease may concede to the lessees the right of preëmption where another wishes to buy the land in accordance with the present law; such right must be exercised by the lessee within one month after notification by the Department of its intention to sell the land. (**Art.** 3.)

Art. 870. Surveys — Reservations. — The Executive, through the Department of Fomento, will order the survey and measurement of all *terrenos baldíos* yet remaining in the Republic, by official commissions paid out of the appropriations for that purpose, and, through said commissions, will proceed to the rectification of the surveys of all national lands, complementing such rectification with the geographical data prescribed by the regulations or administrative orders. The national lands and *baldíos* so surveyed and measured shall be destined preferentially for colonization and other purposes of general interest, reserving such lands as may be adequate for forests. The Executive may sell the lands not destined for the above purposes, but no sale to any one person shall exceed 5,000 hectares. In all sales of lands belonging to the Nation the occupants of the same should be preferred, provided that for ten years or more they have inclosed the lands they occupy with fences, hedges or stakes, or have cultivated or used the same for any agricultural purposes, and have moreover for the last five years paid the taxes imposed on said lands by the respective local laws; such occupation under the above terms must be proven before the Judge of the proper District, after citation to and the attendance of the Ministerio Público, who will be guided by the general or special instructions given by the Department of Fomento. (Arts. 5–7.)

Art. 871. Provisions Continued in Effect.— The provisions of the law of 26 March, 1894, affording possessors of *baldíos* and *demasías* means of perfecting their rights and obtaining lawful titles, are continued in force. The Department of Fomento will continue to effect compositions in respect of such lands which are held under the terms of said law; and said Department is empowered to make such provisions as it deems proper in order that the plans and expert works in general which must be made for the purposes of such compositions, shall conform to new requisites in order to assure their accuracy; in all cases such plans must be made and works must be done by an expert appointed by the Department of Fomento, before the same can be approved. The provisions of law in regard to the subdivision of commons (*ejidos*) are continued in force, but the titles issued by virtue thereof shall impose the obligation of cultivating or making use of the lot during ten years, and shall contain the necessary conditions to the end that the grantee or his heirs-at-law shall only have the usufruct of said land for the term of ten years, without the power to lease or sell the same or grant its use until after such term, during which time neither the land itself nor any of the rights therein granted, shall be subject to embargo by any third party. Violation of these provisions renders the title void, and the Nation may reclaim the land by the preper judicial proceeding, so that it may be granted to the head of a family who possesses the legal qualifications. (Arts. 8-9.)

Art. 872. Tariff of Prices.— For the Sale of Public Lands:

1909–1910. (Sales Suspended.) Hectare.

In the State of **Aguascalientes**	$ 7.00
In the State of Campeche	4.00
In the State of Chiapas	4.00
In the State of Chihuahua	4.00
In the State of Coahuila	4.00
In the State of Colima	6.00
In the State of Durango	4.00
In the State of Guanajuato	12.00
In the State of Guerrero	5.00
In the State of Hidalgo	5.00
In the State of Jalisco	9.00
In the State of Mexico	21.00
In the State of Michoacán	14.00
In the State of Morelos	27.00
In the State of Nuevo León	4.00
In the State of Oaxaca	5.00

In the State of Puebla 11.00
In the State of Querétaro 9.00
In the State of San Luis Potosi 4.00
In the State of Sinaloa 4.00
In the State of Sonora 4.00
In the State of Tabasco 7.00
In the State of Tamaulipas 4.00
In the State of Tlaxcala 17.00
In the State of Veracruz 12.00
In the State of Yucatán 4.00
In the State of Zacatecas 4.00
In the Federal District 100.00
In the Territory of Tepic 4.00
In the Territory of Baja California 2.00
In the Territory of Quintana Roo 2.00

TITLE III.

LAWS CONCERNING WATERS AND WATER RIGHTS.

CHAPTER 1.

PUBLIC WATER WAYS AND RIGHTS THEREIN.

(Law of 5 June, 1888.)

Art. 873. General Ways of Communication.
　874. Regulation — Public and Private Rights.

Art. 873. General Ways of Communication.— Besides the national highways, railroads, etc., the following are general ways of communication under fraction 22 of Article 72 of the Constitution: The territorial seas; the estuaries and lagoons along the coasts of the Republic; the canals constructed by the Federation or with aid from the national Treasury; interior lakes and rivers, if navigable or floatable; lakes and rivers of any class and for their whole length, which serve as boundaries of the Republic or of two or more States of the Union. (Art. 1.)

Art. 874. Regulation — Public and Private Rights.— The guarding and policing of the foregoing general ways of communication depends upon the Federal Executive, who has also power to regulate the public and private uses of the same, on the following bases: a, The towns along their course shall have the free use of the waters needed for the domestic service of the inhabitants; b, the rights of private persons in respect to easements, use and supply of waters created in their favor upon rivers, lakes and canals will be respected and confirmed, provided such rights are founded on lawful titles or civil prescription of more than ten years; c, the concession or confirmation of private rights upon lakes, rivers and canals can only be granted by the Department of Fomento when it neither produces or threatens to produce any change of their course, nor deprives the lower riparian dwellers of the use of their waters; d, fishing, pearl-hunting, and the use and utilization of the estuaries, lagoons along the shores and on public lands, and of the other territorial seas, will be specially regulated by the Federal Executive. Ordinary crimes committed on interior lakes, rivers and canals, and jurisdiction over controversies between private persons in regard to the application of the Regulations issued by the Fomento, belong to the competent local tribunals. (Arts. 2–3.)

CHAPTER 2.

CONCESSION OF WATER RIGHTS.

(Law of 6 June, 1894.)

Art. 875. Concessions — Conditions.
  876. Franchises and Exemptions.

Art. 875. Concessions — Conditions.— The Executive is

authorized in accordance with the present Law and that of 5 June, 1888, to grant concessions to individuals and companies for the better utilization of the waters under federal jurisdiction, for irrigation and as power adaptable to various industries. Such concessions will be granted on the following conditions: 1, Previous publication of the petition in the official newspaper of the Federation and of the proper State; 2, without prejudice of third parties, any oppositions arising being first decided by the competent tribunals; 3, presentation of plans, profiles and descriptive reports for the complete understanding of the projected works, within the time prescribed in the concession; 4, the admission of an engineer appointed by the Executive and paid by the *concessionaire,* as inspector of the work of planning and construction of all the works; 5, making a deposit of bonds of the public debt to guarantee the performance of the obligations contracted by the *concessionaires;* 6, the submission of the tariffs for the sale and leasing of the waters to the examination and approval of the Department of Fomento. .(Arts. 1–2.)

Art. 876. Franchises and Exemptions.— The Executive may grant to the *concessionaires* the following franchises and exemptions: 1, Exemption for five years from all federal taxes except stamp taxes, on the capital employed in laying out, construction and repair of the works defined in the concession; 2, the importation at one time free of duty of the machinery, scientific instruments and apparatus necessary for the laying out, construction and operation of said works; 3, the right to occupy without cost the public lands for the passage of canals, for the construction of dams or 'dikes, and for the formation of deposits; 4, the right of expropriation from private persons because of public utility, upon indemnity and on the same terms as railroads, of the lands necessary for the foregoing uses. The Executive may also grant the free importation of machinery and apparatus necessary for the utilization of water for irrigation or motive·

power, under concessions granted by the States for that purpose, provided the *concessionaires* give security for carrying out their works, and under such rules and limitations as may be prescribed by the Executive, who will also issue regulations for the utilization of waters in the Federal District and Territories, and who may also grant concessions for constructing dams and forming deposits in accordance with the principles of the Civil Code. (Arts. 3–5.)

CHAPTER 3.

STATE CONCESSIONS OF WATER RIGITS.

(Law of 17 December, 1896.)

Art. 877. Revalidation — Conditions.
878. Futuie Concessions.

Art. 877. Revalidation — Conditions.— The Executive will revalidate for this one time the concessions granted up to this date by the State authorities to private persons to utilize the waters of rivers or streams classified as under Federal jurisdiction by Art. 1 of the Law of 5 June, 1888, provided that they comply with the following requisites: 1, That the revalidation be solicited within one year from the promulgation of this law; (other detailed requirements of the petitions and proceedings are omitted, as now of no concern). (Arts. 1–3.)

Art. 878. Future Concessions.— Where concessions are sought from the States in respect to a water course of a doubtful character, whether in regard to its being navigable or floatable, or as to its situation as the probable boundary between two or more States, the State authorities, before granting a concession for the use of its waters, must consult the Federal Government in respect to the definitive character of such water course; concessions made without observing this requirement can hereafter under no circumstances be confirmed. (Art. 4.)

BOOK XIV.

NEW MINING LAW.[1]

(Ley Minera de los Estados Unidos Mexicanos, of 25 November, 1909, effective January 1, 1910.)

CHAPTER 1.

MINING PROPERTY AND ITS CHARACTERISTICS.

Art. 879. Scope of Law — Public and Private Property.
880. Mining Claims — Unit and Extension.
881. Mining Rights — Public Utility.

Art. 879. Scope of Law — Public and Private Property.— The following are of the direct ownership (*dominio*) of the Nation and subject to this law: 1, Deposits (*criaderos*) of all inorganic substances which in veins or masses of any form constitute deposits whose composition is distinct from that of the rocks of the earth, such as those of gold, platinum, silver, copper, iron, cobalt, nickel, manganese, lead, mercury, tin, chrome, antimony, zinc and bismuth ; those of sulphur, arsenic and tellurium ; those of rock salt and those of precious stones ; 2, placers of gold and of platinum. The following are the exclusive property of the owner of the soil: 1, Beds or deposits of all kinds of combustible minerals ; 2, those of bituminous materials ; 3, those of salts which show (*afloren á*) on the surface ; 4, springs of surface and subterranean waters, subject to the provisions of the common law and to

[1] See comparison of the present with the former Mining Law, in the Appendix, Chap. 3, p 981.

the special laws of waters, and to the provisions of Art. 881;
5, the rocks of the earth and materials of the soil, such as
slate, porphyry, basalt and calc (*caliza*), and earths, sands
and clays; 6, bog and drift iron and tin and ochres. The
Department of Fomento may enter into contracts, on such
conditions as may be proper in each case, for the exploitation
of metalic substances found in the beds of waters under Federal jurisdiction, unless otherwise provided in the special laws
of waters. The provisions of the Civil Code in regard to
ordinary property and its subdivisions are applicable to mining property unless otherwise provided herein. (Arts. 1–3,
135.)

Art. 880. Mining Claims — Unit and Extension.— The
unit of mining property is called a "*pertenencia*," which is
a solid of unlimited depth, and limited on the earth by the
four vertical planes corresponding to the projection of a
horizontal square of one hundred meters on each side; [2] it is
indivisible in all acts and contracts concerning its ownership. A mining property, or "*fundo minero*," is one or
more contiguous *pertenencias* covered by the original grant
or by conveyance thereunder. Where it is impossible, in
laying out a mining property, by reason of adjoining properties, to secure the *pertenencias* entire, the surplus (*irre-
ducible*) portion is called *demasía,* and is considered for all
legal purposes, as composed of as many *pertenencias* as there
are hectares embraced in its horizontal projection, and any
fraction of a *hectare* which may result will be considered as
an additional *pertenencia;* where such surplus portion is less
than an *hectare,* it is also called *demasía* and considered for
legal purposes as a *pertenencia;* the form and manner of locating *pertenencias* and *demasías* will be prescribed by the Regulations. (Arts. 4–6.)

Art. 881. Mining Rights — Public Utility.— The owner of
a mining property has the right to extract and make use of all

[2] A mining *pertenencia* contains 10,000 square meters, or 1 *hectare,*
and is equal to 2.47 acres.

the substances above mentioned found on the surface or in the subsoil of his property, but cannot extend his workings beyond its limits although surrounded by free ground; he may also make use of the waters encountered in the workings, and extract and dispose of the same with all the substances which they hold in suspension or solution, but cannot claim indemnity where such waters are exhausted or diminished through the drainage of other mining properties. Where the striking of waters in the interior workings causes the exhaustion or diminution of springs belonging to another owner, the latter may recover the waters belonging to him, provided he does not deprive the owner of the mine of the water he needs for his own work, and the former cannot require indemnity for the same; the conveyance or loss of a mining property carries with it the right to the interior waters. The mine " dumps " constitute an accession of the mining property from which they arise; if their origin cannot be determined, their ownership will be governed by the common law.

The mining industry is of public utility, hence the owners of mining property have the right of expropriation (eminent domain) in the cases and conditions prescribed in this law.[3] (Arts. 7–10, 134.)

CHAPTER 2.

ACQUISITION AND FORFEITURE OF MINING PROPERTY.

Art. 882. Denouncements — What Subject To.— Mining property is acquired originally from the Nation by means

3 *Post,* Arts. 895–896.

of a grant (*título*) issued by the Executive Power through the Department of Fomento, after denouncement (*denuncio*) and the other requisites herein prescribed. Denouncements can only be made on free (i. e., unoccupied) ground; land is not considered free which has already been granted or as to which another denouncement is pending, nor, in the following cases, until after thirty days after the date of posting the proper declaration on the bulletin of the Mining **Agency**: 1, *Pertenencias* the title to which has been declared forfeited; 2, *pertenencias* the denouncement of which has been finally disapproved; 3, *pertenencias* declared free by the Department of Fomento in accordance with this law. A denunciant who has been declared in default (*moroso*) in respect to a previous denouncement of all or part of the same property, will not be permitted to again denounce it within one year from the date he was declared in default. (Arts. 11–14.)

Art. 883.   Form and Requisites of Denouncement.[4] — A denouncement must be framed in writing and in duplicate, and must set forth the name, age, occupation, nationality, domicile and residence of the denunciant; the principal substances which he expects to exploit; the number of *pertenencias,* and their position on the ground so indicated as to be identified; the description of the adjacent mining boundaries, and the location of the *pertenencias;* the denouncement must be accompanied by a certificate of the deposit of the value of the stamps which, according to the Stamp Law, must be attached to the title.[5] The number of *pertenencias* may be stated approximately: 1, Where the boundaries of the property are so clearly defined in the denouncement that they can be readily identified on the ground; 2, where the *pertenencias* denounced are entirely surrounded by properties already titled (granted) or by *pertenencias* denounced and measured; in such cases, if the deposit for stamps is greater than re-

[4] See Art. 910.
[5] See Stamp Law, *voc.* " Titles," *post,* p. 744, and Art. 930D.

quired the excess will be returned, or if less, the denunciant must put up the difference, or his denouncement will be held as abandoned. Each denouncement must embrace only one *pertenencia* or group (*conjunto*) of contiguous *pertenencias;* the *pertenencias* need not be contiguous provided: 1, That within the limits of the denouncement there are mining properties previously granted or *pertenencias* denounced; 2, that all the *pertenencias* denounced are located upon the same deposit (*criadero*) and within the jurisdiction of the same Mining Agency. (Arts. 15–19.)

Art. 884. Presentation — Proceedings. — The denouncement must be presented personally by the denunciant or by his lawful representative or by attorney-in-fact with power-of-attorney or letter-of-attorney; the latter must be ratified by the principal through *escritura pública* or *apud-acta* within sixty days after the denouncement is presented. The Mining Agent will receive the denouncement and record it in his register, noting therein and on the original and duplicate denouncement the day and hour of presentation; if in the Agent's opinion it is not sufficiently definite he may request any necessary explanations and note them in the same way, but the denouncement will be registered in any event; the same rules apply in case of denouncements presented at the same time or successively in respect to the same *pertenencias;* in the latter event, one of them will be selected by lot to be proceeded with, unless the parties agree upon one. Within three days after presentation, the Agent will decide whether the denouncement is to be admitted; if so, he will proceed to make up the record (*expediente*); if refused, he will state in writing the reason of his decision, which, together with all other decisions of the Agent, is reviewable by the Department of Fomento on the petition of the denunciant. The procedure (*tramitación*) includes the appointment of an expert to measure and make plans of the land, the publication of an extract of the denouncement and of the announcement of the filing in the **A**gency of the expert report and of any opposition which may have been presented. (Arts. 20–25, 48.)

Art. 885. Proceedings in Department of Fomento.— At the close of the proceedings before the Agency, if no opposition has been presented to suspend their course, the Agent will forward a copy of the record to the Department of Fomento, which will examine the same, and if approved will fix a time within which the denunciant must erect the proper monuments (*mojoneras*) and to prove their erection; upon so doing the title will be issued to him, which confers the legal possession of the property, without need of other formality; if he fails to comply he will be declared in default (*moroso*).

The Department will disapprove the *expediente* where the denouncement or proceeding is defective for failure to observe the law or regulations through the fault of the denunciant, and he will be declared in default; if the Department is satisfied from the proofs presented that the denunciant is not at fault, it will order any defects in the record to be amended; any defects not involving infraction of the law or regulations may be ordered supplied by the person at fault; if the denunciant is at fault, and he fails to comply with the order, he will be held to abandon the denouncement; if the Agent or expert is at fault the Department will enforce their liability, and the denunciant may recover indemnity for all damages he has incurred.

If the denunciant fails to attend the meetings or proceedings provided by law or regulations he will be declared desisted, but may be excused upon proof that it was due to causes beyond his control, and the proceeding may again be had so far as necessary, but if he again fails to attend no excuse will be admitted. A denunciant who is not in default (*morosidad*) may withdraw his denouncement before the Department renders its final decision on the record. Failure to provide stamps will not suspend the proceedings, the pages of the record being legalized temporarily with the seal of the **Agency**, but the Department will require the stamps to be attached before rendering its final decision; if the denunciant does not provide them within the time allowed he will be declared desisted; the same results from failure to pay the fees of the Mining **Agent** as prescribed in the regulations. In every case of desistment, and of default, the deposit made when the denouncement was presented will be applied, first to payment of the stamps due on the *expediente,* and second to the fees of the Mining Agent, the denunciant remaining liable for any deficiency. (Arts. 26–36.)

Art. 886. Oppositions — Procedure.— Causes of opposition to a denouncement are: 1, Total or partial invasion of already granted *pertenencias* the titles of which have not been declared forfeited (*caducos*); 2, a pending denouncement of all or part of the same *pertenencias.* The opposition for the foregoing causes will be formulated before the Mining **Agency** within the time fixed by the regulations; thereupon the parties will be cited to a meeting for purposes of composition, under rules prescribed in the regulations; if no agreement is reached the parties will be notified that they may choose either administrative or judicial proceedings for the settlement of the opposition; if they do not at once choose the administrative proceeding, the proceedings on the *expediente* will be suspended, and it will be forwarded within forty-eight hours to the judicial authority to be proceeded in by suit as hereinafter provided; if they select the administrative proceeding, the proceedings on the *expediente* will be carried forward so that in due time the Department of Fomento, after hearing both parties, in accordance with the regulations, will definitely decide the opposition. If the parties choose the administrative proceeding, they cannot afterwards have recourse to the judicial, but if they choose the latter, they may before final judgment submit the opposition to the decision of the Department.

Any cause of opposition other than above mentioned must be alleged before the Agency, but the proceedings on the *expediente* will not be suspended; the Department will, when the record reaches it, examine the cause alleged and decide whether or not it will be considered; if so, it will proceed and decide as provided above in this Article, otherwise it will disregard the opposition without prejudice to the rights of the oppositor. Oppositions may be presented during revision directly to the Department, where the oppositor proves that it was not his fault that he did not go first to the Mining Agency; the oppositor will be held as desisted if he fails to attend upon the proceedings, being excused if it was not through his fault, but no excuse will be admitted if he fails for a second time to appear. (Arts. 37–45.)

Art. 887. Issuance of Title — Forfeiture.— The title will be issued to the denunciant without prejudice to the rights of third persons; in order to be issued to any other person, the latter's right must be evidenced by *escritura pública*. The Department of Fomento may refuse the issuance of a mining title although the *expediente* is in legal form, for reasons of public utility established by law justifying the refusal, and upon reimbursing the denunciant for all legitimate expenses incurred; if such reasons cease to exist, the Department will so declare, and publish the declaration as provided by the regulations, in order that the denunciant may present himself within ninety days to request the issuance of the title; if within that time he fails to apply, the *pertenencias* will be considered as free ground.

Mining property will be forfeited by failure to pay the tax (*impuesto*) as prescribed by the tax law.[6] (Arts. 49–51.)

---

[6] See Arts. 930D and 930E.

37

CHAPTER 3.

REDUCTION, RECTIFICATION AND DIVISION.

Art. 888. Reduction of Denouncements and of Pertenencias.
    889. Rectification of Localization.
    890. Division of Mining Properties — New Titles.

Art. 888. Reduction of Denouncement and of Pertenencias.
—A petition to reduce the number of *pertenencias* included
in a denouncement may only be presented within the first
forty days of the proceedings before the **Agency**; it cannot
have the effect of changing the time for the filing of plans;
a denouncement cannot be modified by increasing the number
of *pertenencias,* a separate denouncement being required for
every amplification.

Where it is desired to reduce the number of *pertenencias*
in a mining property, the petition for reduction, accompanied by the mining title, will be presented to the proper
Mining Agency, it being necessary to make new plans and
issue a new title cancelling the former one; upon the issuance of the new title being awarded, the excess of land covered by the former title will be declared free, and a time will
be fixed for the erection of new monuments, observing the
same procedure as in the issuance of the original titles.
(Arts. 46-47, 52.)

Art. 889. Rectification of Localization.— The localization
on the ground of *pertenencias* already titled may be rectified
so as to make it correspond to that shown in the denouncement and title, without the issuance of a new title; but
where the localization of the *pertenencias,* as indicated in the
title, does not correspond with that shown by the denouncement, the title will be rectified and a new one issued, although
the localization on the ground agrees with that shown by the
denouncement; also where neither the localization of the
pertenencias on the ground nor that shown by the title agrees

with that indicated in the denouncement, the localization
will be rectified and a new title issued.   Such rectifications
will be made upon petition of the owner of the mining property, of the adjoining owners interested, or *ex officio* by order
of the Department; in the latter event the action of the Department will not prejudice the rights of any of the parties.
In all cases of rectification of the localization of the *pertenen-*
cias on the land, the Department will fix a term for the erection of the proper monuments, and will not issue the new title
until the same is done; the Department may also at the petition of the owner, and without prejudice to the rights of others, order the administrative correction of any errors in the
title not affecting the localization of the *pertenencias* on the
ground, issuing in such cases a new title and cancelling the
former one; all corrections will be made on the basis of the
data contained in the denouncement.   (Arts. 53–59.)

Art. 890. Division of Mining Properties — New Titles.—
In order that the division of a mining property into two or
more be legally effective, new plans must be presented as
provided in the regulations, and new titles must be issued in
the same manner as originally, cancelling the former one.
(Art. 60.)

CHAPTER 4.

LEGAL MINING EASEMENTS.

Art. 891. Nature and Extent of Easements.
 892. Rules for Use of Easements.
 893. Establishment of Easements.

Art. 891. Nature and Extent of Easements.— Common
properties are subject, in favor of mining properties, to the
legal easements (*servidumbres*) of passage, drainage, aqueduct, ventilation, and transmission of electric power; mining
properties are only subject, in favor of other mining proper-

ties, to the legal easements of drainage and ventilation. The easements of passage, drainage and aqueduct are governed by the provisions of the Federal Civil Code in respect of the rights and obligations of the dominant and servient estates, except that the easement of passage may consist not only in the right of transit through the common properties, but in the permanent establishment across them of lines of transmission by cable or by any other method of transportation authorized by the regulations, intended exclusively for the operating needs of the mining property and to establish communication between it and the public roads, railroads or smelting plants, such right of way not to exceed ten meters in width unless otherwise agreed.

The easement of ventilation, over common properties, consists of the right of communication from the surface to the interior workings of the mining properties for the sole purpose of affording necessary ventilation; such easement over mining properties, consists of the right to establish communication through them for the purpose of ventilating other mining properties, and to make use of the works of the servient estate for that purpose where not incompatible with the use for which they are intended.

The easement of transmission of electric power over common properties consists of the right to establish overhead or underground lines from the point of production of the power to the mining property where it is to be utilized, across the intervening properties, together with the right of passage for their construction, maintenance and guarding, the rules as to the easement of passage being applicable to this easement so far as practicable.

The easement of drainage to which other mining properties are subject, consists of the right to establish through them mining tunnels (*socavónes*) or countermines for the purpose of draining other mining properties, also the right to make use of the tunnels or countermines used by the servient estate for the same purpose, and the servient estate may make use for its own drainage of the tunnels and countermines opened for that purpose by the dominant estate; but this easement does not authorize the running of such tunnels or countermines through or under a shaft (*tiro*) of a mine. The rights to open and exploit tunnels are ineffective where the parties undertaking to exercise such rights fail to comply with the requirements of the laws or concessions under which such rights were acquired. (Arts. 61–69, 148.)

Art. 892. Rules for Use of Easements.— In making use of the easements of drainage and ventilation above referred to, the following rules will be observed: 1, While the work is being done, the owner of the servient estate has the right to have an interventor for the protection of his interests, and as long as the easement lasts, to require that doors be put in according to the regulations at points where his works are intersected, also where his own works cut into those put on his property in the exercise of the easement; 2, if during the work any of the minerals mentioned in the first two clauses of **Art.** 879 are encountered in paying quantities, the owner of the dominant estate must bring them to the surface and notify the Department of Fomento and the owner of the servient estate, and if the latter does not dispose of them within sixty days after such notice they will remain on the surface at his risk; 3, if such substances are encountered while working in free ground, the owner of the dominant estate, after notice to the Department, may dispose of such as it is necessary to extract in order to carry on the work, but cannot exploit the deposit unless he obtains a title, for which purpose he shall have a preferential right to present his denouncement within thirty days from the discovery, within a zone of one hundred meters on each side of the axis of the shaft. (**Art.** 70.)

Art. 893. Establishment of Easements.— The easements herein referred to may be established in any of the following ways: 1, By consent of the owner of the servient estate evidenced by public instrument; 2, by resolution of the Department of Fomento; 3, by judicial judgment. If the owner of the servient estate refuses to consent, the owner of the dominant estate may apply to the Fomento, which, after hearing both parties, will decide whether the easement shall be established; if in the affirmative, the Department will fix the use and extension of the easement, the material conditions of its establishment and the amount of indemnity to be paid to the owner of the servient estate, such decision being final unless objected to within thirty days. If within that time objection is made, the Department may authorize the work upon giving bond for all damages and losses which may be caused; such resolution will be notified to the owner of the servient estate, who may bring his action in court within thirty days, failing to do which, the easement will be taken as definitely established and the bond will be cancelled. If the Department decides that the easement is not to be established or established on different terms than as solicited, the applicant may bring his suit within thirty days or will lose his right.

In authorizing the establishment of easements the Department will observe the provisions of the Federal Civil Code so far as not otherwise provided herein; in respect to easements of drainage and ventilation the Department will take into account the advantages and disadvantages of the system proposed as compared with those of other known systems. The amplification of easements already established will conform to the rules for their original establishment. (Arts. 71–78.)

.

CHAPTER 5.

MINING CONTRACTS. REGISTRY.

Art. 894. Acts of Commerce — Lesión.

Art. 894. Acts of Commerce — Lesión.— All mining enterprises, and all contracts in regard to the transfer and exploitation of mines and in regard to the products of mines, are "acts of commerce" and governed by the provisions of the Code of Commerce, unless otherwise specially provided herein. The valuation placed upon mining properties and rights by the incorporators in organizing a mining company shall be considered as proven, and no mining contract shall be subjcet to rescission on account of lesión. The offices of the Commercial Register in the States, Territories and Federal District will keep a special book in which they will record: 1, The titles of mining property; 2, *escrituras públicas* and judicial and administrative decisions which transmit or affect the ownership of mining properties or real rights concerning the same; 3, *escrituras públicas* concerning promises to transfer mining properties or *pertenencias;* 4, *escrituras públicas* and judicial decisions concerning the exploitation of mining properties; such registry will be made in the office of the Municipality where the mining property is located; documents concerning mining easements upon common properties will be registered in the office of the place where the servient estate is located. The registry of documents mentioned in clause 3 above will be effective as to third persons for the term stated in the contract, from the date of registry, but not to exceed two years, although the time fixed for the subsistence of the promise is longer. Where the document to be registered is presented for registry within thirty days of its date, if an *escritura pública,* or from the time the judicial decision was rendered, the registry will produce its effects from such date, but only from the time of presenta-

tion if after thirty days; the registry of foreign documents
is effective from the date on which the certified copy of its
protocolization is presented at the proper registry office.
(Arts. 79–86.)

CHAPTER 6.

EXPROPRIATION.

Art. 895. Right of Expropriation.
    896. Proceedings — Incidents.

Art. 895. Right of Expropriation.— The owner of a mining property (*fundo minero*) has the right to occupy, within
the limits of his *pertenencias,* so much of the surface of the
ground as is strictly necessary for the use and exploitation of
superficial deposits, and for the buildings and works necessary for mining operations, and for treating or smelting the
ores produced on the property or on its annexes belonging to
the same owner, and to occupy, within and without the limits of his *pertenencias,* subject to the regulations, the necessary land for the establishment of permanent railways for the
purposes of the enterprise.   (Art. 87.)

Art. 896. Proceedings — Incidents.— Where the owner of
the mining property is unable to come to an agreement with
the owner of the surface property in regard to acquiring it,
he may apply to the Department of Fomento for its expropriation; after hearing the landowner, the Department will
decide whether or not the petition is to be granted, and if
in the affirmative, it will fix the extent of land to be expropriated and the amount of indemnity to be paid by the
mine owner; the latter may provisionally occupy the portion
of land designated upon depositing to the landowner's order,
in an ofhee of the Treasury indicated by the Fomento, the
amount of indemnity fixed.   If the landowner opposes the
occupation, the mine owner may apply to the competent

judge for an order to put him into immediate possession of the land designated by the Department. The landowner may oppose the administrative order of the Department upon notifying it of his opposition and filing his suit at law within thirty days, failing in which he will be held to definitely consent to the order of the Department; the mine owner may also bring suit within thirty days to review the decision of the Department refusing his application for expropriation.   .

If the landowner consents to or does not oppose the administrative order as above provided, or such order is confirmed or modified by final judicial decision, the mine owner may apply to the competent judge requesting the execution of an *escritura pública* of adjudication, which will be signed by the judge upon failure of the landowner to appear and sign it within a reasonable time to be fixed by the judge. If the owner of the land is unknown or uncertain, the petition for expropriation will be published for thirty days as provided by the regulations; if within such time the landowner appears the foregoing procedure will be observed, but if he does not appear, the Department of Fomento may authorize the expropriation upon deposit of the fixed indemnity, and the mine owner may apply to the judge for the *escritura* of adjudication; if the landowner subsequently appears, he may receive the deposit, but cannot contest the administrative decision decreeing the expropriation. The landowner or his assignee (*causahabiente*) may, however, within one year, recover the land expropriated, or the part affected, in the event: 1, That the mine owner, within one year, has not begun the work for which the land was taken, or has suspended it for a like time except through *vis major;* 2, that all or part of the land taken is used for a purpose different from that for which it was expropriated; 3, that the title of the mining property for the use of which the land was taken has been forfeited. In such cases the landowner will only refund the amount of indemnity re-

ceived or its proportional part, as the case may be. The suit
for recovery cannot be brought if the cause for which it lies
has ceased. (Arts. 88–96.)

CHAPTER 7.

PENAL PROVISIONS.

Art. 897. What Law Applicable — Penalties.

Art. 897. What Law Applicable — Penalties.— Crimes
committed in violation of this law, and civil liability arising
under it, are subject to the Federal Penal Code, except as
herein provided — certain fines and penalties imposed on
Mining Agents and experts for violations of the law and
regulations are omitted. Any person who without right exploits any of the substances mentioned in Art. 879, unless
through justifiable error, is subject to the following penalties: 1, If the exploitation is made in free ground or
in *pertenencias* denounced or titled, by imprisonment from
one to two years and a fine from one to two thousand pesos;
2, if the denunciant exploits the property before obtaining
the title, by " arrest " for thirty days to eleven months, and
fine from sixteen to one thousand pesos. Disposing of ores
encountered in easement works is subject to the penalty in
clause 1 above; the theft of ores by operatives or employés
of mining concerns is subject to two years in prison; the
destruction or changing location of mining monuments on the
surface or inside the mines is punishable under Art. 497 of
the Penal Code; and interference by private persons with
the operations of the mining experts is subject to the penalties
of Arts. 904 to 908 of said Code.   (Arts. 97–106.)

CHAPTER 8.

SUITS — JURISDICTION.

Art. 898. Federal and Local Courts.

Art. 898. Federal and Local Courts.— The Federal Tribunals have jurisdiction of suits in respect to: 1, Opposition to denouncements or to issuance of titles; 2, opposition to rectification of titles or localization of titled *pertenencias;* 3, nullity of mining titles; 4, expropriation for mining purposes; 5, legal mining easements; 6, crimes committed under chapter 7 of this law; 7, crimes endangering the safety of mining works or the life of operatives in the interior workings. (Details of determining jurisdiction are omitted.) The Department of Fomento may bring suit to declare nullity of a mining title for fraud or deceit within three years from its date; like suit may be brought by third persons interested. In all cases under this chapter the *Ministerio Público* will be heard, following instructions from the Department of Fomento. All final judgments rendered in such suits will be communicated to the Department.

All suits in regard to mining contracts referred to in chapter 5, will be brought before competent local judges (*del órden común*) in accordance with the Code of Commerce, also all other mining suits not included in the seven clauses above, in accordance with local legislation, the Code of Commerce or the Federal Civil Code, as the case may be. (Arts. 107–123.)

CHAPTER 9.

MISCELLANEOUS PROVISIONS.

Art. 899. Mining Explorations — Rules.
900. Inspections — Police Regulation.
901. Foreigners and Mining Rights.

Art. 899. Mining Explorations — Rules.— Mining explorations are subject to the prescriptions of the Regulations of this law and to the special police regulations, in accordance with the following bases: 1, To determine the zone of exploration, a fixed and easily identifiable point will be taken as the center of a circumference not to exceed five hundred meters; 2, explorations cannot be made on private property without the permission of the owner; if he refuses it, the applicant may apply to the Mining Agent, who, after hearing the landowner, and in observance of the regulations, will grant the required permission, if there is no legal cause to the contrary, upon the explorer giving bond to cover any damage caused to the owner; 3, explorations on public lands can only be made with the permission of the Mining Agent, who cannot refuse it without legal cause; 4, the period for exploration cannot exceed sixty days, which cannot be extended, from the date of granting the permit, where granted by the Mining Agent, or from the date the permit from the owner is registered in the Agency; 5, during the period of exploration only the explorer can present denouncements for mining *pertenencias* within the zone; 6, new permits to explore all or part of the same zone cannot be granted within six months after the expiration of the former permit; 7, in case of controversy between the explorer and the landowner as to the limits of the zone, the former must make the proof; 8, zones of exploration cannot be granted in lands on which mining work has been done although the *pertenencias* have been abandoned, nor within a distance of two hundred meters of a mining property, nor within the boundaries of towns; 9, the Mining Police Regulations will determine within what distance from buildings, railroads and other public or private constructions, mining explorations may be carried on, also in what cases and under what conditions mining works may be carried on in the subsoil pertaining to buildings and public or private constructions. (Arts. 124–125.)

Art. 900. Inspections — Police Regulation.— The Department of Fomento may send its inspectors to visit mining properties and their annexed installations used directly for mining works, for the purpose: 1, Of determining whether the mining police regulations are duly complied with; 2, to obtain scientific and statistical data concerning mining; also at the request of any interested party, or *ex officio* where it suspects that free lands are being invaded, to ascertain whether other mining properties or such free lands are being invaded; in no event can the inspectors inquire into the commercial status of the business.

The Department of Fomento may order the suspension of mining works which do not conform to the police regulations if the life of the mine operatives is endangered; such order of suspension must be based on the reports of the inspectors who have visted the place, or investigations made by the local authorities, and will be limited to the point or zone of danger, and the suspension will continue until the cause is removed; in grave and urgent cases the suspension may be decreed at the instance of the Governor or *Jefe Político* without the necessity of such report or investigation; in such cases the Department will order an official inspection to be made in the shortest time possible. Coal mining works which may endanger the life of operatives, the safety of the workings or the stability of the soil are subject to the mining police regulations. (Arts. 126–133.)

Art. 901. Foreigners and Mining Rights.— Without previous special permission from the Executive of the Union, no title of mining property can be issued to foreigners who denounce *pertenencias* within a zone of eighty kilometers along the boundary line with foreign countries, even when the denouncement is made jointly by foreigners and citizens; nor without such permit can foreigners acquire by any other title mining property or real rights in or to the same within such zone; foreign corporations are incapable of denouncing or otherwise acquiring mining property or real rights in and to the same within such zone of eighty kilometers; all acquisitions made in contravention of the foregoing provisions are void, and the suit for nullity may be brought by any person interested or by the Ministerio Público under instructions from the Department of Fomento. The Regulations [7] will prescribe the time within which the permits above referred to must be solicited and the conditions under which they will be granted; if permit is refused the land denounced will be declared free, and the money deposited will be applied as provided in cases of desistment.

Where a foreigner acquires mining properties or real rights to the same, within such zone, by inheritance or through judicial adjudication in payment of debt, he must dispose of the same within one year, unless within that time he obtains the permit above referred to; where a foreign corporation obtains such property or rights in the same way, it must in all cases dispose of it within one year. The judicial authorities before whom the heredity proceedings or adjudication are conducted will give due notice to the Department of Fomento of the existence of such proceedings. The Executive of the Union, through the Ministerio Público, will proceed to obtain the seizure of such mining property and rights acquired or held in contravention of the foregoing provisions, and the same shall be sold at public auction in accordance with the provisions of the Federal Code of Civil Procedure; the proceeds obtained, after deduction of costs and taxes, will remain subject to the disposition of the interested parties. (Arts. 136–144.)

[7] See Art. 925.

Art. 902. Payment of Mining Taxes.— Any person may pay the property tax on a mining property, but only one having a legitimate interest in preventing the forfeiture of the title has the right to require the owner to reimburse him for what he may pay; in the latter event the claim for repayment shall have preference over all other debts payable out of the value of the mining property, including mortgage debts.   (Art. 145.)

Art. 903. Computation of Time.— Unless otherwise provided herein, the terms fixed in this law and in the regulations will begin to run from the day after the notice is given or the act done, and the last day will be counted, Sundays and national holidays and fast-days being excluded; but the terms for prescription and for judicial proceedings are computed according to the provisions of the respective laws on the subject. (Arts. 146–147.)

Art. 904. Mining Agents — Fees.— The Department of Fomento will determine the number of Mining Agents and the territory within which each is to act, and will decide all questions arising in regard to their jurisdiction; their services will be paid according to the schedule of fees issued by the Department.[8]   (Arts. 149–150.)

Art. 905. Mining Titles — Loss.— Mining titles issued by the Fomento will be signed alone by the Secretary of the Department.   Where the loss or disappearance of a mining title is satisfactorily proven to the Department by the mine owner, a duplicate may be issued to him at his cost, reciting in it the reason for its issuance.   (Arts. 151–152.)

Art. 906. Regulations of Mining Law.— The Department of Fomento will issue the general Regulations of this law, the special mining police regulations and other reglamentary

[8] See Arts. 926–930.

provisions intended to make effective the provisions of the
law. (Art. 153.)

Art. 907. Transitory Provisions.— This law will go into
effect January 1, 1910; contracts for explorations will continue in force according to their provisions; pending mining
applications will be disposed of according to the terms of
this law. Pending lawsuits will be transferred to the Federal Courts; pending cassation proceedings will proceed to
decision according to the general laws applicable. Six
months are allowed for mine owners who have not complied
with the first part of **Art.** 2 of the law of 6 June, 1892, to
prove their compliance therewith to the Department, after
which time, if not complied with, their titles will be forfeited
and the land freely subject to denouncement; one year **is**
allowed to mine owners in which to set up monuments; any
one failing to comply is liable for all damages caused to **a**
third person, and to a fine of from one hundred to five hundred
pesos to be imposed by the Department, and if he persists for
thirty days in failure to comply he will be liable to criminal proceedings, and the Department may construct the monuments at his expense.

Mining titles, acts and contracts registered prior **to**
January 1, 1910, in accordance with existing laws or regulations, need not be registered anew; those subject to registry
under this law must be registered, and will take effect as
to third persons from the date of registry. After **January**
1 all laws relating to mining, mining rights and denouncements, except those of a fiscal character, which will remain **in**
force in so far as they are not modified by the present **law,**
are repealed. (Arts. 1–9.)

TITLE II.

MINING REGULATIONS.

(Decreto de 15 de Diciembre de 1909.)

CHAPTER 1.

MINING AGENTS.

Art. 908. Appointment and Qualifications.
  909. Duties of Agents — Fees.

Art. 908. Appointment and Qualifications.— The Agents of the Mining Bureau of the Department of Fomento must be Mexicans in the exercise of their rights; they will be appointed by the Department, and will receive, and act upon (*tramitar*) the denouncements of mining properties filed with them, and perform the duties assigned to them by the mining law and regulations and by the orders of the Department, and in cases of doubt as to their application they will consult the Department. The Department will establish the Districts within which the **A**gents are to act, and besides the principal Agent, will appoint one or more deputies (*suplentes*) as required by the volume of business in the mining agency, who shall have the same qualifications as the Agent. (Details of supplying the service in case of absence or death of the **A**gent are omitted.) The Agents cannot act in case of any legal impediment, which are: 1, Having an interest direct or indirect in the matter; 2, any such interest on the part of any consanguineous relative in the right line in any degree; by collaterals within the fourth degree and by affinity within the second degree, both inclusive; 3, being the agent, partner, clerk or administrator of any of the parties; 4, to have been an agent, lawyer, attorney or expert in the matter under consideration; in such cases they will make a note of the fact and call upon the *suplente* to act. In places

38

not within the district of any Mining Agency, denouncements of mining property, notices (*avisos*), and exploration
permits (*constancias de permisos*) will be presented to the
Postmaster, who will endorse thereon the day and hour of
presentation, and will immediately notify the Department
of Fomento by telegraph, if there is one, and by mail.   (Arts.
1–6, 8–10.)

Art. 909.   Duties of Agents — Fees.— Mining Agents must
observe the following requirements: 1, To affix on the exte-
rior of the Agency in a place easily visible to the public, a
sign with the words: "*Agencia de Minería de la Secretaría
de Fomento*"; 2, to keep on the outside of the Agency a
permanent announcement of the office hours, which cannot
be interrupted except on Sundays and national holidays; 3,
to keep on the outside of the Agency, or if not possible, at
the entrance, in a place easily visible and accessible to the
public, a bulletin board on which they will make the publications required by the Law, Regulations and other legal provisions; 4, to keep inside the Agency in a visible and easily
accessible place, a clock showing the local time; 5, to make
and keep up to date an inventory of the records (*archivo*)
of the Agency; 6, to keep a register of denouncements, entering them therein in strict order of dates and numeration
and without leaving blank lines between the entries; 7, to
keep a register of mining explorations, entered in the same
way as above; 8, to keep a register of licensed experts, such being those who have been received in some official establishment
of the Republic to exercise the profession of engineer, or whose
diplomas (*títulos*) have been accepted or recognized by the
Government; 9, to forward to the Department of Fomento,
within the first ten days of each month, a detailed report of
denouncements admitted, of notices and applications for
exploration permits, or of applications for the rectification,
reduction or division of patented mining properties presented
to them during the previous month.

The revision of the decisions of the Λ ining **Agent**, under Art. 48 of the Law, does not operate to suspend the proceedings in a case except where specially so provided in the Law, Regulations or otherwise. The Λ ining Agents will collect their fees in accordance with the Schedule of Fees issued by the Department of Fomento.[1]   (Arts. 11–12.)

CHAPTER 2.

DENOUNCEMENTS OF MINING PROPERTIES.

Art. 910. Presentation — Requirements.
911. Expert — Selection.
912. Appointment — Proceedings.
913. Proceedings of Expert — Plans.
914. Same — Reports — Monuments.
915. Proceedings on Report — Setting Monuments.
916. Issuance of Titles — Publications.

Art. 910. Presentation — Requirements. — Denouncements must be filed with the Λ ining Agency of the District in which the property denounced is located, or before the Agency of either District where the property lies in two or more Districts. If several denouncements of the same property are presented before different Agencies having jurisdiction, only the one filed first is valid, and it must be proceeded with before the Agency in which it was filed. Besides the data specified in Art. 883, the denouncement must state the fixed point from which measurements are to start, and in order to readily identify the land where the *pertenencias* are to be measured, will mention any well known points in the vicinity. No denouncement shall be admitted which does not set out specifically the names of all the denunciants, or which is not signed by such persons or by their legal representatives.   (Arts. 13–17.)

[1] See Arts. 926–930.

Art. 911. Expert — Selection.— Within three days after the admission of a denouncement, the Mining Agent will appoint an expert to measure the *pertenencias* and *demasías* denounced and to make a plan of the same, which shall clearly show the points on the boundaries of the property where monuments must be constructed, as well as all the monuments found within a zone of one hundred meters around the same and belonging to adjoining or neighboring mining properties. The Agent will appoint the expert named in the denouncement if he is licensed; but if none is named in the denouncement or he is unlicensed, the Agent will freely make the appointment, giving the preference to licensed experts of the place, and only if there are none he may appoint practical persons of the locality if in his judgment they are competent to discharge their duties satisfactorily. If the Agent rejects the expert proposed he must state his reasons, and the party interested may make complaint about it to the Department within three days after notice of the same, after which time it is irrevocable; the Agent will forward the complaint to the Department within three days after it is filed; the proceedings will be suspended from the filing of the complaint till the Agent receives the decision of the Department; the Agent will make the proper entry on the record.

The expert must advise the Agent within eight days after notice of his appointment whether he accepts it or not; if he does not accept or reply, the Agent will notify the denunciant so that he may appoint another licensed expert, if he had named one in the denouncement, and a new expert will be appointed as above prescribed, within the unextendable term of fifteen days, at the end of which, if no expert accepts, a copy of the record will be forwarded to the Department, which will declare the discontinuance of the denouncement, such declaration being published for eight days on the bulletin of the Agency, after which time any person may denounce the property; the Agent will enter the facts in his record. (Arts. 18–20.)

Art. 912. Appointment — Proceedings.— The appointment being accepted by the expert and duly recorded, the **Agent** will fix an unextendable term of sixty days within which he must present in quadruplicate the plan above required, accompanied by an explanatory report. The **A**gent will issue in duplicate an extract which will contain: 1, An abstract of the denouncement, showing clearly the name and domicile of the denunciant and the serial number of the record; 2, the name, domicile and acceptance of the expert; 3, the statement that the unextendable period of one hundred and twenty days, counted from the date of the extract, has been assigned within. which the record in the Agency must be made up. A copy of the extract will be posted on the bulletin of the **Agency** for thirty days; another copy will be delivered to the denunciant to be published at his cost three consecutive times in the official newspaper of the respective State, Territory or Federal District, within forty days after the date of the extract, and within said one hundred and twenty days the denunciant must file copies of the papers containing said publication, to be added to the record; of all which due record will be made; such publication has the effect of citation to all parties concerned in opposing the denouncement of the mining property in question. A certified copy of his appointment will be given to the expert, concluding with a warning that whoever resists the performance of the field-work to be done by the expert will be liable to the penalties prescribed in **Art.** 897, and in case of resistance the expert will call upon the local authorities for assistance. (Arts. 21–23, 29.)

Art. 913. Proceedings of Expert — Plans.— The field work of the expert on the land will be done in such a way as to obtain the lengths (*longitudes*) of the horizontal projections of the boundary lines of the mining property, and the angles formed by such lines with the astronomical meridian; and so that one or more of the vertices of the perimeter shall refer each to at least two fixed points on the ground, or **to** only one fixed point if the distance thereto is also determined; and data necessary to verify the work will be gathered. The location and measurement of the property on **the** land confers no right to occupy the same, but only serves to define the boundaries of said mining property.

The plans of mining properties must be drawn **on** linen-mounted paper, for their preservation, and the copies on drawing-linen; said plans shall contain: 1, The name of the mine; the place where it is located; the 1unicipality, District, *Partido,* Cantón or Department, and State, Territory or Federal District, together with other data serving to identify the mining property; 2, the lengths (*longitudes*) of the sides of the perimeter of the mining property, and the azimuths of said sides, or their directions with respect to the astronomical meridian; 3, the area in *hectares* comprised within its boundaries; 4, the scale, which must **be** entirely decimal; 5, although a compass was used, only the astronomical meridian will be indicated, which will be represented by a line parallel to the right edge of the paper of the plan and so oriented that its upper end will indicate the astronomical north; 6, the pointers or references (*visuales de referencia*) to fixed and notable points of the land; **7,** the adjoining mining boundaries; 8, the date and the signature of the expert. (Arts. 24–25.)

Art. 914. Same — Reports — Monuments.— The explanatory report in regard to the measurements of the mining properties must contain the description of the technical operations conducted and all the data shown on the plans, so that if necessary the plans could be reconstructed from the data of the report, and in addition the report must show the location of the property and the relative position of the *pertenencias* comprised in it, as indicated in the denouncement, with pertinent remarks in the event of any discrepancy. The expert will cause solid foundations of masonry (*mampostería*) to be constructed at the places where monuments are to be set up, such foundations not to be less than fifty centimeters high, level on top and square in shape with sides not less than fifty centimeters, and signs will be placed thereon so that each of the monuments may be easily recognized and identified in accordance with their designation on the plan. The experts will follow the terms of the denouncement in making the locations and measurements, and will indicate on the plans not only the monuments of the adjoining mining properties outside of the *pertenencias* denounced but those within such *pertenencias,* and will set out all matters called to their attention by the denunciant, the adjoining owners or by anyone considering himself prejudiced by the expert operations. Upon the filing of the expert's report in the Agency, notice of the fact will be published for fifteen days on the bulletin of the Agency. (Arts. 26–28, 30.)

Art. 915. Proceedings on Report — Setting Monuments.— At the expiration of the one hundred and twenty days above provided, if there has been no opposition, or if it was based on any of the causes stated in Art. 886, or where final judgment has been rendered by the tribunals in favor of the denunciant, the Agent, on his strictest responsibility, and within the next fifteen days, will make up a copy of the record and forward it, with three copies of the plan, by registered mail to the Department of Fomento; such copy of the record will include a complete copy of the extract of the denouncement. The denunciant will be notified, in accordance with Art. 885, that a period of thirty days is allowed him within which he must set up the monuments and to certify that he has done so, for which purpose a copy of the plan will be furnished him, which he must return certified, and with exact indication of the places where the monuments have been set and the distinctive signs placed thereon; said certification shall show as a certain fact that the monuments have been set up at the places on the ground indicated on the plan, and will be attested, if possible, by the expert who made it, and if not, by some other licensed expert, or if there is none, by some practical expert of recognized ability.

In setting up the monuments the following requisites will be observed: 1, Their position shall not be changed unless the mining properties of which they mark the boundaries are themselves changed; they must be solidly constructed and always maintained in good condition; 2, they must be set up in convenient places, in such number as may be necessary so that from each one the next monument on either side may be seen, and by their size, shape, color or other characteristics may be distinguished from the monuments of adjoining mining properties. (Arts. 31–33.)

Art. 916. Issuance of Titles — Publications.— Upon the issuance of a title to mining property, it will be delivered to the denunciant or forwarded to him in care of the Mining Agent, together with a copy of the plan sealed by the Department of Fomento, which will notify the Treasury Department of the issuance of the title. As soon as the Mining Agent receives a title for delivery to the denunciant, he will post a notice for thirty days on the bulletin notifying the denunciant to call for it; if the latter does not call for it within such time, the title will be added to the record together with the notice; the title will remain in the Agency at the disposition of the interested party until receipt by the Agency of the notice of forfeiture of the property, in which event the document, if not reclaimed, will be returned to the Department of Fomento.

The publication referred to in **Art.** 887 will be made for thirty days on the bulletin of the Agency, and for ten consecutive times in the official newspaper of the respective State, Territory or Federal District. The notice that a mining property is free will be published for twenty days on the bulletin, counted from the day and hour that the notice is posted, until the same hour of the last day, excluding Sundays and national holidays. (Arts. 34–36.)

CHAPTER 3.

OPPOSITIONS.

Art. 917. When to be Filed — Proceedings.

Art. 917. When to be Filed — Proceedings.— Oppositions based on any of the grounds stated in clauses 1 and 2 of Art. 886, can only be allowed within ninety days from the date of publication of the extract. Upon the filing of opposition, the Agent will at once notify the denunciant by notice posted for ten days on the bulletin, stating the names of the oppositor and of the denunciant and the number of the record, in which he will enter the fact of publication and attach the original notice. On the same day of the receipt of the expert's report and plans, the Agent will cite the interested parties to a meeting to be held within fifteen days; such citation to be made by an order sent by registered mail and posted also for three days on the bulletin, adding the registry receipt and the notice to the record; at such meeting the Agent will endeavor to bring the parties to an agreement and avoid litigation, an entry of everything done being made in the record; if at the meeting the parties do not come to an agreement nor choose to settle the matter through administrative proceedings, the Agent will transmit the record to the tribunals within forty-eight hours as provided in **Art. 886.** If after transmitting the record to the tribunal before the ninety days is elapsed, a new opposition is filed based on any of the grounds stated in Art. 886, the Agent will not admit the same but will refer the oppositor to the tribunal to establish his claims; if based on any other grounds than as above, the Agent will retain the opposition and add it to the record when returned from the tribunal.

If at the meeting the parties choose the administrative proceedings, a record (*acta*) of the same will be made and signed by all parties, and the proceedings will be continued until the end of the term of one hundred and twenty days. Where the Department of Fomento decides to consider an opposition based on any of the grounds stated in Art. 886, it will order that the same be proceeded with in the Agency as in other cases of oppositions under **Art.** 886. The Department of Fomento, in deciding oppositions submitted for administrative action, shall have entire freedom to order such proceedings taken as it may deem advisable in order to inform itself, and after hearing the parties, who may submit anything in support of their interests, will render such decision as may be just. (Arts. 37–44.)

CHAPTER 4.

PETITIONS FOR REDUCTION, EASEMENTS, ETC.

Art. 918. Reduction of Denouncements.— Petitions **for the** reduction of pending denouncements must be published for twenty days on the bulletin board of the Agency, and one time, during said period, in the Official Newspaper of the State, District or Territory, at the cost of the applicant, **who** must file one copy of the newspaper containing the **adver**tisement within the 120 days of the proceedings. If at the time the reduction is requested, the expert has not filed his plans, the **Agent** will notify him in order that he may make new measurements and deliver his plans and report within the remaining time of the period of sixty days provided in Art. 912. At the expiration of the publication on the bulletin board, the Agent may admit denouncements of the excess lands released by the reduction. (Art. 45.)

Art. 919. Reduction and Rectification of Pertenencias.— In case of reduction of *pertenencias* of a mining property already titled, as provided in the Law, Art. 888, the appointment of the expert and the delivery of the plans and report will be made in accordance with Arts. 911 and 912; and upon their receipt by the Agent he will within fifteen days forward a copy of the *expediente,* together with the title and its plan and the other documents hereinafter required, to the Department of Fomento.

The proceedings for the rectification of a titled mining property, as provided in the Law, Art, 889, will be the same as for a new denouncement, and the monuments must be located as hereinbefore prescribed. When the proceedings are ended, the Agent will forward a copy of the *expediente* to the Department of Fomento, and upon its approval the Agent will be directed to deliver to the interested party the certified copy of the record to be added to his title papers. (Arts. 46–48.)

Art. 920. Division of Mining Properties.— Petitions in regard to the division of a mining property into two or more will be addressed to the Department of Fomento, either directly or through the proper Mining Agent, with as many plans, in quadruplicate, as may be required by the division, together with a report rendered by a licensed expert, or if there is none, by a practical one of recognized ability, the plans being authenticated by the expert. The applicant will also forward the documents required by the following Article, and the stamps for the issuance of the new titles. Upon the approval of the plans by the Department, it will allow a reasonable time for the erection of the monuments to mark the new mining properties, failing to comply with which during said time the applicant will be held to have abandoned **his** application. (**Art. 49.**)

Art. 921. Documents Required with Petitions.— Petitions for the reduction, rectification or division of mining property the titles of which have already been issued, must be accompanied by the following documents: 1, The title and plan of the property; 2, a voucher showing that the Federal taxes on the property are paid up to date; 3, document showing that the applicant is the owner of the mining property or is legally authorized to make the application; 4, in case of reduction, it is also necessary to produce the certificate showing that the property is unencumbered, or a document showing the consent of any mortgage creditors to the reduction. (**Art. 50.**)

Art. 922. Easements — Proceedings.— Petitions to the Department of Fomento for the establishment of easements in accordance with the Law, Art. 893, must be accompanied by a report of a licensed expert, or if there is none, by that of **a** practical one of recognized ability, showing the necessity **for** and extent of the easements. Upon filing the petition, **a** citation will be issued to the owner of the servient estate, notifying him that if he does not appear on the day fixed, the petition will be granted; if he does not appear on said day, or after a hearing if he does appear, and after such proceedings as it deems proper, the Department of Fomento will render its decision. Petitions for easements of passage must be accompanied by such plans and expert reports and other data as the applicant deems material and necessary; and **the** Department will allow such means of transportation in each case as it may deem proper. (**Arts. 51–52.**)

Art. 923. Explorations — Permits.— Petitions for exploration permits must be filed in duplicate, together with a certificate issued by a licensed expert showing that no mining works have been carried on in the zone of exploration, and that the limits of said zone are at least two hundred meters distant from the boundaries of the nearest mining property; the duplicate will be returned to the applicant by the Agent after he has noted thereon the day and hour of its presentation. If the exploration is to be made on private property, the explorer must solicit the permission of the owner or of his representative, and if granted, the evidence of the same will be presented to the Mining Agent that he may take note of the same; the explorer must make proof that the person granting the permit is the owner of the land or is authorized to grant it. If the owner or his representative does not grant the permission, the explorer will solicit it of the Mining Agent, stating in his petition the residence of the owner, and the name of the surety who is proposed by the applicant for any damages he may cause by the works of exploration; the petition will be published by the Agent on the bulletin board for fifteen days, and he will notify the owner that unless he makes objection his consent will be taken as granted. At the expiration of the time of publication the Agent will allow thirty days for the execution and approval by him on his responsibility, of the bond, upon the giving of which he will issue the permit, which shall indicate the zone and the fixed point to serve as its center. The Agent will publish on the bulletin board for thirty days an extract of the permit, stating the name of the explorer, the location of the zone and its fixed central point, the day the exploration is to begin and the termination of the sixty day period; and in all cases the Agent will declare in the permit or in the proof of publication, that the exploration works must be strictly subject to the provisions of the Mining Police Regulations. (Arts. 53–56.)

Art. 924. Expropriation — Proceedings.— Petitions for expropriation under the Law, Art. 896, must be presented to the Department of Fomento directly or through the proper

Mining Agent, accompanied by a report of a licensed expert, or if there is none, by a practical one of recognized ability, and by plans authenticated by the expert, to the end that the Department, in view of all the data and after hearing the owner of the land, may make the proper decision. If the owner of the land is unknown or cannot be found, notice of the petition shall be published for thirty days on the bulletin board and in the *" Diario Oficial "* of the Federation. (Arts. 57–58.)

Art. 925. Permits to Foreigners — Conditions.— Petitions for permits to foreigners to denounce or acquire mining property or real rights therein, as provided in the Law, Art. 901, shall be directed to the Department of Fomento directly or through the Mining Agent, upon filing the denouncement or within sixty days after its admission. Such permits will be granted upon the condition, which shall be expressed therein, that the mining properties remain subject in all respects to the Mexican laws, and that no right or claim based on foreign citizenship (*extranjería*) can be urged in respect thereof, and that the Tribunals of the Republic alone have jurisdiction to decide all questions which may arise in respect to such properties, to the exclusion of all foreign intervention. (Art. 59.)

CHAPTER 5.

SCHEDULE OF FEES OF MINING AGENTS

(Issued 16 December, 1909.)

Art. 926. Explorations — Denouncements. — Upon filing

notice of exploration on private lands, accompanied by permit of the owner, or petition for permit to explore on national lands, there will be paid, for the entire proceedings, $4.00; but where permission is refused by the owner and permit is solicited of the Agent, $8.00. For the entire proceedings on a denouncement, including copy of the *expediente,* up to the delivery of the title, where no " incident " of opposition or reduction of *pertenencias* arises, fees will be paid in the order as follows: 1, Upon filing and registry of the denouncement, $2.00; 2, on acceptance by the Agent of the denouncement, $10.00; 3, upon receipt by the denunciant of the copy of the extract of the petition for its publication, $18.00. (Arts. 1–2.)

Art. 927. Reductions, Rectification and Division.— For the proceedings for the reduction of *pertenencias* of a pending denouncement, upon filing the petition, $8.00. For the entire proceedings under a petition for rectification of a titled mining property, in any of the cases under Article 923, where no opposition is filed, up to the delivery of the new title or copy of the proceedings to be added to the title, fees will be paid in the order as follows: 1, Upon filing the petition, $10.00; 2, upon receipt by the applicant of copy of extract of the petition for its publication, $18.00. For proceedings under petition for division of mining property, up to delivery of new titles, on filing petition, $5.00. For proceedings under petition for reduction of *pertenencias* of titled mining property, upon filing petition, $10.00. (Arts. 3–6.)

Art. 928. Expropriations — Easements.— For all proceedings under petitions for expropriations or easements, where the Agent intervenes in them, on filing petition, $.... (the amount is omitted in the text.) (Art. 7.)

Art. 929. Oppositions — Copies — Searches.— In cases of oppositions to a denouncement, the denunciant will pay, for the proceedings before the Agency, when the meeting **for** agreement is held, $10.00, which amount he may recover by suit from the oppositor. For copies of final judgments (*ejecutorias*) rendered in suits of oppositions to mining denouncements, such copy to be added to the copy of the *expediente* forwarded by the Agent to the Department of Fomento, for each sheet or fraction, $2.00. For certified copies of expert reports, or of all kinds of documents issued by Mining Agents **at** the instance of interested parties, for each sheet or fraction, $2.00. For comparison and authentication of plans, $2.00. For taking note of any document, $1.00. For searching **the** *expedientes* or other documents in the archives, $1.00; **and** where insufficient data are furnished for finding it, $1.00 additional for each year the records of which must **be** searched. (**Arts.** 8–11.)

Art. 930. Right to Fees — Irregularities.— Mining Agents have the right to receive only the fees fixed by this Schedule, and in cases not covered by it, they must consult the Department in regard to the amount to be collected. Where proceedings on an *expediente* are interrupted without the Agent's fault, no fees paid to him shall be refunded. Where on **account** of any irregularities committed by **Agents**, it is **necessary** to repeat any proceeding, it shall be done at the cost of the Agent, who cannot collect new fees for the same. (Arts. 12–14.)

MINING TAX AND FRANCHISE LAW.

(Ley sobre Impuestos y Franquicias á la Minería, de 25 Marzo, 1905.)

CHAPTER 1.

Art. 930A. Stamp Tax on Gold and Silver.— Gold and silver produced in the Republic or coming into it from a foreign country, shall be subject to the internal Stamp Tax, except only as herein provided; said tax being hereafter paid as follows: A. At the rate of $3\frac{1}{2}\%$ on the value of the gold and silver which are not treated (*beneficiados*) within the country, but are exported in any form in which they are combined or mixed with substances not properly metals; B. at the rate of $2\frac{1}{2}\%$ on the value of the gold and silver which are treated in the country up to the point where they are not combined or mixed except with other metals, and whatever the fineness (*ley*) of the product. For the purposes of such tax, gold will always be of the value of $1.00 for each 75 centigrams of pure gold, and the value of silver will be fixed by taking its average cash sale price in London during the previous month, and converting such price into Mexican money at the rate of exchange during said month; the "*Diario Oficial*" will publish the price of silver which shall serve each month as the basis for the payment of the tax. Smelters which refine gold or silver up to at least 999-1000ths fineness shall be entitled to a rebate on the $2\frac{1}{2}\%$ tax upon the gold and silver so refined, the amount of such rebate to be fixed

39

by a decree of the Executive after a hearing of the interested parties. (Arts. 1–4.)

Art. 930B. Same — Exemptions.— But the Stamp Tax will not be paid on: A. Refined gold presented to the mints for coinage or to the Government offices in exchange for silver money, at the rate of 75 centigrams of pure gold per *peso;* B. Mexican and foreign gold and silver moneys of current coinage; C. silver exported in the form of ore, earth or dust, whether in their natural state or mechanically concentrated, and in the form of cyanides, sulphides or furnace slag, where the amount of silver contained in such substances does not exceed 250 grams per ton; D. silver and gold imported into the Republic in any of the above forms or with a beginning of treatment and exported within four months in the form of cakes, disks or bars after smelting operations in Mexican establishments; E. gold and silver used in national industries; F. samples of ores in their natural state exported under the conditions prescribed by the Regulations. (Art. 5.)

Art. 930C. Assay and Other Duties —Tax Franchises.— Assay duties are only payable where the operation is performed at the request of the interested parties, or is required by law or regulation; the smelting duties, where on account of want of homogeneity of the bars or pieces it is necessary to remelt them in order to assay and appraise the same; the duties of refining and separation, where such operations are performed at the request of the interested parties in the Government offices which are disposed for such service; the amount of such duties will be fixed in a Tariff to be issued by the Treasury Department, based on the cost of the respective services.

Smelting establishments which through special concessions granted by the Government and which are in force at the time of this law, enjoy franchises in respect to federal and local taxation, may avail themselves of this law provided that they unreservedly renounce such franchises before the Treasury Department; in the meanwhile they shall not enjoy the benefits of this law, and shall continue subject to the terms of their concessions, to the law and regulations of 27 March, 1897, and to the other provisions of law now in force, including the payment of the coinage duty. Said Law of 27 March, 1897, in respect to the tax on coinage is repealed. Upon the expiration of the aforesaid concessions, they shall not be extended or renewed, but said establishments shall remain subject to all the common fiscal legislation. (Arts. 6–8.)

Art. 930D. Mining Stamp Tax — Fixed and Annual.— The amount of special stamps which according to present laws must be affixed to the titles of mining properties, shall be $5.00 for each *pertenencia* protected by said titles, whatever minerals are exploited.

The annual tax on mining properties shall be paid as follows: A. The *cuota* shall be six ($6.00) *pesos* a year per mining *pertenencia,* or two *pesos* for each third of a year (*tercio*), whatever minerals are exploited; B. if the number of *pertenencias* of a single mining industry exceeds 25, and said *pertenencias* are contiguous, the rate of $6.00 shall be paid only by the first twenty-five *pertenencias,* and will be reduced to $3.00 on each *pertenencia* in excess of twenty-five.

Petitions for concessions of mining *pertenencias* and *demasías* must be accompanied by the certificate issued by the local Stamp Tax office showing that the amount of the stamps for the title, according to the number of *pertenencias* solicited, has been deposited with said office; such certificate will be returned to the interested parties as soon as the stamps have been cancelled on the titles or that the denouncement has been finally rejected.

The maximum amount of tax which the States or the Federation shall impose on mines, under **Art.** 4 of the Decree of 6 June, 1887, is reduced to 1½%.[1] (**Arts.** 9–12.)

[1] The regulations of this law, for the collection of the Stamp Tax

Art. 930E. Payment of Tax — Penalties — Forfeiture.— The annual mining tax shall be paid in advance by *tercios* in each fiscal year, and within the first month of each *tercio,* to the Offices of the Hacienda to be fixed by the Regulations, at which the mine owner must present himself to make the payment, without the necessity of notice or any other requisite which might serve for delay or excuse. The *tercios* above mentioned shall begin with November 1st (Amendment of 31 December, 1892); the tax for each *tercio* must be paid before November 30th, March 31st, and July 31st of each year. For this purpose, the respective principal or subaltern Stamp Offices will deliver to each mine owner interested a *Boleta,* which shall contain: 1, The heading *"Impuesto Minero";* 2, the name of the State and Municipality to which the issuing Office belongs; 3, the name of the Mine, number of *pertenencias* on which the tax is paid, Municipality in which it is located, name of the owner, company or concern in whose possession it is, and ordinal number of the registry of the title; 4, the quota of tax to be paid each *tercio;* 5, three columns in blank in which the stamps for each *tercio* will be attached and duly cancelled; such *Boletas,* showing the stamps duly cancelled, must be kept in a visible place in the business Office of the mining concern.

Failure to pay the annual mining tax within the first month of each *tercio* incurs a fine against the owner of the mining property, equal to 50 per cent. of the amount of the tax, if same is paid during the second month; if paid within the third month the fine will be 100 per cent., or double the amount of the tax due; if within such time the tax and penalties are not paid the mining property will be forfeited *ipso facto,* without any recourse, and the declaration of forfeiture will be made by the Department of Hacienda, and published in the *Diario Oficial,* whereupon the property is subject to denouncement by any other person. (Law 6 June, 1892; Arts. 5–6; Regulation 30 June, 1892, Art. 22.)

and of the Smelting and Assay Duties on Precious Metals, are of date 30 March 1905.

BOOK XV.
NOTARIAL LAW. PUBLIC INSTRU-MENTS.

(*Ley del Notariado,* of the Federal Government,[1] of

19 December, 1901.)

CHAPTER 1.

PRELIMINARY PROVISIONS.

Art. 931. Qualifications — Appointments, Etc.— The profession of Notary is a public function which can only be conferred, in the Federal District and Territories, by the Executive, and is incompatible with any other business or public office. A Notary is an official appointed for life (**Art. 72**), whose acts and instruments authorized by him are entitled to public faith and credit; such acts and instruments must be kept written and signed in his protocol, together with such documents as the parties may present, to whom he will issue such copies as may legally be issued. Such a number of Notaries may be appointed as the public interests from time to time may require; in places where there is only one Notary, and he is absent or disqualified, the Executive may authorize the Minor Judges in places where there is no Notary to act as

---

[1] The Notarial Laws of the several States are substantial copies of this Federal Statute, and the functions of the Notaries identical.

notary within the limits of their jurisdiction; where there
are several Notaries in a place each may act anywhere
within the jurisdiction; a Notary cannot act outside
his jurisdiction, but instruments to have effect elsewhere may be authorized by him. Notaries receive no
public salary, but are entitled to collect the fees fixed by the
tariff (*arancel*) of Notary fees. A Council of Notaries is
established in Mexico City, composed of a President, Secretary and nine members, elected January 1st of each year,
for the purposes of assisting the Department of Justice in
overseeing the compliance with this law, and to propose any
measures for the improvement of the system. The Notariate
is responsible to the Executive through the Department of
Justice, but the Department of Hacienda may inspect the
notarial offices for the purpose of observing compliance with
the revenue laws, or otherwise as may be provided
by law, and will notify the Department of Justice whenever a Notary is to be proceeded against. Besides the duties
prescribed in this law, Notaries must comply with the requirements of the general laws in regard to examination of
documents, execution of instruments, and issuance of certified and other copies. (The details of qualifications and
appointment of Notaries, etc., are omitted.) A Notary in
Mexico City must give a bond of $5,000, and outside of the
city of $2,000, deposited with the Department of Justice.
The seal of the Notary must represent in the center the national coat of arms, and have inscribed around it his name,
number and place of residence. (Arts. 1–29.)

Art. 932. Exercise of Functions — Disqualifications.— A
Notary must reside in the place wherein he acts, and cannot
leave for longer than thirty days without leave from the
Department of Justice. The Notary's office is called "*No-
taría Pública,*" and must be kept open at least from nine
till one o'clock and from three till six, and over the door,
which must be of easy access from the public street, there

must be a sign with the name, official designation and number of the Notary. The Notary is obliged to exercise his functions whenever required, but must refuse: 1, If the act required is prohibited by law or is manifestly contrary to good morals, or is one which should only be performed by some other official; 2, where any of the parties is his wife, relation by consanguinity or affinity in any degree, or collateral within the fourth degree inclusive; 3, where the Notary, his wife, or any relation as above prohibited, is interested in the act or in any of its stipulations, or is attorney or legal representative of any party thereto. He may also refuse to act if the parties do not advance the charges and fees, except in urgent cases 'of last wills he can only require advance payment for the necessary stamps. He cannot act while another is filling his place during leave of absence. (Arts. 30–35.)

Art. 933. Protocols and Records — How Kept.— All juridical acts of a Notary must be recorded in his protocol, which he may keep in one or more books, not to exceed five, according to the needs of the business of his office, and which must be numbered and kept in strict numerical order of his notarial acts, and special authorization of the Department must be had to keep more than one. In connection with the protocols he must also keep a portfolio (*carpeta*) or " Appendix " in which to file all documents relating to his notarial acts, which will be arranged in bundles numbered to correspond with the acts, and each document specified with an alphabetical letter. He will also keep a special book in which Powers of Attorney (*Poderes*) only will be recorded, each page of which will contain a proper printed form, with blanks to be filled according to the requirements of the parties, and printed certified copies of which, with corresponding number, will be delivered to the parties, who may either use such forms, or execute their powers of attorney in the same way as other contracts. The Notary will also keep an " Abstract Book " (*Libro de*

Extractos) which will contain a brief synopsis of the act, its number and date, the names of the parties, witnesses and interpreters, with their signatures, and that of the Notary and his seal, and will be always preserved in the office of the Notary. (Other details of keeping these books, which are merely of administrative concern, are omitted.) When a book is closed, or a Notary dies or goes out of office, all his protocols and records, except the " Abstract," are deposited and kept in the *" Archivo General de Notarías,"* in the Department of Justice of the Nation or of the several States. The Notary will also keep an index of all acts, in duplicate, one to be kept in his office, the other delivered to the General Archives. The protocols cannot be taken out of the office, except as herein expressly provided for the purpose of having it signed by parties unable to come to the office, and the records must be inspected, even by official inspectors, in the office and in the presence of the Notary. (Arts. 36–48.)

CHAPTER 2.

NOTARIAL INSTRUMENTS AND COPIES.

Art. 934. Form and Manner of Execution.— The Notary must himself compose or reduce to written form his notarial acts or instruments (this original form being called the *matriz*), and record them in the proper book of his protocol, attended by his assistant, or if none, by two unexceptionable witnesses who can read and write, who are over twenty-one years of age and residents of the town where the act is executed, and he must issue the proper copies. Every notarial act must be " extended " in conformity with the following rules: 1, It must be composed in the Spanish language and be written with indelible ink, in clear hand-writing, without abbreviations, arithmetical figures, erasures, corrections or blanks; 2, the Notary must state his name and surname and the place of execution; 3, the date of execution, name and surnáme, age, status, business or occupation and residence of the parties, of his assistant or of the witnesses to the instrument, and of any other witnesses required by law; 4, he must certify that he knows the parties and their legal capacity, or that these matters are vouched for by two witnesses whom he knows; if there are no such witnesses or they are not qualified to attest, the instrument cannot be executed, except in grave and urgent cases, the reason for which must be recited, and if any document is presented in proof of the identity of any of the parties, it will also be entered; the assistant or instrumental witnesses can in no event act as witnesses to identity; 5, the act or contract must be set forth in clear and concise clauses, avoiding all useless and antiquated formulas; 6, the subject-matter of the contract must be distinctly stated so as not to be confounded with anything else, and if it be real estate, its nature, location in its proper municipality, district and State, its boundaries, and as far as possible its topographical limits and superficial area must be stated; 7, any document presented will be literally transcribed, compared, sealed and rubricated, and in the proper case filed in the Appendix; 8, the renouncement or waiver by the parties of any law, which is not prohibitive, or affecting the public interests, rights, or good morals, must be precisely stated, observing the provisions of the law on the subject; 9, it must appear that the force and effect of the several clauses were explained to the parties; 10, the hour must be stated where required by law; 11, the Notary must certify that the instrument was read to the parties and witnesses; if any party is deaf he must himself read it, and the fact be recited; if he cannot read it, he will designate some one to read it in his name, and the fact will be certified; 12, if any party does not know the Spanish language, he will select an interpreter, who must "protest" before the Notary that he will faithfully perform his duty; the other party who knows the language may also have an interpreter; the interpreters will be named and described in the act and will sign it, and all the circumstances will be recited; 13, at the end of the instrument all words crossed out or interlined will be mentioned and their number stated: words must be so crossed out as to remain legible; 14, the parties and witnesses of identity will sign, if they can, if not, the circumstance will be recited; the instrumental witnesses or the assistant will then sign, and finally the Notary, who will also affix his seal; 15, if the parties wish to make any addition or alteration before the Notary signs, it will be written in without leaving any blank spaces, with the statement that it was read, and all will sign and the seal be affixed as above provided. (Arts. 49–50.)

Art. 935. Same — Original Contracts.— An *escritura pública* may also be extended in respect to any contract already made between the parties, where the original is presented, in writing, signed by the parties and properly stamped; but for such *escrituras* to be valid, it is necessary, besides the conditions required by law: 1, That the parties are present in person or by attorney with special power; 2, that the written contract comply with the requirements of clauses 1, 5, 6, 8, 13 and 14 (as to signatures of the parties) of the preceding Article; 3, that the Notary extend in his procotol an act explaining briefly in abstract the nature of the contract, and complying with the requirements of clauses 1, 2, 3, 4, 7, 9, 10, 11, 12, 13, 14 and 15 of the preceding Article, and reciting moreover that the original contract, read and explained to the contracting parties, agreed to and ratified by them, signed and sealed on the margin of each of its pages by the Notary and signed in the same way by the parties, remains added to the Appendix under its proper number and stating the number of pages it contains; 4, that he shall send within three days to the *Archivo General de Notarías* a notice of the execution of the contract, noting that fact on the margin of the act, which he will sign and seal. The paper and writing of said original contract must be, like the pages of the protocol, 35 centimeters in length by 24 in width in their utilizable part, and contain not more than forty lines of writing, at equal distance apart, leaving a blank space of one-third part to the left of the writing; failure to observe these requirements does not affect the validity of the contract, but is subject to the penalties fixed by the Stamp Law, besides a fine against the Notary of from $25 to $100; Notaries must conform as far as possible to the same forms in respect to judicial documents which they are required to protocolize. (Arts. 51–52.)

Art. 936. Foreign Documents — Protocolization.— Foreign public instruments may be protocolized in Mexico upon order of the judge, who will first cause the document to be translated into Spanish, and require the legalization of signatures, and will see that it complies with the requirements of Art. 145, unless otherwise provided by treaties with the foreign country from which it comes. (**Art.** 53.)

Art. 937. Other Documents and Records — Form.— Every *escritura* will be numbered on the margin in progressive order, with the names of the parties and the nature of the instrument; no space shall be left between one *escritura* and another than is necessary for signatures and seal. Instruments

other than contracts and wills, which the laws permit or
require a Notary to authorize, will be extended under their
proper number in the protocol, and observing the requirements and form which such laws prescribe, and those
of clauses 1, 2, 4, 7, 10, 13 and 15, and the material por--
tions of clauses 3, 5, 6, 11, 12 and 14, of Art. 934. (Arts.
54–55.)

Art. 938. Failure to Sign — Effects.— Notaries are prohibited to authorize an *escritura* unless the parties sign it within
the unalterable term of thirty days from its date; where
the signatures are collected by separate acts on different
days, the day and hour of signing must be stated, on the
Notary's responsibility; those acts which according to law
may be protocolized without the appearance and express
consent before the Notary of all the parties, can only be
reduced to *escritura pública* by judicial order. In the urgent
cases stated in clause 4 of Art. 934, the *escritura* and its certified copies will be valid, if the identity of the maker is
afterwards proven. (Arts. 56–58.)

Art. 939. Minutes of Contracts —" Blotter."— Notaries are
not required to keep a " Blotter " or Minute-book of *escrituras,* but they must accept all minutes presented by the
parties, and certify that they were signed in their presence
or proceed to verify the signatures; the minutes will be
kept on file, and when the notarial instrument is signed
will be cancelled; minutes of contracts have no other effect
than to require the parties to execute the corresponding
escritura or make compensation in damages. (Art. 59.)

Art. 940. Compelling Signature — Minutas.— Wherever it
is required by law or by the agreement of the parties, that
a contract be executed in *escritura pública,* and one of them
refuses to sign it, the other may compel him to sign or to
pay all damages caused. For this purpose Notaries shall

extend no instrument in their protocols without first requiring the interested parties to sign the minute or blotter
(*minuta ó borrador*) of it before him, or if they cannot
write, to express their consent before the Notary and two
witnesses, which fact will be recited in the instrument.
Where the foregoing requirements have been complied with,
and the party refusing to sign fails to justify his refusal,
the judge will sign, and such fact will be stated in the
escritura, which will be considered perfect upon the judgment becoming final. (Code Civil Proc., Arts. 9–10.)

Art. 941. Certified Copies of Notarial Acts.— The Notary
must issue under his signature and seal the first copy (*testimonio*) of any act, upon compliance with the requirements
of the Stamp Law and payment of all other taxes, indicating at its close and on the margin of the matrix, the number
of sheets of paper it is on, the name of the party to whom
issued and for what reason, and the date of issuance, and
must deliver it to the party ordering it within three days
if of not more than five sheets and within six days if containing more; each sheet of the copy must be sealed by the
Notary, and all words crossed out or interlined will be
mentioned at the end the same as on the record; the proper
amount of stamps must be affixed to the copy, except where
the copy is ordered by authority for use in criminal or revenue matters, in which cases he will authorize it with his seal
on each page and his signature at the end, and it can be used
for no other purpose. Second and other copies (*copias*)
may be issued at the request of the proper parties where it
does not prejudice third persons, such copies being numbered in order; the paper used for all copies must be of the
size required by law, each page containing at most forty lines,
and having on each side a margin of one-eight the width of
the page. No other contract, including assignments, sub-
rogations, and substitutions of powers of attorney, can be extended at the end of the certified copy of another *escritura,*

but only in the protocol, making the corresponding notation on the matrix and on the copy of it, and a copy of the new contract must also be issued; nor can any notarial act be revoked or modified by simple notation on the margin, but a new *escritura* must be made and notation of it made on the old, unless otherwise provided by law; and such annotation must be made on all earlier records in the protocols when later ones are made referring to the former. (Arts. 60–65.)

Art. 942. Legal Effect of Notarial Acts — Authentication. All public instruments issued by the proper Notary in conformity with this law are full proof in and out of court; in order to have such effect outside the Federal District, or Territory wherein extended, the signature and seal of the Notary must be legalized, without charge, by the Department of Justice in the Federal District, and by the proper *Jefe Politico* in the Territories (and in the States, for the same purpose, the signature of the Notary will be legalized by the President of the Supreme Court, and that of the latter by the Governor of the State). Notaries as such are prohibited from issuing certifications of any act or fact not appearing in their protocols, and they are only entitled to public faith in respect to the exercise of their proper functions. (Arts. 66–67.)

Art. 943. Wills — Special Records.— Notaries will immediately advise the *Archivo General* of the execution of all public wills, giving the name of the maker and the date of its execution, and if it is closed, the name of the person or place where it is deposited; said *Archivo* will keep a special book for such matters, and judges before whom cases of intestate succession are brought will at once inquire from the *Archivo* if there is any record in said book of a will made by the deceased. (Art. 68.)

Art. 944. Nullity of Escrituras — Liability of Notary.—

An *escritura* is void: 1, If the Notary authorizing it is not at the time duly in the exercise of his functions; 2, if written in a foreign language; 3, if the Notary fails to certify that the act was read to the parties; 4, or where any party is deaf or deaf-mute, that he read it for himself or ascertained its contents by other legal means; 5, if the signature of any party, witness or interpreter is missing, if he could sign, or if he could not, that fact is not recited; likewise if the signature or seal of the Notary is wanting, or the signature of the assistant, when he acts instead of instrumental witnesses; 6, if the place and date of its execution are not stated; 7, if the act was authorized by the Notary outside the district for which he was appointed; 8, if the Notary is disqualified by reason of relationship, as provided in Art. 932, but if his fault relates to clause 3, only the forbidden clause or stipulation is void; 9, wherever any internal or external requisite is wanting which makes it void under this or any other law. In all other cases the document is not void, although the Notary who violates any legal requirement may be liable according to law; where any notarial act must be corrected on account of the error or default of the Notary, he is liable for the costs.[1] (Arts. 69-70.)

Art. 945. Responsibilities of Notaries.— Notaries are liable for crimes and defaults committed in the discharge of their duties, in both civil and criminal proceedings, at the instance of the injured party, and to administrative penalties for the infraction of any provisions of this law not involving penal liability; the latter are inflicted by the Department of Justice, which may consist of warnings, fines from $25 to $500, or suspension not to exceed one month, according to the gravity of the offense, a record of all such offenses being kept in the Department; where the punish-

---

[1] Articles 71 to 84 and 123 to 132 inclusive, in regard to resignation, death, etc. of Notaries, of " Complementary " provisions, and the " Transitory " provisions, of no general concern, are omitted.

ment involves loss of office the penalty must be imposed by the proper judicial authority. (Arts. 85–90.)

Art. 946. Archivo General — Functions.— An *Archivo General de Notarías* of the Federal District is established in Mexico City, dependent upon the Department of Justice, and may be extended to the Territories, with a Keeper or *Archivero* appointed by the Department. (In the several States like *Archivos* are established also in connection with the Department of Justice, and with similar functions.) In such *Archivos* will be kept: The documents which the Notaries are required to remit to the Archives; the closed protocols and annexed documents, which must be remitted within six months; the archives of suspended Notaries, and other documents belonging to the General Archive; the seals of Notaries which must be deposited or rendered useless as required by law. Details of organization and internal administration are omitted, only these of public interest being stated; among the duties of the Directors of the *Archivo* are: To keep a register of·the seals and signatures of Notaries within the jurisdiction; to keep all the records of the Office properly classified; not to allow the protocols and annexed documents to remain out of their proper place, and to allow only the Notaries to take, in their presence, memoranda necessary for the preparation of any new *escritura* which they may have to make; to obtain from the Department of Justice the new books which the Notaries require for their business; to issue, in proper cases, to the interested parties, certified copies of *escrituras* and notarial acts registered in the protocols deposited, and to issue such copies as are required by judicial decree, which will be inserted in the copy; to keep general indexes according to the rules prescribed by the Department. The Director will use on such copies and on other official documents a seal, reading in the center *" Estados Unidos Mexicanos,"* and on its circumference, *"Archivo General de Notarías del Distrito Federal — México."* (Arts. 91–102.)

Art. 947. Tariff of Notarial Fees.— Notaries in the Federal District and Territories will receive the fees (*honorarios*) prescribed in the following *Arancel,* which varies in the several States: For the preparation or simple authorization of *escrituras* and notarial acts of ascertained value, not otherwise taxed herein: Where the value does not exceed $500, $5; not exceeding $2,000, $10; not exceeding $5,000, $20; not exceeding $7,500, $30; not exceeding $10,000, $35; not exceeding $20,000, $40; from $20,000 to $50,000, $40 for the first $20,000 and $2 per thousand of the excess; from $50,000 upwards, the above rates on the first $50,000, and $1 per thousand on the excess, but the total fees are not to exceed $200 in any case. Where the principal amount is determined, interest or other periodical return is not counted; in leases for an indefinite period, the amount of three annual payments will be taken as the basis; in case of life annuities in which the capital is not fixed, the basis will be the amount of capital which at six per cent. a year would produce the same income for a time not to exceed five years. Where the *escritura* or notarial act contains several correlative contracts, the full fees will be paid on the amount of the principal contract and one-half on each of the accessories, according to their pecuniary value. Where it is not possible to determine the money value of the act or contract, there will be paid for its redaction and authorization the sum of $8 for each sheet.

Powers of Attorney: For the preparation and authorization of a power of attorney for collections or lawsuit or both, $5; special powers for a particular matter, $8; general powers for suits, collections, compromises and accounts, without clauses for administration or alienation of property, $12; unlimited powers, $15; for all such powers where printed forms are used the only fee will be $5.

40

Protests: For protest of mercantile documents required by law: If the amount does not exceed $250, $4; from $250 to $1,000, $5; up to $10,000, $10; up to $20,000, $20; over $20,000 to any amount, $30; none of the foregoing amounts is to be added to the preceding, but each is subject only to the fee fixed.

Wills: For open public wills and codicils of the same kind, if executed during business hours in the Notary's office, $20; if at the testator's house on account of his inability to go to the Notary, $25; if because he does not want to go, $50; if out of business hours, up till eleven o'clock at night, $10 for each hour employed will be added to the above amounts; if the testator has an infectious disease, $100 will be added to the foregoing amounts; for notation and authorization on the wrapper of closed wills, $10, applying the foregoing rules in the respective cases.

Protocolization: For the protocolization of a power of attorney, $5, and for that of a will, document or legal proceedings, $10; and in addition to said charges, for the matter written and compared in the protocol or copies, $1 per double sheet (*pliego*), and if amounts are stated in the copy which must be summed up on the front or turn of the page, $2 for each sum.

Miscellaneous Acts: For taking signatures outside the office, $3 for one signature, and $1 for each additional if in the same house and in the City, and double the amount if outside the City. For the examination of every document not exceeding ten sheets (*fojas*), $3, and 10cts. for each additional sheet, and if made for good cause outside his Office, double rates. For communications which they are required to direct to any office, $1 each. For the authorization of copies and certifications, and rubrication of the corresponding documents, $1 each. For annotations placed on or in regard to instruments, $2.50 each. For the preparation and authorization of every *escritura* of cancellation, extinction of obligations, or redemption of *censos,* where the amount is less than $1,000, $5; if over $1,000, the fee will be one-half the amount of the tax on the said *escritura,* not to exceed $30. For the simple search for *escrituras* or other documents or records in his Archives, for the current year, or a specified past year, 50cts.; if not of the current year and the party does not designate the year, for each year up to five, $1, and for each additional year, 50cts. For the authorization and deposit of a minute of contract, $5. The prescribed fees cannot be doubled in any case.

The entire amount of fees in bilateral contracts will be paid by the party agreed upon when the *escritura* is extended, or pro rata by all if no one is agreed on; the total amount of fees will be stated in the note of " Taxes and Fees " on the margin of the matrix and at the foot of the certified copy issued. (Arts. 103–122.)

BOOK XVI.
REGISTERS AND REGISTRY.[1]

CHAPTER 1.

THE PUBLIC REGISTER. (REGISTRO PÚBLICO.)

(*Código Civil*, Arts. 3184–3226.)

Art. 948. General Provisions.— In every place where there is a court of first instance there shall be an office called *" Registro Público"*; it shall be composed of four sections: 1, Register of Conveyances of real estate and real rights, other than mortgages; 2, Register of Mortgages; 3, Register of Leases; 4, Register of Judgments; also an Index of private documents of sales of real estate under five hundred pesos, of which a special record will be kept; the section of mortgages and their registry is governed by the provisions of Arts. 415–418.

The registry must be made in the office of the district where the land is located, and if located in several districts, the registry must be made in each. No registry can be made unless it appears that the person requesting it is the actual

[1] See Arts. 156, *et seq.*, in regard to the Register of Civil Status; Arts. 415–418 in regard to the Registry of Mortgages, and Arts. 859–863 for the Grand Register of Property.

owner of the property or his lawful attorney-in-fact, or has legal right to demand the registry. Only instruments constituted by *escritura pública,* and duly certified judgments and judicial records, can be registered. Acts and contracts required by law to be registered are of no effect against third persons unless they are registered in the proper office. (Arts. 3184–3191, 3193.)

Art. 949. Foreign Instruments.— Acts and contracts executed and judgments rendered in a foreign country can only be registered under the following circumstances: 1, When they would require registry if executed or rendered in in Mexico; 2, when they are duly legalized as required by the Code of Civil Procedure; 3, where the judgments are such that their execution would be ordered by the Superior Tribunal of the Federal District. (Art. 3192.)

Art. 950. Instruments Subject to Registry.— All the following acts, contracts, instruments and documents must be registered:

All acts and contracts between living persons which transmit or modify the ownership, possession or enjoyment of real property or of real rights imposed upon it, except where the value does not exceed five hundred pesos; leases for more than six years or in which the rent is paid in advance for more than three; last wills and testaments, after the testator's death, which transfer real property or rights, and in cases of intestacy the judicial declaration of heirship and deeds of partition, the fact of the death being noted on the register; instruments constituting usufruct, use, habitation, easements, concessions of mines, quarries, beds of mineral substances, and others of similar nature; matrimonial and dowry capitulations, in which community of real property is established between husband and wife, or one of them acquires such property by way of dowry, antenuptial donation or otherwise; compromises, reservations, conditions, of absentees and judgments declaring absence and the presumption of death; judgments decreeing separation of property on account of necessary divorce and approving that in cases of voluntary or consent divorce; judgments declaring bankruptcy or permitting an assignment of property; judgments or decrees ordering the posting of mortgage notices, attachments, *sequestros,* receivership (*intervención*) or expropriation. (Arts. 3194–3207.)

Art. 951. Manner of Making Registry.— The interested party must present to the proper section of the registry office the instrument or certified copy of judgment, together with his power of attorney if he represents another person; if the registrar does not find such documents in due form, he will advise the party and require the judicial declaration.

The register must contain: 1, The names, ages, residence and business of the contracting parties, " moral persons " being designated by their official name and companies by their firm name; 2, the date and nature of the instrument registered, the authority or notary authorizing it, and the day and hour when it is presented; 3, the nature and value of the property or rights transferred or modified, stating exactly its location, and all facts in regard to income, encumbrances, rents, annuities, terms and other circumstances concerning the instrument. In the Index above mentioned must appear the names of the parties, the location and boundaries of the property, the price and date of the sale, and the date of registry.

When the document has been registered, it will be returned to the party presenting it, with an endorsement of its registration on the date and at the number and page of the register when and where it is registered. Contracts registered within fifteen days after their date are effective as against third persons from their date, but if registered after fifteen days they are only effective as to third persons from the time of registry; the documents required to be entered in the Index [2] are only effective as to third persons from the time they are presented in the ofhee. If the act registered is annulled or rescinded by judgment, it must be noted on the margin of the register within thirty days after it becomes final, otherwise it will only be effective as to third persons from the time it is noted.

The rights and obligations of registrars, and the forms and manner of keeping the registers, will be fixed by a special Regulation. ' (Arts. 3208–3218.)

Art. 952. Extinction of Inscriptions.— Inscriptions are only extinguished as to third parties by their cancellation or by the registry of the transfer of the property or right to another person.

Cancellation may be total or partial; total cancellation may be required and must be ordered: When the estate or right affected by it is extinguished; when the title which it concerns, or its inscription, is declared void; when the property encumbered is judicially sold; [3] when in the case of a notice (*cédula*) of mortgage or of attachment, three years have elapsed from date of registry. Partial cancellation may be required and must be decreed, when the estate or right affected is reduced. The cancellation may be made by consent of the rightful parties where they are capable of contracting and clearly indicate their intention; if any condition is attached to the cancellation, it must be performed.

When the title of the purchaser is registered that of the grantor will be cancelled; upon the registry of a judgment declaring ineffective a former one registered, the former registry will be cancelled. (Arts. 3219–3226.)

[2] See Art. 948.
[3] See Art. 803.

(Código de Comercio, Arts. 18–32.)

Art. 953. Where and How Kept.
954. What Register must Contain.
955. Double Registry.
956. Registry of Foreign Corporations.
957. How Registered.
958. Failure to Register — Effects.
959. Effects of Registry.
960. Are Public Records.
961. Correcting Entries.

Art. 953. Where and How Kept.— A *Registro de Comercio* shall be kept in the principal town of each judicial district, by the official having charge of the Public Register of Property, as provided by Art. 948, or if there be none, by the Recorder of Mortgages, or by the ordinary judges of first instance. Inscription in the Register is optional for individuals engaged in commerce, who are considered as inscribed upon registering any document subject to be recorded; but is obligatory for commercial companies and ships. The Register must be kept in the chronological order of the presentation of documents. (Arts. 18–20.)

Art. 954. What Register Must Contain.— The inscription of each merchant or company must contain: 1, The name of the person, firm or corporation; 2, the kind of business in which engaged; 3, the date of beginning business; 4, its domicile; with that of any branches, which must also be inscribed in their own district; 5, the articles of association of mercantile companies of every kind, as well as all amendments, and the dissolution of said companies; 6, in case of stock companies formed by public subscription, the record of the first general meeting, with all annexed documents; 7, the general powers of attorney and appointments, with their revocations, if any, conferred upon managers and other employés; 8, the documents emancipating minors and authorizing them to engage in commerce; 9, marital licenses and other documents authorizing women to engage in commerce, and revocations of the same; 10, the documents relating to dowry, marriage settlements, paraphernalia, etc., of the wives of merchants, to separation of interests between married persons, and any modifications in the same; 11, documents in regard to the estate or patrimony of children or wards who are subject to the *patria potestad* or guardianship of persons engaged in commerce; 12, the increase or diminution of the capital of *sociedades anónimas* or *en comandita por acciones;* 13, the titles of industrial property, patents and trade-marks;[1] 14, the issue of shares, bonds and obligations of all kinds of companies, as well as individuals, stating the series and number of certificates of each issue, their interest and time of maturity, the total amount of the issue, and the property, rights or mortgages charged with their payment; 15, the issues of bank-notes, stating their date, kinds, series, denomination, and amount of each issue; 16, ships, stating their name, class, kind and power, and date of construction; principal dimensions; and names and residences of the owners; 17, all changes in the ownership of ships or in the other particulars specified; 18, the creation, modification and cancellation of any kind of encumbrances upon ships; the bonds of brokers.   (**Art. 21.**)

Art. 955. Double Registry.— When any of the foregoing matters or contracts are also required by law to be registered in the Public Register of Property or of Mortgages, their inscription in such Register shall be sufficient for all legal purposes of the commercial law, provided that a note of such other entry is made in the special Register of Commerce.   All such inscriptions should be made in the judicial district of the merchant's domicile, except when real property

---

[1] Repealed by Patent and Trade-mark Laws of 25 August, 1903, requiring registration in the Patent Office.

Art. 956. Registry of Foreign Corporations.— Foreign corporations desiring to locate or establish branches in the Republic, must present and record in the Commercial Register, in addition to the certified copy of the protocolization of their by-laws, contracts and other documents in regard to their charter, their inventory or last balance sheet, if any, and a certificate of their being constituted and authorized according to the laws of their respective countries, issued by the minister of Mexico in such country, if there be one, or by the Mexican consul. (Art. 24.)

Art. 957. How Registered.— The registration must be made upon presentation of a certified copy of a public document, or of the written document or declaration of the merchant when the document is not required to be public. All documents subject to registration, coming from a foreign country, must first be protocolized in Mexico. (Art. 25.)

Art. 958. Failure to Register — Effects.— Documents required to be registered, which are not registered, are only effective between the parties to them, but cannot prejudice a third person, who may avail himself of them so far as favorable to him. Documents relating to real property **and** rights will affect third persons, although not registered **in** the Commercial Register, if they are registered in the proper Register of Property or of Mortgages. Failure to register documents raises the presumption of fraud in case of bankruptcy, in the absence of proof to the contrary. If a merchant fails to register the documents requiring registry, his wife, her parents or ascendants who have exercised the *patria potestad* over her, or her guardian, may demand their registry. (Arts. 26–28.)

Art. 959. Effects of Registry.— Registered documents

produce their effects from the date of their registration,[4] and cannot be invalidated by prior or subsequent unregistered documents. (**Art.** 29.)

Art. 960. Are Public Records.— The Commercial Register is a public record, and the registrar must furnish information of its entries to all who request it, and must issue certified copies of all inscriptions to those who apply for them. They cannot refuse under any pretext to register all commercial documents presented for registry. (Arts. 30–31.)

Art. 961. Correcting Entries.— Any corrections of form or substance may be made summarily by the judge of the merchant's domicile, according to the proofs adduced, the registrar being in the position of defendant. (Art. 32.)

[4] See Art. 951 as to civil documents.

BOOK XVII.

PATENTS, TRADEMARKS AND COPYRIGHTS.

TITLE I.

PATENTS AND REGULATIONS.

CHAPTER 1.

PATENTS OF INVENTION.

(New Patent Law of 25 August, 1903.)

Art. 962. What is and is not Patentable.— All persons, making new inventions of any industrial character, may acquire the exclusive right, by virtue of **Arts.** 28 and 85 of the Constitution, to exploit them for their own benefit, during a certain time, subject to the rules and conditions contained in this law, it being first necessary to obtain a patent of invention. The following are patentable: A new industrial product; the application of new means, or the new application of known means, to obtain an industrial product or result; also every *new form* of an industrial product, piece of machinery, tool, statue, bust, high or low relief, which by reason of its new artistic arrangement or novel arrangement of its materials, forms a new and original industrial product; also every new design or drawing used for purposes of industrial ornamentation in any substance and applied thereto by any mechanical, physical or chemical process, so that it gives to such industrial products on which such designs are used a peculiar and distinctive appearance. The following are not patentable: A discovery or invention consisting simply in making known or evident something already existing in nature, although previously unknown to men; scientific principles or discoveries of a purely speculative nature; inventions or discoveries the use of which is contrary to prohibitive laws, to public safety or health, and to good customs or morals; chemical products, except new methods of obtaining or new industrial applications of the same. (Arts. 1–3, 102.)

Art. 962. Novelty — Exceptions.— An invention cannot be considered new which prior to the application for patent, whether in Mexico or abroad, has been used for commercial or industrial purposes, or through any printed publication has received sufficient publicity to enable it to be used, it being in such cases considered public property; but this rule does not apply to the inventor or owner of the patent obtained in a foreign country: 1, Where such publicity arises from the exhibition of the invention in some official or officially recognized exposition, provided that prior to its exhibition the documents required by the regulations are filed in the Patent Office and that the proper application is presented to said Office within three months after the official closure of such exposition; 2, where the owner of the foreign patent files his application for a Mexican patent within three months from the day that said invention was made public according to the law of the country where the patent was issued, or where there are several foreign patents, within three months after the first was made public; 3, where such application is made within the time provided by international treaties on the subject, or within the twelve months referred to in Art. 965; such treaty provisions supersede those herein prescribed, and the interested party is entitled to the full time therein provided; if the publicity arises in more than one of the ways mentioned, the application must be filed within the shortest period. (Arts. 4–5.)

Art. 964. Rights of Patentee.— The owner of a patent has the exclusive right to exploit it himself, or through others with his permission, during the time herein granted; to prosecute in the Courts those who infringe his rights, either by the industrial manufacture of the patented article, by the industrial use of the patented process or method, or by having in their possession, selling, offering for sale, or bringing into the country any of the manufactured articles without his consent; a fraudulent intention is not requisite to criminal liability in case of industrial manufacture, but is in the other cases mentioned. But such patent is not effective against similar articles in transit through the country or remaining in its territorial waters; or against a third person who exploited such patented articles in the country prior to the filing of the application for patent, or had made necessary preparations for doing so, or who for purposes of experiment or study makes an article or adopts a process similar to the one patented. A patent may be issued in the name of two or more persons jointly if they jointly apply for it. (Arts. 6–8.)

Art. 965. Application and Granting of Patents.— Everyone wishing to obtain a patent must file in the Patent Office an application accompanied by two copies of a description, a claim (*reivindicación*), and drawings if he thinks them necessary; and in case of models or industrial designs, will also present a copy or model, or where it is difficult or costly to do so, a photograph may be permitted, or dispensed with entirely where the design itself gives a clear idea. The Patent Office will make a purely administrative examination of the documents presented for the purpose of ascertaining whether they are complete and in the form required by the regulations, but in no way concerning the novelty or utility of the thing proposed to be patented nor as to the sufficiency of said documents; if such documents are not in due form or the article proposed is such as is forbidden to be patented, the documents will be considered as not presented, and the applicant will be notified, and if not satisfied he may have recourse to the courts as hereinafter provided; if the documents are found in due form the applicant will likewise be notified.

The legal date of a patent is that of the filing of the application and accompanying documents, or depositing the documents in case of an article on exhibition as above provided, from which times the patent is presumed to be granted and produces its legal effects; but where a patent is solicited in Mexico and the same person has already made application in one or more foreign countries, the legal date will be that of the foreign patent, provided that the application in Mexico is made within twelve months from the first foreign application in case of invention, or within four months in case of a drawing or industrial model, and that such foreign country concedes the same right to citizens of Mexico; and patents applied for in Mexico on such conditions shall have absolutely the same force and legal effect as if they had been applied for on the day and hour of their legal date. Patents shall be issued without prejudice to the rights of third persons, and without guaranty of their novelty or utility, such qualities and the rights of the patentee being only presumed until proof to the contrary. One not the inventor applying for a patent must establish his right as representative by letter of attorney (*carta-poder*) signed by the inventor and two witnesses, but the patent office may require ratification of the signatures if deemed necessary. (Arts. 9–14, 103.)

Art. 966. Duration of Patent — Fees.— Patents of invention are granted for twenty years from their legal date; this period is divided into two, the first for one year and the second for nineteen years; the fees for the first period are five pesos, for the second thirty-five pesos; the regulations will fix the fees for copies, certificates, replacing the patent papers, etc. All charges will be paid by means of Federal revenue stamps as prescribed by the regulations. The twenty year period may be extended for five years, at the discretion of the Executive, upon the payment of such additional fees as he may require; application for such extension must be addressed to the Patent Office within the next to the last six months of the original period, accompanied by proof that the patent has been in uninterrupted use in the national territory during at least the last two years previous to the date of said application. Patents for models or industrial designs will be granted for five or ten years, at the election of the applicant, and the term cannot be extended; for five-year patents the fee is $5 and for ten years $10; all rights expire at the end of said term. (Arts. 15–18, 104–106.)

Art. 967. Exploitation of Patents.— The exploitation of a patent is not obligatory, but if within three years from its legal date it is not industrially used in the national territory, or if after such time its use is suspended for more than three consecutive months, the Patent Office may grant to a third person license to exploit it as herein provided. Any person wishing to obtain such license will make application to the Patent Office stating the grounds of his petition, copy of which will be served upon the owner of the patent, and a period of one month, which cannot be extended, will be fixed within which both parties must present their proofs to said Office, and within that time the Office may call for reports, appoint inspectors and take such other administrative steps as it may deem proper to ascertain the truth of the facts. If the owner of such patent shall not have made proof of having begun the industrial exploitation of the same within the 15 days hereinafter provided for that purpose, he will not be permitted to make any proof, and the said license will be forthwith granted to the petitioner. Within fifteen days after the said time for offering proofs, or within eight days after the presentation of the petition for license in the event the original proofs of user have not been presented, the Office will decide whether or not the requested license shall be granted; if the interested party is not satisfied with such decision, he may apply to any of the District Judges of the City of Mexico for the revocation of such decision, he taking the part of plaintiff and the other party that of defendant; the former must file his suit within the fixed period of eight days after notice of the administrative decision, and if he does not, he will be held to have abandoned his claim and to accept the decision; such suit will be conducted as provided in this law; the effects of the administrative decision granting the license are not suspended by the suit brought by the owner of the patent, but the licensee has the right to the immediate user of the patent without giving bond or any other requisite; but he must begin to exploit the patent within two months after the decision of the Patent Office or of the Court respectively, and must not suspend such user for more than two consecutive months. (Arts. 19–24.)

Art. 968. Rights and Duties of Parties.— One-half of the net profits obtained by the licensee from such exploitation shall belong to the owner of the patent, and he has the right to keep a watch on the user of the patent and to sue for his half of the proceeds, unless the parties otherwise agree about the matter. If the owner of the patent is absent

41

or does not appear to exercise his rights, the licensee must deposit said one-half of the profits every two months in a bank or institution of credit to be designated by the Patent Office for that purpose, and must also file with the Patent Office bi-monthly reports of the proceeds and net profits of said exploitation, and upon failure to comply with these requirements the Patent Office shall revoke said license at the request of the owner of the patent; the above notices will be published in the *Gazeta Oficial de Patentes;* if the licensee makes a false report to the Office he will be liable to the penalty of major arrest, and a fine of the second class, or either such penalty, at the discretion of the Judge, and for all damages and losses caused to the owner of the patent. Such license granted by the Patent Office does not deprive the owner of the patent of the right to exploit his invention himself and to issue such licenses as he may desire.

The owner of the patent may request the revocation of the license granted by the Patent Office after two years if he or some one else in his name is exploiting it industrially, provided he has made the proof of user as herein required, otherwise his petition will be rejected without recourse; the licensee must also have made like proof of having begun exploitation within two months, or no evidence will be admitted on his part; in other respects the proceeding to revoke the license will be conducted in the same way as the proceeding for granting it. If the licensee does not begin the exploitation within two months, or has suspended the same for more than two months, unless in case of accident or force, and continues to exploit it, the owner of the patent may prosecute him in the courts as an infringer or illegal exploiter of his patent. Both the owner of the patent and the person licensed by the Patent Office to use it, must within fifteen days after beginning to exploit it, make proof of that fact to the Patent Office by some legal means. (Arts. 25–30.)

Art. 969. Issuance of Patent — Mark.— Patents will be issued in the name of the President by the Patent Office and be countersigned by the Secretary of Fomento, and will recite: The number of the patent, the name of the person or persons to whom it is granted, its duration, the purpose for which it is granted, its legal date and the date of issuance, and will be sealed with the special seal of the Patent Office, to be kept for the purpose; such patent, together with a copy of the description, claim and drawings, if any, will constitute the title evidencing the rights of the patentee; the patent is effective only as to the subject-matter covered by the claim, the description and drawings, if any, only serving as explanatory of the claim. Every patented article must bear a mark stating the fact that it is patented and the number and date of the patent. (Arts. 31–34.)

Art. 970. Examination — Assignment of Rights.— The Patent Office will make an examination, without guaranty, in the manner provided by the regulations, at the request of the interested party, as to the novelty of a proposed patent, and on behalf of any person, to ascertain if any thing is already patented or is public property in Mexico, the result of such examination being reported in writing to the party requesting it. The rights conferred by a patent may be transferred in whole or part in the same way as other rights, but to be effective as to third parties such assignment must be registered in the Patent Office, upon payment of a fee not to exceed $20 to be fixed by the regulations. (Arts. 36–37.)

Art. 971. Expropriation of Patents.— A patent of invention may be expropriated for public use by the Federal Executive, the invention becoming public property, upon proper indemnity to the inventor, and observing as near as may be the procedure relating to expropriation of real property. Where the invention is a new or improved weapon, explosive, or other material of war adaptable to public defense,

and which in the judgment of the Executive should be kept
secret, the patent, and the invention even before being
patented, may be taken over in the same way, becoming the
exclusive property of the Government and not public property, and in such case the Patent Office will not give publicity to the patent.   (**Arts.** 38–39.)

Art. 972. Expiration and Nullity of Patents.— Patents
expire: 1, At the end of the first one-year period unless the
fees for the second period have been paid; 2, at the end of the
second nineteen-year period; or, 3, at the end of the five-
year extension if any was granted; the name and number of
each patent expiring will be published in the " Gazette."

Patents are void: 1, Where issued on a non-patentable article, or one wanting in novelty; 2, where the claim is not
sufficiently clear and explicit to ascertain from it what is
claimed as new; 3, where the description and drawings are
not sufficiently clear, in the judgment of experts, to enable
the thing described to be constructed or produced therefrom;
4, where the purpose for which the patent is obtained is
different from that for which it was solicited; 5, where a
similar patent has been previously granted in exico or
abroad, although it has expired.   A patent can be declared
void only by judicial authority, and for one of the foregoing
causes; the action may be brought by any one prejudiced by
it, or by the *Ministerio Público* where the Federal interest is
concerned; the District Judges of exico City have jurisdiction of such causes, except that where the nullity or expiration
is urged as a defense, and in criminal proceedings hereunder,
the judge before whom the suit or prosecution is pending
will decide upon the nullity, expiration or ownership of
the patent, and the final judgment or sentence will be notified to the Patent Office, published in the *" Diario Oficial "*
and " Gaceta de Patentes," and entered in the Register of
Patents, with annotation of all references to the patent.
(Arts. 40–47, 62.)

Art. 973. Official Publications — Museum.— The Patent Ofhee will publish a periodical called " Gaceta Oficial de Patentes y Marcas," in which, at least every two months, will be published a list of the patents and trade-marks granted, and everything concerning them, together with indexes, memorials, and other matter on the subject, and at least annually will publish a special book containing the claim and one or more drawings of every patent; and will establish a Public Museum in which will be deposited all models, plans, drawings, etc., relating to all patents granted. (Arts. 35, 101.)

Articles 48 to 100, relating entirely to penalties for infringement, administrative, civil and penal procedure, and Articles 108 to 121, which are " transitory " administrative regulations, are omitted as of no practical purpose in this work.

CHAPTER 2.

REGULATIONS OF PATENT LAW.

(Issued 24 September, 1903.)

Art. 974. Application — Requisites.— Every one wishing to obtain a patent must present to the Patent Office, in person or by attorney, a petition (*solicitud*) accompanied by the following documents: 1, A description; 2, a claim; 3, a drawing or drawings, if necessary; 4, two copies of the foregoing documents. The applicant will be given a receipt showing the date and hour of their filing, their filing number, and the terms within which the applicant must appear at the Office to be notified of the result of the examination and to pay the fiscal dues; failure to comply with the requirements indicated in the receipt will be considered as an abandonment of the case. The application must be in the form shown by the model; where the patent is solicited by several persons jointly, the name of the one who is to represent the others will be stated first in the application and so noted in the description. (Arts. 1–3.)

Art. 975. Description and Claim — Contents. — The description must begin: (a), with the name of the inventor or inventors, their occupation, nationality, residence, and place in Mexico City for the receipt of notifications; (b), next the name, nature and object of the invention, with an enumeration of the drawings; (c), the invention must next be described completely, clearly, exactly and as concisely as possible, and omitting all mathematical, philosophical or other demonstrations; (d), after the description will follow the claim; (e), the claim must be signed by the inventor or his representative; (f), the forms annexed to the Regulations must be strictly followed.

The Claim (*Reivindicación*) must define and express clearly and precisely the process, combination or product which constitutes the invention, or the article (*órgano*) or piece which forms the essential part of the invention, and indicate its relations with other organs or elements which are not the direct object of the patent. (Arts. 4–5.)

Art. 976. Drawings — Requisites. — The drawings (*Dibujos*) must be made on white paper of the thickness of three sheets of Bristol paper, of smooth and pressed surface, approximately 350 mm. in length by 254 mm. in width; a heavy line 25 mm. from the margin of the paper will form a square within which the drawing must be made; in the upper part of the square must be left a blank of about 25 mm. in which the Patent Office will put the name of the invention, its number, etc.; the inventor must write with a soft pencil on the back of the sheet the title which he gives to his invention; in the lower part of the square towards the right the inventor will sign his name. If possible the paper should be used lengthwise, its narrow ends being top and bottom, but if considered best it may be used sidewise, with the long sides at top and bottom; if one sheet is not sufficient, several may be used, but the complete invention must appear on at least one of them. Only China ink and grafio must be used, the ink being perfectly black; shading should be avoided as far as possible, but if absolutely necessary, it should be done with as few lines as possible; the light will be supposed as coming from the upper left corner of the paper at 45 degrees, so that the lines on the side of the shadow should be heavier than those on the side of the light. It is preferable and is expressly recommended, that the invention should be presented in a single drawing of the largest size possible, in conventional and free perspective, without the necessity of adhering to any scale, even between the parts of the same figure, as clearness is desired above everything else. Pieces represented in cross-section (*en corte*) should be marked with oblique lines at not less than 1.5 mm. apart. Reference signs should be letters or figures not smaller than 3 mm.; if at places there is not room for them or they may cause confusion, they should be placed as near as possible and connected with the point which they indicate by a straight or curved line; if notwithstanding it should be necessary to place a sign or letter in a space marked with oblique lines, a small circle in blank should be left in which to put it. If there are pieces or details which in the general figure appear too small, they should be marked with a single letter or sign, and represented sufficiently enlarged in special figures with the same sign.

Duplicates should be made on drawing-linen with China ink. Where photographs are admissible instead of drawings, they and their duplicates should be on blue paper, sepia, or other inalterable heliograph, of the size above indicated; the negative, which should be on a thick film, will also be presented.   The drawings must not be folded but presented extended between two heavy cardboards.   All the particulars of drawings annexed to the Regulations should be followed. (**Arts.** 6–10.)

Art. 977.   Rules for Particular Inventions.— A person wishing to obtain the rights granted by the law under clause 1 of **Art.** 962, must forward to the Patent Office a description, claim and drawings of the article to be exhibited, in the form and manner as above provided, and which may be used in the application for the patent.   Two or more independent inventions cannot be patented in a single patent, but where several distinct inventions are related to each other, in a single machine or process and mutually contribute to produce a single result, they may be included in a single patent.   In general every organ or combination of organs susceptible of separate exploitation, and the use of which in connection with the machine in which they are used is not absolutely necessary, forms the object of an individual patent.   Individual patents are required for: A machine and its product; a machine and the process in which it is used; an industrial drawing and the process by which it is obtained; an industrial model and the process for obtaining it; a process in which one substance or organ requires other processes in order to obtain it, but if the substance results as a necessary consequence of the process itself, a single patent is sufficient; also a process and its product may be covered by a single patent; in all doubtful cases two or more patents should be solicited.   (**Arts.** 11–20.)

Art. 978.   Issuance of Patents and Marks — Stamp Tax.— If the result of the examination is favorable, the party interested must present at the Patent Office within the time indicated in the receipt for the documents filed, a stamp **for**

$5.00, surcharged "*Patentes,*" for the fiscal dues for the first period of one year, and attach and cancel the same as directed; on any business day within the first year he may request the issuance of the definitive patent, presenting to the Patent Office three stamps of $10.00 and one of $5.00, all surcharged as above, which he will also attach and cancel, and the Patent Office will issue the Patent Title. The same will be observed in respect to patents for industrial Models or Drawings, paying a stamp of $5.00 if issued for five years and $10.00 if issued for ten years. Patents will be registered in a special register. (Arts. 21–23, 31.)

Art. 979. Extension of Patents — Proceedings.— Anyone wishing to obtain the extension granted by **Art. 966**, must address a petition to the Patent Office, on any business day during the six months next before the last six months of the natural period of the patent which he wishes to renew, together with all documents deemed necessary to prove that the patent has been exploited for at least two years uninterruptedly in the country, and stating any other reasons in support of his petition. The Patent Office will transmit the petition and documents to the Department of Fomento, with such report as it may make; if the Department finds the documents or proofs insufficient in any way, it will grant the applicant, through the Patent Office, not less than eight days or more than one month in which to supply the deficiency, after which time, whether or not the applicant avails of it, the Department will definitely decide whether the extension shall be granted. The Patent Office will notify the applicant of the decision; if favorable, the applicant will attach and cancel on the document indicated to him the number of surcharged stamps required to cover the tax fixed by the Executive; the notice and stamps must be presented to the Patent Office within one month from its date, together with the Patent Title on which to annotate the extension;

lost.

Under no circumstances will any documents or any taxes paid be returned in case of forfeiture, nullity, or other default, nor any copy or model filed in the Patent Office. (Arts. 24–25, 29.)

Art. 980.   Lost Patents — Sundry Documents.— If the Patent Title is lost or destroyed, it may be replaced at the instance of the interested party, who at his cost will have made a copy of the description, claim and drawings, and will pay $15.00 in surcharged stamps, attached and cancelled as indicated; the new Title will be marked duplicate.

To secure the examination mentioned in the **Law, Art.** 970, a petition stating clearly the applicant's domicile, and with a 50ct. stamp, must be presented, and the applicant will attach and cancel on the document indicated two surcharged stamps of $10.00 each, and the Patent Office will send to the applicant a document stating the number and date of any patents which it deems like or similar to the one applied for, or such references or indications as it deems material.   A like stamp for $5.00 will be attached to the petition for the registry of any other instrument mentioned in said **Article.**

The petition, description and claim, with their duplicates, and all other documents and papers presented to the Patent Office must be typewritten on one side only of paper 330 mm. by 215 mm., in blue or dark violet ink, non-copying, or well printed.   The Patent Office will fix the prices at which printed copies of patents granted may be sold to the public. (Arts. 26–28, 30, 32.)

TITLE II.

TRADE MARKS, NAMES AND ADVERTISEMENTS.

(Law of 25 August, 1903.)

CHAPTER 1.

INDUSTRIAL AND COMMERCIAL TRADEMARKS.

Art. 981. Defined — What May Be Registered.
    982. Who May Obtain — How Registered.
    983. Issuance of Trademarks — Effects.
    984. Assignment — Effect.
    985. Nullity — Actions.

Art. 981. Defined — What May Be Registered.— A trademark is a peculiar and characteristic sign or name used by manufacturers, agriculturists, or merchants on the articles which they produce or sell, for the purpose of identifying them and indicating their origin; but the following cannot be registered as trademarks: 1, Generic names or denominations, when the trademark covers objects embraced within the genus or species to which the name or denomination refers, for the mark must necessarily distinguish the articles protected by it from all others of the same species or class; 2, everything contrary to morals, good manners or prohibitive laws, or which tends to ridicule persons, ideas or objects worthy of consideration; 3, coats of arms, escutcheons and emblems, of Mexico, or of foreign countries, or of Mexican or foreign States or cities, without their consent; 4, the names, signatures, seals or pictures of individuals, without their consent. (Arts. 1, 5.)

Art. 982. Who May Obtain — How Registered.— Any Mexican or foreigner, including companies, corporations and all moral persons, may register a trademark, upon application to the Office of Patents and Trademarks in person or reservations as may be made of it; the name of the owner, and of his factory or business place, if it has a name, its location, and a statement of the objects or products on which the mark is to be used; he must also present a " *cliche* " or " cut " of the mark, and twelve copies of the mark as it is to be used. The registry will be made without examination of its novelty, on the exclusive responsibility of the applicant and without prejudice to third persons; the examination made will be simply to determine whether the documents are complete and in due form; if not in proper form, or wanting in any other requirement, they will be considered as not filed; whether approved or not, the applicant will be notified, and if not satisfied with the finding he may have it reviewed by the court as hereinafter provided. (Arts. 2–4, 10.)

Art. 983. Issuance of Trademarks — Effect.— The certificate of registry of a mark will be issued by the Office, and together with the annexed documents, will be the title evidencing the exclusive right to use it; the right relates back to the date of presenting the application and documents; where the application is made in Mexico within four months after like application in foreign countries, the registry relates back to the date of the first foreign application granted, provided such foreign country grants similar rights to Mexicans, and produces full force and effect from such time.

Registered trademarks must bear visible inscriptions as follows: Those used by manufacturers, industries, agriculturists, etc., " *Marca Industrial Registrada,*" or simply " *M..*

Ind. Rgtrda," with number and date; those used by mer-chants, *" Marca de Comercio Registrada "* or *M. de C. Rgtrda,"* with number and date; marks consisting of names, denominations, legends, signs connected with names, etc., initial letters or abbreviations, must display the name of the owner of the business, the name of the establishment or fac-tory, if any, and its location; any change of location or new establishment must also be registered, and indicated on the mark. The registry of a trademark must be renewed every twenty years; delay in renewing does not forfeit the right to its exclusive use, but incurs extra tax charges as fixed by the regulations, and prevents any penal action on account of infringements during the lapsed time. (Arts. 6–9, 11, 14.) .

Art. 984. Assignment — Effect.— Registered marks may be transmitted or assigned as any other right, but such assignment must be registered and the name of the new owner indicated on the mark as above provided; the new owner acquires all the rights secured by the trademark. (Arts. 12–13.)

Art. 985. Nullity — Actions.— Registration of a trade-mark is void where made in contravention of this law or its regulations, or where it has been registered by another more than two years previously, or for less time with better right; the action of nullity may be brought by anyone prejudiced, or by the *Ministerio Público* in cases of general interest. Final judgment declaring a trademark void must be notified by the judge to the Patent Office and published in the official " Gazette." (Arts. 15–17.)

Art. 986. Trade Names — Incidents.— The owner of a trade name has the exclusive right to use it, without registration or other requisite, and he, or any one who is injured thereby, may recover damages and have penal action against any one appropriating or imitating it; but any native or foreign merchant may nevertheless publish his trade name in the " Official Gazette," renewing the publication every ten years; such publication creates the presumption of fraud against any person wrongfully using or imitating such trade name, and dispenses with proof of fraud which must otherwise be made in cases of infringement. Any one who in any way makes use of a trade name not belonging to him, or who imitates it in such way as to produce confusion, is subject to minor arrest or to second class fine, or both, at the discretion of the judge, besides the penalty prescribed in case the trade name is improperly used in connection with and as part of a trademark, where the use of the latter is made a crime by this law, and cumulative penalties may be imposed as provided in the Penal Code. (Arts. 73–78.)

Art. 987. Commercial Advertisements.— Any person making use of any distinctive or original advertisement of his business or goods, may acquire the exclusive right to use it and prevent any one else from using anything similar which at first sight is likely to cause confusion, upon compliance as nearly as may be with the provision of this law applicable to trademarks, for a term of five or ten years, as he may elect, subject to other extensions for like periods, by applying for them before the expiration of the time, and publishing same in the " Official Gazette," and may have civil action for damages against any infringer, who is also liable to criminal punishment, with first class fine, as provided in the preceding Article. The printers or other makers of falsified commercial advertisements which are improperly used, and all who sell or put them in circulation, are guilty as principals or accomplices according to circumstances, and liable to punishment as prescribed in the Penal Code; the civil and criminal proceedings herein prescribed in regard to falsification of trademarks are also applicable to trade names and advertisements. (Arts. 79–84.)

Art. 988. Revenue Taxes.— The registration or extension of a trademark is subject to a tax of $5; the publication of a trade name, $1; the registration of a commercial advertisement will pay: For five years, $2; for ten years, $4; for each extension of five years, $4; all such taxes are payable in Federal Revenue Stamps as provided in the regulations, which will also fix the charge for other acts of the Patent and Trademark Office. (Art. 85.)

CHAPTER 3.

REGULATIONS OF TRADE MARK LAW.

(Issued 24 September, 1903.)

Art. 989. Applications — Requisites.— Commercial trademarks and advertisements will be registered in the Office of Patents and Trademarks at the instance of the interested party, a separate petition in the prescribed form being presented for each device to be registered; a receipt will be issued for all documents and cuts, showing the date and hour of **filing** and the corresponding number. The Office will make **an** administrative examination of the documents, in accordance with the Law, **Art.** 982, and if favorable, the applicant must present to the Office, within the time indicated in the receipt, a stamp surcharged " *Marcas,*" to cover the amount of tax, which he will attach and cancel on the document indicated to him, failing to do which within the time allowed the case will be held as abandoned. If the documents presented are not in proper form, the applicant will be **notified** so that he may replace them or proceed as provided in **the** Law.

The descriptions of the trademark must be authenticated by the signature of the applicant or his attorney, and if comprising more than one page, each page will be rubricated on the margin. **A**ll petitions and other documents must be typewritten, on only one side of the paper, with black, blue or dark violet non-copying ink; the paper must be 330 mm. long, 215 mm. wide, and have a margin of 54 mm. on the left hand side. The length or breadth of the " *cliché* " cannot be less than 15 mm. nor more than 100 mm., and its height 24 mm. If the trademark consists of several separate parts, a " *cliché* " for each part must be furnished, the colors being indicated as far as possible as indicated in the prescribed form. The twelve copies of the mark required to be filed must not have any erasures, corrections or **modifica**tions. (**A**rts. 1–9.)

Art. 990. Registry — Certificates.— If a trademark or part of it is of metal or other substance, or is to be **affixed** by means of seals in lead by fire or otherwise, twelve copies of its impression on paper must also be filed. **A**lthough several registries are sought in the name of the same person, the applicant must accredit his personality on each application. **A** person presenting himself as the agent or representative of a company, corporation or moral person must be accredited in the manner required by law; if the applicant acts as mandatary under a general power of attorney, he need only present a certified copy of the material part thereof.

The certificate of registry of a trademark must contain, in addition to the matters required by law: The number of the trademark; the date and hour of the filing of the petition and other documents; the name of the person to whom issued (*titular*); the seal of the Office of Patents and Marks; a copy of the registered trademark; a description of the trademark. If the certificate of registry should be lost or destroyed, it may be replaced at the cost of the grantee, upon his filing a petition with a surcharged stamp for $3.00, which he will attach and cancel on the document indicated; the new certificate will be marked duplicate. (Arts. 10–13.)

Art. 991. Transfers — Renewals.—To obtain the registry of a transfer of a trademark, a petition must be presented to the Office stating: The number of the registered trademark; the name of the former owner; the name of the mark, if any; the article or product which it covers; the name of the new owner; together with a copy of the trademark, and surcharged stamps for $3.00, which must be attached and cancelled as indicated. To prove the acquisition of the trademark or advertisement, the original and a copy of the *escritura* of assignment must be presented, the original being returned and the copy forming a part of the *expediente*.

To obtain the renewal of registry of a trademark or commercial advertisement, a petition must be presented, accompanied by surcharged stamps covering the amount of tax, and a copy of the mark or advertisement, within the first six months of the last year for the which the registry was granted; if the renewal is solicited after the expiration of such time, in addition to the stamps covering the tax, as many other like stamps must be paid as there are years or

42

fractions of a year elapsed after the expiration of such time. (Arts. 14–16.)

Art. 992. Advertisements — Registry.— To obtain the registry of a commercial advertisement, a petition must be presented to the Office, accompanied by: A *" cliché "* of the advertisement; twelve copies of the advertisement as it is to be used; twelve copies of said advertisement, printed on paper, where such advertisement is to circulate, made on crystal, plates, leather, card-board, etc. The petition must be in the prescribed form, and accompanied by surcharged stamps for $2 if the registry is for five years and for $4 if for ten years, and attached and cancelled as indicated. Application for the extension of the registry must be made within the next to the last six months of the period for which the registry was granted, and accompanied by a printed copy of the advertisement, and surcharged stamps for $4 for each extension of five years. For the publication of a commercial or trade name, the applicant will present a petition in the prescribed form, accompanied by a surcharged stamp for $1, to be attached and cancelled as indicated. (Arts. 17–20.)

Art. 993. Sundry Provisions.— The number of the trademark or registered advertisement must always be stated in every document relating to the same. Parties wishing the publication of any judgment rendered in regard to trademarks or advertisements must personally present a petition to the Office, accompanied by surcharged stamp for $1 to be cancelled as indicated. The Office will fix the prices at which printed copies of marks and advertisements and descriptions may be sold to the public. All documents which do not comply with the requirements of the Law and Regulations must be replaced at the cost of the interested party. On no account will any documents or stamps be returned. The public may examine registered trademarks and advertisements at such hours as the Office may allow.

Trademarks registered under previous laws remain valid, but in order to avail of the penal actions provided by the present law the owner of the marks must renew their registry every twenty years as provided in **Art.** 989. The provisions of the Code of Commerce, Art. 958, and clause 13 of Art. 954, no longer apply to the registry of trademarks, but the same must hereafter be registered in the Patent and Trademark Office; inscriptions made in the latter office shall have preference over those made in the Commercial Registry although of earlier date. Articles 700, 701, 702 and 708 of the Federal Penal Code, so far as concerns crimes in respect to trademarks, are repealed. (Arts. 21-27, 87, 91-92.)

TITLE III.

REGULATIONS FOR REGISTRY OF INTERNATIONAL TRADEMARKS.

(Issued 9 November, 1909.)

CHAPTER 1.

INTERNATIONAL REGULATIONS.

'Art. 993a. Requirements for Registration.
    993b. Registry — Notices — Publications.
    993c. Changes — Nullity.

Art. 993A. Requirements for Registration.— Every person or corporation domiciled in Mexico, owning a manufacturing or commercial trademark (*marca de fábrica ó de comercio*), registered in accordance with the laws of 28 November, 1889, (repealed by the following) or of 25 August, 1903, who wishes to secure protection for said trademark in the countries which have or shall hereafter adhere to the Convention (*Arreglo*) signed in Madrid on 14 April, 1891, relating to the international registry of such trademarks, will forward to the Office of Patents and Trademarks, in Mexico City, D. F.: 1, A petition for registry, in duplicate, made on the official form, which shall contain the name and address of the owner of the trademark, its number, the date of its issuance, and the articles which it protects; 2, three facsimiles of the trademark, separate from the petition, and authenticated by the signature of the petitioner, said facsimiles not to be larger than ten centimeters each side; 3, a *cliché* or cut of the trademark to be published in the publication of the International Office in Berne; such *cliché* must be an exact reproduction of the trademark registered in Mexico, showing clearly all its details; it must not be less than fifteen millimeters nor more than ten centimeters in width or length, and must be exactly 24 millimeters in thickness, which is the height of the printing types; such *cliché* will be preserved in the International Office; 4, a sight draft in favor of the " *Bureau International de la Propieté Industrielle,*" payable in Berne, for the amount of the international emolument, which is 100 francs for the first trademark and 50 francs for each additional one in cases where several are filed at the same time by the same owner; 5, a letter-of-Attorney (*carta-poder*), if the petition for registry is made through an attorney in fact. The Patent and Trademark Office will furnish gratuitously the necessary forms for registry to any person applying for same in writing. Any incomplete or irregular petitions will be returned immediately to the interested party.

The international registry of a trademark can only protect articles identical to those for which the trademark was issued in Mexico. The petition must not contain either a description or reservation of the trademark, as the facsimile will suffice to make it known, except when a description is necessary in case that a color or combination of colors is claimed as a distinctive feature of it; in such event the description shall be brief and will only state what is in relation to the color, and the interested party will remit forty-two examples (*etiquetas*) of the trademark printed in the color or combination of colors claimed. The renewal of registry is subject to the same requirements as a new registry except as to sending *clichés*. (Arts. 1–3, 11.)

Art. 993B. Registry — Notices — Publications.— As soon as the Office in Mexico admits an application for international registry, it will enter the same in a special book and will forward it to the International Office, and will notify the applicant of such fact. The legal date of the international trademark will be that of its registry in Berne. Upon receiving advices from the International Office of the registry of the trademark, the Mexican Office will make a record of the same and will send to the owner a certified copy of the official certificate issued by the International Office. All documents relating to the international registry of trademarks will be separately classified according to their nature in numerical order. An album containing them will be open to the public in the Patent Office during business hours, and a supplement containing all international trademarks registered will be published in the *Diario Oficial*. (Arts. 4–6, 9–10.)

Art. 993C. Changes — Nullity.— At the request of the owner of an international trademark, the Patent Office will notify the International Office of any changes made in the ownership of the trademark or in the firm-name of the owner, upon compliance with the requirements of the present trademark law in regard to such changes; the petition requesting such notification must bear a duly cancelled internal revenue stamps for 50cts., and a similar stamp for $1.00 with the surcharge " *Marcas.*"

All renunciations or decrees of nullity affecting trademarks registered in the International Registry must be notified to it by the Patent office *ex officio* and without charge; and will give like notice of the institution of any suit of nullity against a Mexican registry of trademark, arising from an international registry, so that the International Office may notify the interested party. Whenever the Patent Office has notice of the international registry of a trademark which is in violation of the provisions of clauses 2 and 3 of Art. 989 of the Trademark Law, said Office will within one year send to the International Office a declaration that protection cannot be given to such trademark in Mexico. (Arts. 7–8, 12–13.)

TITLE IV.

COPYRIGHT LAW.

(Civil Code, Arts. 1130–1271.)

CHAPTER 1.

LITERARY PROPERTY.

Art. 994. A Constitutional Right.
 995. Scope of Right.
 996. Duration of Copyright.
 997. Assignment of Copyright.
 998. Joint Authorship.
 999. Translations.
 1000. Unauthorized Reproduction.
 1001. Anonymous and Posthumous Works.
 1002. Newspapers — Laws.
 1003. Dramatic and Artistic Copyright.

Art. 994. A Constitutional Right.— The Mexican Constitution, Art. IV, secures every man in the enjoyment of the products of his labor; this right is governed by the ordinary laws in respect to ownership of property, with the exception of the special rules on the subject of literary, artistic and dramatic property, or the special Copyright Law, established by the Civil Code. (Arts. 1130–1131.)

Art. 995. Scope of Right.— The inhabitants of the Republic, native as well as foreign, have the exclusive right to publish and reproduce their original works as often as they wish, in whole or in part, by manuscript copies, printing, lithograph or any other like means, in conformity with the laws regulating the exercise of the freedom of the press. The right includes manuscript works, and oral and written lessons and all kinds of public speeches; but speeches delivered in political Assemblies are only subject to copyright when collections of them are intended. Private correspondence can only be published by consent of both correspondents or their heirs, except when necessary for the proof or defense of legal rights, or when required by the public interests or the advancement of the sciences. Dramatic authors also have the sole right of production of their work on the stage.

Authors of all kinds of maps, plans and drawings; architeets, painters, engravers, lithographers, photographers, sculptors, both as to completed works and models and molds, musicians, and calligraphists, enjoy the same exclusive rights to reproduce their original works. (Arts. 1133–1137, 1168, 1191.)

Art. 996. Duration of Copyright.— Copyright of all literary, artistic and dramatic works continues during the life of the author, and on his death passes to his heirs according to law; in the case of dramatic works, the author also has the sole right of stage representation of the work during his life, and his heirs shall enjoy it for thirty years afterwards; assignees shall have this right during the author's life and for thirty years afterwards. Non-residents of the Republic publishing their works abroad, may reserve the right of translation for ten years. The editor of a work which is already public property, may have copyright while his edition is

being published and for one year afterwards, but this will **not**
prevent the publication of editions in other countries.   Scientific and literary organizations are entitled to copyright of
their publications for twenty-five years.   The terms which **in**
these cases are indicated for the duration of copyright are to
be counted from the date of the work, or if the date does **not**
appear, from the first of January of the year following **the**
publication of the work or of its last volume or part.   (Arts.
1138,.1156, 1162, 1167, 1169, 1192.)

Art. 997. Assignment of Copyright.— The author or **his**
heirs may assign the copyright, the assignee acquiring all **the**
rights of the author according to the terms of the assignment.   If the assignment be for a shorter term than the
copyright, the author regains his rights at the expiration of
the assignment.   If after the assignment the author makes
substantial changes in the work, the assignee cannot prevent
it from being also published or assigned.   (Arts. 1139–
1140, 1145.)

Art. 998. Joint Authorship.— In case of a cyclopædia or
other work composed by different known authors, but **the**
part contributed by each one can not be indicated, the copyright belongs to all jointly, and on the death of any without
heirs or assigns, his interest goes to the others.   If **the**
portions contributed by each can be designated, each owns
his portion, but the consent of the majority must be given to
its re-publication.   If such work be undertaken or published
by a single person or corporation, the latter owns the copyright of the entire work, but each author has the right to
republish his parts, singly or collectively; and such parts
cannot be published singly without consent of their authors.
Either of the joint authors of a dramatic work, or his heirs
or assignees, may authorize its representation unless otherwise stipulated; if there are several heirs or assignees, their

vote is only counted as that of the author whom they represent. (Arts. 1148–1152, 1184–1185.)

Art. 999. Translations.— An author may reserve the right to publish translations of his works, but should state whether the reservation is limited to a certain language or extends to all languages. If the author does not make such reservation, or has granted the right of translation, the translator has all the rights of an author in regard to his translation, but cannot prevent other translations, unless the author also grants that power. The judge will decide all disputes after hearing the opinions of experts. (Arts. 1154–1157.)

Art. 1000. Unauthorized Reproduction.— No one may reproduce the work of another, under the pretext of annotating, commenting upon, or enlarging it or improving the edition, without the permission of the author, but such commentaries or additions may be published separately by their author and copyrighted. Like permission is also necessary to make an abridgment or compendium of a work; but if the former is of such merit or importance as to constitute a new work or one of general utility, the government may authorize its publication, after hearing the parties and experts. In such event, the author or owner of the original work shall receive as indemnity of from fifteen to thirty per cent. of the net proceeds of all editions of such compendium. (Arts. 1158–1160.)

Art. 1001. Anonymous and Posthumous Works.— Anonymous and pseudononymous works are within the terms of the copyright law, upon their authorship being proven; if the author is unknown, the editor of such a work has all the rights of an author. Heirs and assignees will have the same rights in respect to posthumous works as the author. The first publisher of an old manuscript (*códice*) of which he is the legitimate possessor, is entitled to its copyright during his

life. Posthumous dramatic works cannot be represented except by consent of heirs or assignees; the copyright is for
twenty years for dramatic and thirty years for literary works;
that of anonymous dramatic works is for thirty years. (Arts.
1142–1144; 1163–1165; 1181–1183.)

Art. 1002. Newspapers — Laws.— Political periodicals are
not subject to copyright, except as to scientific, literary or
artistic articles; but any person publishing parts of the free
matter must cite the name and number of the paper from
which it is taken.   Laws, regulations, and decisions of the
courts may be published by any one after they are officially
published, the editor using the authentic text; but collections
of the same cannot be published without consent of the general or state governments respectively.   (Arts. 1153, 1166.)

Art. 1003. Dramatic and Artistic Copyright.— These divisions of the copyright law are in the most part entirely
covered by the principles already stated in regard to literary
copyright, the few minor exceptions being of no importance
to our treatment; they are to be found scattered between Articles 1168 and 1200, most of which have been cited above.

CHAPTER 2.

INFRINGEMENT OF COPYRIGHT.

(Falsificación.)

Art. 1004. What is Infringement.
    1005. What is not Infringement.
    1006. Penalties for Infringement.

Art. 1004. What is Infringement.— Infringement takes
place when anyone, without the consent of the lawful owner,
publishes any copyrighted literary matter or translations of
it, and represents, executes or reproduces dramatic, musical

or artistic matter or objects, whether by the same or a different process than that employed in the original; omits the name
of the author or translator; changes the title of a work or
suppresses or varies any part of it, or publishes a greater
number of copies than stipulated; reproduces a piece of
architecture to do which it is necessary to enter a private
house; publishes or executes a piece of music made up of
extracts from others, or arranges a musical composition for
separate instruments. Also when works are published, reproduced or represented in violation of the provisions of the copyright law. Also the advertisement of a dramatic or musical
work without consent of the owner, although the author is not
named and the representation never takes place. The dealing in infringed works, either within or without the country,
is also an infringement. So likewise is the publication of a
work contrary to the law regulating the liberty of the press;
together with every publication or reproduction which is not
literally embraced in the next following Article. (Arts.
1201–1206.)

Art. 1005. What is not Infringement.— The following are
not infringements: Literal quotation or insertion of extracts
or passages from published works; the reproduction or
abridgment of articles in reviews, dictionaries, periodicals
and works of this class, provided the work from which taken
is cited, and that the part reproduced is not excessive in the
judgment of experts; the reproduction of poems, reminis-
cences, addresses, etc., in works of literary criticism, of the
history of literature, in periodicals, and in books for educational establishments; the publication of a collection of literary compositions taken from other works; that of additions
and changes of the work of another, made separately; that
of uncopyrighted works, and those of a dead author without
heirs or assignees, and anonymous and pseudononymous
works, except as stated in Art. 1001; the reproduction of dramatic or musical works, without stage effects, in private houses

or in public concerts where there is no paid attendance, or the proceeds of which are intended for charity; the publication of librettos of operas and the words of other musical compositions, unless the owner has reversed that right; the translation of works already published, except as provided in Article 999; the reproduction of sculptural works, if the difference between the copy and the original is such that it may be considered a new work in the judgment of experts, or of those found in public places; the reproduction of works of painting, engraving or lithography made by moulding (*en plástica*), and of works of this class made by those processes; that of a model already sold, if there are substantial differences; that of architectural works on public buildings or on the outside of private houses; the use of artistic works as models for manufactured products. (Art. 1207.)

Art. 1006. Penalties for Infringement.— The infringer of a copyright forfeits to the owner of the work all copies of the infringement and the price of any sold, or must pay the price of all at the owner's option; and all plates, molds, and matrices used in the fraudulent edition, except the types themselves, shall be destroyed. The infringer of musical or dramatic works shall pay the owner all the proceeds which he has derived, without deduction for expenses; and the owner may attach the receipts at any time and may prevent the rendition of the work; and all copies of the work distributed to those taking part shall be destroyed, and the owner may also recover damages; besides all which, the infringer is subject to the penalties prescribed for fraud by the Penal Code. The details of estimating and enforcing the damages are omitted. (Arts. 1208–1233.)

CHAPTER 3.

PROCEEDINGS FOR COPYRIGHT.

Art. 1007. Copyright — How Acquired.— To secure copyright, the author, translator or editor, as the case may be, must file in person, or by his attorney having due power of attorney, with the Department of Public Instruction and Fine Arts,[1] his declaration of the reservation of his rights, and must deposit two copies of every printed book, musical work, engraving, and similar work, or one copy of the drawing, design or plan of works of architecture, painting, sculpture, and similar works, stating the dimensions and all other circumstances which characterize the original, such copies being for the National Library, the National Conservatory, the School of Fine Arts and the General Archives, as the case may be; a like deposit will be made for each new edition or issue of every work. If the work is published without the name of the author, he must, in order to secure its copyright, present with the required copies of the work, a sealed packet, marked as he may deem desirable, containing his name.

The author, translator or editor must also place on the title page of books and musical compositions, at the bottom of prints, and at the base or other visible part of other artistic works, his name, the date of publication, the notice that he has secured copyright through having made the deposit of copies required by law, with such other legal conditions and notifications as he deems advisable. Failure to make such announcement destroys the copyright. Copyright in regard to the representation of dramatic and musical

---

[1] As amended by Decree of 16 May, 1905; See Art. 135.

Art. 1008. General Provisions.— Contracts in regard to publication of a work should stipulate the number of copies, otherwise infringement will not lie on that ground (1247). One directing a work to be made at his expense is considered its author unless otherwise agreed (1253). If the author, translator or editor of a work which has been given to the public, dies without securing copyright, his heirs cannot secure it (1261). Literary and artistic copyright prescribes in ten years, computed as provided in **Art.** 996; dramatic copyright in four years from the first representation or production of the work (1263). Copyright under this law is personal property, unless the law otherwise provides in special instances (1264). When it is desirable to reproduce any work, and its owner will not do it, the government may order it done either at its expense or through public bidding, after payment of indemnity and on the other conditions prescribed for the taking of property for public uses (1265). Copyright cannot be had in works prohibited by law or withdrawn from circulation by judicial decree (1266).

Art. 1009. Foreigners.— There is no distinction of legal rights between Mexicans and foreigners when the work is published in the Republic. If the work is published abroad by a Mexican or a resident foreigner, he may secure copyright upon filing the declaration and making the deposit of copies required by law. The translator of a work written in a foreign language is considered as its author in respect of his translation. Foreign authors residing in other countries enjoy the same rights as Mexicans, if in the country where the work is published Mexicans enjoy the same rights as the former. (**Arts.** 1267–1271.)

BOOK XVIII.
CIVIL RESPONSIBILITY IN TORTS AND CRIMES.[1]

TITLE I.
GENERAL PRINCIPLES OF LIABILITY.

(*Código Penal Reformado,* of 7 December, 1871; Arts. 301–367.)

CHAPTER 1.

EXTENT AND REQUISITES OF CIVIL RESPONSIBILITY.

Art. 1010. Nature and Extent of Liability.
    1011. Suits for Damages — Survival of Action.

Art. 1010. Nature and Extent of Liability.— Civil responsibility arising from an act or omission contrary to a penal

[1] AMERICAN COURT DECISIONS CONSTRUING MEXICAN PENAL CODE.

The provisions of this Chapter in respect to the civil responsibility of railroads for death and personal injuries have several times been before the American Courts in damage suits brought to recover damages for injuries received in Mexico, resulting in a flagrant conflict of authority. The Mexican laws have been given effect in Evey vs. Mexican Central Ry. Co. (C. C. A.) 81 Fed. Rep. 294; 26 C. C. A., 407; 38 L. R. A., 387; Mexican Cent. Ry. Co. vs. Marshall (C. C. A.), 91 Fed. Rep., 933; 34 C. C. A., 133; Mex. Cent. Ry. Co. vs. Mitten, 13 Tex. Civ. App., 653; Mex. Cent. Ry. Co. vs. Gehr, 66 Ill. App. 173. Other Courts, including the Supreme Court of the United States, in Slater vs. Mexican Cent. Ry. Co., 194 U. S. 120; (S. C. 115 Fed. Rep. 593 and 53 C. C. A. 239), have refused to give them effect because of the peculiar method of assessing damages; in this class also are: Mexican Cent. Ry. Co. vs. Chantry, 136 Fed. Rep. (C. C. A.) 316; Mexican National R. R. Co. vs. Jackson, 89 Tex. 107; 31 L. R. A. 276; 59 Am. St. Reps. 28. A number of other Articles of the Mexican Codes and statutes are cited and some of them construed in the above cases.

law, consists in the obligation of the party responsible, to make: 1, Restitution; 2, reparation; 3, indemnization; 4, payment of judicial costs.

Restitution consists in the return of the thing wrongfully taken (*cosa usurpada*), together, in cases where required by the civil law, with its existing " fruits "; if the thing has passed into the possession of a third person, although he acquired it by just title and in good faith, he must restore it to its owner, if it is not yet prescribed, but he has the right to recover indemnity from the person from whom he acquired it.

Reparation embraces the payment of all damages (*daños*) caused to the injured party, to his family or to a third person, by the violation of a substantial right (*derecho formal*), existent and not simply possible, provided such damages are actual and result directly and immediately from the act or omission in question, or there is a certainty that they will result as a proximate and inevitable consequence thereof. If the damage consists in the loss or serious injury (*grave deterioro*) of a thing, its owner is entitled to recover its full value, but if the injury is slight, its estimated amount will be paid and the thing restored.

Indemnization involves the payment of losses (*perjuicios*), that is, of what the injured party is deprived of gaining (*deja de lucrar*) as the direct and immediate consequence of an act or omission which violates a substantial right (*derecho formal*), existent and not simply possible, and of the value of the already consumed " fruits " of the thing wrongfully taken, where the same must be accounted for according to the civil law. The foregoing requirement that the " *daños y perjuicios* " must be actual, does not prevent recovery by a new action of those afterwards accruing, where they result directly and as a necessary consequence from the same act of omission.

The payment of judicial costs is limited to those absolutely necessary incurred by the injured party in the investigation of the act or omission which gives rise to the criminal proceeding, and in asserting his rights in it and in the civil suit. (Arts. 301–307.)

Art. 1011. Suits for Damages — Survival of Action.— Civil responsibility can only be enforced at the instance of a lawful party (*parte legítima*). In deciding upon such liability, the judges will follow the provisions of this Title on all points herein treated; in all other respects they will observe the provisions, according to the nature of the case, of the civil or commercial laws in force at the time of the act or omission which gives rise to the civil responsibility. The right to recover damages forms part of the estate of the deceased and passes to his heirs and successors, except as below provided in respect to *alimentos,* or where it arises from defamation (*injuria ó difamación*), and the injured party did not during his lifetime, if he had the opportunity, bring a suit nor direct his heirs to do so, the offense being thereby remitted. The action to demand support (*alimentos*) from a murderer is personal, and belongs exclusively to the persons mentioned in Article 1013, as directly injured; hence such action is no part of the estate of the deceased, nor is it extinguished although the latter during his lifetime pardoned the offense. In cases of rape or seduction, the woman cannot require, as a reparation to her honor, that the man shall marry or endow her. (Arts. 308–312.)

CHAPTER 2.

COMPUTATION OF DAMAGES.

Art. 1012. Loss or Injury of Property.— The judge who tries a suit for civil responsibility will endeavor to have

43

the parties agree upon the amount of damages and the terms
of payment; if they do not agree, the rules herein prescribed
will be observed.

In cases of loss or injury of a thing, for which any of the
persons mentioned in clause II of Art. 1017 is liable by reason of its having been formally delivered to him as provided in clause III of Art. 1018, if the person so delivering
it fixed a value on it at the time, such valuation shall be
taken as its legitimate value, provided that a copy of the
entry required by said Art. 1018 was issued at the time;
otherwise the ordinary value of the thing at the time when
it should have been delivered to its owner, shall be paid,
whether greater or less than it had before, and disregarding
any " value of affection " which its owner may set upon it;
and where the injury to the thing is slight, it shall be estimated in the same way, and the thing returned to its owner.
But if it is proven that the thing was purposely destroyed
or injured with the intention of hurting the owner in his
affection for it, the foregoing rules will not apply, and the
" estimative " value put upon it by the owner will be assessed, but not in excess of one-third of its ordinary value.
(Arts. 313–317.)

**Art. 1013.   Death by Wrongful Act —" Alimentos " as Dam-
ages.—** Civil responsibility arising from death by wrongful
act (*homicidio ejecutado sin derecho*), embraces: The payment of necessary burial expenses; of the necessary costs
and expenses of medical care to the deceased; of the damages (*daños*) occasioned by the person causing the death
(*homicida*) to the property of the deceased; and the payment of support (*alimentos*) not only to the widow, descendants and ascendents of the deceased whom he was sup-
porting under legal obligation, but also to any posthumous
descendants he may leave.   The obligation to provide such
alimentos shall continue for the whole time that the deceased
should have lived if he had not been killed; such time will

be calculated by the judge according to the Table of Life Expectancy hereto annexed, but taking into consideration the state of health of the deceased previous to the homicide. In order to determine the amount of the *alimentos* which must be provided, the means or ability (*los posibles*) of the party liable, and the necessities and circumstances of the persons who are to receive them, will be taken into consideration. The obligation to provide support shall cease: 1, At any time when it is not absolutely necessary for the subsistence of those receiving it; 2, when they marry; 3, when male children attain their majority; 4, in any other event, in which, according to law, the duty of the deceased to provide it, if alive, would have ceased. (Arts. 318–320.)

TABLE OF LIFE EXPECTANCY,

ACCORDING TO AGE.

Years of Age.	Expectancy of Life.
10	40.80
15	37.40
20	34.26
25	31.34
30	28.52
35	25.72
40	22.89
45	20.05
50	17.23
55	14.51
60	11.05
65	9.63
70	7.58
75	5.87
80	4.60
85	2.00

Art. 1014. Personal Injuries — Disabilities.— In case of blows or wounds from which the injured party is not crippled, lamed or deformed, he may recover from the person inflicting the same the expenses of treatment, the damages (*daños*) which he has suffered, and whatever he has been prevented from gaining while, in the judgment of medical experts (*facultativos*), unable to engage in his work of livelihood, but such disability to work must be the direct result of his injuries or of a cause which is the immediate effect thereof. If such disability to follow his habitual work is permanent, but upon the healing of his wounds he can engage in a different work, which is lucrative and adequate to his education, habits, social position and physical constitution, the amount of damages will be reduced to the difference between what he can earn in such work and what he earned daily in the work in which he was formerly engaged. If the blows or wounds cause the loss of some member not indispensable for his work, or the injured party is otherwise crippled, lamed or deformed (*baldado, lisiado ó deforme*), he may by reason of such circumstance recover not only his " *daños y perjuicios,*" but also such amount as extraordinary indemnization as the judge may award him, taking into consideration the social position and sex of the injured person and the part of the body in which he is so injured. The amount of earnings (*lucro*) which the injured party was prevented from receiving while disabled from working, will be computed by multiplying the amount which he was earning daily by the number of days he was disabled. The foregoing rules for computing the amount of damages for wounds or blows will be applied in all other cases where, through the violation of a penal law, one person causes to another any sickness or disability to work. (Arts. 321–325.)

CHAPTER 3.

PERSONS CIVILLY RESPONSIBLE.
\

Art. 1015. Essential Grounds of Liability.— No one can be declared civilly responsible for an act or omission contrary to a penal law, unless it is proven: That he wrongfully took (*se usurpó*) the property of another; that by himself or through another he wrongfully (*sin derecho*) caused damage and loss (*daños y perjuicios*) to the plaintiff; or that, being able to prevent it, the damage and loss were caused by another person under his control. Where any of the foregoing conditions exist, the defendant is civilly responsible, whether he is convicted or acquitted of criminal responsibility. This rule applies not only to the principals in a duel which results in wounds or killing, but also to the seconds or witnesses, but not to the physicians or surgeons who attended the combat in such capacity. But the rule does not apply to persons who fail to use all the lawful means in their power to prevent the commission of crime, or to aid in its investigation and in pursuit of the criminals, as required by Article 1 of the Penal Code, as such persons do not thereby incur civil responsibility. (Arts. 326–328.)

Art. 1016. Persons Liable — In Loco Parentis.— In accordance with the preceding Article, the following are civilly, but not criminally, responsible for acts and omissions: 1, The father, mother and other ascendants, for the descendants under their *patria potestad,* in their company, or under their immediate care, except in cases where their teachers or masters are responsible as below provided; 2, guardians for the acts or omissions of insane wards or minors who live with them under their authority, with the above exception in respect of minors; 3, school and shop masters who receive scholars or apprentices under eighteen years of age, who are responsible for their acts or omissions committed during the time they are under their care; but the persons mentioned in the three foregoing clauses will not be responsible if they prove that they were without fault (*culpa*), and could not prevent the act or omission complained of, and in order to determine whether they were at fault the circumstances of the act or omission and of the persons mentioned and of those for whom they are responsible, will be taken into consideration; 4, the husband will be responsible for his wife only in the event that the plaintiff proves two things: (a), That the husband had previous knowledge that his wife was going to commit the crime in question, or that he saw her commit it; (b), that he had the actual ability to prevent it, or that if he did not have, it was for his own fault. (Arts. 329, 333.)

Art. 1017. Master and Servant — Carriers — Innkeepers, etc. — In order that masters shall be responsible for their clerks and servants it is precisely necessary that the acts or omissions of the latter, which give rise to the responsibility, be committed in the service for which they are employed (*á que han sido destinados*). Upon the above conditions, the following are responsible:

1, Members of a company, for the acts or omissions of its managing members, on the same terms as, according to the civil or commercial law, they are liable for other obligations contracted by them; married women are excepted from this rule, as she is in no event responsible for the crime of her husband.

2, Owners of stages, coaches, carts and all kinds of vehicles, for their own use or for hire; the owners or drivers of pack-trains; railroad companies; the managers or contractors of mails and posts; the owners, outfitters and captains of canoes, boats and vessels of all kinds; the owners and keepers of hotels, inns, boarding-houses, or any kind of house engaged in whole or part in constantly receiving guests for pay, and of cafes, eating-houses, baths and livery-stables, for the acts or omissions of their clerks or servants; liability in all the cases hereinbefore mentioned being subject to the rules stated in the succeeding Articles.

3, The State, for its public officials, employés and clerks, but such obligation is subsidiary and will be paid out of the indemnization funds.

4, Municipal Councils (*Ayuntamientos*), out of their funds, on the same terms as the State, for their employés and clerks, provided: That said employés or clerks caused the damage or loss in the discharge of their duty, that they are appointed and paid by the *Ayuntamientos,* and are under their orders and subject to be removed by them.

The civil responsibility of all the persons above mentioned in this Article does not relieve those on account of whom they incur it, and the injured party may enforce the liability in the terms prescribed in Arts. 1024–1025; but this rule does not apply to the case where the person causing the injury acts in the name and by the order of another, doing in good faith an act not criminal in itself, and in excusable ignorance of the circumstances which constitute it a crime; in such event the agent is not responsible either to the injured person or to the person in whose name he acted. (Arts. 330–332.)

Art. 1018. Inn-keepers and Carriers — Valuables.— The owners and keepers of inns and houses of all kinds destined in whole or part to constantly receive guests for pay, do not incur civil responsibility in the following cases: 1, Where they prove that the damage was due to accident (*caso fortuito*), or that without their fault or that of their clerks or servants, it was caused by armed force or by other *vis major* which they could not resist; 2, where it concerns effects left outside of the establishment; 3, where the loss is of money, precious jewels, bank notes, or other securities which the passenger carries with him, and which should not prudently be a part of his traveling baggage, and are not necessary for his expenses, considering his social position, the object of the trip and other circumstances, unless he delivered such valuables in detail, for safekeeping, to the keeper of the establishment, and the latter issued to him a copy of the entry below mentioned; 4, where the damage is caused to one passenger by another, or by a person not in the service of the establishment, if the keeper or his clerks or servants were not at fault, or if the person injured is himself at fault. Persons living regularly (*que vivan de pié*) in such establishment, and not as passengers, are bound by the provisions of clause 3 above, except that they may keep in their rooms such amount of cash as is absolutely necessary for their expenses for one month.

The keepers of all such establishment must keep a register in which they must enter: The money, securities, jewels and other effects delivered to them for safekeeping, stating the value put on them by the owner if he wishes to state it; if he does so and the parties agree upon it, it will be so stated in the entry, and the innkeeper will be responsible for such price; but if they disagree about it, or it is not fixed, he will be liable for the value assessed by the judge upon the testimony of experts. A copy of the foregoing entry will be given to the owner of the objects deposited. This requirement, and those of clauses 1, 3 and 4 above, are applicable to all carriers mentioned in clause 2 of the preceding Article. (Arts. 334–337.)

Art. 1019. Liability for Costs — Avoiding Injuries.— Only those are responsible for costs against whom a criminal action or suit for civil responsibility has been prosecuted and who have been adjudged liable by final judgment, in which event the following rules will be observed: 1, If all have been convicted of the same offense they are jointly and severally liable for the costs; 2, if besides of the offense common to all, some one is convicted of a different offense, the costs thereby accrued will be borne by him.

One who upon a valuable consideration (*á título lucrativo*) and in good faith shares in the effects or products of a crime or misdemeanor (*delito ó falta*), is obliged to respond for the damage and loss only to the extent of the value which he has received.

Where damage or loss has been caused to the property of one person in order to save the property of others, the latter are civilly responsible pro rata, in the opinion of the judge, in proportion to the damage from which each has been saved; but if the injury was not avoided only the person who committed or ordered the damage will be responsible. Where the damage has been caused in averting damage to an entire district or town, the town or towns from which the damage has been averted will make indemnity in the terms prescribed in the Civil Code; but if the damage is not averted, the indemnity will be paid by the public Treasury and not from the common indemnity fund. (Arts. 339–342.)

Art. 1020. Damage by Animals and Things — Telegraphs. — For loss and damage caused by an animal or thing, the person who was making use of the same when the damage was caused is responsible, unless he proves that he was without any fault; the injured person may take possession of or even kill the animal which injured him, in cases where the law gives him such right.

Telegraph companies and their employés are civilly liable only in the cases and terms which will be prescribed in a special law concerning telegraphs. (Arts. 338, 343.)

Art. 1021. Damages to Persons Acquitted or Wrongfully Accused.— Where a person accused *ex officio* is acquitted, not for failure of proof, but by having established his complete innocence of the crime of which he was accused, and his former conduct was not such as to induce the belief that he was guilty, it will be so declared *ex officio* in the final judgment; and if the accused so requests, and after hearing the representative of the Ministerio Público, the judgment will fix the amount of "*daños y perjuicios*" which he has suffered by the prosecution; in such event, the damages will be paid from the common indemnization fund, if the officials mentioned in the following Article are not responsible or are unable to pay.

The acquitted party has a like right against the person who complained or informed against him, subject to the following rules: 1, He will be entitled to the costs of the criminal process only when the complainant or informer has acted as assistant to the Ministerio Público or Promotor Fiscal, and the complaint or denouncement has given place to the prosecution, or where, without becoming assistant to the prosecution, his complaint or denouncement was calumnious or rash; 2, the costs incurred by him in a suit for civil responsibility, if he is successful, will be repaid to him by the party who made the complaint or denouncement; 3, the complainant or informer will be liable to him for "*daños y perjuicios*" only when the complaint or denouncement was calumnious or rash. The amount of judicial costs will be precisely fixed in the judgment which orders their payment. (Arts. 344–346.)

Art. 1022. Same — Liability of Judges and Officials.— The provisions of the preceding Article apply to public officials who, in the exercise of their office, rashly or calumniously make an accusation or denouncement, or give notice of a crime. Judges and every other public authority, employé or official, shall be civilly responsible: For arbitrary detentions made by them by improperly ordering the arrest of a person; for detaining a person in prison longer than the law permits; for the damages (*perjuicios*) caused by their want of skill or knowledge (*impericia*) or by their delay (*morosidad*) in the dispatch of business; and for every other misdemeanor or crime (*falta ó delito*) committed in the exercise of their functions, by which they cause "*daños ó perjuicios*" to others. (Arts. 347–348.)

Art. 1023. Transmission of Liability.— Upon the death of the party responsible, to his heirs is transmitted the obligation to satisfy the civil responsibility, to the extent of the property inherited, which shall pass to them subject to this encumbrance. ·(Art. 349.)

CHAPTER 4.

DIVISION AND ENFORCEMENT OF LIABILITY.

Art. 1024. Joint and Several Liability — Contribution.— Where various persons are condemned for the same act or omission, all and each of them will be liable for the whole amount of damages, and the plaintiff may sue them all jointly or any one or more of them, as he pleases; but if he does not sue all, those who pay may recover of the others the share which they should pay in accordance with the following rules: If the law does not establish the share of liability of each party, the criminal judges will fix it in proportion to the penalties they impose, and the civil judges in proportion to the penalties imposed by the former, or which should be imposed if not yet decreed; if no penalty is to be imposed because they are acquitted of any criminal offense, but they are nevertheless civilly liable, it will be divided among them pro rata. Such division of liability among themselves does not affect their joint and several liability to the plaintiff as above provided, but only concerns their contribution where one pays more than his share. (Arts. 350–352.)

Art. 1025. Same — Exceptions.— In cases of restitution suit can be brought only against the party in possession of the thing or its fruits, but if he is not the wrongful taker, he may recover from the person from whom he acquired it. The rule of joint and several liability does not apply to those receiving stolen property (*encubridores*) except in respect to the damages and losses resulting with regard to the property received.

The provisions of the preceding Article do not apply to minors or insane persons who are under *patria potestad* or guardianship, nor to masters or employers, in respect to all of whom the following rules will be observed: Those deprived of reason and minors without discernment, will only be responsible when the persons having them in charge are not civilly responsible or have no property to satisfy it; but if they are not under guardianship or *patria potestad* they alone will be responsible; 2, where the minor acts with discernment, neither he nor his guardian can recover from the other more than one-half of the amount of damages, where one of them has paid the entire amount; 3, where clerks or servants act against the orders of their master, or without exactly complying with them, the latter may recover from the former all damages and losses which he may have paid. But if such damages and losses are caused as the necessary consequence of the master's orders, and the clerk or servant acts in good faith in doing an act which is not criminal in itself, and in ignorance of the circumstances which make it a crime, he does not incur civil responsibility to the injured party, nor can the master recover of him any damages he may have had to pay. (Arts. 353–355.)

Art. 1026. Enforcing Liability — Property Subject.— The entire property of the party responsible is subject to the satisfaction of the damages, with the exception of the reserve fund created by Art. 85 of the Penal Code, the wearing apparel of himself and family, his household furniture, and instruments, tools or books used in his trade or profession, together with all other property exempt from embargo by the laws, and without prejudice to the " benefit of competency " allowed to insane persons and to minors and deaf-mutes acting without discernment. If such property is not sufficient to satisfy the damages, the balance will be taken from the twenty-five per cent. fund provided for that purpose by clause 1 of **Art.** 85 of the Penal Code; if the amount is not yet satisfied, and the defendant has served out his term of punishment, the judge will compel him to pay the entire balance in monthly payments such as, in his judgment, he is able to pay after the necessary living expenses of himself and family; or if he afterwards acquires property sufficient to satisfy the damages, the injured party may require him to pay in a lump sum all that is due him.

Where a party adjudged to make restitution, reparation, indemnization, the payment of judicial costs, and a fine, has not sufficient property to satisfy all these liabilities, they shall have preference of payment in the order named. (Arts. 356–360.)

Art. 1027. Extinction of Liability and Actions.— The several actions for the enforcement of civil responsibility, or for obtaining execution against the defendant adjudged by final judgment to be liable therefor, shall be extinguished within the terms and in the manner prescribed by the Civil or Commercial Codes according to the nature of the case, subject to the following limitations: Civil responsibility, nor the actions for its recovery, nor the lawful rights acquired by third persons, are not extinguished by amnesty; but where the responsibility has not yet been made effective, and the object is not restitution but the reparation of damages (*daños*), the indemnization of losses (*perjuicios*), or the payment of judicial costs, the defendant is discharged from these obligations only where it is so declared in the amnesty and it is expressly left to the charge of the Treasury; nor are such liability, actions and rights extinguished by a pardon (*indulto*). Prescription is interrupted by the criminal proceeding until final judgment is pronounced, whereupon its term will begin to run anew (*de nuevo*). The right to civil responsibility is extinguished by set-off (*compensación*), except where the thing wrongfully taken (*cosa usurpada*) exists in the possession of the party responsible and he is sued for its restitution. (Arts. 363–367.)

TITLE II.

CRIMINAL BASIS OF CIVIL RESPONSIBILITY.

(*Código Penal Reformado.*)

CHAPTER 1.

CRIMES AND MISDEMEANORS IN GENERAL.

Art. 1028. General Rules — Definitions.
1029. Classes of "*Culpa*"— Intent.

Art. 1028. General Rules — Definitions.— A crime (*delito*) is the voluntary infraction of a penal law, by doing what it prohibits or failing to do what it commands. A misdemeanor (*falta*) is the infraction of the regulations or edicts (*bandos*) of police and good government. There are intentional crimes and crimes of negligence (*delitos de culpa*).

An intentional crime is that committed with the knowledge that the act or omission of which it consists is punishable.

Crimes of negligence (*de culpa*) arise:

1, When an act or omission is done, which although lawful in itself, is not so by reason of its consequences, if the culpable party did not avert them because of want of foresight (*imprevisión*), negligence (*negligencia*), by want of reflexion or of care, because of not making the proper investigations, by reason of not taking the necessary precautions, or on account of want of skill or knowledge (*impericia*) in an art or science, the knowledge of which is necessary so that the act shall produce no damage; but the "*impericia*" is not punishable where the person doing the act does not profess the art or science which it is necessary to know, and acted under pressure of the gravity and urgency of the case.

2, By violation of the provisions of the Code requiring every person to use all means in his power to prevent the commission of crime and to aid in their investigation and in the pursuit of criminals, except in cases that it cannot be done without danger to the person or interests of the culpable party or of some near relative.

3, Where the act is only punishable on account of the circumstances under which it was done, or *por alguna persona* (*sic*) of the injured party, if the culpable party was ignorant of them because of not having previously made the investigations which the duty of his profession or the importance of the case required.

4, When the defendant infringes a penal law while in a state of complete drunkenness, if he is in the habit of becoming intoxicated, or has previously committed some punishable infraction while drunk.

5, Where there is excess in legitimate defense. (Arts. 4–7, 11.)

Art. 1029. Classes of " Culpa "— Intent.— For the crime of negligence (*delito de culpa*) to be punishable, it is neces-

sary: 1, That it shall be consummated; 2, that it is **not**
so light (*leve*) that, if it were intentional, it would only
be punished by one month of arrest, or by a first-class fine.[1]
Culpa is of two classes: Grave or light.   In the above cases
of preventing crime it is always light; in all other cases it
is left to the prudent discretion of the judges to decide
whether the " *culpa* " committed is grave or light, and in so
deciding they will take into consideration: The greater or
lesser facility to foresee and avert the damage; whether for
such purpose ordinary reflexion or attention and common
knowledge in some art or science would be sufficient; the
sex, age, education, intelligence and social position of the
culpable parties; whether they have previously been **delin-**
quent in similar circumstances; and whether they had time
to act with the necessary reflexion and care.   Misdemeanors
(*faltas*) are punished only when they are consummated,
without regard except to the material fact, and regardless of
intention or negligence (*culpa*).   (**Arts.** 12, 14–17.)

TITLE III.

LIABILITY OF RAILROAD COMPANIES.

(Railroad Law, of 29 April, 1899.)

CHAPTER 1.

GENERAL FREIGHT AND BAGGAGE PROVISIONS.

Art. 1029a. Railroad Rates — Regulation.
    1030. Duty to Receive and Transport — Conditions.

[1] Fines (*multas*) are of three classes: 1st, from $1 to $15; 2nd,
from $16 to $1,000; 3rd, of amount fixed in the law, or basis fixed for
determining the amount of the fine. " *Arresto*," which is distinguished
from " *prisión*," is " *minor*," or from 3 to 30 days, and " *major*," from
1 to 11 months. Where by accumulation of penalties the time exceeds
11 months, it is converted into " *prisión*." Código Penal, Arts. 112, 124.

Art. 1029A. Railroad Rates — Regulation.— Railroads have only the right, under their concessions, to receive the rates fixed in the tariffs, and to enforce the conditions of transportation legally established by the Companies, after the same are duly approved by the Department of Communications and Public Works and published as herein provided. Therefore are prohibited: 1, All contracts by which one or more persons are granted a rate of passage or carriage lower than that authorized by the tariff approved and published; 2, the refund of all or any part of the price of carriage or passage collected when the contract is made, for the purpose of rebating or reducing the tariff rates; 3, rebates of passage or freight rates made out of their commissions by agents who are paid commissions on sales of tickets or contracts for transportation; all such agents will be considered for all legal purposes as agents of the Companies, and such sales or contracts are embraced under clause 1 of this Article; 4, every act or contract the effect of which is to decrease or rebate directly or indirectly the rates of passage or carriage prescribed in the respective tariffs; all contracts made in violation of this law are void, except as expressly herein excepted. The Company, as well as its agent or employé, in their respective cases, will pay as *" daños y perjuicios "* double the amount of the difference of rates, to all those who, within two months before and two months after the shipment made at reduced rates, have made like shipments of goods between the places where said shipment was made.   (Arts. 99, 163.)

44

Art. 1030. Duty to Receive and Transport — Conditions.—
From the moment that a railroad and its rates have been
approved by the Department of Communications and Public
Works, it cannot refuse, except as expressly herein provided, to transport merchandise to another station on its own
line: 1, If the goods, considering their class and nature, are
proper to be transported, if they are properly packed, and if
their handling does not require special appliances which the
railroad does not and is not required to possess; 2, if the
shipper conforms to the tariffs and to the rules in respect
to delivery of goods and other conditions which the railroad
has the right to fix; 3, if the normal means of the railroad
are sufficient to make the transportation.

Railroads are not obliged to accept goods for transportation before it can be done; but in the stations which the
Department, after a hearing of the company, may designate,
it is bound, within the time fixed by the Department, to have
and maintain sheds or other kinds of shelter, as it may elect,
in which, under the vigilance and responsibility of the owner,
goods may be protected against the dampness of the soil
and rain, until their turn comes and they are received by
the railroad for transportation; for the use of such shelter
the company may collect a compensation according to its
tariff approved by the Department. No shipment shall be
given preference over another in the order of transportation,
except for reasons connected with the installation and repair
of the road, with the circumstances of the transportation or
with the public interests. The infraction of the foregoing . .
rules renders the company responsible for damages and losses
thereby occasioned. (Arts. 106–110.)

Art. 1031. Bills of Lading — Limiting Liability.— The bill
of lading, besides the requirements of **Art.** 696, must contain the following: 1, The declared value, if the railroad
company guarantees a fixed sum in case of responsibility;
2, the conditions under which the goods are transported,

whether according to those of the general tariff or to those of a special tariff, stating which, whether with full or limited liability, and any other particular stipulations in such cases as the law permits them; 3, the number of the car or cars, where they are taken whole, and the numbers of their seals.

Railroad companies have not the right, except in cases where specially authorized by law, to limit, in their regulations, bills of lading or other documents issued by them, the responsibility and obligations in respect to transportation, imposed upon them by law, or to relieve themselves therefrom; all rules, clauses or conditions inserted in any of said instruments in violation of this Article are void.

The liability of railroad companies will be limited in the following cases: 1, The liability will be fixed on the basis of the goods declared for the issuance of the bill of lading, where the shipper declares goods subject to a lower rate than those actually contained in the shipment; 2, the liability shall be based on the merchandise really contained in the shipment where the shipper declares different goods or of a higher value than the shipment contains; 3, where it is stipulated that the liability, or loss, shortage or damage shall not exceed a certain sum, but the railroad will nevertheless be liable for the full value of the shipment in case of fraud, bad faith or culpability of the company or its employés; 4, where the company is released of liability for delay in delivery imputable to the railroad, or such liability is limited to a certain sum, except in the instances in clause 3 stated. (Arts. 111, 119, 123.)

Art. 1032. Exceptions from Liability — Freight.— Railroad companies, unless otherwise contracted, and except in cases of fraud, bad faith or negligence (*en caso de dolo, mala fé ó culpa*), are not responsible for the loss, shortage (*desfalcos*) or injury (*averías*), or risks to which on the trip are exposed: 1, Live animals; 2, merchandise, which at

the written request of the shipper, is transported in open
cars in cases where the nature of the goods requires for
its protection to be transported in a closed or covered car;
3, goods shipped unpacked or with defective packing, which
by their nature should be properly packed, the want or defect
of packing to be stated in the bill of lading; 4, goods which
from their particular nature, from the fact of their transportation by railroad, from their inevitable exposure to bad
weather, or on account of heat or other natural causes, are
exposed to special risks of total or partial loss or injury,
and particularly to breakage, oxidation, internal deterioration, waste (*merma*), etc., the following rules being observed:

A. The Department of Communications and Public Works
will form a table of merchandises subject to waste, taking
into consideration the duration of the trip and the seasons,
fixing for each article the proportion of waste to which the
liability of the company shall be limited; B. such normal waste
so fixed shall be counted separately for each package included
in the same bill of lading, where the weight or dimensions of
each package is stated therein; C. the railroads may reserve,
with the approbation of the Department, the right of non-
liability, although the waste exceeds the normal limit, in
case the goods are loaded by the shipper or unloaded by the
consignee; D. such non-liability shall not be allowed when
the losses, shortage or damage are due to stealage, or when
they do not arise from the nature of the goods, or if the
normal waste is not in keeping with their nature or with the
circumstances; E. in case of total loss the railroad is not
entitled to reduction on account of waste; 5, explosives, inflammable substances and all other articles of a dangerous
character, a list of all such articles being formulated by the
Department; 6, articles placed in coaches or other vehicles
transported by the railroad; 7, merchandise transported
under the care of a person placed in charge for that purpose
by the shipper with the consent of the railroad; 8, merchan-

dise which by the tariff òr agreement with the shipper is loaded or unloaded by him or by the consignee, provided the car has no external lesion which may have caused the loss or damage; the shipper under this paragraph has the following rights:

A. To load the car at the point of shipment; B. to seal the car with his own seal or that it be sealed in his presence with the company's seals; C. to have the car unloaded at its final destination by the person authorized to receive the freight; D. to have the car unloaded in the presence of such person, or in his absence in the presence of the Treasury employé in charge of the fiscal inspection, or if neither is present, in the presence of any judicial authority; the company has the right to require that such person, employé or authority, before the seals are broken, issue to it a document without stamps or other formality, showing the state of the seals.

Where in accordance with the fiscal laws a car must be opened in transit, the Treasury employé in charge of fiscal inspection will examine the state of the seals before they are broken, making a note of their number, and after the inspection the car will be again sealed in his presence, and he will issue to the conductor of the train a document stating the number and condition of the seals before being broken and the number of the new seals put on in his presence. The company, in such case, does not guarantee the number of packages stated in the bill of lading. (Art. 120.)

Art. 1033. Exceptions from Liability — Baggage.— Neither are railroad companies liable, unless otherwise contracted, and except in cases of fraud, bad faith or negligence (*en caso de dolo, mala fé ó culpa*), for the loss, shortage or injury (*pérdida, desfalcos ó averías*) of baggage: 1, When it is not delivered at the office of the railroad to be transported, but is kept by the passenger in the coach; 2, although it has been delivered at the office, if the passenger does not claim the baggage within fifteen days, in case of interior passage, and within thirty days in case of international passage, such terms being counted from the day after the arrival of the train on which the baggage should be carried.

In the cases of this and the preceding **Article** the presumption is in favor of the railroad company until it is proven to the contrary, that the loss or injury was caused by the fraud, bad faith or culpability of the management of the railroad or its empolyés. The Department of Communications and Public Works will fix by Regulations the limit of the responsibility of railroad companies for the loss or damage of baggage the value of which has not been declared; where the value has been declared, the company has the right to require that the packages with declared value shall not be included in the baggage which the passenger is allowed to carry free, but that such packages shall be sent by express with the obligations and rights thereto annexed. The free baggage shall include all packages of undeclared value, whatever the contents may be, which the passenger presents as baggage, up to the limit of weight fixed by the concession, or by the regulations of the company if they allow a greater weight than the concession, but merchandise intended for traffic or other commercial purposes cannot be included in the free baggage.

The provisions of Art. 1036 apply, with the exceptions in this law contained, to the loss, shortage or damage to baggage, but the time after which the same shall be considered lost is fifteen days in interior passage and thirty days in international, counted from the day following the arrival of the train on which it ought to be carried. (Arts. 121–122, 124–125, 137.)

Art. 1034. Connecting Carriers — Liability.— In case of connecting lines of railroads, or of connections between a railroad and water transportation companies, the last carrier is bound to deliver the freight, which shall be done as prescribed by law in accordance with the bill of lading issued by the first carrier, and with the responsibility fixed by the law, but with the following restrictions: 1, If the bill of lading fixes a charge based on a different rate than that fixed by the tariff, the last carrier will nevertheless collect the rate according to the legal tariff; 2, the liability of the last carrier begins when it receives the freight; 3, the liability includes the loss of packages and shortages or damages occurring on the last or any of the connecting lines, saving the right of the last carrier against the company on whose line the act or omission occurred out of which the liability arises, and against any other line afterwards receiving the goods; the same applies in cases of connection between a railroad and a ship line making voyages between Mexican ports, in respect of hauls made from one of said ports to another in the national territory partly by ship and partly by rail. The same rules apply where a railroad receives goods to be shipped under a bill of lading designating as the place of delivery a point not on its own line nor on any of its connecting lines, but the liability of the railroad ends at the point where the transportation by rail terminates. In delivering freight or baggage from one line to another, the roads will exchange documents, the one showing receipt and the other delivery, and stating the date, number and conditions of seals or number and marks of packages, no stamps or other special formalities being required; such documents raise a legal presumption against which no evidence is admissible, in respect to the date of the receipt of the goods, their condition and the number of packages of which they consist, at the time of their delivery to the respective carrier. (Arts. 126–130.)

Art. 1035. Foreign Shipments — Liability.— In shipments of merchandise coming from a foreign country into Mexico, and which are transported from a port or the frontier to the interior by railroad, the Mexican road or roads shall be liable for losses, shortages and injuries in the following terms and cases: 1, The responsibility is governed by the laws of the country where the bill of lading was issued, if it is so provided in the document, but even in such event, if the existence of the foreign law and its applicability to the case is not proven, the rights and liability of the last carrier making a haul on Mexican territory will be governed, in respect to delivery, by the preceding Article; 2, the same rule applies where the bill of lading does not state to what law the rights and obligations arising from the contract are subject. The Mexican line, whether or not the last carrier, to which freight is delivered by a connecting line, national or foreign, by land, sea or river, shall have the right, in case of loss, shortage or injury, at its election: 1, To refuse the freight, notifying the consignee, if his name and address are known, so that he may give instructions regarding the transportation, whereupon the Mexican line shall be exempt from all liability on account of such loss, shortage or injury on other lines; 2, to receive the freight, issuing for it a bill of lading stating the condition of the freight, the liability of the last carrier, in such case, being limited to delivering the freight according to said bill of lading, except as provided in Art. 1032. In the transportation of merchandise from Mexico to a foreign country, over lines connected with the Mexican line which issued the bill of lading, the latter is liable according to the Mexican laws before the competent Mexican tribunals, for losses, shortages and injuries, saving its right, where the same occurred on another line, to recover indemnization from it; but the shipper or holder of the bill of lading may if he prefers have recourse to the courts of such other country to assert such rights as their laws afford him. (Arts. 131–133.)

Art. 1036. Loss of Goods — Measure of Damages.— The freight or baggage is considered lost if it is not delivered, in case of freight, within the month after the end of the term in which delivery should be made, and in case of baggage within fifteen days in interior, and thirty days in international passages, after the day following the arrival of the train on which it should arrive; but if it is found after such time, the party entitled to receive it has the right to require, within eight days after notice, that the freight or baggage be delivered to him without costs at the shipping point or at its original destination as shown by the bill of lading; upon delivery of the goods he must repay without interest any indemnity he has received. Where the railroad is not liable for the loss, shortage or injury, it may require payment of the full freight charges for the transportation made by it.

The responsibility of railroads, in cases of loss, shortage or injury, includes the obligation to pay the commercial value of the merchandise at the place and time of delivery, according to the terms of clause 9 of Art. 698, less customs duties, other expenses not due to the loss, and any unpaid freight charges, together with interest on the amount of indemnity at the rate of six per cent. per annum from the day on which delivery should have been made. Where the liability is due to the fault of several roads, the amount of indemnity will be divided among the roads responsible in proportion to the length of haul on each; the last carrier is in all cases bound to pay the indemnity to the holder of the bill of lading, but it has the right to have the other lines cited in any suit brought by the holder, and to require them to contribute their proportion of what it may have paid. (Arts. 134–137, 142.)

Art. 1037. Delays in Shipment — Weighing Freight.— The consignee or person entitled to receive freight may require it to be weighed in his presence upon delivery, and at the cost of the railroad if the weight is less than stated in the bill of lading; otherwise the cost will be paid by him according to a tariff to be approved by the Department and duly published.

In cases of delay for which the carrier is liable, the party entitled to receive the freight must prove the real and effective damages and losses which have been caused by the delay; in default of such proof the railroad will not pay other damages than a fraction of the freight charges, which will be fixed in the Regulations by the Department of Communications and Public Works. In such Regulations the time of duration of the trip, after which the delay begins, will be fixed on the basis of a certain number of kilometers daily, and the time shall begin to run from the day after the freight was delivered to the railroad. In no case shall indemnity for losses and damages for delay exceed the whole amount of freight charges, except in case of fraud, bad faith or grave negligence of the railroad management or its employés, in which case all damages and losses proven shall be paid. (Arts. 138–141.)

Art. 1038. Change of Shipping Directions.— The shipper having possession of the bill of lading, or the lawful holder of the same, may order that the freight be delivered or stored at a point on the line of the original or some connecting carrier other than the destination stated in the bill of lading. In such case the holder will endorse on the bill of lading the new point of delivery or storage, and will present it to the office of the road making the transportation, to which he will also give written notice of the change; and the railroad also has the right to note such change on the bill of lading; and if there are several carriers, the bill of lading and notice will be communicated to the railroad on which is the final destination shown in the bill of lading and to the railroad on which the newly designated point is located. In all cases the entire amount agreed in the bill of lading will be paid, unless by the terms of this law a higher rate is charged for transportation to the new point; the railroad will endorse on the bill of lading the amount which is to be paid.[1] (Art. 143.)

CHAPTER 2.

BAGGAGE REGULATIONS.

(Regulations for the Construction, Maintenance and Operation of Railroads, of 1 June, 1883.)

Art. 1039. Free Baggage — Checking.
    1040. Loss of Baggage — Limit of Liability.

Art. 1039. Free Baggage — Checking.— Every passenger may retain in his possession, without submitting them for checking (*á registro*), such packages as by their size or nature cannot molest or cause damage to other passengers, provided the weight of such packages does not exceed fifteen kilograms. The company shall not be responsible for packages of baggage which have not been duly checked (*registrados*) in its office. The checking of baggage shall be effected by presenting the passenger ticket, in view of which a baggage check (*resguardo*) will be issued to the passenger, showing the name of the stations of departure and destination, the number of packages composing the baggage, their corresponding number, their total weight, and the amount of excess paid, if any; this check will serve the passenger for claiming his baggage on arrival at its destination, where it shall be delivered to him with only the delay necessary for removing it from the baggage car; if left in the station for more than forty-eight hours, the passenger must pay storage charges.

[1] The omitted Articles of the Railroad Law and Regulations treat of concessions, construction, maintenance, operation, and similar technical matters, not of concern to the shipper, passenger or business public, all provisions of general interest being herein stated.

If the passenger cannot present the check, he can only obtain his baggage upon fully proving that it belongs to him, which must be done by presenting the keys and precisely describing the external marks on the packages and some of the articles contained in each, and paying any costs occasioned thereby.   If any of the packages of baggage stated in the check is missing upon the arrival of the train, the passenger will notify the station master, giving him the description and all details which may facilitate finding it, and in exchange for the check will require a document stating the kind of package missing, its weight, initial station, and the agreement of the company to deliver it on a train leaving there within twenty-four hours after the claim is made, the company being obliged to indemnify the claimant for any damages and losses caused by the delay in delivering the baggage.   (Arts. 138–141.)

Art. 1040.   Loss of Baggage — Limit of Liability.— In case of the loss (*extravío*) of packages delivered as baggage, the company will be responsible to pay for it, according to the following classification, unless proved to the contrary: For each large trunk (*baúl mundo*), $200; for each trunk or chest (*petaca*), according to its size, from $50 to $100; for each traveling grip or valise (*maleta*), $25; for each hat box, $5.   The traveler who carries in his baggage jewelry, bank notes, money, corporate stock, public bonds, or other objects of value, must make it known by exhibiting them before the baggage is checked, and state the total value of the same, either their sale value or the value in which he esteems them; failure to comply with this requirement releases the company from responsibility in case of theft or loss (*sustracción ó extravío*), and it will be bound to pay only the amount corresponding to the above classification.   The declaration made by the traveler in regard to the contents of the packages may be accepted by the company, unless from special circumstances it appears to be incorrect; in which event the same will be inspected, and if there is disagreement between the parties, the company may cause a record thereof to be made by an administrative or judicial official, who will set forth the differences between the parties, stating the contents, condition and value given by each party, to the end that such record may be used for the proper purposes in case of loss or otherwise. (**Arts.** 142–144.)

BOOK XIX.
INSURANCE LAW.[1]

TITLE I.

THE CIVIL CONTRACT.

(Código Civil, Arts. 2705 to 2771.)

CHAPTER 1.

GENERAL PROVISIONS.

Art. 1041. Definitions — Incidents.
    1042. Insurers and Insured.
    1043. Settlement of Indemnity.
    1044. Loss — Proof of Fault.
    1045. Premiums.
    1046. Life Insurance — Incidents.
    1047. Insurance of Rights and Actions.
    1048. Fire Insurance.
    1049. Insurance of Transportation.

Art. 1041. Definitions — Incidents.— The contract of insurance is that by which one party undertakes, for a certain price, to indemnify another for damages caused by some accident which may befall him; the former is called the insurer, the latter the insured, the price charged is the premium, and the writing containing the contract is the insurance policy; the contract is void if not in writing. Insurance

---

[1] There is now pending before the Mexican Congress a thorough revision of the general Insurance Law, which renders useless the insertion of the several existing enactments, other than the Codes.

may cover life, rights and actions, real and personal property, and may be effected by the owner or any one having an interest in the property, and for the insured personally or for his heirs or other persons, who must be expressly named in the policy; either party may require collateral securities. Insurance must be for a definite time expressly stated or determined by an event limiting it; the policy must specify the premium and amount of indemnity, the property insured, and the events insured against, and only covers the property and risks stated, and may cover its total loss or damages to it only; in the latter event only the specified damage shall be indemnified although the loss is total. The right to the indemnity is assignable. (Arts. 2707–2715, 2732, 2749.)   .

Art. 1042. Insurers and Insured.— Any person or company able to contract may be an insurer; an administrator of another's property cannot insure it in the latter's name without special authority; guardians, even with judicial authority, cannot make their wards insurers, but may insure them without such authority. If there are several insurers, each is liable for his own obligation, and cannot be subrogated to the insured's rights against the others; if they are severally liable, the rules of mancommunity apply; two or more owners may insure each other against the accidental loss of their property; in mutual insurance each party is liable in proportion to his own property insured. Accident does not embrace superior force (*vis major*) unless expressly stipulated. The insurer must pay the agreed indemnity, which neither party can alter, whether greater or less than the value of the property lost. (Arts. 2716–2724.)

Art. 1043. Settlement of Indemnity.— If so authorized by the contract, the insurer may replace the thing lost, where its kind and value are undisputed, by another of the same kind; if he undertakes to replace, he must do so whatever the cost; the judge may award a reasonable time for the work if necessary. Upon payment of the value or agreed indemnity of the thing lost, the insurer is entitled to any remains of it; if the property is wholly or partly saved, both parties will pay any costs of salvage pro rata unless the insurer prefers to pay the insurance. Where the property is consumed or its form changed by the insured, the liability of the insurer ceases. Where the property is insured by a third person having an interest in it, the indemnity will be paid to the insured, but he can only retain sufficient to cover his interest, paying the balance to the owner. (Arts. 2725–2728, 2730–2734.)

Art. 1044. Loss — Proof of Fault.— Within six days after loss the insured must give notice to the insurer or he loses his right of action; he must prove that the loss occurred by accident and without his fault. Besides ordinary cases of negligence, the insured is at fault where he makes an undue use of the thing insured, or makes no effort to avoid or diminish the loss where he might do so. Any action against a third party on account of the loss must be brought by the insured and insurer jointly, the amount realized being first applied to reimburse the insurer; but he cannot delay or diminish the payment by reason of such action.

The policy is void if the insured knew at the time it was made that the damage insured against has happened, and if the insurer knew that the property insured has escaped the damage; if both acted in good faith the contract is valid although at the time the damage had occurred or the property had been saved. (Arts. 2729, 2735–2741.)

Art. 1045. Premiums.— The policy must state the premium and amount of indemnity; if the latter covers deterioration, its extent will be fixed by experts unless otherwise agreed. The premium may be fixed freely by the parties, and may be paid whole or in installments; if paid in a lump sum, the insured cannot require the repayment of any part of it; if paid in installments, the insurer may deduct any unpaid installments to accrue until the end of the term, from the amount of indemnity he must pay in case of loss, unless otherwise agreed in the policy. Where payable in installments during the term of the policy, the insurer is not liable for a loss occurring during a period for which the installment is unpaid, and the insured can only claim indemnity for loss occurring before the end of the period. (Arts. 2742–2748.)

Art. 1046. Life Insurance — Incidents.— Life insurance may cover natural death only or death in any form even by violence, except by suicide; in case of suicide, the heirs may demand the return of the premiums paid. Life insurance can only be effected by the person whose life is insured; upon his death the insurance money becomes a part of the deceased's estate and is distributed according to law. A person procuring the death of the insured can never take the insurance money even where expressly made payable to him; any stipulation to the contrary is void. Where the term of the insurance has expired the insurer is released although the insured was at the point of death and died immediately afterwards. (Arts. 2750–2755.)

Art. 1047. Insurance of Rights and Actions.— Rights and actions, except in future inheritances, may be insured, and although they are in litigation, but the insurer in such case is only bound by a final judgment on the merits not rendered by default or upon compromise. (Arts. 2756–2759.)

Art. 1048. Fire Insurance.— A person conducting business in premises belonging to another, cannot insure his own effects without insuring the premises in favor of the owner, the indemnity in case of loss to be paid to the insured and divided according to their interests. Where combustible or inflammable material is kept in a storehouse in a town, the

45

policy must contain a certificate from the police authority of the due observance of the regulations, and one showing that the adjoining owners have been notified and acknowledged receipt of such notice; the insurer may reserve the right to inspect the premises and said materials at any time. The insurance of consumable (*fungible*) goods is void unless they are clearly described. (Arts. 2760–2763.)

Art. 1049. Insurance of Transportation.— Insurance of transportation is void if the goods are shipped in a different manner or route from that specified, or through accident or force are not shipped; in the latter event the insurer will return the premium received, and if the failure to ship is due to his fault he is liable for damages; where for any other cause the shipment is not made the insurer is only entitled to ten per cent. of the premium agreed. If the shipment is begun but abandoned, the contract is valid, but if the insurer is at fault he must return the premium and pay damages. If the insured property is lost, but after payment of indemnity is found, the insured may elect between keeping the money or the property; if found before payment, the insurer is only liable for any injury to the property. Maritime insurance is governed by the Commercial Code. (Arts. 2764–2771.)

TITLE II.

THE COMMERCIAL CONTRACT.

(Código de Comercio, **Arts.** 392 to 448.)

CHAPTER 1.

INSURANCE CONTRACTS IN GENERAL.

Art. 1050 Nature and Form of Contract.

Art. 1050. Nature and Form of Contract.— All contracts of insurance, when made by companies, are mercantile. Insurance contracts are rendered void by the bad faith of either party in making them; where the assured, even in good faith, makes any untrue declaration which affects the risks, or omits or conceals any facts or circumstances which might affect the execution of the contract.

The contract of insurance must be in writing, in a policy or other public or private document, and signed by the contracting parties; the contract must contain: 1, The names of the insurer and the assured; 2, the terms and conditions under which the insurance is given; 3, the description and valuation of the property insured, and such indications as may be necessary to determine the nature of the risks; 4, the amount in which the objects insured are valued, apportioning the amount, if required, to the several classes of articles; 5, the amount of premium and the form, manner and place of its payment; 6, the duration of the insurance; 7, the day and hour when the contract takes effect; 8, the amount of insurance already on the same property; 9, any other terms upon which the parties have agreed.[1] Any changes which may be made in the contract during its term must be precisely written on the policy of insurance. The contract of insurance will be governed by the lawful terms contained in it, and in the absence of such by the provisions of this title; and may cover all classes of risks arising from natural accidents or mishaps. (Arts. 392–397, 448.)

CHAPTER 2.

FIRE INSURANCE.

[1] See Arts. 1056 and 1058.

Art. 1051. Objects Insurable — Identity.— Every species of movable and immovable property subject to destruction or. injury by fire is insurable, including, where so stipulated, all kinds of public, private and corporate securities, bank notes, precious stones and metals, and objects of art, the value and circumstances of the same being stated in the policy. The substitution or change of objects insured for others of different kind not embraced in the contract, renders it void from the moment such change is made; if such change is made by accident, or by a third person, either party has the right to rescind the contract. (Arts. 398–399, 403–404.)

Art. 1052. Premiums.— For the contract of fire insurance to be binding, the premium must be received by the insurer, in advance, either by a single whole payment or in such installments as may be agreed, which become upon payment the property of the insurer, whatever be the duration of the insurance. If not paid, the insurer may rescind the contract within the first forty-eight hours, notifying the assured; if he does not exercise this right, he may sue in executive action to recover the premiums due, first obtaining the acknowledgment of the signature to the policy. Movables are charged with a lien for the payment of the premium, immovables being only liable as at common law. (Arts. 400–401, 415.)

Art. 1053. Effect and Extent of Contract.— In cases of total loss by fire, the amounts at which the objects insured are valued, the premiums paid by the assured, the descriptions and valuations contained in the policy, constitute the proof of the existence of the goods insured at the time and place of the fire, in the absence of proof to the contrary; in cases of partial loss, the assured must adduce additional proof to ascertain the yet remaining value of the objects.

The contract of insurance shall embrace indemnity for

all material losses and damages caused by the direct action of the fire and its inevitable consequences, and particularly, the expenses incurred by the assured in removing goods in the attempt to save them, and the injuries sustained by such goods, together with damages caused to the insured goods by the authorities in efforts to limit or extinguish the fire; but it does not embrace, unless otherwise stipulated, losses to the assured through the suspension of his work or business, loss of rents of the burned property, and other similar losses or injuries. The insurer is liable although the fire is caused by accident, wrongful act of a third person, or by the negligence of the assured or of those for whom he is civilly responsible; but unless otherwise stipulated, he is not liable where the fire is caused by the crime of the assured, by military forces in time of war, by popular tumults, nor as the result of eruptions, volcanoes and earthquakes. In insurance against meteorological accidents, explosions of gas or of steam apparatus, the insurer is only liable for the consequences of the resulting fire, if any, unless otherwise stipulated.

The liability only extends to the objects insured in the place where they were, and in no case shall exceed the amount in which the property was valued or the risks estimated. (Arts. 402, 405–409.)

Art. 1054. Incidents of Insurance — Rescission.— The assured must notify the insurer of all other insurance taken and of any modifications of that contained in the policy, and of any changes in the condition of the property insured which may affect the risks. Property insured for its full value cannot be further insured during the term of the first policy, except by way of guaranty of the first contract. If the same property is covered by several policies each for a part of the value, the insurers will pay any losses pro rata. The insurer may assign part of the insurance to other insurers, but remains directly or exclusively liable to the assured; in such cases of assignment of part of the insurance, or of reinsurance, the assignees receiving part of the premium are liable to the first insurer to contribute equally to the losses sustained, and assume responsibility for the arrangements and compromises made between the assured and the first insurer.

The insurance will not be increased by the death, liquidation or bankruptcy of the assured, or by the sale or transfer of the insured property, if it is real property; but if personal property, factory or store, the insurer may in such events rescind the contract, upon giving notice to the assured or his representatives within the certain term of fifteen days. If the assured or his representatives should not notify the insurer within like time of the circumstances above mentioned in cases concerning personal property, the contract will be void as of the time such event occurred. (Arts. 410–414.)

Art. 1055.   Adjustment of Losses.— In case of loss, the assured must immediately notify the insurer, and at the same time make a comprehensive statement before the competent judge, of the property existing at the time of the fire, and of the effects saved, together with his estimate of the amount of the loss suffered.   The appraisement of the damages sustained will be made by experts as provided in the policy or by agreement between the parties, or in default of these, in accordance with the Code of Civil Procedure.   The experts will determine: The cause of the fire; the actual value of the property insured on the day of the fire before it occurred; its value after the fire, and all other matters submitted to them.   Their decision has the effect of an " executive title " against the insurer, when it is rendered before a notary, or is established by the judicial declaration of the experts, and the recognition of their signatures and of the truth of their report.

The insurer must pay in cash the loss fixed by the experts within ten days after their decision is agreed upon, with interest thereafter on the amount due in case of default in payment; or, if the parties so agree, he may repair, rebuild or replace wholly or in part, as the case may be, the property insured and destroyed by the fire. The insurer may acquire the effects saved upon paying the insured their actual value as fixed by the experts; and is subrogated fully to all rights and actions of the assured against anyone responsible for the loss; he may also cancel the policy as to future losses, and any other policies he may have with the same party, upon giving him fifteen days notice and returning the unearned part of the premium.

The costs of adjustment and settlement shall be equally divided between the insurer and assured, unless the latter has manifestly exaggerated the loss, in which event he must pay all the expenses. (Arts. 416–425.)

CHAPTER 3.

LIFE INSURANCE.

Art. 1056. Nature and Form of Contract.
1057. Premiums — Incidents of Contract.

Art. 1056. Nature and Form of Contract.— Life insurance embraces all combinations which may be made, stipulating for payment of premiums or capital in exchange for annuities for life or until a certain age, or the receipt of money upon the death of a certain person, in favor of the assured, his assignee (*causahabiente*) or of a third person; or any like combination; it may be taken upon the life of one or more persons, irrespective of age, condition, sex or state of health. Where in favor of a third person, the policy shall name or otherwise identify the beneficiary, the person taking out the insurance being obliged to comply with all conditions of the insurance and the provisions of the next Article, and to pay premiums, but the beneficiary shall have the right to enforce the contract against the insurance company.

Besides the contents required by Article 1050, the policy of life insurance must state the amount, in capital or income, assured, and the decreases or increases to which such amount is subject, and the date when they take effect.

Only such risks as are clearly specified in the policy are covered by it; but it shall not cover death as the result of a duel, suicide, or capital punishment for common crimes; nor, unless specially stipulated and an extra premium paid, . does it cover death occurring when traveling in foreign countries, in the military service on land or sea in time of war, or as the result of some extraordinary undertaking (*empresa*), or act notoriously dangerous or imprudent. (Arts. 426–434.)

Art. 1057. Premiums — Incidents of Contract.— Failure to pay the premiums or other amounts due deprives the assured of all rights under the policy if the contingency occurs while he is in default. If the assured is unable to continue, after making several payments, he may so notify the insurer, and may receive a paid-up policy for an amount in just proportion to the premiums paid, in accordance with the Company's schedule of rates, considering the risks assumed, unless otherwise agreed. The assured must notify the insurer of all other insurance effected by him, or the policy is void except as to its paid-up value. The insolvency of the assured does not avoid the policy, but it may be reduced at the instance of his representatives to its paid-up value.

The proceeds of life insurance belong to the beneficiary and his heirs and are exempt from all claims of the heirs or creditors of the assured. Life insurance policies may be assigned after payment of premiums, by written endorsement on the policy, authentic notice of such fact being given to the insurance company by the endorser and endorsee.

The life insurance policy gives rise to the " executive action " in favor of both parties; where the assured is in arrears of premiums, the insurer may sue to recover the amount due, or may rescind the contract upon giving him notice within twenty days after default and returning any amounts received. (Arts. 435–441.)

CHAPTER 4.

INSURANCE OF FREIGHT IN TRANSIT.

Art. 1058. Nature and Form of Contract.

Art. 1058. Nature and Form of Contract.— All property transportable by land carriage may be insured, by the owners or by anyone having an interest in it, the nature of the interest being stated in the policy. Besides the contents required in Art. 1050, the policy shall contain the name of the carrier, an exact description of the property insured, stating the number of packages and any marks on them; and the place where the property insured is to be received and delivered.

The policy may cover all kinds of risks however arising; but the insurer is not liable, unless otherwise provided, for injuries due to inherent defects in the goods or by lapse of time; in such cases the insurer must judicially establish the condition of the insured property within twenty-four hours after its arrival at the place of delivery; if he fails to do this he cannot relieve himself of his liability as insurer. The insurer is subrogated to all the rights of the assured to recover damages for which the carrier is liable under the Code. (Arts. 442–447.)

BOOK XX.

THE FEDERAL STAMP TAX.

(*Ley de la Renta Federal del Timbre,* of 1 June, 1906,
with all **A**mendments.)

CHAPTER 1.

GENERAL PROVISIONS.

Art. 1059. What Subject to Stamp **Tax.**
  1060. Issuance of Stamps — Kinds.

Art. 1059. What Subject to Stamp Tax.— The Federal
Stamp Tax (*Impuesto del Timbre*) is payable, by means of
stamps:

I. On all acts, contracts and documents, specified in the
law, which are executed or issued in the Republic, although
they are to be used or take effect in a foreign country.

II. On like acts, contracts and documents which are executed or issued in a foreign country, when they are to be
used or have any effect in Mexico, with such exceptions as
the law prescribes.[1]   Also such other taxes and dues as may
be imposed by special laws to be paid by stamps.

All contracts and documents subject to the Stamp Tax
must be in writing so that the stamps may be affixed to and

---

[1] Although a contract is made and is to be performed in a foreign
country, it must be "validated" by attaching the corresponding value
of stamps, before suit can be brought on it, or other legal effect be
given to it, in Mexico. This is true of notes, bills and all other forms
of contract. See *post*, Arts. 1097–1099, as to "validating" such documents, and Art. 1090.

cancelled on the paper, except where the execution of a writing is optional under the Stamp Law; failure to do so is punishable as in case of omission to attach stamps. (Arts. 1–3.)

Art. 1060. Issuance of Stamps — Kinds.— Stamps can only be issued by the Federal Government; no other authority can issue or use them nor issue receipts for payment in the form of stamps; nor can the Federal Government sell stamps at a discount or on credit, or use them to make payment, advances or otherwise. The Department of Hacienda will annually authorize the issue, and fix the value, form and denominations of the stamps, which shall be of three classes: 1, Common stamps of the General Stamp Tax; 2, stamps of the Federal Tax; 3, stamps for special taxes; the common stamps may be used for some special taxes or dues, as may be provided, in which event they must bear a special restamp designating their object. The Treasury may authorize the Stamp Printing Office to print stamps directly upon stock certificates, bank notes, bonds, checks, cigarette wrappers, titles and other documents, upon payment of the value of the stamps such documents should bear and the cost of the work, on such terms as said Department may prescribe.

The stamps can only be used during the fiscal year for which they are issued, except as provided in regard to manufactured tobacco and yarns and cotton goods; but the Executive may under special circumstances legalize the use of the stamps for a longer time, and may authorize their issuance for two fiscal years. All common stamps and those of the Federal taxes will bear the restamp of the Main Office (*Administración Principal*) which sells them, and they can only be used on documents executed in the respective District; they must bear the restamp of the Principal Office (*Dirección del Ramo*) when sold by it. The stamp tax may be paid by one or more stamps of the required class equaling the amount to be paid; documents bearing stamps

of a different class from that of the tax, or with the restamp
of the Main Office of another District than that in which
they are executed, will be revalidated upon payment of a
fine as herein provided. (Arts. 4–12.)

CHAPTER 2.

STAMP TARIFF.

TAXES IN FORM OF COMMON STAMPS.[2]

Art. 1061. Amounts of Tax Required.

Art. 1061. Amounts of Tax Required.— The acts, documents and contracts herein mentioned are subject to the
payment in common stamps of the rates prescribed, on the
following basis: 1, A rate on each sheet of the document;
2, a rate in proportion to the value stated in the document;
3, a fixed rate, irrespective of the number of sheets or the
value stated. The rates of Taxes will be as specified in the
following: (Arts. 13–14.)

TARIFF.

33.— ACCOUNTS, of Division and Partition. (See
"Inheritances and Legacies.")

34.— ACCOUNTS, (*Cuentas*) of every other kind, which
serve as receipts or are presented for collection, for
each $20 or fraction, 2 cts.

[2] N. B. In order to arrange the subjects of stamp taxation as translated in the following schedules, in alphabetical order to facilitate
reference, as they are in the Spanish text, it is of course necessary
to change the original numerical sequence of the paragraphs; but their
original numbering is retained for purposes of reference to the original
text. Some of the "Special Rules for Application of the Tax," where
they are brief, are inserted in the following table, others follow in
their regular place in the Articles referred to in parentheses after the
subject-heading in the Tariff. All sums are stated in current Mexican
PESOS, equal to 49.8 cts., U. S. currency.

18.— ACCOUNTS, Statements of (*Carta-cuenta*), for each $20 or fraction, 2 cts.

56.— ACCOUNT BOOKS. (See " Books of Account ").

5.— ADJUDICATION of Property in Payment, or to the Bidder at Auctions; pays the same rate as " *Compra-venta*," on the price bid. Includes adjudication of pledges not sold at auction, made by interventors in favor of pawnshop owners. The tax will be paid on the minute or document evidencing the adjudication, unless an *escritura pública* is required, in which event it will be paid as provided for the latter instruments. (Art. 36.)

22.— ANNUITIES. (*Censos.*) 1, The *consignativo*, for each $100 or fraction of the capital, 50 cts.; 2, the *enfitéutico*, on the amount of the annuity capitalized at the agreed rate or at six per cent. if not stipulated, for each $100 or fraction, 50 cts. If the amount is payable in a certain portion of products, the rules in clause V under " Leases " are applicable. (Art. 54.)

94·— ANNUITIES, Life, Contract of (*Renta Vitalicia*). 1, Where the consideration is cash or property, on the amount resulting from capitalization at ten per cent. a year, for each $100 or fraction, 50 cts.; 2, if the product of the capitalization is less than the amount of capital or value of the property delivered, the above rate will be paid, and on the difference, the rate applicable to Donations; 3, those created gratuitously will pay the rate on Donations, on the amount resulting from capitalization of the annuity at ten per cent. a year.

37, 65 & 73.— APPOINTMENTS and Commissions to Public Office or Employment. (*Despachos, Nom-bramientos y Patentes.* See Arts. 131 to 135 of Stamp Law.) Where the salary, emoluments or annual pension is between $500 and $1,000, $1; from $1,000 to $2,000, $2; from $2,000 to $4,000, $5;

popular election; appointments of Secretaries of State and of diplomatic representatives resident in the Republic; military and naval appointments, minor employés, etc.

10.— APPRAISEMENTS. (*Avalúo.*) Those made to be presented to any public authority or office, 50 cts. per sheet; where presented together with the inventory of the property appraised a single rate of 50 cts. per sheet is paid. (**Art.** 49.) Exempt from tax: Those made by tax officers for the collection of taxes, unless made at the request of interested parties, or made necessary by their objection to the tax.

26.— ASSIGNMENTS. (*Cesión.*) 1, Upon onerous title: a, Of real rights, same rate as *Compraventa;* b, of personal rights, for each $10 or fraction, 2 cts.; 2, gratuitous: Of rights of any kind, same as Donations. Exempt from tax: The sale of shares of stock or titles to bearer. (See "Endorsements," 40.) For taxing purposes an assignment in which no consideration is expressed is presumed gratuitous; if made subject to encumbrances estimable in money it is considered gratuitous only as to any excess of value over encumbrances, and the above rates are payable; where the assignee makes a subsequent declaration that he holds the property in trust for another who furnished the money or on whose behalf the property was acquired, it is considered an assignment upon consideration and will pay the above rates. (Arts. 59–61.)

72.— AUCTION BIDS. (*Papel de Abono.*) Where the valuation serving as basis of the auction is from $200 to $1,000, 50 cts.; from $1,000 to $5,000, $2; over $5,000, $5. Exempt from tax: Bids where the basis of sale does not exceed $200.

11.— BALANCES. (*Balance.*) Copies made by judicial or administrative order or to be presented before any public authority or office in matters of private interest, 50 cts. per sheet.

13.— BANK NOTES. (*Billetes de Banco.*) Up to $20, 2 cts.; over that amount, for each $50 or fraction, 5 cts.; except banks having franchises in regard to stamp tax in their concessions, which will govern.

54.— BILLS OF EXCHANGE. (*Letras de Cambio.* See Art. 1088.) Up to $100, 2 cts.; from $100 to $500, 5 cts.; from $500 to $1,000, 10 cts.; over $1,000, for each $1,000 or fraction, 10 cts. Exempt: Bills of exchange drawn by public offices.

Duplicates and triplicates of bills and drafts may be legalized by presenting them, with the original properly stamped, to the Stamp Office of the place, where the seal of the office will be impressed on them, with a memorandum of the fact; if the original is not presented properly stamped, the copies must bear stamps; but the drawer may use coupon-stamps, putting the stamp on the original and the coupon or stub on the duplicate, any other copies being legalized by the official seal; brokers intervening in the transaction must take care that the stamps are attached and the foregoing rules observed, and in case of neglect are liable to the same penalties as the drawer and taker of the bill. (Arts. 165–166.)

30.— BILLS OF LADING. (*Conocimientos de fletes y de portes.* See Art. 1074.) On the amount of freight charges: From 50 cts. to $2, 1 ct.; from $2 to $10, for each $2 or fraction, 1 ct.; from $10 up, for each $10 or fraction, 5 cts. Exempt from tax: a, Bills of lading for freight from a Mexican port to a foreign country; b, documents issued by maritime transportation concerns for charges for carrying freight between wharves and vessels, or from one

Mexican port to another, which documents will pay
same as receipts; c, bills of lading on account of the
Federal Government.

68.— BILLS OF SALE. (*Nota.*) Bills or memoranda of
sale, if signed and taking the place of receipts or
invoices, will pay same as " Receipts " or " Invoices." Exempt from tax: Notas of merchandise
sent to buyers for the sole purpose of proving the
delivery and receipt of merchandise.

15.— BONDS. (*Bonos.*) Those evidencing indebtedness
of any company or business concern: 1, If issued by
virtue of a contract on which stamps have already
been paid, on each bond not exceeding $100 par
value, for each $20 or fraction, 1 ct.; if over $100,
for each $100 or fraction, 5 cts.; 2, if not issued
under such contract already stamped, on the par
value of the bonds, for each $10 or fraction, 5 cts.;
3, the several kinds of bonds issued by Institutions
of Credit will pay in accordance with the special laws
and concessions. Bonds must be stamped although
issued in exchange for others previously stamped
which are to be retired, but if the original issue have
been stamped at the rate provided in clause 2 above,
the reissue will only pay as provided in clause 1.
Exempt from tax are the bonds, obligations and certificates of credit of the Federal, State and Municipal
governments.

45.— BONDS, Surety. (*Fianzas.*) 1, Where the amount
is stated: a, If executed in *escritura pública,* for
each $100 or fraction, 20 cts.; b, if executed in
any other form, for each $20 or fraction, 2 cts.;
2, where the amount is not ascertained when the
contract is made: a, If by *escritura pública,* $2 per
sheet; b, if otherwise, $1 per sheet; 3, bonds given to
carriers to obtain delivery of freight when the bill of
lading is missing, or to pawnbrokers when the ticket

is lost, where the amount is not stated, 25 cts.; 4, those executed, although by mortgage, to insure the responsibility of public employés, except as provided in favor of bonding companies, for each $20 or fraction, 2 cts. Exempt from tax: a, Bonds executed in the same instrument with the principal obligation; b, bail and prison bonds.

56.— BOOKS OF ACCOUNT. (See Art. 1080.) Account books, Journal, Ledger, Inventory and Balance Books, required by mercantile law to be kept by merchants, where the assets of the business amount to $2,000 or more, 5 cts. per sheet; 2, sales books required by the Stamp Law to be kept by those habitually engaged in making sales by retail or wholesale, 1 ct. per sheet; 3, books required to be kept by pawnbrokers, of whatever capital, towit: Books of valuation, reception and disposition of pledges, journal, ledger, inventories and balances, 5 cts. per sheet; 4, Brokers' Registers; stock certificate books and minute books of companies; books of private corporations or associations organized for profit; books kept in railroad stations for entering their daily operations; books of carriers for recording receipts from freight and passenger tolls, where they are not required to keep all the books of account named in clause 1, 5 cts. per sheet. Exempt from tax: a, The books of *Montes de Piedad* and other establishments of public charity and instruction, or of private charity under the patronage or supervision of the Federal or State governments; b, account books of industrial establishments dependent upon the Federal, State or Municipal governments, although such establishments sell their own products.

55.— BOOKS of Deposit or Pass-books. (*Libretas.*) Books of deposits, with or without interest, issued by institutions of credit, savings banks, and banking and

46

business houses, on the understanding that the debit
and credit accounts therein are not subject to the
stamp tax, 25 cts. per book.

63 & 80.— BROKERS' Minutes or Policy of Contracts,
will pay same rate as that corresponding to the contract.

69.— BUILDING CONTRACTS. (*Contrato de Obras.*)
1, Contracts for work on real estate, by the job: a,
Where the contractor is to do the work and furnish
materials for a fixed price, upon the contract price,
for each $10 or fraction, 1 ct. ; b, where he only gives
his work or skill for a fixed fee, upon the amount of
the fee, for each $10 or fraction, 1 ct. ; 3, contracts for
work on personal property are governed by the rules
of *compra-venta* where the contractor furnishes the
materials, unless they are only accessories and not
the principal element of the transaction, or are simply for repairs, and by the rules as to " unspecified
contracts." (**Arts.** 107, 129.)

16.— CANCELLATIONS. Of mortgages or real encumbrances, only where made on account of payment, for
each $20 or fraction, 2 cts. Exempt from tax: The
cancellation of a mortgage made in the same *escritura*
in which the mortgaged property is sold or otherwise
disposed of, upon which a higher rate is paid than
for cancellation. The stamps representing the tax
on cancellation may be affixed either to the receipt
which is to be protocolized, or to the minute sent
to the stamp office when a special *escritura* is to be
executed, or on the margin of the protocol entry of
the cancellation, wherever such cancellation need not
be by *escritura pública*. (**Art.** 52.)

23.— CERTIFICATES or CERTIFICATION. (See
Art. 1063.) Those of any kind issued by a public authority, official or office, or by a private person to be
presented to a public authority, officer or office, **50**

cts. per sheet. Exempt from tax: a, Medical certificates for use in the offices of the Civil Register or to show compliance with some sanitary regulation; b, acts of civil status; c, those concerning military and police matters; d, those issued to show the closing of any establishment or other exemption from taxation; e, those concerning the survival of public pensioners; f, those issued by military commanders in regard to billeting of troops; g, all certificates issued *ex officio* by public offices in compliance with any law or regulation of general observance; h, those issued by public offices in regard to fines and other fiscal matters; i, those issued by primary schools in regard to educational matters; j, those relating to excuses from jury service; k, those issued to ships sailing in ballast.

24.— CERTIFICATES, Provisional, of Stocks or Bonds. These will pay a tax of ten per cent. of the rate for Stocks and Bonds under Sections 1 and 15 of the Tariff, on the total par value represented by the same, but in no case to be less than one cent nor more than five pesos on each certificate. Such provisional certificates can only be legalized at the above ten per cent. rate if they are exchanged within one year from their date for the stocks or bonds which they represent; if not exchanged within that time, they must be revalidated with the stamps corresponding to the stocks or bonds, which if not done within the fixed term of fifteen days, the holders as well as the company issuing them will be subject to the penalties herein prescribed. (Art. 58.)

25.— CERTIFICATES OF DEPOSIT. Where the deposit is of a specific chattel or of cash in chest or sack closed and sealed: 1, On the amount of the bailee's fee or compensation, for each $20 or fraction, 2 cts.; 2, if the deposit is gratuitous, 50 cts. per sheet, except as otherwise provided by the concessions of Institutions of Credit. Exempt from tax: a, Those issued by public offices; b, those issued under Art. 5 of the Decree of 23 November, 1905, and Art. 3 of that of 22 December, 1905.

32.— CERTIFIED COPIES (of Documents other than " public," as provided for in Section 100, below) : 1, Except as herein provided, the rules in Section 23 as to " Certificates and Certification " are applicable; 2, those issued under Section 37 in regard to " Appointments," for use in paying offices, 10 cts. per sheet; 3, those issued for use in legal proceedings to parties authorized to plead as " poor persons," 5 cts. per sheet, but the balance of the rate of 50 cts. per sheet must be paid when the record is completed and the charges paid. Exempt from tax: a, Those issued in applications for pardon, commutation of sentence or release on bail; b, those issued in criminal cases at the instance of the defendant or his attorney for the purpose of applying for *amparo* or to present as proof of said action; c, those of original documents accompanying reports forming military records, or made for a like purpose because of the loss of the originals, from other copies or minutes in the archives; d, those of military documents in regard to grades in the Army; e, those of appointments and commissions which are exempt from stamp tax, for use in the pay offices; f, those issued for use in court in matters involving less than one hundred pesos.

100.— CERTIFIED COPIES. (*Testimonios.*) Those of any protocolized document, *escritura pública,* will, or minute entered in the protocol, per sheet, $1. The sheet added to such copy for recording legalization of signatures, entries from the Public Register and other proceedings, will only pay 50 cts., besides the tax on the legalization. (**Art.** 208.)

9.— CHARITABLE ASSOCIATIONS or Foundations, Private. Their Constitutions and the protocolization of their By-laws are exempt from tax where such institutions are duly authorized by law; if they do not obtain such authorization within six months, or an extension not to exceed six months granted by the Department of Hacienda, they are subject to the same rates as civil and commercial companies under Sec. 96, in case of Associations, and to the rates applicable to " Donations " under Sec. 39 or to " Legacies and Inheritances " under Sec. 48, in cases of foundations. (Art. 48.)

35.— CHECKS. Those issued in conformity with the provisions of the Code of Commerce: Up to $100, 2 cts.; over $100, 5 cts.

96.— COMPANIES AND CORPORATIONS. (*Sociedades*. See Art. 1089.) Civil and Commercial Companies will pay upon the capital stated in the Contract: 1, a, When the capital does not exceed $500,000, for each $1,000 or fraction, $1; b, between $500,000 and $1,000,000, for the first $500,000, at the rate of $1 per thousand, and for the balance, for each $1,000 or fraction, 50 cts.; c, where the capital exceeds $1,000,000, the first million will pay according to clauses " a " and " b," and on the excess, for each $1,000 or fraction, 10 cts.; 2, where from the nature of the company's object there is no capital, or the company is formed for profits only, or the contributions do not belong to the company, $2 per sheet; 3, by-laws which are protocolized separately from the articles of association, $2 per sheet.

38.— COMPANIES AND CORPORATIONS, Dissolution of. Upon the dissolution of a company either before or at the expiration of the term fixed for its duration, the tax will be paid only on the amuont received by the partners in excess of their share of capital contributed and profits obtained, in whatever form such excess is realized: For each $1,000 or fraction, $2. Where one partner pays the others with his own money the amount of their respective shares, the tax corresponding to " onerous " assignments of personal property will be paid although real estate forms part of the company capital; this rule also applies where, without dissolution, one partner withdraws and the others pay him the amount of his interest or an agreed sum in lieu thereof; in the division of community property, of that acquired *pro indiviso* (undivided), or in which the owners represent aliquot parts, the rules as to dissolution of companies apply and the above rate will be paid. (**Arts.** 136–139.)

28.— *COMPRA-VENTA.* (Purchase and Sale Contracts. See Arts. 1064 to 1073.) I. When the price is less than $20, and the transactions are by merchants or mercantile, industrial, agricultural or mining concerns, subject to Arts. 1064 to 1069, in regard to sales by retail, the tax will be paid as therein **provided** at the rate of $\frac{1}{2}$ per cent.

II. Where the price is less than $20 and the transactions are not of the kind stated above, for each $2 or fraction, 1 ct.

III. When the price is $20 or more: a, If the contract is in *escritura pública,* for each $100 or fraction, 70 cts.; b, in other cases, for each $10 or fraction, 5 cts.

IV. Where from the nature or conditions of the contract, the amount involved cannot be determined when the contract is made, the rates above **specified** in I, II and III will be paid as provided in Art. 1073, and in addition, there will be paid at the time the contract is made: a, If in *escritura pública,* $2 per sheet; b, in other cases, 50 cts. per sheet.

Exempt from Tax: a, Sales by retail amounting altogether to less than $100 a month; b, sales made in stalls or booths in public markets, streets and other places for which a daily floor-rent is paid; c, sales effected within club-houses or private meeting-places, provided such sales are for the immediate and direct account of the association, and not for that of third persons, contractors or lessees; d, supplies of seeds made to peons and workmen on account of wages; e, sales of periodical publications; f, sales of their own products made by industrial schools, offices and establishments maintained by the Federal, State or Municipal governments, or by the Public Beneficence; g, sales of the products of animals killed in slaughter-houses, provided the sales are made within said places; h, the first-hand sales of articles subject to the special tax on cotton yarns and fabrics. The sales referred to in clauses g and h are also exempt from the tax on sales by wholesale.

29.— CONCESSIONS. 1, Those for utilization of water for Motive Power, $5 per sheet; and, in addition thereto, for each horse-power effective in the place where the plant is installed, according to the previous calculation of the authority granting the concession, which estimate must be recited in the concession for the purpose of determining the tax: a, If the concession is for thirty years or more, $2; b, if for less than thirty years, $1.

2, Those for Use of Water for Irrigation, $5 per sheet; and, in addition thereto, in respect to the volume of water granted, calculated and stated as above; for each cubic meter or fraction per minute: a, If the concession is for thirty years or more, $5; b, if for less than thirty years, $2.50.

3, Those for the construction and operation of railroads of any kind, $5 per sheet; and, in addition thereto, for each kilometer of main line or branches, whether of obligatory or optional construction, the estimated number of which kilometers must be stated in the concession, $10.

4, All others issued as authorizations or permits. by the Federal or State government or by political authorities or Municipal Councils, for any kind of enterprise or industry, except such as are embraced under " Licenses " in Sec. 57 or " Permits " in Sec. 76 of this tariff, $5 per sheet; and, in addition thereto: a, Upon the capital to be invested in such enterprise, or where this is not stated, upon the amount of cash paid by the *concessionaire,* or if such amount is to be paid in installments for more than a year, then only on the amount payable in one year, for each $100 or fraction, 50 cts.; b, where the capital or cash payment is not stated, in case of concessions granted by the Federal or State governments, $5 per sheet; if granted by political authorities or municipal councils, $1 per sheet.

5, Concessions for the use and exploitation of forests, *terrenos baldíos,* salt beds and other national properties, and, generally, all concessions dependent upon any contract specially rated in this Tariff, will pay the rate corresponding to such contract.

62.— CONTRACTS, Minutes of. (See " Minutes of Contracts.")

28.— CONTRACTS, of Purchase and Sale. (See " *Compraventa.")*

92.— CONTRACTS, Rescission of. (See " Rescission.")

69.— CONTRACTS, for Work. (See " Building Contracts.")

31.— CONTRACTS, Unspecified. (See Art. 1075.) 1, Where the amount involved is stated: a, If the contract involves the transfer of real property or rights, it will pay the rates of *Compra-venta;* b, if it does not involve such transfers, and is in *escritura pública,* for each $100 or fraction, 20 cts.; if in a document other than *escritura pública,* for each $10 or fraction, 1 ct.; 2, where the amount is not stated: a, If the contract is in *escritura pública,* $2 per sheet; b, if not in *escritura pública,* 50 cts. per sheet. Exempt from tax: a, Contracts of enlistment or reënlistment in the army, navy or police forces; b, contracts of affreightment made outside the Republic, which foreign merchant vessels have to present to Mexican port officers on arriving or clearing.

86.— CONTRACTS, Extensions of. (See Arts. 1085 and 1089.) The simple extension of time, without altering other substantial conditions of the contract, and unless otherwise provided in this law: Upon the amount of the obligation extended, for each $20 or fraction, 2 cts.

74.— CUSTOMS HOUSE PETITIONS. I. For the loading or unloading of sea-going vessels: a, For ships of 10 gross tons burden or less, $1; b, from 10 to 50 tons, $2; c, from 50 to 100 tons, $4; d, ships of more than 100 gross tons burden, $8. II. For loading or unloading coasting vessels: Those of up to 50 gross tons burden, 50 cents; b, those of more than 50 gross tons, $2. III. Petitions for the dispatch of foreign merchandise; for its transit through the national territory; for shipment for exportation; for reshipment of foreign merchandise unloaded on account of landing under stress; for the clearing of vessels put in under stress; for loading at uninhabited places along the coast; for the deposit of foreign merchandise, or its transportation from one warehouse to another; for the final shipment of such warehoused merchandise, and for taking of samples from the deposit, each 50 cts. per sheet. IV. Petitions for shipment of national goods in the coasting trade; for shipment of samples or articles of commerce carried by passengers in their baggage; and those presented by Express companies for the shipment of goods, 25 cts. per sheet. V. For transshipment of merchandise, $1.

Exempt from tax: A. Petitions for shipment of effects by express for diplomatic representatives in Mexico; B. for transshipment of effects brought into Mexican ports for warships of a friendly nation; C. for the shipment of such effects which have been unloaded; D. for transit through foreign territory of national or nationalized merchandise to be reimported through another Mexican customhouse; E. for shipment of provisions for use on coastwise vessels.

50.— DEPOSITIONS. (*Informaciones ad perpetuam.*) Pay the same rate as " legal documents," although intended to prove title to real estate.

38.— DISSOLUTION OF COMPANY. See " Companies and Corporations, Dissolution."

39.— DONATIONS. (See **Art.** 1076.) Upon the **net** amount of the gift: I. When in favor of ascendants, descendants or husband or wife, 1%; II. when in favor of collateral relations from the second to the eighth degree, 2%; III. when in favor of other relations or of strangers, 3%; IV. where the amount of the gift cannot at all be determined: in the case of clause **I,** $2.50 per sheet; in case of clause II, $5 per sheet; in the case of clause III, $10 per sheet. V. where the amount cannot be determined when the contract is made, but may be afterwards: a, on the document in which the gift is made, $2 per sheet; b, on the document or receipt which necessarily must be executed upon ascertaining the amount or receiving the donation, the tax will be paid according to clauses I, II and III above respectively. VI. Ante-nuptial gifts made by one of the parties to the other, pay as in clause I.

Exempt from tax: A. Gifts to the Nation; B. gifts to public charitable or educational establishments or private ones recognized by law and under the supervision of the Federal or State governments; C. gifts of less than $200, but where repeated or periodical between the same persons, they must pay the proper rate when their amount reaches $200 or more; D. ante-nuptial gifts consisting of wearing apparel, jewelry and furniture.

54 *bis.*— DRAFTS. (*Libranzas.* See Arts. 165–166 under "Bills of Exchange," No. 54.) 1, Those drawn at sight or at not to exceed thirty days sight (same as checks), up to $100, 2 cts.; for more than $100, 5 cts.; 2, those drawn for over thirty days sight (same as notes), for each $100 or fraction, 2 cts.

102.— DUE-BILLS: "I. O. U." (*Vales.*) Those issued under the Code of Commerce pay same as "Notes." Those referred to herein only include those issued by one merchant obligating himself to deliver to the order of another named a certain amount of money or goods; such goods, for the purpose of determining the tax, will be taken at the valuation put on them by the parties in executing the document, and if no value is fixed, at the current market price at the time and place of issuing the due-bill. (Arts. 209–210.)

40.— ENDORSEMENTS. (*Endoso.*) The irregular endorsement of documents which according to law are not endorsable, will pay, when in fact effect is given to them, the same as the "onerous" assignment of personal rights, for each $10 or fraction, 2 cts. (See "Assignments," 26, I, b.) Exempt from tax: The endorsement of shares of stock, bills of exchange, drafts and other instruments which according to law may be transferred by endorsement.

41.— *ESCRITURA PÚBLICA.* (See **Art.** 1077.) These will pay the rate corresponding to the act or contract contained in them, provided that the tax on such act or contract has not already been paid on another document, in which event the rules stated in **Art.** 1077 will be observed.

77.— EXCHANGES. (*Permuta.*) Pay same rate as " *Compraventa.*" In contracts having for object the reciprocal transfer of property, the tax will be computed only on the property of greater value delivered by either of the parties, without including any cash money which he may pay or promise to pay to the other party or to a third person for him. (Art. 118.)

86.— EXTENSIONS OF CONTRACTS. (See " Contracts, Extensions of.")

39.— GIFTS. (See " Donations.")

93.— INCOME OR PENSIÓN, Temporary. (*Renta ó pensión temporal.*) I. If for an indefinite time, will pay same as " Life Annuities." II. If for a definite time and gratuitous, the annual amount will be multiplied by the number of years it has to run, and on the amount obtained the same rates will be paid as for " Donations "; but if such amount is greater than a life annuity would be, it will be taxed the same rate as a life annuity. III. If for a definite time and upon " onerous title," it will be taxed as " *compraventa.*"

48.— INHERITANCES AND LEGACIES. (See **Art.** 1079.) On the net amount of the estate inherited: I. On the shares by inheritance or legacy in favor of ascendants, descendants or husband and wife, 1% ; II. on such shares of collateral relations, by consanguinity, from the second to the eighth degree, 2% ;

III. on the shares of other relations or of strangers, 3%. Exempt from tax: Inheritances and legacies in favor of the Federal, State, or Municipal treasury, and of public charity and education, or of private charities recognized by law and under the supervision of the Federal or State governments.

52.— INVENTORIES. Those which have to be presented before any public authority or office, 50 cts. per sheet.

42.— INVOICES, Wholesale. (*Factura.*) Pay same as "*Compraventa,*" and must be issued in the form prescribed in Arts. 1070–1071. Exempt from tax: Those relative to transactions of *compraventa* for which the tax has been paid on the document con-taning the contract, but this fact must be stated in them.

43.— INVOICE-PETITIONS. (*Factura-Pedimento.*) Those accompanying foreign merchandise imported through frontier customs-houses, whatever the size of the sheets, 50 cts. per sheet.

7.— LEASES AND SUB-LEASES. (See Art. 1062A.) I. Those made for a definite time not exceeding five years: Upon the amount of rents during the term, for each $10 or fraction, 5 cts; II. if made for more than five years, up to fifteen, which is the limit for paying the tax, although made for a longer term, the above rate will be paid for the first five years, and upon the remaining, for each $10 or fraction, 1 ct.; III. if the amount of rents for the first five years exceeds one million pesos, there will be paid upon the million the rate of $5 a thousand, and on the excess, for each $10 or fraction, 1 ct., and in addi-tion the rate prescribed in clause II for the time beyond five years.

IV. If the contract is for an indefinite time: Upon the rent for one year, for each $10 or fraction, 5 cts.; V. where the amount of rent cannot be determined when the contract is made, and a basis only is established for afterwards ascertaining it, whatever the term of the lease or if it is indefinite: a, on the the document containing the contract: if *escritura pública,* $2 per sheet; if not, 50 cts. per sheet; b, on the receipt which must be given on payment of the rent, for each $10 or fraction, 5 cts.; VI. the renting or hiring of personal property is subject to the rates above prescribed respectively.

Exempt from tax: A. The renting of real estate for less than $100 yearly; B. that of personal property where the amount, whether paid in one or more installments, is less than $20.

3.— LEGAL PROCEEDINGS. (*Actuaciones.* See Arts. 28–34.) I. Administrative and judicial documents, as provided in Arts. 17–27, 50 cts. per sheet; II. those issued at the instance of persons judicially habilitated on account of poverty, 5 cts. per sheet. The tax on administrative proceedings is payable only on those had in regard to adjudication of *baldíos* and properties of the *Ayuntamientos,* the denouncement of mines, treasures and of vacant and unclaimed properties; and, in general, in all those brought by private parties in regard to matters of purely private interest and which must be conducted in accordance with the procedure established by law. (Art. 17, as amended 25 October, 1909.)

Exempt from tax: A. All judicial documents in which the amount involved is less than $100; B. administrative documents in controversies over the application of fiscal laws, the distribution of communal lands and those belonging to the town common lands (*ejidos*); C. all kinds of criminal proceedings; D. proceedings brought by defendants for *" amparo "* against criminal procedure or sentences; E. proceedings in respect to release on bail or to obtain pardon;

F. writs (*oficios*) directed, although at the instance of a party, by any tribunal, court or public official to a public authority or private person; G. memoranda of reports of hearings or oral arguments before judges or tribunals; H. reports with the proofs and exhibits attached, rendered by the authorities in proceedings for "*amparo.*"

27.— LEGAL SUMMONS. (*Citas judiciales.*) Those issued to summon the defendant in cases only where the amount involved equals or exceeds $100, 25 cts.

53.— LEGALIZATIONS, of Signatures. Of officials, chiefs of offices, notaries, public employés, and of private persons: same rate as " Certifications."

21.— LETTERS OF ATTORNEY. (*Carta-poder.* See Art. 1083 relating to Powers of Attorney.) Whether the amount involved is stated or not: I. Where signed by only one person in favor of one other, 5 cts.; II. where there are three parties either principal or agent, 10 cts.; III. if four parties as above, 15 cts.; IV. if five or more parties, 20 cts.; V. substitutions pay the same rates as above respectively.

19.— LETTERS OF CREDIT AND LETTER-ORDERS. (*Carta de Crédito y Carta-órden.*) Up to $100, 2 cts.; for more than $100, or uncertain sum, 5 cts.

20.— LETTERS OF PAYMENT. (*Carta de Pago.*) For each $20 or fraction, 2 cts.

57.— LICENSES. Those for carrying weapons, and all others issued in matters of police by the political and municipal authorities, and for their renewal, 10 cts.

84 & 64.— LOANS OF MONEY. (See Art. 1085.) I. Where executed in *escritura pública,* for each $100 or fraction, 50 cts.; II. when in other kind of document, for each $20 or fraction, 2 cts. Loan contracts made by or in favor of institutions of credit

or general warehouses, pay such rates as are provided in their franchises.

58.— LOTTERIES OR RAFFLES. Those which issue tickets: On the value of the prizes including the *reintegros,* 5%.

4 & 59.— MANIFESTS, of Customshouses, Additions, Corrections, etc. The principal copy, 50 cts.

17.— MARRIAGE SETTLEMENTS. (*Capitulaciones Matrimoniales.*) I. Those made for the purpose of regulating voluntary conjugal partnerships: Upon the net value of the property brought in by the couple: a, If not exceeding $500,000, for each $1,000 or fraction, $1; b, from $500,000 to $1,000,000, on the first $500,000, the above rate, and on the balance, for each $1,000 or fraction, 50 cts.; c, if exceeding one million pesos, the above rates on the first million, and on the excess, for each $1,000 or fraction, 10 cts.

II. Those made for the purpose of terminating the voluntary or legal partnership, will pay the same rates as " Dissolution of Companies."

III. Those made before marriage for the purpose of regulating the separation of properties, $2 per sheet.

60.— MEMORIALS. (See Art. 1081.) I. Memorials, petitions and other written applications presented to any authority or chief of office of the Federation, States or Municipalities, 50 cts. per sheet; II. those presented by soldiers and by " poor persons," 5 cts. per sheet. Exempt from tax: A. Pleadings, briefs and other documents of prisoners or their attorneys, and by the prosecutor or complainant in all criminal proceedings, and petitions for pardon, commutation and bail; B. those in civil proceedings where the amount is less than $100; C. resignations of public officials and employés; D. those presented by private persons in matters of public administration, in the capacity of agents of the Government or commissioners, but not as contractors; E. memorials presented to the Board of Private Beneficence in regard to creating charitable institutions, although they are not established; F. manifestations presented to any public authority or office in compliance with law or regulations; G. memorials presented by owners or possessors to the proper officials in regard to taxation of real estate.

61.— MINES. (See " Titles.")

2.— MINUTES. (*Actas.* See **Art.** 1062.) I. Those executed before any authority, official or public employé, or between private persons, besides the rate payable on the act or contract therein contained, 50 cts. per sheet; II. company or corporate minutes entered in their books; See " Books of **Account.**"

Exempt from tax: A. Those not relating to lucrative matters; B. those relating to matters under $100; C. those kept by public officials and relating to public affairs; D. those entered in duly stamped protocols; E. the second and later copies of those executed before any public official, and issued in compliance with some law or regulation, provided the originals were duly stamped.

62.— MINUTES, of Contracts. (*Minutas.* See **Art.** 1082.) Those executed before or deposited with Notaries, *Escribanos* or judges acting as such, 10 cts. per sheet.

47.— MONEY ORDERS. (*Giros postales.*) For whatever amount, 3 cts.

49.— MORTGAGES. I. On the amount of the obligation secured, same rate as " Bonds, Surety," No. 45; II. extensions of mortgages, same rate as above; III. those given to secure loans of money, where tax is not already paid on the loan (See " Loans," I), for each $100 or fraction, 50 cts. Exempt from tax: A. mort-

47

gages and extension's executed in the same instrument in which the original obligation is created or extended, already duly stamped; B. extensions granted to new owners of mortgaged property, where granted in the instrument under which the property is acquired; C. mortgages constituted in the same deed of purchase in favor of a third person who lends the money to make the purchase, the tax in such case being only imposed on the sale, and not on the mortgage or loan.

71.— NOTES, Promissory. (*Pagaré.*) For each $20 or fraction, 2 cts. Exempt from tax: Those given in transactions between institutions of credit and the Federal, State or Municipal governments.

70.— OPTIONS. (See " Promise of Sale," No. 85.)

8.—PARTNERSHIPS. (See No. 96, " Companies and Corporations.")

6.— PARTNERSHIPS, Rural. (*Aparcería.*) I. On the document containing the contract, 50 cts. per sheet; II. on the receipt which the owner must give for the products received under the contract, for each $10 or fraction, 5 cts.; III. on the document issued by the owner for part of the products received on any other account, same as II. Exempt: A. In cases of I and II above where the area of the ground does not exceed four hectares; B. in cattle partnerships, of not exceeding 100 head of " *ganado menor* " (smaller animals), or 20 head of " *ganado mayor* " (larger cattle).

14.— PAWN TICKETS. On pawn tickets, or memorandum of renewal: for loans less than $1, 1 ct.; from $1 to $20, 2 cts.; over $20, for each $20 or fraction, 2 cts. Exempt: Those of public or private charitable institutions, the latter if authorized by law.

36.— PAYMENT, by Delivery of Property. (*Dación en Pago*). Same rate as " *compraventa.*"

.67.— PAY-ROLLS. (*Nómina.*) Will pay the same rate as " Receipts " for each item of salary, fees or pension, except where covered by a separate voucher properly stamped. Exempt from tax: A. Those of soldiers in active service under rank of sergeant, and military musicians; B. those of auxiliary forces, police, etc., whose daily pay does not exceed $1.50; C. those of the daily allowance from the Federal Treasury to prisoners; D. those of day laborers and operatives.

76.— PERMITS. For sales in Pawnshops, $1.

83.— PLEDGES AND ANTICRESIS. Same rules as " Bonds, Surety," No. 45. Warehouses and institutions of credit enjoy their special franchises in respect to these contracts.

79.— POLICY. (*Póliza*). That issued by private persons to public offices pay the same rates as " Receipts." Exempt: That to which a duly stamped receipt or pay-roll is attached; the policy or receipt issued to evidence the return of advances and loans without interest, of amounts improperly entered, and of deposits made to secure public interests.

81.— POLICY, of Insurance. I. Of life insurance, 10 cts.; II. of fire or other risk, upon the value insured, for each $100 or fraction, 1 ct. Exempt from tax: Fire insurance and other risks for less than six months.

78.— POWERS OF ATTORNEY. (*Poder jurídico.* See " Letters of Attorney," No. 21. See Art. 1083.) Whether or not any amount is stated and although a fixed compensation is stipulated: I. If only one principal and one attorney, $2 per sheet; II. if three parties, either principal or attorney, $4 per sheet; III. if four parties as above, $6 per sheet; IV. if five or more parties, $8 per sheet; V. substitutions of powers pay same rates as above respectively. Exempt from tax: Revocations of powers of attorney.

12.— POWERS OF ATTORNEY, Inspection of. (*Bastanteo de Poder*). 50 cts.

82.— PREMIUMS OF INSURANCE. (See Art. 1084.) I. Premiums received by Insurance Companies on all kinds of policies issued before December 16, 1892, 2%; II. those on policies issued since above date, and not included in clause III, 3%; III. those received on policies other than life, for less than six months, 5%.

85.— PROMISE OF SALE or Purchase; Options. I. On the amount paid for the promise or option, for each $10 or fraction, 2 cts; II. if no payment is agreed: a, in *escritura pública,* $2 per sheet; b, in other document, 50 cts. per sheet.

87.— PROTESTS. The protest of bills of exchange and other commercial paper, when made in a document not in protocol, 50 cts. per sheet.

88.— PROTOCOLS. (See Art. 1086.) Those kept by notaries, *escribanos públicos,* or judges acting as such, $1 per sheet.

89.— PROTOCOLIZATION. (See Arts. 1087 and 1092.) I. The protocolization of all instruments, whether executed in Mexico or abroad, will pay the rate prescribed for the act or contract therein contained, except as herein provided:

II. The protocolization of documents in relation to the organization of foreign companies which wish to do business or establish agencies or branches in Mexico, will pay on the amount of capital, when not exceeding $1,000,000, the same rates as prescribed for " Companies and Corporations " (No. 96); if exceeding that amount, the above rates will be paid on the first million pesos, and on the excess, for each $1,000 or fraction, 5 cts.

III. Where such companies have no capital, the tax will be paid on the difference between the assets and liabilities as shown by the last annual balance.

IV. The protocolization of documents already stamped, or which are exempt from tax, will only pay the protocol tax on the number of sheets contained.

28.— PURCHASE AND SALE, Contracts of. (See *"Compraventa,"* No. 28.)

44.— RAILROADS AND OTHER CARRIERS OF PASSENGERS. (See Art. 1078.) I. On the gross receipts from passenger fares on railroads within the Republic, 2%; II. on like receipts from street-cars, diligences and other vehicles for land transportation of passengers, with regular service and fixed itinerary, 1%. Exempt: Fares chargeable to the Government.

90.— RECEIPTS. (*Recibos.* See Art. 1088.) Every kind of document issued to evidence the delivery of a sum of money or a payment in cash or effects, where such document is not taxed otherwise in this Tariff, for each $20 or fraction, 2 cts.

Exempt from tax: A. to E. all kinds of receipts and vouchers in regard to governmental and public transactions; F. those receipts which are contained in all kinds of commercial paper, invoices and nominative titles, although such instruments are exempt from tax, but in such cases the provisions of Art. 1088 referring to clause "II," will be observed; G. those for installments of the purchase price of shares of stock, endorsed thereon or on the provisional certificates, as well as those entered in deposit books legalized under Sec. 55; II. those contained in correspondence by letter or telegram sent from one place to another; I. those given to carriers to evidence receipt of packages containing money or val-

uables; J. those given for domestic wages; K. those
of a routine nature passing between employés of the
same establishment covering delivery of funds for
expenses of the different departments, proper receipts being required upon the ultimate paying out
of the money; L. those recited in the document evi-
deucing the original contract; LL. statements,
invoices or receipts presented upon payment of
coupons, stock, bonds and other securities payable to
bearer; M. duplicates, where the originals are duly
stamped, observing the provisions on this point in
Art. 1088; N. those issued for subscriptions for
relief in cases of public calamities; NN. those for
amounts not exceeding $5 issued by charitable, mu-
tual and savings institutions having such authorization from the Treasury Department; O. those for
alms and gifts of all kinds less than $20.

51.— REGISTRY. (*Inscripción.*) In the books of the
Public Register of Property, Commerce and others
of the kind: I. For each inscription, 25 cts.; II.
for each entry in the index of private instruments
which under the civil law must be filed in the Public
Registry, 10 cts. Exempt from tax: Entries or
annotations of simple reference or explanation.

46.— RELEASES. (*Finiquito.*) Those between private persons: I. Where the amount is stated, same
rate as receipts; II. where no amount stated, 50 cts.
per sheet.

91.— REMISSION OF DEBT BY CONTRACT. I.
Where the amount of debt is determined, for each
$20 or fraction, 2 cts.; II. where amount not deter-
minable when contract is made, 50 cts. per sheet;
III. if the remission is gratuitous, it will pay the rate
corresponding to the contract in which it is stipulated. Exempt from tax: Releases granted by

creditors to a common debtor, or reductions made in favor of the debtor.

95.— RESALES. (*Retroventa*). Pay same rate as Rescission of Contracts.

92.— RESCISSION OF CONTRACTS: $2 per sheet.

28.— SALE AND PURCHASE, Contract of. (See "*Compraventa*.")

85.— SALE, Promise of. (See "Promise of Sale.")

1.— STOCK, SHARES OF. Certificates of Stock, nominative or to bearer, evidencing and representing a part of the capital of any concern or company: I. Where the amount is stated, for each $20 or fraction of par value, 2 cts.; II. where amount is not stated, $1; III. stock or bonds issued to promoters, and any other document which, without representing capital invested, evidences rights to share in the profits, will pay the above rates. Certificates of stock are subject to the above tax although they are issued in exchange for others already stamped which are retired and cancelled (*hayan de amortizarse*). (Art. 15.)

97.— SUBROGATION, Conventional. Pay same rate as assignments upon onerous title, on the amount paid to the creditor by the party subrogated.

98.— TELEGRAMS. I. On the original, not containing a petition to any public official, 1 ct.; II. if the telegram contains such petition, on the original copy, 50 cts.

Telegraph operators must require the original messages filed to be properly stamped; if a telegram contains a petition to a public official, they must state on transmitting it that the stamps are affixed to the original; when the stamp is paid on the original, further tax is not required on copies received by intermediate offices for forwarding where the transmission is not direct. (Arts. 206–207.)

101.— TITLES. I. Of ownership of Mines of any kind: For each *pertenencia,* or fraction of one-half or more, $5; II. professional titles, $1; III. those **of** *terrenos baldíos, demasías* and *excedencias,* pay **the** same rates as *" compraventa."* Exempt: Professional titles of primary instruction.

66 & 75.— VESSELS. Original copy of appointment **of** consignees made by ship-captains under customs regulations, 5 cts. Petitions to port or naval authorities for permit to sail: I. Vessels of ten gross tons or less, 50 cts.; II. of from ten to thirty tons, $1; III. from thirty to fifty tons, $2; IV. vessels of over **fifty** tons, $4. Exempt: War vessels, fishing boats, **and** launches and other minor craft which ply about **the** port, and ships sailing in ballast.

99.— WILLS. (*Testamentos.*) I. Public closed wills, executed in Mexico, on the wrapper, $5; II. public open, private, military and maritime wills, and wills executed abroad to take effect in Mexico, pay only **the** protocol tax.

CHAPTER 3.

SPECIAL RULES FOR APPLICATION OF SOME TAXES.

Art. 1062. "Actas"— **Minutes.**— The tax payable on the minute or contract executed before a public functionary or employé, besides the rate per sheet, must be paid by affixing and cancelling the stamps before the act is authorized or judicially approved, as the case may be, where *escritura pública* is not required for its validity, in the latter event, the tax will be paid in the form and manner prescribed for such instruments. (Art. 16.)

Art. 1062A. **Leases and Sub-leases.**— In order to compute the tax on leases for a definite time, in the cases under fraction 7 of the Tariff, the time fixed for the duration of the contract will always be taken into consideration, although the contract is obligatory on only one of the parties. The tax will be paid upon the rent stipulated, and also on the amount of the real-property tax according to the laws in force at the time the contract was made, when the payment of this tax, or of all others to which the estate is subject, is chargeable to the lessee. The value of improvements other than those of mere preservation of the leased property, made by the lessee by virtue of the contract, is also considered as a part of the rent, provided that the amount so expended on

the same is determined, and also upon such amount the tax
will be paid at the rate of 5 cents, or of 1 cent, for each
ten pesos or fraction, according to the time when the improvements are to be made. Where the value of such improvements is not determined in the contract, there will be
paid, in addition to the rate prescribed for the respective
cases stated in fraction 7, that of $2.00 per sheet if the con-
tract is in *escritura pública,* or of 50 cts. per sheet if in private document. If for any reason the lessee continues in
the use and enjoyment of the leased premises after the expiration of the term, without executing a new contract duly
legalized, the lessor must, after two months from the expiration of the term, re-stamp the former contract in accordance with clause IV of fraction 7 of the Tariff.

Contracts of lease for an indefinite time do not need to
be renewed although the year for which they have been
stamped has expired. If the contract was for a definite time,
with a provision that after the end of the term the lessee
should continue at will of the parties, there will be paid, in
addition to the rate for the fixed term, the rate provided in
fraction 7 on leases for indefinite time. Where the parties
do not expressly fix the duration of the contract, but make
reference to the legal term, and some term is fixed by the
civil law, the contract will be considered as for a definite
time, and will be stamped for such legal term.

Where the lessee, under the terms of the contract, assigns
it to a third person, a new tax will not be paid; but where
the lessee, without such authorization, assigns the contract
with the consent of the lessor, and in general wherever there
is a novation of contract, either by increase or decrease of
the rental or by substitution of lessee, the corresponding tax
will be paid anew. The tax will also be paid in case of an
expressed extension, such extension being considered as a new
contract; but the stamps will be attached to the original document on which the renewal will be noted. The provision by
which the lessee agrees to insure the premises in favor of the

owner, is not subject to tax where it is made at the same time as the lease. Where the rent is not paid in money but in specific things agreed upon, such articles will be appraised at the current market price at the time and place of delivery. Contracts in regard to the exploitation of forests, quarries, and other natural products, whether periodical or not, for an amount expressly determined, will pay the same rates as leases in the respective cases; but if there is only fixed a basis of price with relation to a determined portion of the products to be obtained, the contract will be rated as a *compra-venta*. (Arts. 38–47.)

Art. 1063. Certificates or Certifications.— These are subject to a single rate although several parties join in them; for taxing purposes a certificate is any document issued to prove facts or declare any thing or circumstance, in whatever form and although the word "certify" is not used. Certificates of any kind contained in a document otherwise stamped, must nevertheless be stamped as provided in section 23 of the Tariff, except such as are made in judicial decrees, which pay the rate for legal proceedings. Assay certificates procured by private persons at the federal assay offices will be legalized with the matrix of coupon stamps and the stub will be attached to the copy forwarded with the accounts to the general Treasury. (Arts. 55–57.)

COMPRAVENTA BY RETAIL.

Art. 1064. Retail Sales — Statements.— For the purposes of taxation, a retail sale (*venta al por menor*), is one made for an amount less than $20; whether for cash or on time, they will pay the rate prescribed by clause I of sec. 28 of the Tariff, in the manner herein provided. All merchants, and in general, the owners or managers of any commercial, industrial, agricultural or mining business or establishment, habitually making sales by retail, and not embraced in the exceptions B to H

inclusive of said sec. 28, must present to the proper Stamp
Tax office, within the first fifteen days of June of each year,
a statement of the amount of retail sales effected between
June 1st and May 31st of the immediately preceding year.
(Arts. 62–63.)

Art. 1065. Approving or Proving Statements.— The Stamp
Tax officials will pass upon such statements of sales, taking
into consideration the extent and importance of the business
and the conditions of the market, and be governed by the
following rules:

A. Statements showing an increase over the previous
year, and which in the opinion of the Administrador are
unobjectionable, will be finally approved forthwith, and the
statement so approved cannot be afterwards impeached except as provided in **Art. 1067.**

B. Although showing such increase, if the Administrador
deems the statement too low, he will fix the amount which in
his judgment should serve as the basis of the tax, and if
the interested party is agreed, he will sign the return, and its
correctness cannot be inquired into as above provided; but if
he objects to such estimate, and does not make the proofs prescribed in sec. D, his statement will be accepted, reserving
the right to require proof upon an official visitation to the
establishment, which cannot be made until after six months,
during which time the party making the return may rectify
his statement by declaring the true amount of sales, without any punishment, upon payment of the balance of the
taxes due.

C. Statements showing an equal or decreased amount of
sales over the last year, and apparently unobjectionable,
will be approved with reservation of the right of visitation,
as above provided, and voluntary corrections may likewise
be made within the six months.

D. Where the statement shows an equal or decreased
amount, and the Administrador deems it too low, he will

fix the amount and proceed as provided in B. If the interested party objects, and produces all his books of account and of sales in proof of the correctness of his statement, it will be finally approved as it stands, and cannot be questioned as provided in clause A. If the interested party does not make such proof, he must provisionally pay the tax on the average amount between his return and the amount fixed by the Administrador, until an official investigation is made of the exact amount of sales; if · upon such examination the statement is found correct, the amount overpaid will be refunded; if found incorrect, the full amount of tax will be exacted and the prescribed punishment- inflicted. Merchants not required to keep stamped books of account, may prove their returns by their special book of sales or any other they may have although not stamped; if there is no special book of sales, the amount will be estimated by experts appointed under the regulations. (Arts. 64–65, as amended 27 May, 1907.)

Art. 1066. Tax Receipts —" Boletas."— Upon the approval as above of the tax returns, the Stamp Office will issue to the interested party, before July 1st, a printed " *Boleta,"* bearing its corresponding number, and reciting the amount of sales, and whether definitely approved or accepted subject to proof, and also stating the annual bi-monthly amount of the tax assessed; and stamps equal to the bi-monthly quota will be attached to the *boleta* and cancelled bi-monthly in advance. (**Art. 66, as amended 27 May, 1907.**)

Art. 1067. Correction of Returns — False Returns.— Before the *boleta* is issued, any party may correct his return without penalty; but after the *boleta* is issued no claims will be allowed and the tax assessed must be paid, subject only to be amended during the year, if as provided in the law, or by admission as in Art. 1065, it appears that sales were concealed, or when sales of some separate department are discontinued, in which events, in the first case, the *boleta* will be corrected upon payment of the omitted taxes, with or without penalty as circumstances may warrant, and in the second, the provisions of Art. 1069 will be observed.

Neither the approval by the Stamp Office of the return filed, even when it conforms to the books, nor the amount fixed by the Administrador as the basis of the tax, relieves the taxpayer from the penalties incurred, if within the period of prescription it is discovered that he made a·false return to defraud the revenue or failed to enter in his books all the sales really made; but in the cases mentioned in Art. 1066 no visitation will be made for the purposes of investigation, unless formal complaint is made, or official instructions received, or positive information is had of concealment of sales, or an extraordinary general visitation is ordered; in such cases the concealment may be investigated and punished even within the six months above allowed for voluntary corrections.   (Arts. 67–68, as amended 27 May, 1907.)

Art. 1068. Payment of Taxes — Loss of Boleta.— If the sales do not amount to $100 a month, a certificate of exemption will be issued to the interested party, which will be exposed in a visible place in the establishment.   Merchants, owners or managers of establishments must procure their *boletas* in due time, and attach thereon and cancel the proper stamps within the first ten business days of each bi-monthly period.   The stamps must be cancelled by hand or with seal, stating the date and place and the name of the person or establishment making the cancellation, or it may be by perforator, but always showing the date of cancellation.   If the *boleta* is lost, or destroyed totally or partially, it cannot be replaced except upon payment anew of the tax for the bi-monthly periods elapsed, and the issuance of a new *boleta* by the Stamp Office, which will affix the proper amount of stamps for the tax due for such period; only the Department of Hacienda can remit such second payment upon proof that the *boleta* contained all the stamps for the time elapsed and that they were destroyed or rendered entirely useless; if within the fiscal year the tax-payer should present the missing *boleta,* the value of the stamps will be repaid him in cash less the fees paid to the Stamp Office.

With the statement previously mentioned, the tax-payer will present the *boleta* for the last past year for the purpose only of proving payment of the last year's tax; but failure to present it does not affect proceedings on the current returns, or the separate proceeding to impose the penalty for failure to pay the former tax, which will be presumed in the absence of the last *boleta,* except upon proof to the contrary. The Tax Office will examine the *boletas* immediately upon receiving them, and if found correct will issue to the interested parties a receipt to that effect; but if found that all taxes have not been paid or the stamps not properly cancelled, the penalties prescribed will be imposed; such receipt exempts the tax-payer from all liabilities, and if upon revision any stamps are found missing, the employé who issued the receipt must make the amount good. (Arts. 69–74.)

Art. 1069. Opening, Close or Transfer of Business.— Upon the opening of any retail establishment, shop or business house of any kind, written notice must be given the Stamp Office within three days, and within the first fifteen days of the fourth month after such opening a statement of the sales made within the first three months must be filed, which if approved will be taken as a basis for calculating the sales for one year, and the tax will be paid on the amount of the statement from the date of opening business; in the case of pawnshops, the statement will be made within the above time after the first auction sale. (**Art. 75**, as amended 27 May, 1907.) If the business is transferred to another person or company, the latter will notify the Stamp Office in writing, and the *boleta* must be presented to show that the current taxes have been paid, and it will be returned to the new owner who will pay the subsequent taxes; failure to give notice and present the *boleta* will subject the new owner to the payment of any taxes in arrears and any penalties incurred by the former owner. If the establishment is closed during the fiscal year, the interested party will give written notice to the Stamp Office, stating the date of closure, and the proper political or municipal official will certify on the same document that said establishment was actually closed on the date mentioned, and the *boleta* will also be presented for examination and receipt as provided in the preceding Article. If the stamps for the current bi-monthly period have already been attached to the *boleta,* no part of the tax will be refunded, but if they have not yet been attached, the bi-monthly period will be divided into four parts, and the tax will only be paid for the fifteen days current when the establishment was closed, and no penalty will be imposed for the failure to attach the stamps within the proper time. If notice of closure is not given, the establishment will be reputed open, and the taxes must be paid until such notice is given although the place was actually closed.

If any new establishment is opened during the year, the provisions of Art. 75 herein above will be observed, but a new statement must be made for the current fiscal year if the establishment was opened more than three months before the first of June; such statement shall state the amount of retail sales effected between the day of opening and May thirty-first, and if the statement is approved, the sales for one year will be calculated upon the amount shown, and a *boleta* issued for the amount calculated. The rate established for the year will not generally be diminished or increased by the discontinuance or addition of any article to those usually sold in an establishment; but if a house should cease to sell articles of a certain kind, opening an entirely separate branch or department for their sale, it must present a statement of the sales made by the latter within the time fixed by Article 75 above, and the main house may request the reduction from its *boleta* of the amount upon which the branch house is paying, such reduction being effective from the date of the opening of the branch.

If the closure of a mercantile establishment is only temporary, it will continue upon reopening to pay the same rate which it paid at closing; but if on reopening it has not the same stock of goods, or if the capital has been increased or diminished, the provisions in regard to new establishments must be observed; the change of ownership or removal to the different location is not considered as opening a new business, but notice of such change must be given to the Stamp Office. Where an establishment is closed within three months after it is opened, a statement of its sales must be presented with the notice of closure, and if approved by the Stamp Office a special *boleta* with the proper stamps duly cancelled will be issued, the settlement being made on the fifteen-day basis above provided, and the *boleta* will be taken up and a receipt issued to the interested party; the same procedure will be followed in case of an establishment opened during a fair or by others beginning a retail business, who must notify the Stamp Office within three days, and upon closure within three months, unless exempt from tax because of sales of less than $100 a month, will pay on the basis above provided.

Where retail sales are made by persons not habitually engaged in making them, and who are therefore not required to observe the foregoing requirements, the tax provided by clause II of Section 28 of the Tariff is only payable where the parties voluntarily execute some document, invoice or receipt evidencing the sale, and which it is optional with them to do or not. (Arts. 75–85.)

48

COMPRAVENTA BY WHOLESALE.

Art. 1070.   Wholesale — Invoices.— For the purposes of
taxation, a sale by wholesale (*venta al por mayor*), is one
made in a single transaction with the same buyer for a
price of $20 or more, or the aggregation in a single receipt,
invoice or document of several transactions made on the
same day and amounting together to $20 or more; the
omission of the dates of several items joined in the same
document raises the presumption that they were had on the
same day unless proven to the contrary.

In every sale by wholesale effected by merchants or in
any mercantile, industrial, agricultural or mining business
or establishment habitually making such sales, the seller,
whether on his own account or on commission, must issue
an invoice (*factura*) evidencing the sale and legalized with
coupon stamps for the proper tax on the amount of the sale
in accordance with clause III of Section 28 of the Tariff;
the buyer must require such invoice, and if refused, he must
notify the proper Stamp Office within eight business days
after such invoice should have been issued, and if he fails
to give such notice he is subject to the same penalties as
the seller for failure to pay the tax.   Such invoice must be
issued at latest within fifteen business days after the sale
if the parties live in the same place or within one month
if they live in different places.   Where the price cannot
be fixed when the contract is made, the invoice will be
issued, as provided in **Art.** 1073, upon receipt of payment,
but the stamp per sheet required by clause IV of Section 28
must be attached to legalize the document.   All such merchants, owners of estates, establishments or business-con-
cerns as above, must keep one or more stub-books of invoices, which will be legalized gratis by the Stamp Office,
which legalization is good till the books are used up; such
books must be kept although the sales are only made period-
ically.   (**Arts.** 86–89.)

Art. 1071. Same — Notes.— The invoices must be issued within the time above provided, although the goods have not been delivered, or the sale is on time; in the latter event the seller must require, and the buyer execute promissory notes, which must be stamped as required for notes; such notes must be delivered within three days after the sale is effected, to the seller or broker making the sale, where both parties reside in the same place; if residing in different places, the seller must send the notes already duly stamped and cancelled, to the buyer to be signed, the buyer being obliged to repay the value of the stamps unless otherwise agreed; the entire transaction must be completed within one month. If a broker conducted the sale, he must see that these requirements are complied with, but neither he nor the seller is subject to the penalties if they prove that the notes were remitted duly stamped to the buyer.

Where sales by wholesale are made by persons not required to keep the stub-book of inventories, the seller may issue an inventory or any kind of document to which to affix and cancel the stamps, which may be either stub-stamps or without stubs; if the former they must be affixed entire. If the contract of sale is evidenced by broker's policy, minute deposited with notary, or by *escritura pública,* the provisions of the law applicable to those cases will be observed; if sales on time are evidenced by any of the foregoing documents or by other than inventory, the execution of notes is not obligatory. Where the proper tax is already paid on any such document, the invoices issued by the seller need not be again stamped, but an annotation referring to such document will be made on the invoice, and on duplicates of them if taken from the stub-book. (Arts. 90–96.)

COMPRAVENTA — GENERAL PROVISIONS.

Art. 1072. Special Sales Books.— Every mercantile, industrial, agricultural or mining establishment, shop, sales-office or business place, together with their separate branches, doing habitually either a wholesale or retail business, also all merchants having no fixed establishment, and all those doing retail business who are not exempt under Section 28 of the Tariff, must keep, in addition to the books of account required by law, one or more special sales books, as their business may require, and keeping separate books for wholesale transactions, if they prefer, which must be authorized by the Stamp Office and stamped as required by clause II of Section 56; in case the interested party should request a new book because of the claimed loss or theft of the former, it shall be authorized, but he is subject to the penalty for not keeping such book unless he proves the actual loss or theft of the former one.

In such special sales book must be entered daily, or at the latest within seven days, the total amount of sales of each day, and in a separate column, unless a separate sales-book is kept for the purpose, an abstract of all sales by wholesale must be entered within seven business days from the issuance of the respective invoices. Any one failing to observe these requirements, or who omits sales or makes false entries, is subject to the penalties of law and to continual inspection of all his books and correspondence so far as deemed necessary to detect all violations for the past five years. (Arts. 97–101.)

Art. 1073. Sales — What So Considered.— For the purposes of taxation every instance of goods going out of the establishment or place is considered a sale, unless the interested party proves to the satisfaction of the Stamp Office that it was only for the purpose of removal from one place to another of the same owner, or was sent out as a sample, or on commission for sale, or some other operation not subject to taxation; also the supplying of materials by mining concerns to laborers for the working of mines, where the same are charged even at cost against their wages, is taken as a sale for the purposes of taxation. Also the acquisition of ores by smelting concerns for treatment on their own account, and although for sale abroad, and whether to be paid for before or after sale, or according to the value after assay or on any other conditions; the Executive may make arrangements with such smelters and exporters by which the taxes may be paid in cash, at the reduced rate of $2 on the thousand, taking as the basis for computing the tax the total amount of metals or ore brought into the establishment or exported during the previous year, whether on own account or that of others, or on commission or otherwise; but smelting concerns, whether or not they have made such arrangements in regard to payment, have the right granted by the decree of 24 November, 1905, and other like regulations, to the refund of three-fourths of the tax paid on metals.

The making or manufacture of articles, for an agreed price, where the workman or contractor furnishes the materials, is considered a sale and subject to all the rules of *compraventa,* unless such materials are the accessories and not the prinicpal feature, and excepting work of mere repair. The costs of insurance, cartage, freight, packing, etc., paid by the seller for the purpose of shipping goods from one place to another, do not form part of the price, and if included in the invoice for the purpose of collection or otherwise are only subject to tax as a receipt. The transfer of personal property made after a number of periodical payments in the nature of rent or hire, does not require a stamped invoice where the original contract is duly legalized. In cases under clause 4 of Section 28 of the Tariff, as soon as the price is ascertained, the parties must execute a supplementary document in the same form as the original contract and pay the tax for the sale on the same; if the determination of the price depends upon periodical deliveries or upon the number, weight or measure of the thing sold, the seller, upon receiving the price either in one or several payments, must upon each payment issue an invoice or receipt

duly stamped at the rate prescribed in clause 3, according
to the kind of instrument evidencing the contract; where at
the time of sale part of the price is determined, the corresponding part of the tax will be then paid, and the foregoing
provisions will be observed as to the undetermined balance.

Orders of goods for third persons made to factories or
commercial houses in Mexico are considered made on commission only when such goods pass to the purchaser at the
same price paid for them by the person placing the order,
irrespective of any commission he may receive; in such cases
the sale is legalized by an invoice issued by the seller to either
the purchaser or his agent; if the transfer is made for a
different price, the purchaser must issue and stamp a new
invoice. Orders placed abroad for third persons are not
subject to tax where the seller issues and sends the invoice
and shipping-bill directly to the buyer, and only the receipt
for the agent's commission will be stamped; but if the seller
issues such documents in the name of the agent, he must
stamp the foreign invoice if he presents it for collection to
the person ordering the goods, or he must issue to him a new
invoice duly stamped, besides the stamps on his receipt for
commissions. If the agent contracts personal obligations
with the buyer in regard to the transaction, it will be considered as a *compreventa* between the two unless satisfactorily
proven that such obligations were contracted by authority
and on account of the seller of the goods.

Sales made by traveling agents of Mexican or foreign
houses are subject to tax when the house accepts the orders
and ships the goods; but where the agents themselves deliver
the goods, or in case of sales made on their own account by
persons having no fixed place who travel about selling their
wares, the tax must be paid and all formalities complied
with as soon as the sale is made; such persons must comply
with the requirements in regard to statements and stub-
books and sales books in whatever place they may be, and
before beginning business in each place must give written

notice to the Stamp Office, stating at what house or hotel they are stopping, as well as of any change of address; and they must go in person to the Stamp Office every eight days of their stay with their *boleta* and book of sales and settle accounts for the preceding eight days, being subject to the oversight and inspection of the officials at any time.

The transfer of a business is subject to the tax on *compraventa,* and the stamps will be affixed to the document or invoice issued, or to the inventory of stock or balance taken upon which the purchase price is determined. In the transfer of estates subject to encumbrance which is assumed by the purchaser, the amount of encumbrance is taken as part of the price on which the tax must be paid; in case of exchange of properties, the tax is computed only on the one of greater value delivered by one of the parties, without regard to any amount of cash paid or to be paid by the other or by any one for him.

As a general rule the tax on *compraventa* is payable by the seller, subject to reimbursement by the buyer if so agreed; but in sales by wholesale made by Government offices or establishments, the tax must always be paid by the buyer. (Arts. 102–119.)

BILLS OF LADING.

Art. 1074.— Bills of lading as herein provided must be issued in all cases by carriers and persons habitually engaged in transportation for the public; those who only occasionally make such contracts need only issue and stamp bills of lading when the amount of charges is $20 or more; but if they do issue a bill of lading it must be stamped; the tax will be paid by the person paying the freight unless otherwise agreed. Railroad, express, and street car companies may, if they prefer, with the authorization of the Department of Hacienda, make their payments in cash directly to the Treasury, which will fix the amount to be paid upon the basis of verified returns, but reserving the right to require the rate on each document under Section 30 of the Tariff; the rate on such cash payment will be $7 per thousand, payable bi-monthly in advance within the first ten business days of each period, and deducting any amounts of freight paid by the Federal Government, or occasioned by carrying materials owned by the company, and the value of any stamps charged to the shippers.

Where a new carrier begins business, or a new section of railroad is opened during the fiscal year, and wishes to make payment of taxes in cash as above, it must notify the Principal Tax Office and secure the authorization of the Department of Hacienda, if not already obtained for existing lines, and must within the first fortnight of the fourth month file a statement of its receipts for the first three months, upon the basis of which the Department will fix the tax to be paid, from the time of opening business.

In cases where the direct carriage corresponds in part to national and in part to foreign lines, and in those where the freight charges are partly within the exemptions of clauses A. and B. of Section 30, the amount of carriage or freight subject to the tax will be stated in the bill of lading or receipt, and the tax must be paid on one-half the total amount, although the proportion is less.

The tax must be paid on freight carried in street-cars or by any other means of transportation, where carried by contract with and under the responsibility of the carrier, but not where it is carried at the owner's risk in vehicles hired for the purpose, in which event only the tax on the contract itself is required. Small carriers not required to keep stamped books of account must however keep the book required by clause 4 of Section 56 of the Tariff. (See " Books of Account.") (Arts. 120–127.)

CONTRACTS.

Art. 1075. When Subject to Tax.— It is optional with the parties to execute in writing or not the contracts not specified in the Tariff, provided they do not involve the transfer of real property or rights, so that the rates prescribed in Section 31 are only payable when the parties voluntarily reduce such contracts to writing in whatever form; said Section including contracts in regard to the temporary use of waters, the creation of easements, the furnishing of electric light and power, including the necessary work of connections; the execution of lithographic, typographic and photographic works and of book-binding; dentistry work, works of all kinds subject to payment of toll, lodging, and generally all kinds of contracts not specified in the Tariff; but if the houses, establishments or shops doing such kinds of work also sell merchandise whether of their own line of business or otherwise, such sales are subject to the rules in respect to *compraventa*. (Arts. 128–130.)

Art. 1076. Donations — How Taxable.— Donations subject to " resolutory " conditions pay the same as if unconditional; where the condition is " suspensive," one-half the tax is payable when the donation is made and the balance when the condition is fulfilled; no part of the tax paid is refundable upon the revocation or reduction of the donation for any cause. If the gift is of the bare title with reservation of the usufruct, the donee will pay one-half the tax when the gift is made and the balance when the usufruct is extinguished; if the gift is of the usufruct with reservation of the title, the tax is payable only on one-half the value of the property; if the title is given to one person and the usufruct to another, each will pay one-half the tax. (Arts. 140–143.)

ESCRITURA PÚBLICA.

Art. 1077. When and How Stamped.— Whenever a contract is made by *escritura pública,* the stamps for which have not been affixed on the minute of the contract or other document, as provided by law, the proper tax will be paid by affixing the stamps on the liquidation-note which the notary, *escribano* or judge acting as such remits to the Stamp Office; if the tax has already been paid in whole or part, the notary will certify the fact at the foot of the *escritura,* stating the document on which the stamps are affixed and their amount; if such amount is insufficient, the difference must be paid on the liquidation-note. Notaries and other officials must cause their instruments to be properly stamped under their responsibility, and in cases of doubt must submit the question of rate to the Hacienda. The liquidation-note sent to the Stamp Office must contain the statement of the amount of tax payable, stating the number of the *escritura* in its proper order, its date, the kind of contract and the amount involved, the number of sheets it occupies in the protocol, the Section of the Tariff applicable to the case, the names of the contracting parties, and the amount to be paid for tax. The Stamp Office will limit itself to receiving the payment made by the parties and to affixing and cancelling the corresponding amount of stamps on the *nota,* returning it at once duly receipted; if it should be of opinion that a higher rate should be paid it will notify the Hacienda.

If less stamps than the contract requires have been cancelled on the minute, the *nota* will be issued for the difference between the amount paid and that required by the Tariff, also in cases where in an *escritura* of partition a greater value is put on the property than in the inventory or accounts, or a higher value is put on property for the payment of annuities under wills or donations, than that taken as the basis for payment of the tax; in the latter cases if the greater value of the property is determined after the *escritura* is authorized, the proper rectification will be made in the same protocol and a supplemental *nota* containing the balance of the tax will be sent to the Stamp Office.

Payment must be made within one month after the instrument is begun to be extended in the protocol, regardless of the time when it is signed by the parties, and it cannot be authorized by the notary until the *nota* with the stamps and voucher of payment are returned; if the payment is not made within the month, except only where the question of proper rate is pending in the Hacienda, it cannot be afterward received, and the notary must, under penalty of five hundred pesos, mark the *escritura* " Not passed " (*No pasó*), and it can in no event be revalidated, but the protocol tax must be paid on it; if the parties wish to proceed with the contract they must execute a new *escritura.* Within the time allowed for payment the notary may issue a supplemental *nota* or rectify the one previously issued if erroneous, without being subject to penalty, but after that time he cannot do so except in the cases of overvaluation above mentioned, or when because of error in the rate he is required to revalidate the *escritura.*

When the *nota* and voucher of payment are returned, they will be protocolized along with the *escritura,* or added to the appendix where the protocol is kept in books already bound and paged, in which case the notary will note in the *escrituras* the page where they are recorded; the *nota* and voucher will be copied in full in all certified copies of the *escritura* issued. Simple ratifications, rectifications and explanations of an *escritura* already stamped, only pay the protocol tax; also an acceptance made separately from the original contract duly stamped. (Arts. 144–154.)

RAILROADS.

Art. 1078. Railroads and other carriers must file with the proper Stamp Ofhee a statement of their receipts for passenger service during the previous civil year, indicating any amounts paid by the Federal Government; and the Department of Hacienda, upon verification of its correctness, will fix the amount on which tax must be paid, which payment must be in cash by bi-monthly periods in advance within the first fifteen days of each period. Where any new carrier begins business or opens a new branch within the fiscal year, it must at once notify the Stamp Office, and

within the first fifteen days of the fourth month it must file
a statement of its receipts for the first three months, as the
basis upon which the Hacienda will fix the proportional
amount upon which taxes will be paid during the remainder
of the year.   If the traffic is suspended, notice will be given
the Stamp Office so that it may fix the proportion of tax
which will be paid, as in the case of retail sales; if such
notice is not given the company must continue paying the
tax although the traffic was suspended.   (Arts. 155–157.)

INHERITANCES AND LEGACIES.

Art. 1079. The tax will be paid by the executors or
those making the distribution and charged against the several shares, the stamps being affixed and cancelled by the
parties on the partition account, before its approval by the
judge, who will require it to be done; in cases where heirs
may withdraw from the probate proceedings, the judge
will not permit their withdrawal until the inventory is approved and the tax paid on the true net value of the estate,
which will be done by affixing the stamps to the copy of the
inventory which is on file in the proceedings, as also in
cases where there is no partition account; the judges before
whom any probate proceeding is brought must give notice
to the proper Stamp Office within eight days.   For the purpose of taxation the heirs must make an inventory although
the testator otherwise provides; likewise in regard to real
estate in Mexico although the proceedings are had in a
foreign country.   The tax will be paid on the net value
of the estate, that is, after deduction of debts and three per
cent. for expenses; if not paid within three years after the
death of the deceased, the date of which must always be
stated, a penalty of ten per cent. for each subsequent year
or fraction of a year will be imposed.   The Executive may
appoint special commissioners who, without the consent of
the local authorities, may inspect the court records and
take proper steps to insure payment of the tax.   Conditional

inheritances and legacies, and those of the bare title or of the usufruct, are subject to the rules regarding donations. A legacy of a life annuity will be capitalized at ten per cent. a year, and the tax will be imposed on the resultant amount as provided in Section 48, and the amount will be deducted on computing the rate to be paid by the heir or legatee charged with the payment of the annuity. Where the taxes have been paid as therein provided, on the inventory or partition account, no other tax will be paid upon executing the *escritura* of partition than the protocol tax, except as provided in Art. 1077 in respect to the overvaluation of the property of the estate. (Arts. 158–164.)

BOOKS OF ACCOUNT.

Art. 1080. Stamped Books — By Whom and How Kept.— In order to determine whether a merchant must keep stamped books as provided in Section 56, the assets of his commercial business and not his other property will be considered, but if he has several establishments whose combined capital is $2,000 or more, although separately less, he must keep stamped books. If the Stamp Officials have data indicating that any one ought to have stamped books, and the latter claims exemption, they may require from the local tax office a statement of the amount of taxes paid to the State or municipal government, and if the amount of assets cannot be determined in this way, they may have recourse to the evidence of experts in the *juicio pericial,* or expert inquest, and if the party interested fails to appear in the proceeding, he will be bound without further recourse to keep stamped books, although the capital which he uses belongs to other persons. The branches of any establishment which keeps stamped books are required to keep only the special sales book when they are engaged in making sales at retail or wholesale. Farmers, artisans and in general all who have a store or shop in town for the sale of the products of these country estates or of their industry or work, must keep the books required by law, but are exempt if they do not maintain such store or shop.

The account and sales books must be presented in blank to the Stamp Office to be authorized; the authorization must be written and stamps for the amount of the tax must be affixed and cancelled on the first page, and the seal of the Office impressed on the other pages; when new books are brought in to be authorized, the former ones must be presented to show that they are filled up or nearly so with the proper entries. All books must be kept in Spanish, and always at hand in the office, store or shop, and the principal Stamp officials are empowered to impose the penalties and enforce the requirements provided in the Code of Commerce (**Art.** 571). Books once authorized may continue to be used after the time fixed for the currency of the stamps used in them, provided there has been no total suspension of entries during the year, in which event they must be revalidated by payment of the quota corresponding to the blank pages, or new books must be authorized; in respect to balances and inventories the suspension may extend to two years. If the books are not used during the legal term of the stamps, except where authorized within the last three months of the fiscal year and which may be used during the next year without revalidation, they are considered as not stamped, and their owners are subject to the duties and penalties prescribed by law. Where an establishment is removed, although into another revenue district, or changes owners or business-name, the books already authorized may continue to be used. (Arts. 167–175.)

Art. 1081. Memorials.— Officials and employés making petitions in private matters must do so by memorial properly stamped, but consular petitions presented to customs-houses are considered official and not subject to stamp; memorials sent from foreign countries by mail directly to public authorities will be admitted without stamps, but if presented by some one authorized for the purpose or afterwards appointed to represent the petitioner in the matter, he must pay the proper tax. (Arts. 178–179.)

Art. 1082. Minutes of Contracts.— Only minutes executed before or deposited with notaries, where the contract is required to be in *escritura pública,* are subject to the tax; if a public instrument is not necessary under the civil law, and the contract is contained in the minute so deposited, the tax corresponding to the private contract will be paid at the time upon the minute, and if afterwards it is transferred to *escritura pública,* the requirements in such cases provided in Art. 1077 will be observed. (Art. 180.)

Art. 1083. Powers of Attorney.— To determine the rate to be paid where there are more than two parties to a power, the capacity in which a party appears will be taken into consideration, so that if one person executes it for himself and as the representative of another, he will be considered as two parties, except where by virtue of law he represents various persons, in which event, and in cases of joint agency, he is considered as a single party. The tax on substitutions made in accordance with law on the foot of the certified copy of the power, will be paid by attaching the stamps to the page on which it is written, or in the legal proceedings in which it may be made, and all subsequent substitutions will pay the same rate. (Arts. 181–183.)

Art. 1084. Insurance Premiums.— Premiums and policies of reinsurance pay the same rate as those of insurance, penalties (*recargos*) being considered as premiums for taxing purposes. Companies and individuals engaged in insurance must pay each six months the tax upon the amount of receipts during the past six months, affixing the stamps to the statement filed, which will be verified by the Stamp officials from the account books of the tax-payer; insurance not engaged in the insurance business, but which with the permission of the Hacienda insure specified merchandise against maritime risks for their regular customers, will pay the tax by means of coupon stamps which must be attached in all cases to receipts taken from stub-books, the principal part of the stamp being cancelled on the receipt and the coupon on the stub in the book. (Arts. 184–187.)

Art. 1085. Loans of Money.— The renewal of loans evidenced by *escritura pública,* made before maturity without alterations of the terms of the original contract, are not considered for taxing purposes as a new loan and will only pay the rate of 20 cts. per $100 or fraction as provided in clause 1 of Section 31 of the Tariff, although the debt is secured by mortgage. The rate provided by Section 84 must be paid on *escrituras públicas* providing for the issuance of bonds and on documents authorizing the issuance of obligations against any company or concern, besides the rate provided by clause 1 of Section 15 when the same are put into circulation. (Arts. 188–189.)

Art. 1086. Protocol.— When a page of the protocol is once legalized it may be used throughout, whether for one or more *escrituras,* and although the period of legal currency of the stamp is expired, provided that some instrument was entered in it during the currency of the stamp. (Art. 190.)

Art. 1087. Protocolization.— The provisions of Art. 1077 in regard to *escritura pública* are applicable to protocolization. Foreign corporations wishing to protocolize their by-laws and documents, must prove to the satisfaction of the Hacienda, in order to enjoy the privileges of clause 2 of Section 89, that their principal place of business is in the foreign country and that they are conducting business there. (Arts. 191–192.)

Art. 1088. Receipts.— A receipt must be demanded and issued, duly stamped, for every delivery of money or payment in cash or securities, subject to tax under Section 90; but private persons and those not required to keep a book of sales, need not issue receipts for payments less than $20, nor merchants who do keep such books, for like sales when the payment is made in the store or shop at the time of the purchase; but if a receipt in any form is issued it must pay the tax unless within some of the exemptions of said Section 90. Notwithstanding the provisions of clause II of said Section, if the payment or delivery of money or securities is made by a third person, on account and order of a house or person domiciled in another place, the letter, receipt or document which must necessarily be issued as a voucher for such third person making the payment, must be stamped at the rate prescribed for bills of exchange. To determine the tax on receipts issued for payments made in securities, the latter will be taken at the valuation given them by the parties in the contract out of which the payment arose, and if no such valuation was made, then at their par value. When original receipts must be sent away, or it is wished for any reason to keep copies, they must be presented at the Stamp Office, and upon it appearing that the original is properly stamped, the copies will be legalized by the seal of the office, a note being made on them of the fact. (Arts. 193–196.)

COMPANIES AND CORPORATIONS.

Art. 1089. The tax on companies is only payable on the net capital contributed by the members, and when once paid on the *escritura* of association, those by which the members make their contributions, even of real estate, are only subject to the protocol tax. *Escrituras* of association which provide for future increase of capital, pay upon the original capital,

49

and when the increase is made pay the corresponding tax on the *escritura* or documents protocolized in relation thereto; the tax will be paid on the increase, with the proper reductions in view of the amount of the old and new capital; reorganization is only subject to tax in case increase of capital results, and then only on the increase, except where other taxable operations are involved. In partnerships between capitalist and industrial partners, only the capital contributed by the former is subject to tax, the right of the latter to participate in the profits not being figured in the firm assets. The consolidation or fusion of two or more companies is not subject to tax, whether a new company results or one of the former ones absorbs the others, except where increase of capital or other taxable operation results, in which event the corresponding tax must be paid; likewise in cases of the coming in or retiring of members, which does not necessitate a new company, but in proper cases the provisions in regard to dissolution of companies will be observed. The simple extension of the company existence, agreed upon before the time has expired, is only subject to the protocol tax; but if agreed on afterwards, or if the members are changed or the terms of the original contract substantially modified, it will be considered a new company and the corresponding taxes must be paid. (**Arts. 197–205.**)

CHAPTER 4.

GENERAL RULES IN REGARD TO THE COMMON STAMP TAX.

Art. 1090. Foreign Documents — Revalidation.— Notwithstanding the provisions of clause 2 of **Art. 1059**, contracts made abroad and documents in regard to payments made abroad on account of the Federal Government, and intended to have only administrative effects in the Republic, are exempt from tax, as also are contracts and documents which have paid consular fees as provided by law; as to memorials, see **Art. 1081.** Foreign documents produce effect in Mexico, for purposes of taxation, when they must be presented before any public office or authority, when they must be protocolized or registered, or are presented for acceptance or collection; also whenever they are to be performed wholly or partly in Mexico; such documents must be stamped by the person making use of them. Where the form and denomination of such foreign contracts are not clearly defined in Mexican law, they must be submitted to the Department of Hacienda for its decision as to the rate of tax to which it is subject by analogy to the contracts embraced in the Tariff. (Arts. 211–213, 215.)

Art. 1091. Who Must Pay Tax.— Concessions and contracts entered into between official authorities or bodies of the Republic are not subject to tax, but those between the Government and private persons are subject to the tax, which must be paid in every case by the private contracting party. As a general rule the tax must be paid by the party issuing the document, unless otherwise provided by law or agreed between the parties, but such agreements cannot relieve the parties from their several liability to the government for the payment of the tax; the tax on foreign documents must be paid by the person making use of them. (Arts. 214–215.)

Art. 1092. Methods of Determining Values.— In transactions for which the Tariff fixes the rate only for determined values, the parties must express in the instrument the value and other circumstances of the transaction affecting the tax so that it may be properly taxed, and if such valuation appears to be fictitious the parties are subject to the penalties pro-

vided for partial failure to pay the tax. Contracts involving not to exceed one million pesos will pay the full rates
fixed by the Tariff; if in excess of one million but not exceeding five million, the Tariff rates will be paid on the first
million, and half such rates on the excess; and if exceeding
five millions, the first five million will be taxed in the foregoing proportion, and on the excess at the rate of ten per
cent. of the rate on the first million; this rule applies also
to the concessions embraced in clause 4 of Section 29, but
not to leases, articles of association and matrimonial capitulations, which in all cases will pay the Tariff rates. In
contracts not specified in the Tariff, providing for periodical
payments which must be taken as the basis for the payment
of the tax, the amount of such payments for not exceeding
five years will be taken as the basis, but where the time
is indefinite the tax will be paid on one annual payment.
Interest will not be considered in computing the tax unless
where past due interest is compounded or is the principal
object of the contract. Except as provided in **Art. 1076** in
case of donations, the tax must be paid on conditional contracts as if they were unconditional and taxes paid will not
be refunded upon failure of the condition. Where a contract states both determined and undetermined values, the
proper rate will be paid on the former, and one peso for
each sheet of the document if in *escritura pública* or fifty
cents if not, unless the Tariff also fixes the rate for indeter-
minate values. Except as provided for surety contracts,
where several transactions or contracts intimately related
and subject to tax are contained in one document, the tax
will be paid only on the one causing the highest rate or on
one of them if several pay the same rate; if they are not intimately related the tax will be paid on the total amount
involved in the document; among other instances of such
intimate relation with the principal contract are provisions
relating to the subject-matter of the contract itself, or modifying its natural conditions, or in regard to such incidental

conditions as *retroventa,* penal clauses, liquidated damages, the *derecho del tanto,* and similar matters; like rules apply to the protocolization in the same act of foreign documents relating to contracts and transactions intimately connected, although appearing in different documents executed on different dates. (Arts. 216–223.)

CHAPTER 5.

USE AND CANCELLATION OF STAMPS.

Art. 1093. Tax per Sheet — Size of Paper.
1094. Coupon and Common Stamps.
1095. Cancellation of Stamps — How and By Whom.
1096. Neglect to Cancel — Defective Cancellation.

Art. 1093. Tax Per Sheet — Size of Paper.— The sheet of paper for documents taxable by the sheet,, including protocols, must not exceed 35 centimeters in length by 24 in width, regardless of the dimensions of the written part, and the number of written and printed lines on both sides cannot exceed eighty; sheets of greater size or number of lines will pay double the rate; excepted from these requirements are account books and other books authorized under Section 56, customs-house documents and others permitted by law to have other dimensions, balances, and statistical documents in tabulated form, all which pay the single rate per sheet of whatever dimensions and number of lines. In determining the amount of tax payable on acts and contracts taxed per sheet, the number of sheets on which they are written will be counted, although not fully covered and although the tax has been already paid on another act or contract written partly on the same sheet, but not counting the words usually written at the bottom of a page to connect it with the following; the full rate will be paid on all copies of such document, except copies required by law to be made for use in public offices, those which under this law may be legalized by the use of coupon-stamps, and duplicates to be presented before some public authority or office, the originals of which are duly stamped. (Arts. 224–227.)

Art. 1094. Coupon and Common Stamps.— On contracts and concessions executed in duplicate in documents other than *escritura pública,* and subject to tax on the value, coupon-stamps must be used, affixing the principal part of the stamp on one copy and the stub on the other, such fact being noted at the foot of the document, other copies if any being legalized as provided in Sec. 54 of the Tariff; but duplicates and other copies of documents issued to be presented with the originals duly stamped *ad valorem* before public officials for proving accounts do not need to be stamped or otherwise legalized; with the exceptions herein provided, all duplicates must pay the same rate as the originals. Common stamps with or without coupons may be used indiscriminately, but the former must be affixed entire except in cases where this law requires them to be divided for use on duplicates or stub-books; coupon-stamps may be used on receipts, drafts, notes, etc., where the parties wish to keep stub-books bound and paged, affixing the principal part of the stamp on the document and the coupon on the stub, which must contain a statement of the transaction. If by mistake of the parties or notary a greater amount of stamps than required is cancelled on an instrument, the excess cannot be refunded, but the notary may be required to reimburse it if he is at fault. (Arts. 228–233.)

Art. 1095. Cancellation of Stamps — How and By Whom.—. Stamps and coupons used separately must be cancelled by hand or seal, or may be by perforating seal, which form must be used by the federal revenue offices; expressing in all cases the date and place, and the name of the person, concern or office making the cancellation, which must cover all the stamps and extend on both sides on the paper to which they are affixed. Except as otherwise provided, the cancellation must be made: 1, On private documents, by the party executing them; 2, on drafts and bills of exchange, by the drawers; 3, on notes given for sales on time, by either buyer or seller; 4, on the pages of the protocol, by the notary or judge acting as such; 5, in other cases herein provided, by the judges, notaries or chiefs of office charged with the legalization or revalidation of proceedings or documents; 6, on the *boletas* issued for retail sales, by the seal of the firm or the name of the owner, with the other requirements above specified. Stamps imprinted by the Printing Office under authority of the Department of Hacienda, directly upon the documents enumerated in Art. 1060, do not need to be cancelled. (Arts. 234–236, 239.)

Art. 1096. Neglect to Cancel — Defective Cancellation.— Where a document is properly stamped, but one or more stamps are not cancelled or are defectively cancelled, without any indication of fraud, the office receiving the document will cancel such stamps without imposing any penalty, except in case of *boletas* of sale, the stamps on which must be cancelled in strict observance of the manner herein prescribed, and every failure to cancel or irregular cancellation of which is subject to penalty. Where a document appears without stamps, but it is evident that it had been properly stamped and cancelled, and no indication of fraud appears, the official to whom the document is presented may record the fact and the circumstances proving it, and affix his seal in the place where the stamps had been affixed, without imposing penalty. (Arts. 237–238.)

CHAPTER 6.

REVALIDATION OF UNSTAMPED DOCUMENTS.

Art. 1097. When Revalidated — Double and Triple Rates.
1098. How Revalidated.
1099. Effects of Failure to Stamp and of Revalidation.

Art. 1097. When Revalidated — Double and Triple Rates.— Any book or document, except *escrituras públicas,* wanting any or all the stamps it should have, may be voluntarily presented within eight days after its date to the Stamp Office, which will revalidate it by affixing and cancelling stamps in double the amount missing, upon receipt of their value, the usual time required for the mails being added to the eight days where the document is presented at a place other than where it was executed; if presented after such time, but within one year from its date or that of the first entry in the book, it will be revalidated upon payment of three times the rate. In the above cases no penalty will be imposed provided that the presentation is voluntary, that the omission had not previously been discovered by any official or empolyé, nor reported, and that no official visit of inspection against the delinquent had been undertaken or announced, in all which cases the revalidation will be made through the recovery of the taxes omitted and the imposition of the prescribed penalties. Documents executed prior to the law of 1 December, 1874, on unstamped paper, are regarded as validated by law, and those executed since may be revalidated as above provided on the terms herein prescribed; if the document were not taxed it need not be revalidated. (Arts. 240–243.)

Art. 1098. How Revalidated.— In all cases of revalidation the proper stamps will be affixed to the document and cancelled by the Office, a statement to that effect will be re-

corded on the document and signed by the Stamp Agent
under the seal of the Office; such revalidation may be made at
any office, although the document comes from another revenue
district; in case of *escritura pública* the stamps will be
affixed to the supplemental *nota*.   If there are no stamps at
any place the document or book will be presented to the Stamp
Office and will be legalized upon the payment of the amount
due, and an order of legalization signed by the chief of the
Office, who will issue to the interested party a certificate
of payment in cash because of want of stamps; such legalization will only be effective for two months, after which
time the document or book will be considered as unstamped
unless the proper stamps are affixed to it; for this purpose
the parties must go within the two months to the Stamp
Office and exchange the said certificate for stamps which will
be supplied without other payment and will be affixed and
cancelled by the Office to the document or book; if it is not
in possession of the party asking its legalization, he will
get the stamps in exchange for the certificate and send them
to the person holding the document that they may be affixed
and cancelled in legal form.   (Arts. 244, 246–247.)

Art. 1099.   Effects of Failure to Stamp and of Revalidation.
—No instrument or book not legally stamped, or which involves an infraction punishable under this law, shall be
evidence for any purpose in or out of court, nor be given any
effect, nor can it be registered or admitted by any public
authority, office or employé; but upon payment of the omitted
taxes it will be held as revalidated and be given effect,
although fines which might be imposed have not been paid;
but *escrituras públicas* marked " Not Passed " are not subjcet to revalidation.   The revalidation of any document only
implies the recovery of the stamp tax and does not in any
wise affect its character and validity in law as the basis of
any action or defense.   (Arts. 245, 248.)

CHAPTER 7.

FEDERAL CONTRIBUTION.

Art. 1100. What Subject to — Rate.
    1101. Exempt from Federal Contribution.
    1102. Payment of Federal Contribution.

Art. 1100. What Subject to — Rate.— On every payment made on any account whatever into the revenue offices of the States and Municipalities, there will be paid in addition, for the use of the Federation, twenty (20%) per cent. of its amount, which must be paid in special stamps called "Federal Contribution Stamps." When such payments arise from fines, abandoned property, escheats, treasure-trove or anything other than the payment of a tax or duty in some form, the federal contribution is included in such payments, of which amounts sixteen and two-thirds per cent. will be paid in the above stamps. In cases where the State or Municipal government farms out or contracts the collection of any of its taxes, the twenty per cent. of federal contribution will be collected in addition upon the sum stipulated in the contract, as the payments are made, without the separate collection of the same from the taxpayer by the contractor, nor is he required to cancel stamps for each collection of local revenue which he makes, although he is considered subrogated to the attributes of the revenue ofhee. (Arts. 249–251, as amended 27 May, 1907.)

Art. 1101. Exempt from Federal Contribution: — Revenues belonging to the Federation and to the municipalities of the Federal District and Territories; deposits not on account or in guaranty of payments which may in some way be subject to the contribution according to the preceding Article; payments for the part of the price of *baldios* which is applied to the States according to law; payments arising from military or civil rooms in hospitals; reimbursements; payments made on account of records of the Civil Register; the tuition of students in establishments of public instruction, and the income from funds of such establishments and those of public charity; income received by States and Municipalities from their property or lands, the proceeds of its sale or of the products of its establishments, or arising from its financial operations; gifts to any official work of charity of the States or for objects of public interest in the opinion of the Department of Hacienda; ground rent not exceeding 75 cts. daily in public markets; receipts from fees for authorizing and verifying weights and measures; receipts from distribution of water and for use of woods and pastures; penalties or surcharges for default in payment of local taxes; payments of four cents or under; all capitation or poll-taxes amounting to less than 25 cts. a month, subject to the detailed provisions which are omitted as of negligible importance. (**Arts.** 252–255.)

Art. 1102. Payment of Federal Contribution.— The federal contribution must be paid immediately that the local payment is made, in whatever form or portion it is made, and in all cases must be paid by special coupon-stamps, rescaled by the Principal Administrators of the Revenue, the matrix of the stamps being affixed to the voucher of payment, and the coupons remitted to the Principal Stamp Offices, both matrix and coupon being cancelled with perforating seal or that of the office receiving the payment. (**Art.** 256; the remaining **Articles** up to 265 are omitted as containing only administrative features of accounting in the Stamp Offices.)

CHAPTER 8.

SPECIAL TAXES AND DUES PAYABLE IN STAMPS.

Art. 1103. Special Stamp Taxes.

Art. 1103. Special Stamp Taxes.— The following taxes and dues will be paid in accordance with the laws on the subject at present in force, and those which may be promulgated in the future, by means of special stamps or common stamps bearing a special seal:

I. Annual mining tax. (Law of March 25, 1905.)

II. Tax on gold and silver. (Law of March 25, 1905, and decrees of November 23 and 24 of the same year.)

III. Tax on yarn and cotton fabrics. (Law of November 17, 1893, and decree of October 30, 1902.)

IV. Tax on manufactured tobacco. (Law of December 10, 1892, and decrees of May 12, 1896, May 7, 1903, and May 20, 1904.)

V. Tax on alcoholic liquors manufactured by the distilling process. (Law of May 4, 1895, amended by **Art.** 3 of the law of June 20, 1905, and decrees of May 7, 1903, and May 11, 1905.)

VI. Tax on dynamite and explosives. (Decree of February 21, 1905.)

VII. Dues on patents of invention. (Law of **August 25,** 1903, issued by the Department of Fomento, and Regulations of September 24, 1903.)

VIII. Dues on trademarks. Law of August 25, 1903, issued by the Department of Fomento, and Regulations of September 24, 1903.)

IX. Dues on weights and measures. (Regulations of the law of June 6, 1905, issued by the Department of Fomento on November 16 of the same year.)

In cases not provided for by the laws and Regulations in regard to the taxes and dues above enumerated, the provisions of this law will be observed whenever applicable. (**Arts.** 266–267.)

CHAPTER 9.

Art. 1104.   Classification — Simple   Infractions.— Liabili-ties for failure to comply with the provisions of the Stamp Law are of two kinds: 1, Simple infractions; 2, infractions with criminal liability. Simple infractions are committed: I, By failure to observe the formalities and requisites of this law; II, by lack of vigilance in compliance therewith; III, by failure to pay the tax. Liability under Section I is incurred by: 1, Those failing to properly cancel the stamps on *boletas,* books and documents, except as provided in **Art.** 1096; 2, those using stamps of a different kind than required by law or with the re-stamp of another revenue district; 3, those presenting inaccurate statements, where the error is discovered before the *boleta* is issued or before the tax is payable, except as provided in Art. 1067; 4, those failing to give notices or to present books, *boletas* or documents within the required time; 5, those failing to make proper entries in their books in the time and manner required; 6, those failing to keep their *boleta* or certificate of exemption in a visible place; 7, those failing to keep the required books accessible in their establishments; 8, those failing to comply with any other requisite or formality not above specified; the foregoing infractions are punishable by a fine of from one to one hundred pesos for each violation. (Arts. 268–271.)

Art. 1105.   Same — Sections II and III.— Simple infractions under Section II are committed by public officials and

employés who admit or give effect to any documents or books
not properly stamped, or permit same to be registered, or fail
to cancel stamps, or pay out public money or transmit telegrams, on unstamped documents, or fail to give the notices
required by law, or fail to require stamps on foreign documents, and by judges who fail to require the proper stamps
in matters of inheritance; the penalty for such infractions
under Section II is a fine of five times the value of the
stamps omitted where their value can be determined, provided such fine is not less than one peso nor exceeds five
hundred, and where the amount of stamps cannot be determined, the fine will be from one to five hundred pesos.

Under Section III simple infractions are committed by:
1, Those who fail wholly or in part to purchase the stamps
required for any document; 2, those who fail to execute any
receipt, invoice or other document subject to tax which they
are required to issue, and those who fail to demand the
same when it is their duty to require it; 3, those who
execute any document subject to tax, although its execution
is optional, and fail to stamp it; 4, those who fail to file
returns and pay the tax, or who file returns for less than
their sales books show, where the tax is assessed on that
basis, except in cases of retail *boletas* issued as provided in
Art. 1065, and those who fail to affix and cancel the proper
stamps on such *boletas* within the legal time; 5, those who
make entries of retail or wholesale sales in less than their
actual amount, unless they correct the same as provided in
said Art. 1065; (Clauses 4 and 5 are as amended 27 May,
1907); 6, those who fail to revalidate within ten business
days from the expiration of a year of suspension; 7, those
who fail to secure their *boletas* and to return them properly
stamped within the times required; 8, those who use on
their *boletas,* documents and books stamps which are not
current at the time they should have been stamped; 9, those
who fail to keep books or keep them without stamps, contrary to this law, or destroy them to prevent official inspection;

10, carriers of passengers and freight who do not pay the tax within the legal time; 11, officials, employés and pensioners who collect their salaries or pensions without the proper stamped documents. Likewise included under said Section III of the preceding Article are: 1, Professional persons received in official schools who exercise their profession without properly stamped diploma; 2, notaries, brokers and commission-merchants intervening in any transaction without requiring payment of the proper tax; also notaries, *escribanos* and judges acting as such who fail to exact the correct rate prescribed by law, and brokers who authorize minutes of contracts, issue copies of same, or offer them for registration without the proper stamps; 3, officials or employés violating any of the provisions of law in regard to the federal contribution; 4, those who retain in their possession uncancelled stamps of an old issue after the time when they can be exchanged for stamps of the new issue; 5, those who while not personally bound to stamp a document, receive or retain the same not properly stamped. The penalty for all violations under Section III is a fine of ten times the amount of the omitted stamps, but not to be less than one nor more than five hundred pesos where the value of the stamps is determinable, and where the amount cannot be determined, then from five to three hundred pesos. (Arts. 272–276.)

Art. 1106. Uncurrent Stamps — Revalidation.— Documents bearing stamps of a different class from that required for the tax, may be revalidated upon payment of a fine in amount to be determined by the following proportions: 1, If the stamps do not exceed $1, by paying double their amount; 2, if from $1 to $4, by a fine of $1; 3, if exceeding $4, by a fine equal to 25% of their value up to $100; if exceeding $100, the fine will be $100; where the stamps have the restamp of a different revenue district than that in which the document was executed, it will be revalidated upon payment of like fines, except without the maximum limit of amount.   (Arts. 277–278.)

Art. 1107.   Infractions with Criminal Liability.— Are committed by: 1, Those who keep two or more sets of books, including sales books, whether authorized or not, for the same business, with different entries in them; 2, officials or employés who having received stamps for a document or book fail to affix and cancel them, or remove those affixed to documents in their possesion by reason of their official position; 3, those who sell or use stamps which have been used on other documents or books, by washing, scraping or altering them; 4, those who fraudulently and by reason of their official position, affix to *boletas* or other documents incomplete stamps of a different value than is due; 5, *escribanos* who falsely certify to the proper stamping of any contract or document; 6, those who defraud or assist in defrauding the revenue through any of the acts punished by the Penal Code; 7, officials or employés charged with the collection of the federal contribution who fail to require its payment. The foregoing violations will be punished by a fine of twenty times the amount defrauded, provided the fine be not less than one nor more than five hundred pesos, or from five to fifty pesos where the amount defrauded cannot be determined, without prejudice to criminal liability under the Penal Code and irrespective of the judgment rendered. (Arts. 279–280.)

Art. 1108.   Repeated Offenses — Prescription.— Administrative rules for the application of the foregoing penalties are omitted.   Reincidence, or the second or repeated commission of the offense, is punished as follows: For the second offense 25% more than the fine for the first offense, 50% more for the third, and so successively, provided the total of a single fine does not exceed $500; the commission of any offense equal to the first one, by the same person during two years after the imposition of the penalty is considered reincidence for the purposes of this law. Administrative action for the punishment of every such offense prescribes by the lapse of five years from the day after its commission, or if it were continuous, from the day after it ceased; but at no time can effect be given to instruments, documents or books not properly stamped until they have been presented to the Stamp Office and the proper stamps affixed and cancelled, except where improper stamps have been used it is not necessary to affix new ones; where it is not considered necessary by the parties to issue the document which should have been executed, the value of the stamps it should have borne may be collected in cash. The falsification of stamps is punishable the same as forgery of sealed paper under the Penal Code. The Department of Hacienda may reduce the penalties imposed or pardon any offense committed under this law where in the interest of justice. (Arts. 282–287.)[1]

[1] Articles 288 to 371, dealing entirely with administrative procedure, administration of the stamp offices and official inspections, are omitted as beyond the practical purposes of this work.

BOOK XXI.
WEIGHTS, MEASURES AND COINAGE

TITLE I.

WEIGHTS AND MEASURES.

(Laws of 19 June, 1895, and 6 June, 1905.)

CHAPTER 1.

THE METRIC SYSTEM.

Art. 1109. Metric System Adopted — Standards.
    1110. Old System — Equivalents.

Art. 1109. Metric System Adopted — Standards.— From and after the 16 September, 1896, the International Decimal Metric System of Weights and Measures shall be the only legal system in the Mexican United States. (Law 1895.) The system of weights and measures already established, derived from the international standards of length and mass and from the second of medium time, constitutes the national system of weights and measures, and is the only legal system, and its use is obligatory in the Mexican United States. (Law 1905.) The fundamental units of said system are as follows: 1, The unit of length called the Meter, is equal to the length of the meter recognized and adopted as the international prototype; 2, the unit of mass called the Kilogram, is equal in weight to the weight of the kilogram recognized and adopted as the international prototype of mass; 3, the unit of time is the second of medium time. The Department of Fomento will designate the derived units intended for common use, specifying the conditions with which they must comply, and will also designate the derived units of the national system of weights and measures which are not of common use. (Law 1905, Arts. 1–3.)

Art. 1110. Old System — Equivalents.— The national standards of the new system are those furnished by the International Committee of Weights and Measures, the scientific details of which, being common knowledge, are omitted, (Arts. 4–5); also the details of organization of the Bureau of Weights and Measures of the Department of Fomento, and the provisions for the propagation and conservation of the system, (Arts. 6–16), and the penal provisions, (Arts. 17–21.)

The legal equivalents between the units of the national metric system now in force and those used in the Republic previous to 16 September, 1896, will be those shown in the tables heretofore published by the Department of Fomento and attached to the Regulations of this Law. The teaching of the metric system of weights and measures will continue to be obligatory in all public and private educational establishments. The Executive will issue regulations and orders to secure its strict observance. All former laws on weights and measures are repealed. (Arts. 22–26.)

CHAPTER 2.

OLD MEXICAN LAND AND WATER MEASURES.

(Galvan's *Ordenanzas de Tierras y Aguas,* Chap. X.)

to-day used, and that used formerly.

The Mexican *vara* is the unit of all the measurements of length, the standard of which is the **Castillian** *vara* of **the** "*Marc of Burgos,*" and is the legal *vara* which is used in the Mexican Republic.

The Mexican *vara* is divided into **two** halves, three-thirds or feet, four quarters, six-sixths and thirty-six *pulgadas,* or inches. One *pulgada* is divided into **12** lines, (*lineas*) and one line is considered as divided into **12** *puntos.* We have another division of the legal Mexican *vara* conforming with the division of the ancient *vara* of Toledo, which was used by surveyors and miners. Said division consisted in making two halves of the *vara,* three-thirds or feet, four-quarters, or *palmos* (palms or spans), six-sixths, eighth-eighths and forty-eight *dedos,* or **fingers.** The *dedo* is divided into three *pajas* or straws, or into four *granos.*

Fifty Mexican *varas* is the measurement denominated the *cordel,* which instrument is used for **the meaurement** of land.

The legal league contains **100** *cordeles* or **5000** *varas,* and is divided into two halves or into four quarters, or fourths, the latter being the only subdivision of the same.

The half league has **2500** *varas,* and one-fourth **1250** *varas.*

Formerly the Mexican league was divided into three miles (*millas*), each mile into one thousand paces of Solomon, and one of these paces (*pasos*) was equal to **five**-thirds of the Mexican *vara;* consequently the league contained **3000** paces of Solomon. This was recognized as the legal division, but it has not for a long time been in use.

The same which was understood to be the pace of Solomon was at that epoch termed the *vara,* and served for the measurement of land.

The *marco* is a measure which is equivalent to $2\frac{7}{8}$ *varas,* that is, 8 *marcos* made 23 *varas,* and was used for land measurement.

According to the more ancient Ordinances whenever any titles to land were sold, they should mention the paces of Solomon and the number of *marcos,* and the distances expressed were to be reduced to *varas* in said measurements. For example, if it were measured by the paces of Solomon, it had to be reduced to *varas,* and was written with the number of paces stated and the result was calculated by dividing by six, or that which was equivalent to its sixth part, and the number of *varas* equivalent to the said paces was obtained. By this rule it was found that 2000 paces were equivalent to $3333\frac{1}{3}$ *varas.*

In order to reduce the *marcos* to *varas,* the number was multiplied by 23, and the production divided by 8, or that which was equivalent to its eighth part. By this rule it was found that 384 *marcos* were equivalent to 1104 *varas.*

The *cordel* of 69 *varas* was formerly used for the measurement of the sides of a *caballería.*

Art. 1112. Sitio de Ganado Mayor.— The figure of a *rancho* or *sitio* of the extent of a *ganado mayor* is that of a square, the four sides of which each measures 5000 *varas.* Two of these sides should be laid out in the direction of east to west, consequently the others must be from north to south. The distance from the center of said *sitio* to each of its sides, should be measured directly to the cardinal points of the horizon, and should be 2500 *varas.* The measurement should be then made from the center of said *sitio* to each one of its four right angles, and should be $3535\frac{1}{2}$ *varas,* and the measurement from the right angles to the opposite should be 7071 *varas.* If for this measurement should be used the *cordel* of fifty *varas,* each of the sides of the *sitio* bounding the *ganado mayor* should be 100 *cordeles,* from the center to each one of said sides the measurement should be fifty *cordeles,* from the center of the same, to each one of the angles should be measured seventy *cordeles* and 35½ *varas,* and from one angle to the opposite, it should be one hundred and forty-one *cordeles* and twenty-one *varas.*

The area or superficie of a *sitio de ganado mayor* is 25,000,000 square *varas.* The *criadero de ganado mayor* is a square equal to the fourth part of one *sitio de ganado mayor,* each of the sides of which measures 2500 *varas,* and the area of which is 6,250,000 square *varas.* Formerly the measurement was made by the unit denominated the pace of Solomon, 3000 of which were equal to the league of 5000 *varas.*

Art. 1113. Sitio de Ganado Menor and Caballería.— The figure of the small-stock ranch or *sitio* of the extent of a *ganado menor,* is that of a square, each of its sides measuring $3333\frac{1}{3}$ *varas.* This *sitio* is measured in the same manner as the *sitio de ganado mayor.* The distance from the center of this *sitio* to each of its sides should be $1673\frac{2}{3}$ *varas,* from the center to each of its angles it should be 2357 *varas, and* from each angle to the opposite it should be 4714 *varas.*

If the measurement is made by the *cordel* of fifty *varas,* each of the sides should measure 76 *cordeles* and $32\frac{1}{3}$ *varas.* From the center to each of its sides, it should be 33 *cordeles,* and $16\frac{2}{3}$ *varas;* from the center to each of its angles it should contain 47 *cordeles* and 7 *varas, and* from each angle to the opposite 94 *cordeles* and 14 *varas.* The *criadero de ganado menor* is square, equal to the fourth part of the *sitio de ganado menor,* and measures on each side $1676\frac{2}{3}$ *varas,* and the area of which is 2,777,777 and $\frac{7}{9}$ths square *varas.*

The figure of a *caballería de tierra* is a parallelogram of right angles, the longest sides of which are 1104 *varas,* or 22 *cordeles* and 4 *varas,* and the smaller sides of which measure 552 *varas,* or 11 *córdeles* and 2 *varas.* The figure most common is that of a parallelogram with one of its longest sides of greater length than the other. The length and width of the right angled *caballería,* or the length of its sides when uniform, is the amount before given, the area of said *caballería* being 609,498 square *varas.* One-half a *caballería* is a square of 552 *varas* on each side; area 304,704 square *varas.*

The *suerte* of land, or fourth part of the *caballería* of land, is a figure corresponding to the one-fourth part of said *caballería,* the area of which is 152,352 square *varas,* and measures 11 *cordeles* and 2 *varas* by 5 *cordeles* and 26 *varas.* The *caballería* of land is also divided into 12 Castillian *fanegas,* for the planting of corn (*sembradura de maíz*), and the area of the *fanega* is 50,784 square *varas.* The *caballería* of land is also divided into 69 *fanegas* for the sowing of wheat (*trigo*), each *fanega* occupying a superficial extension or area of 8832 square *varas.*

The *solar* of land is a name given to any portion of land, the area of which is less than a *suerte* of land or less than one-fourth part of the area of a *caballería.*

The *solares* for houses, mills and stores (*molinos y ventas*) should be square lots measuring 50 *varas* on each side, the area of which, is 2,500 square *varas* (50 *vara* lots.)

The *sitio de ganado mayor* contains a little over 41 *caballerías* of land (41.023) or 41 *caballerías* and a square *solar,* the side of which is 119²/₃ *varas;* the *sitio de ganado menor* contains a little over 18 *caballerías,* and one *solar.* the sides of which are 376¾ *varas.* Measuring the *caballería* of land with the *cordel* of 50 *varas* it must measure 22 *cordeles,* and 4 *varas* on the longest sides and 11 *cordeles* and 2 *varas* on the shorter; each side of the square which composes one-half of the *caballería,* should measure 11 *cordeles* and 2 *varas,* the distance from the center of said square (half a

caballería) to each of its sides should measure **5** *cordeles*
and **26** *varas.* The *fundo legal* or town site, for *pueblos,* is
a square, measuring on each side **1,200** *varas,* the area of
which, is **1,440,000** square *varas.* The square should be
laid out with the angles corresponding to the cardinal points.

Art. 1114. Old Water Measures — Terms Defined.— A
buey of water is a volume of water passing through a square
aperture each side of which measures **one** *vara,* the area or
superficie is one square *vara,* hence one *vara* is equivalent
to **48** *dedos* or **36** *pulgadas,* the said superficies being **2,304**
square *dedos,* or **1,296** square *pulgadas.*

The *surco* is the volume of water delivered through an
aperture of rectangular shape, which has for its base or
horizontal width eight *dedos* or six *pulgadas* in measurement,
and measuring from the base perpendicularly, six *dedos*
or four and one-half *pulgadas.* The superficie of a *surco*
is **48** square *dedos* or **27** square *pulgadas,* (each *pulgada*
equals 11-12ths of an English inch); **48** *surcos* make **one**
buey or **2,304** square *dedos.* Forty-eight *surcos* make **one**
buey.

The *naranja* is the measurement of the volume of water
delivered through a rectangular aperture of eight *dedos* in
width and two in height, the superficie of which is **16**
square *dedos* or **9** square *pulgadas.* Three *naranjas* make
one *surco* or **48** square *dedos.*

A *real* of water is the volume delivered through a rectangular aperture, two *dedos* in width and one *dedo* in height,
superficie two square *dedos* or 1⅛ square *pulgadas.* Eight
reales of water make one *naranja,* and the area of one *real*
is two square *dedos,* therefore the area of a *naranja* is **16**
square *dedos.*

A *paja* of water is the measurement of the volume passing
through a square aperture, each side of which measures ¹/₃
of a *dedo,* the area of which is ¹/₉th of a square *dedo* or
¹/₁₆th of a square *pulgada.* The *paja* of water is also one

square *paja,* and is equivalent to one and $^7/_9$ths of a square *grano.*

From the foregoing divisions and subdivisions of a *buey* of water, it results, that one *buey* is composed of 48 *surcos* or 144 *naranjas,* or equal to 1,152 *reales* or 20,736 *pajas.*

TITLE II.

MONETARY LAWS AND COINAGE.

CHAPTER 1.

NEW MONETARY LEGISLATION.

Art. 1115. Gold Standard Adopted.— By the Law of 25 March, 1905, in effect from 1 May, 1905, Mexico passed from its historic championship of the *patrón de plata,* or silver standard, and joined the concert of nations under the régime of the *patrón de oro,* or gold standard of monetary legislation. The principal provisions of this and other kindred laws carrying into effect the new system, are stated in this Chapter.

Art. 1116. Coins — Weight and Fineness.— The theoretic unity of the monetary system of the Mexican United States is represented by seventy-five centigrams of pure gold, and is denominated " peso." The " peso " of silver heretofore coined, and containing 24.4388 grams of pure silver, shall have under the conditions prescribed in this law a legal value equal to the said 75 centigrams of pure gold. The

" peso " is divided into one hundred " *centavos.*"   The coins
to be issued shall have the following values: Gold coins:
$10.00 and $5.00; silver coins: $1.00, $0.50, $0.20, and
$0.10; nickel coin, $0.05; bronze coins, $0.02 and $0.01.
The composition of the gold coinage shall be 0.900 of fine
gold and 0.100 of copper; that of silver coinage: for coins
of $1.00, 0.9027 of pure silver and 0.0973 of copper; that
of bronze monies shall be ninety-five parts copper, four of
tin and one of zinc; the nickel five cent pieces shall be
made of commercially pure nickel.   The limits of tolerance
in the " *ley* " shall be: for gold money, 0.0015; for silver
pesos, 0.003; for fractional silver coinage, 0.0004.

The weights of the coins shall be: Gold: $10.00,
$8.333^1/_3$ grams; $5.00, $4.166^2/_3$ grams; Silver: $1.00,
27.073 grams; $0.50, 12.500 grams; $0.20, 5 grams; $0.10,
2.500 grams; Nickel, $0.05, 5 grams; Bronze, $0.02, 6
grams; $0.01, 3 grams.   (Arts. 1–8.)

Art. 1117.   Coinage and Circulation.— The power to coin
money belongs exclusively to the Executive of the Union,
who will exercise it in accordance with the present law at the
times and in the amounts thereby authorized; hence the right
of private persons to present gold and silver to the mints for
its coinage is abolished.   The coinage of new gold monies will
be limited, until otherwise ordered, to the amounts necessary to exchange for the outstanding gold coins, which will
cease to have legal circulation on July 1st, 1906; however
in the special circumstances hereinafter mentioned, the
Executive may authorize the free coinage of gold monies.
From the time this law goes into effect, and except in case
of recoinage, new silver monies will only be coined and
issued when they are to be received in exchange for gold
coined or in bars, in the proportion of seventy-five centigrams of pure gold for one *peso;* the gold thus received may
be employed in the purchase of bars of silver up to the
amount necessary to coin the silver monies solicited.   The

obligation to issue silver monies in exchange for gold shall cease when the value of silver contained in such coins shall be, in the City of Mexico, greater than that of seventy-five centigrams of pure gold for one *peso;* in other cases such obligation will be given effect in the time and manner fixed by the Regulations.

The new fractional currency shall be manufactured from the metal obtained by the melting down of the current silver coinage, unless its issuance is solicited in exchange for gold as above provided. For the making of the nickel and bronze pieces the necessary metal may be bought in the market; but such pieces shall not be coined where the amount of them in the fund hereinafter mentioned exceeds $200,000.00. The restrictions imposed by the foregoing provisions on the coinage and issuance of silver monies do not apply to the case of recoinage, in which case the amount and kinds of silver monies which may be necessary may be freely coined and put into circulation, provided that the total value represented by the new pieces shall equal that of those delivered for recoinage; the waste occasioned by recoinage shall be covered by the Federal Treasury. Every inhabitant of the Republic has the right to exchange the fractional coinage in order to obtain silver pieces to the value of one *peso,* and *vice versa,* provided he requests the exchange in the amount of one hundred *pesos* or its exact multiples, at the offices to be designated by the Treasury Department. The Department may authorize, but only for exportation, the coinage of *pesos* of the issue previous to 1898, provided that they bear a special countersign; in such cases it will fix the price of the coinage with the interested parties and make such provisions as will insure the exportation of said *pesos.* In all other cases the cost of coinage will be borne by the Government. The mints and federal assay offices will continue performing the functions committed to them by the Mining Tax laws, and will continue to render to private persons the services of assay, smelting, separation and refining, according to the regulations and tariffs issued by the Treasury, in cases where it is so ordered or authorized by law and the regulations. (Arts. 9–19.)

Art. 1118. Legal Tender and Currency of Money.— The obligation to pay any sum in Mexican money is discharged (*se solventa*) by delivery of monies of current coinage at their face value; hence the public offices of the Federation and of the States, and all establishments, companies and private persons are obliged to accept such monies in payment of what is owing them, with only the following restrictions: Gold money to any amount, and silver money of one *peso* denomination, have unlimited legal tender (*tienen poder liberatorio ilimitado*); the fractional silver coins are of obligatory acceptance only up to twenty *pesos* in one payment; those of nickel and bronze up to one *peso*. Foreign money is not of legal currency in the Republic, except where otherwise expressly provided by the law. Obligations payable in foreign money, contracted in or out of the Republic to be performed within the country, are discharged by the delivery of the equivalent in Mexican money, at the rate of exchange current in the place and at the time when payment should be made. The foregoing provisions cannot be waived or renounced, and every stipulation to the contrary is void; the Articles 1453 and 2690 of the Civil Code of the Federal District are repealed.[1] (Arts. 20–23.)

Art. 1119. Withdrawal of Coins — Prohibition of Tokens.— Gold coins and coins of one *peso* which by natural wear have become smooth or decreased in weight, shall be withdrawn at the cost of the Treasury, where such decrease is, in case of gold coins, four times, and in case of silver *pesos* ten times the limit of tolerance provided in **Art. 1116**; the fractional, nickel and bronze coins will be retired when they have become worn smooth. Plugged and clipped pieces, those

[1] See Arts. 452 and 345.

having marks and countersigns, and those which show signs of having been used for other than monetary purposes, shall lose their legal currency, and can neither be accepted nor exchanged at the public offices. The use of tokens, chips, counters and all other objects of whatever material, as conventional signs in place of legal money, is prohibited, and will be punished as herein and in the Penal Code provided, and the voluntary taker can have no action to recover on them; but this does not apply to bank notes and other instruments of credit issued by authority of law. (Arts. 24–26.)

Art. 1120. "Regulatory Fund" — Value of Old Coinage.— A fund called *"Fondo Regulador de la Circulación Monetaria"* is created, the details of which are omitted, and under Art. 32, a decree, of date 3 April, 1905, creating a special *"Comisión de Cambios y Moneda,"* was promulgated, and the "figures and superscriptions" of the coins were established. By Art. 2 of the Transitory Articles it is provided: While they are still in circulation, the gold coins heretofore issued shall be accepted by the public offices and by private persons at the following rates in the new coinage: $20.00 gold as equal to $39.48; $10.00 gold as equal to $19.74; $5.00 gold as equal to $9.87; $2.50 gold as equal to $4.93, and the $1.00 gold as equal to $1.97. (Arts. 27–32; Trans. 1–2.)

Art. 1121. Value of "Peso" in Foreign Moneys.— The equivalence of the Mexican *Peso* with the gold moneys of the several foreign countries which have established the Gold Standard, is, by Decree of 24 May, 1905, as fixed by the following:

TABLE OF EQUIVALENT VALUES OF "PESO."

COUNTRY.	VALUE OF MEXICAN "PESO" IN FOREIGN MONEY
Argentina	0.516 Pesos.
Austria-Hungary	2.45 Kröner.
Belgium	2.58 Francs.
Brazil	0 912 Milreis.
Bulgaria	2.58 Levas.
Canada	0.498 Dollars.
Chile	1.36 Pesos.
Colombia	0.498 Dollars.
Costa Rica	1.07 Colones.
Denmark	1.86 Kröuer.
Ecuador	1.02 Sucres.
England	24.58 Pence.
Egypt	24.24 Pence.
Finland	2.58 Marks.
France	2.58 Francs.
Germany	2.09 Marks.
Greece	2.58 Dracmas.
Hayti	0.516 Gourdes.
Holland	1.23 Florins.
Honduras, British	0.498 Dollars.
India	1.53 Rupées.
Italy	2 58 Lire.
Japan	1.00 Yen.
Liberia	0.498 Dollars.
Monaco	2.58 Francs.
Newfoundland	0.491 Dollars.
Norway	1.86 Kroner.
Panama	0.498 Balboas.
Peru	1.02 Soles.
Philippine Islands	0.996 Pesos.
Portugal	0.461 Milreis.
Russia	0.967 Rubles.
Roumania	2.58 Leus.
Servia	2.58 Dinares.
Spain	2.58 Pesetas.
Sweden	1.86 Kröner.
Switzerland	2.58 Francs.
Turkish Empire	11 36 Piastres.
United States	0.498 Dollars.
Uruguay	0.481 Pesos
Venezuela	2.58 Bolívares.

CHAPTER 2

TABLES OF WEIGHTS, MEASURES AND EQUIVALENTS.

Art. 1122.

TABLE NO. 1.

OLD LAND MEASURES OF THE MEXICAN REPUBLIC.

Spanish Names.	Nearest English Equivalent.	Length in Varas	Width in Varas	Area in Hectares	Area in Acres	Area in Caballerias
Hacienda	Plantation	5,000	5,000	8,778.05	21 697	205.115
Sitio de Ganado Mayor	Cattle Ranch	5,000	5,000	1,755.61	4,339.4	41. 03
Sitio de Ganado Mayor	Ox Farm	2,500	2,500	437.90	1,084.85	10.255
Sitio de Ganado Menor	Sheep Ranch	3,333⅓	3,333⅓	780.27	1,928.464	18.232
Sitio de Ganado Menor	Small-cattle Farm	1,666⅔	1,666⅔	195.777	82.033	4.558
Caballeria de Tierra	Knighthold of Land	1,104	552	.95	105.751	1.
Media Caballeria	Half Knighthold	552	552	21.397	52.875	0.5
Suerte de Tierra	Lot of Land	552	276	10.698	26.438	0.25
Labor	Field	1,000	1,000	70.224	175.532	1.641
Fanega sembradura de maíz	Cornfield for 1 Fanega of Corn	276	184	3.566	8.813	0.833
Fundo Legal para Pueblos	Township or Townsite	1,200	1,200	101.123	244.140	2.36
Solar, para casa ó molino	Building Lot or Site	50	50	0.175	0.434	0.004

Art. 1123.   TABLE NO. 2.

OLD LAND MEASURES OF LENGTH AND AREA.

1 Legua = 3 Millas = 100 Cordeles.

1 Milla = 5,000 piés = 0.88 mile = 1.42 Kilometers.

1 Cordel = 50 Varas = 12.5 Estadales.

1 Estadal = 4 Varas = 12 Piés = 3.38 meters = 3.7 yards.

1 Aranzada = a square of 20 Estadales, or 400 square Estadales.

1 Fanegada = a square of 24 Estadales, or 576 square Estadales; it is divided into 12 Celamines, which is divided into 2 halves and 4 quarters; = .6434 hectare = 1.59 acres.

1 Celámin = .0526 hectare = 0.13 acre.

Art. 1124.   TABLE NO. 3.

RECTILINEAR MEASUREMENTS OF WATER.

Measures of Rectilinear Volumes	Figures of the openings	Width or Basis of the Volumes expressed in *Dedos* or *Pulgadas*		Perpendicular height expressed in *Dedos* or *Pulgadas*		Areas of the Volumes expressed in *Sq'r. Dedos* or *Sq'r. Pulgadas*	
1 Buey or 48 Surcos	Square	48	or 36	48	or 36	2394	or 1296
1 Surco or 3 Naranjas	Rectangular	8	or 6	6	or 4.5	48	or 27
1 Naranja or 8 Reales	Rectangular	8	or 6	2	or 1.5	16	or 9
1 Real or 18 Pajas	Rectangular	2	or 1.5	1	or 0.75	2	or 1 1-8
1 Paja	Square	01-3 or	0.25	01-3 or	0.25	01-9 or	01-16

51

MEASUREMENTS OF DELIVERY OF WATER, SETTING FORTH
THE DIAMETERS OF CIRCULAR APERTURES IN SQUARE
MEASUREMENT, AND THEIR AREAS OR SUPERFICIES.

Volumes of Circular Delivery	Diameters of Circular Delivery or width of circular aperture in square measurements expressed in Pulgadas	Areas of Delivery through the aperture expressed in Square Pulgadas
1 Buey or 48 Surcos ...	40.50	1296
1 Surco or 3 Naranjas ..	5.86	27
1 Naranja or 8 Reales ..	3.38	9
7 Reales	3.17	$7\frac{7}{8}$
6 Reales	2.93	$6\frac{3}{4}$
5 Reales	2.66	$5\frac{5}{8}$
4 Reales	2.39	$4\frac{1}{2}$
3 Reales	2.07	$3\frac{3}{8}$
2 Reales	1.69	$2\frac{1}{4}$
1 Real or 18 Pajas	1.20	$1\frac{1}{8}$
17 Pajas	1.16	$1\frac{1}{16}$
16 Pajas	1.13	1
15 Pajas	1.09	$0\frac{15}{16}$
14 Pajas	1.05	$0\frac{7}{8}$
13 Pajas	1.02	$0\frac{13}{16}$
12 Pajas	0.98	$0\frac{3}{4}$
11 Pajas	0.94	$0\frac{11}{16}$
10 Pajas	0.89	$0\frac{5}{8}$
9 Pajas	0.85	$0\frac{9}{16}$
8 Pajas	0.80	$0\frac{1}{2}$
7 Pajas	0.75	$0\frac{7}{16}$
6 Pajas	0.69	$0\frac{3}{8}$
5 Pajas	0.63	$0\frac{5}{16}$
4 Pajas	0.56	$0\frac{1}{4}$
3 Pajas	0.48	$0\frac{3}{16}$
2 Pajas	0.39	$0\frac{1}{8}$
1 Pajas................	0.28	$0\frac{1}{16}$

[1] Table No. 4 contains the dimensions of circular apertures, expressed in diameters, and may be used for the computation of public and private springs, for this City (of Mexico). The municipal measurement or *toma* is five *pajas*.

Art. 1126.   TABLE NO. 5.   LINEAR MEASURES.

TABLES OF EQUIVALENTS.

OLD MEXICAN, METRIC AND U. S. UNITS.

A

1 **Legua** (league) = 5,000 varas = 4.19 Kilometers = 2.604 miles.

1 **Vara** (yard)   =   3 piés = 0.838   meters   = $\begin{cases} 2.749 \text{ feet.} \\ 32.993 \text{ inches.} \end{cases}$

1 **Pié** (foot)   = 12 pulgadas = 0.279   meters   = $\begin{cases} 0.916 \text{ feet.} \\ 10.99 \text{ inches.} \end{cases}$

1 **Pulgada** (inch) =   12 lineas = 0.023   meters   =   0.916 inches.

1 **Linea** (line)   = 0.00194 meters   =   0.076 inches.

1 **Palmo** or **cuarta**   = 0.2095 meters   =   0.687 **feet.**

B

1 Meter   = 1.1933 varas = 39.37   inches.
1 Kilometer   = .2387 leguas =   .621   mile.
1 Millimeter =   = 0.03937 inches.
1 Centimeter =   = 0.3937 inches.
1 Decimeter =   = 3.937   inches.

C

1 Mile = 1.609 kilometers = 1.14 milla.
1 Yard = 9.144 decimeters = 0.916 vara.
1 Foot = 3.048 decimeters = 1.093 piés.
1 Inch = 2.54   centimeters = 1.093 pulgadas.

D

	Inches.	Feet.	Yards.
Millimeter =	0.03937 =	0.003 =	0.001
Centimeter =	0.39371 =	0.032 =	0.010
Decimeter =	3.93708 =	0.328 =	0.109
Meter =	39.37079 =	3.280 =	1.093
Kilometer =	39,370.79	= 3280.899 =	1093.633

Art. 1127.　　TABLE NO. 6.　SUPERFICIAL OR SQUARE
MEASURES.

A

1 square Legua	=	1755.61	Hectares	= 4339.4	Acres.
1 square Vara	=	0.7022	Sq. meters =	7.559	Sq. feet.
1 square Pié	=	0.078	Sq. meters =	0.839	Sq. feet.
1 square Palmo	=	0.0438	Sq. meters =	68.0309	Sq. inches.
1 square Pulgada	=	0.00054	Sq. meters =	0.84	Sq. inches.

B

1 square Meter	=	1.424 sq. Varas =	10.00 sq. Feet.	
1 Hectare	=	14240.065 sq. Varas =	2.471 Acres.	
1 Are	=	142.40 sq. Varas =	119.603 sq. Yards =	0.02 Acres.
1 Centare	=	1.42 sq. Varas =	10.746 sq. Feet.	

C

1 square inch	= 6.451	sq. centimeters.
1 square foot	= .0929	sq. meter.
1 square yard	= .8361	sq. meter.
1 acre	= .4047	hectare.
1 square mile	= 2.592	sq. kilometers.

Art. 1128.　　TABLE NO. 7.　CUBIC MEASURES.

1 cubic Vara	= 0.5884 cu. meters	= 0.7697 cu. yards.
1 cubic Pié	= 0.0218 cu. meters	= 0.7695 cu. feet.
1 cubic Palmo	= 0.0092 cu. meters	= 0.3246 cu. feet.
1 cubic Meter	= 1.699 cu. Varas	=

Art. 1129.　　TABLE NO. 8.　DRY MEASURES.

1 Carga	= 2 Fanegas	= 181.629 Liters	= 5.154 Bushels.
1 Fanega	= 12 Almudes	= 90.814 Liters	= 2.577 Bushels.
1 Almud	= 4 Cuartillos	= 7.597 Liters	= 0.859 Pecks.
1 Cuartillo (quart)	=	1.891 Liters	= 1.718 Dry Quarts.
1 Liter	=	.0055 Carga.	

Art. 1130.   TABLE NO. 9.   MEASURES OF CAPACITY.

A

	Cubic In.	Cubic Ft.	(U. S.) Dry Pts.	(U. S.) Gallons.	(U. S.) Bushels.
Milliliter	0.06103	0.000	0.0018	0.000	0.000
Centiliter	0.61027	0.000	0.0182	0.002	0.000
Deciliter	6.10271	0.003	0.1816	0.022	0.003
Liter	61.02705	0.035	1.8162	0.227	0.028
Hektoliter	6102.70515	3.531	181.6211	22.703	2.838

The liter is equivalent to 0.2642 gallons (U. S.), or 1.0567 quarts (U. S.), liquid measure.

B

The following are the equivalents of metric measures of capacity in units of the Imperial or British measures of capacity: —

1 Centiliter	= 0.070	gill.
1 Deciliter	= 0.176	pint.
1 Liter	= 1.75980	pints.
1 Dekaliter	= 2.200	gallons.
1 Hectoliter	= 2.75	bushels.

C

1 Gallon (American standard, or 231 cu. in.)	= 3.785 liters.
1 Gallon (Imperial or English standard, 277.3 cu. in.)	= 4.545 liters.
1 Bushel (American standard)	= 35.24 liters.
1 Bushel (English standard)	= 36.35 liters.

Art. 1131.   TABLE NO. 10.   HYDROMETRIC AND LIQUID MEASURES.

A

1 Buey (Ox)	= 48 Surcos.
1 Surco (Furrow)	= 3 Naranjas.
1 Naranja (Orange)	= 8 Reales or Limones.
1 Real (Bit) or Limón (Lemon)	= 2 Dedos.
1 Dedo (Finger)	= 9 Pajas (Straws).

B

1 Cuartillo (for Oil) = 0.506 Liters = 0.5348 U. S. Liq. Qts.
1 Cuartillo (for other liquids) = 0.4562 Liters = 0.4821 U. S. Liq. Qts.
1 Jarra = 8.2127 Liters.
1 Liter = 1.976 Cuartillos (oil).
1 Liter = 2.192 Cuartillos (other liquids).
1 Galón (of 4 Azumbres or 8 cuartillas) = 0.964 gallon.

Art. 1132. TABLE NO. 11. COMMERCIAL WEIGHTS.

A

1 Carga = 3 Quintales = 138.0739 Kilograms = 304.332 U. S. Lbs. Avoir.
1 Quintal = 4 Arrobas = 46.0246 Kilograms = 101.444 U. S. Lbs. Avoir.
1 Arroba = 25 Libras = 11.5061 Kilograms = 25.361 U. S. Lbs. Avoir.
1 Libra (pound) = 16
   Onzas . . . . = 0.4602 Kilograms = 1.014 U. S. Lbs. Avoir.
1 Onza (ounce) = 16
   Adarmes . . . . = 0.0287 Kilograms = 1.014 U. S. Oz. Avoir.
1 Adarme (dram) =
   36 Granos . . . . = 0.0018 Kilograms = 0.063 U. S. Oz. Avoir.
1 Grano (Grain) . . . . = 0.0499 Grammes = 0.771 Grains Avoir.

B

1 Kilogram = 2.1728 Libras = 2.204 Lbs. Avoir. = 2.68 Lbs. Troy.
1 Pound Avoir. = .453 Kilogram.
1 Ounce Avoir. = .028 Kilogram.

Art. 1133. TABLE NO. 12. PRECIOUS METAL WEIGHTS.

				Grams.	Oz. Troy.
1 Marco	=	8 Onzas	=	230.123	= 8.1184
1 Onza	=	8 Octavas	=	28.765	= 1.0148
1 Octava	=	6 Tomines	=	3.596	= 0.1268
					Grains.
1 Tomín	= 12	Granos	=	0.599	= 9.2592
1 Grano			=	0.049	= 0.7716

Art. 1134.   TABLE NO. 13.   WEIGHT AND FINENESS OF
COINS.

Value. (Pesos)	Metal.	Weights. (Grams)	Fineness. (Parts)		Tolerance in Weights (Grams)
$10.00	Gold	8.333⅓	0.900	fine gold	0.025
			0.100	copper	
5.00	Gold	4.166⅔			0.020
1.00	Silver	27.073	0.9027	pure silver	0.100
			0.0973	copper	
0.50	Silver	12.500			0.080
0.20	Silver	5.000			0.080
0.10	Silver	2.500			0.080
0.05	Nickel	5.000	pure nickel		0.250
0.02	Bronze	6.000	0.95	copper	0.300
			0.04	tin	
0.01	Bronze	3.000	0.01	zinc	0.150

Art. 1135.   TABLE NO. 14.   SOME PRACTICAL
EQUIVALENTS.

For practical purposes, it will be found of use to bear in mind the
following table of approximate equivalents: —

1 meter	= 39 ¼ inches = 3 1-4 feet.
1 kilometer	= 3-5 of a mile.
1 liter	= 1 quart (U. S. liquid measure).
1 liter	= 1¾ pints (English liquid measure).
1 kilograme	= 2⅕ lbs. Avoir.
1 grame	= 15½ grains, Troy.
1 hectare	= 2½ Acres.
1 square meter	= 10 square feet.

BOOK XXII.

THE MEXICAN CUSTOMS TARIFF.

*(Ordenanza General de Aduanas Marítimas y Fronterizas,
de 20 de Junio, 1905; with all Amendments to date.)*

CHAPTER 1.

SCHEDULES OF IMPORT DUTIES.[1]

Art. 1136. ANIMAL PRODUCTS.

Notes.	Tariff No.	CLASSIFICATION.	Unit of quantity.	Rate of duty. Pesos.
		I.— LIVE ANIMALS.		
	1	Live animals, not specified		Free.
	2	Geldings	Each	45.00
	3	Swine and sucking pigs (when in cages the weight of the latter shall be taken into consideration)	100 kilos	2.00
		II.— ANIMAL PRODUCE.		
		Alimentary.		
	4	Fresh meat of all kinds	Kilo, net	.10
1	5	Meat, fish, and shellfish, dried, salted, smoked, or pickled	Kilo, legal	.15

[1] All rates are of course quoted in terms of the Mexican *Peso*.

	6	Fish and shellfish, fresh (even when preserved on ice) ....Kilo, gross	.03
		For industrial purposes.	
	7	Animals prepared for collections of natural history	Free.
2	8	Whalebones, raw, and quills without feathers .... —	Free.
3	9	Flock wool ....100 kilos, gross ..	2.00
4	10	Tortoise shells .... —	Free.
5	11	Horsehair, bristles, and cow hair =Kilo, gross	.04
6	12	Horn, unwrought .... —	Free.
7	13	Spermaceti in cakes ....Kilo, legal	.15
8	14	Animal fats not specially mentioned ....Kilo, gross	.08
9	15	Bone, unwrought and grated or powdered	Free.
10	16	Wool, in fleece, unwashed and shoddy ....Kilo, gross	.07
10	17	Wool in fleece, washed and scoured . Kilo, gross	.11
11	18	Wool, carded ....Kilo, net	.14
12	19	Ivory, unwrought, grated or powdered .... —	Free.
13	20	Mother-of-pearl, unwrought, and sawdust and waste of the same .. —	Free.
14	21	Hair, human ....Kilo, net	10.00
15	22	Goat and camel hair ....Kilo, gross	.12
	23	Beaver fur ....Kilo, legal	3.00
16	24	Hair of the vicuña, rabbit, hare, muskrat, and the like ....Kilo, legal	2.00
	25	Pearls, unset ....Kilo, net	100.00
17	26	Beaver skins, with fur, untanned .. Kilo, gross	.30
17	27	Skins of vicuña, rabbit, hare, muskrat, and the like, with hair untanned ....Kilo, gross	.22
17	28	Hides, untanned, not specially mentioned ....100 kilos gross ..	3.50
18	29	Feathers, ornamental ....Kilo, legal	3.50
	30	Feathers and down, for beds, not specially mentioned ....Kilo, legal	.90
		For medicinal purposes.	
19	31	Musk ....Kilo, legal	6.50
	32	Cantharides ....Kilo, legal	.60
20	33	Castoreum ....Kilo, legal	2.25

Notes.	Tariff No.	CLASSIFICATION.	Unit of quantity.	Rate of duty. *Pesos.*

III.— ANIMAL PRODUCE.

Alimentary.

Notes.	Tariff No.	CLASSIFICATION.	Unit of quantity.	Rate of duty
21	34	Animal foods, preserved	Kilo, legal	.18
	35	Eggs, fresh	—	Free.
	36	Milk, fresh	—	Free.
22	37	Lard	Kilo, gross	.12
	38	Butter	Kilo, legal	.25
	39	Honey	Kilo, gross	.06
	40	Cheese of all kinds	Kilo, legal	.15

For industrial purposes.

Notes.	Tariff No.	CLASSIFICATION.	Unit of quantity.	Rate of duty
23	41	Oils, animal, not specially mentioned, in glass vessels	Kilo, legal	.14
23	42	Oils, animal, not specially mentioned, in cans or wooden vessels .	Kilo, gross	.12
23	43	Oils, animal, not specially mentioned, in tank cars and tank ships	Kilo, net	.15
24	44	Albumen, from eggs or blood . .	Kilo, legal	.05
34	45	Charcoal, animal	—	Free.
	46	Wax, animal	Kilo, net	.55
25	47	Glue	Kilo, gross	.05
26	48	Coral, unwrought or powdered	—	Free.
27	49	Sponges, fine	Kilo, legal	2.50
28	50	Sponges, common	Kilo, legal	.50
29	51	Stearin in cakes	Kilo, gross	.11
30	52	Glycerine	—	Free.
31	53	Gelatine (grenetina) and ichthyocolla	Kilo, legal	.12
32	54	Guano	—	Free.
33	55	Silk, raw, of all kinds	Kilo, net	1.10

For medicinal purposes.

Notes.	Tariff No.	CLASSIFICATION.	Unit of quantity.	Rate of duty
35	56	Cod-liver oil in glass vessels	Kilo, legal	.14
35	57	Cod-liver oil in cans or in wooden vessels	Kilo, gross	.12
	58	Bacteriological cultures, vaccine, and serum for hypodermic injections	—	Free.

IV.— INDUSTRIAL PRODUCTS & MANUFACTURES.

Articles of fur and leather.

Notes.	Tariff No.	CLASSIFICATION.	Unit of quantity.	Rate of duty
36	59	Articles of leather not specially mentioned	Kilo, legal . ,...	2.00

Notes.	Tariff No.	CLASSIFICATION.	Unit of quantity.	Rate of duty. Pesos.
37	60	Leather belting for machinery	Kilo, gross	.55
	61	Cowhair belting for machinery	Kilo, gross	.11
38	62	Calfskins, patent leather, kid, chamois, and other common prepared skins not specially mentioned ..	Kilo, legal	1.60
	63	Leather gloves, plain or embroidered, without lining	Kilo, legal	6.00
	64	Leather gloves, plain or embroidered, lined	Kilo, legal	3.00
39	65	Leather gloves, lined or unlined, with strengthened wrists	Kilo, legal	1.50
40	66	Manufactures of tanned skins covered with fine furs.............	Kilo, legal	4.50
40	67	Tanned skins covered with fine fur .	Kilo. legal	2.25
38 -	68	Sole leather	Kilo, legal	1.00

Foot-wear.

Notes.	Tariff No.	CLASSIFICATION.	Unit of quantity.	Rate of duty. Pesos.
41	69	Slippers of all kinds up to 12 centimetres sole length, of leather or other material, not combined with silk, even though ornamented or embroidered with silk or base metal	Pair	.30
41	70	Slippers and shoes of leather or other material, not combined with silk, even though ornamented or embroidered with silk or metal of inferior quality, from 12 to 20 centimetres in length	Pair	.40
47	71	Slippers and shoes of leather or other material, not combined with silk, even though ornamented or embroidered with silk or metal of inferior quality, of more than 20 centimetres in length	Pair	.60
41	72	Leather boots, for men	Pair	3.00
41	73	High and low shoes, up to 12 centimetres in length, of leather or cloth of all kinds and materials, provided they do not contain precious metal	Pair	.70
41	74	High and low shoes, over 12 and up to 20 centimetres in length, of leather or cloth of all kinds or materials, provided they are not combined with fine metal	Pair	1.15

Notes.	Tariff No.	CLASSIFICATION.	Unit of quantity.	Rate of duty. Pesos.
41	75	High and low shoes, over 20 centimeties in length, of leather or cloth of all kinds of materials, provided they are not combined with fine metal ....Pair		1.75
		Miscellaneous Articles.		
	76	Fans with mounting or ribs of horn or bone ....Kilo, legal		1.40
	77	Fans of tortoise shell, mother-of-pearl or ivory, not combined with precious metal ....Each		3.00
	78	Fans of tortoise shell, mother-of-pearl or ivory, with gold, silver, or platinum ornaments or attachments .... Each		6.00
	79	Manufactures of whalebone, horn or bone, not specially mentioned ...Kilo, legal		.45
42	80	Manufactures of tortoise shell, coral, ivory, or mother-of-pearl, not specially mentioned ....Kilo, legal		2.00
	81	Articles or manufactures of human hair ....Kilo, net		15.00
	82	Wax candles or tapers ....Kilo, gross		.70
	83	Candles or tapers of spermaceti, stearin, and of pressed or unpressed tallow ....Kilo, gross		.20

Art. 1137. VEGETABLE MATERIALS.

I.— TEXTILE FIBRES.

	84	Cotton, raw, unginned ....100 kilos, gross ...		3.30
43	85	Cotton, ginned ....100 kilos, gross ...		7.70
44	86	Cotton, carded ....Kilo. legal		.22
45	87	Cotton waste ....100 kilos, gross ...		2.20
	88	Hemp, flax, ramie, and other vegetable fibres, not specially mentioned, raw or hackled ....100 kilos, gross ...		2.20
	89	Artificial silk or " artisela," raw, of all kinds ....Kilo, net		.55
	90	Jute, Abaca or Manila hemp, pita, ixtle, sisal hemp, and New Zealand fibre (Phormium tenax) raw or combed ....100 kilos, gross ...		.55

Notes.	Tariff No.	CLASSIFICATION.	Unit of quantity.	Rate of duty. Pesos.
		II.— FRUITS AND CEREALS.		
		Alimentary.		
46	91	Caraway seed and green aniseed, almonds, sweet or bitter, shelled; cocoa and pepper of all kinds	Kilo, net	.30
	92	Almonds, sweet or bitter, in the shell	Kilo, net	.15
	93	Rice	Kilo, gross	.08
	94	Oats in the grain, and mashed barley	100 kilos, gross ...	1.50
	95	Coffee in the bean, husked or not ..	Kilo, net	.10
	96	Cinnamon of all kinds, cassia and vanilla	Kilo, net	1.10
	96A	Malt	Kilo, gross	.05
	97	Cloves	Kilo, net	.70
47	98	Fruits, dried, not specially mentioned	Kilo, gross	.10
	99	Fruits, pickled	Kilo, gross	.07
	100	Fruits, in their juice, in syrup, and in spirits	Kilo, legal	.80
48	101	Fruits, garden produce, vegetables, and tubers, fresh, not specially mentioned	Kilo, gross	.03
49	102	Fruits, garden produce, vegetables, and tubers, preserved, not specially mentioned	Kilo, legal	.18
	103	Corn	100 kilos, gross ..	.80
	103A	Pressed grapes, for making wines ..	Kilo, gross	.05
	104	Alimentary seeds and grains, not specially mentioned	Kilo, gross	.13
		For medicinal purposes.		
50	105	Medicinal seeds and berries	Kilo, legal	.10
	106	Medicinal seeds and berries, ground, grated, or in pulp	Kilo, legal	.20
		For industrial purposes.		
	107	Oleaginous seeds and fruits, not specially mentioned	Kilo, gross	.01
		Live plants and seeds.		
	108	Live plants, moss, natural flowers, seeds for horticultural and agricultural purposes, of all kinds, when the latter are imported with the previous consent of the Treasury Department	—	Free.

	109	Saffron .... Kilo, net		2.20
	110	Cane for furniture .... Kilo, legal		.10
51	111	Cork, rough, in sheet, or ground ...	—	Free.
51	112	Cork, cut in tubes, for the manufacture of stoppers . ... Kilo, gross		.17
	113	Cork, in sheets and stoppers ...... Kilo, legal		.55
52	114	Vegetable hair, straw of Guinea-corn, or millet .... Kilo, gross		.02
53	115	Firewood, wood shavings, and fodder		Free.
	116	Hops		Free.
54	117	Medicinal roots, barks, flowers, herbs, and leaves .... Kilo, legal		.10
	118	Medicinal roots, barks, flowers, herbs and leaves, ground, grated, or in pulp .... Kilo, legal		.20
	119	Virginia leaf tobacco .... Kilo, net		.55
55	120	Leaf tobacco, filler, not specially mentioned .. .. Kilo, net		.80
55	121	Leaf tobacco, wrapper, not specially mentioned .. .. Kilo, net		2.50
	122	Tea .... Kilo, net		.55

IV.— VARIOUS VEGETABLE PRODUCTS.

Alimentary.

	123	Olive oil in jars or cans .... Kilo, net		.17
	124	Olive oil in glass vessels .... Kilo, net		.22
	125	Sugar, unrefined, rock candy, and refined sugar of all kinds ...... Kilo, gross		.05
	126	Coffee, roasted in the bean or ground, not specially mentioned . Kilo, legal		.05
56	127	Preserves, sweetmeats, and chocolate .... Kilo, legal		.80
	128	Potato meal .... Kilo, gross		.03
53	129	Biscuits of all kinds .... Kilo, gross		.16
57	130	Flour of wheat and other cereals, and meal not specially mentioned .... Kilo, legal		.10
59	131	Molasses of sugar cane or glucose,		

Notes.	Tariff No.	CLASSIFICATION.	Unit of quantity.	Rate of duty. Pesos.
		and sugared preparations for colouring wines, liquors, &c.	100 kilos, gross ..	2.50
57	132	Alimentary pastes of flour	Kilo, gross	.12

Medicinal.

Notes.	Tariff No.	CLASSIFICATION.	Unit of quantity.	Rate of duty.
60	133	Fixed oils for medicinal use, not specially mentioned	Kilo, legal	.22
61	134	Gums, resins, and natural balsams, not specially mentioned	Kilo, legal	.12
62	135	Opium and its extracts	Kilo, legal	3.50

For industrial purposes.

Notes.	Tariff No.	CLASSIFICATION.	Unit of quantity.	Rate of duty.
60	136	Oil, of cocoanut, linseed, corn, and cottonseed, in tank ships or tank cars	100 kilos, net	5.50
60	137	Oil, of cocoanut, linseed, corn, and cottonseed, in drums or cans	Kilo, gross	.05
60	138	Oils, fixed, for industrial uses, not specially mentioned	Kilo, legal	.22
63	139	Oils, essential, not specially mentioned	Kilo, legal	2.20
64	140	Oil of turpentine, and turpentine ..	Kilo, legal	.10
	141	Vegetable tar, and common rosin or colophony	Kilo, gross	.05
65	142	Charcoal	—	Free.
66	143	Vegetable wax	Kilo, net	.25
61	144	Gum arabic, copal, damar, pounce or sandarac, lac, Senegal, and tragacanth	Kilo, legal	.12
67	145	Tannin	Kilo, legal	.10

V.— WOOD.

Notes.	Tariff No.	CLASSIFICATION.	Unit of quantity.	Rate of duty.
68	146	Wood, ordinary, for building purposes, worked into blocks, beams, planks, and ordinary boards		Free.
69	147	Wood, wrought into dovetailed boards	100 kilos, gross ..	.10
70	148	Wood, fine, sawn into blocks, beams, planks, and boards	100 kilos, gross .	2.20
	149	Wood and barks for dyeing and tanning, even though they be pulverized	Kilo, gross	.05
71	150	Wood, fitted for carriage bodies ..	100 kilos, gross ..	2.20
	151	Wood, common, sawn into sheets or veneer	100 kilos, gross ..	1.10

Notes.	Tariff No.	CLASSIFICATION.	Unit of quantity.

VI.— MANUFACTURES OF VEGETABLE MATERIALS.

Wood.

72	152	Articles of common wood, roughly wrought, not specially mentioned .	Kilo, gross ..
72	153	Articles of common wood, when the weight of each exceeds 1 kilo, not specially mentioned	Kilo, legal ..
72	154	Articles of fine or common wood, veneered with fine wood, not specially mentioned, when the weight of each exceeds 1 kilo	Kilo, legal ..
72	155	Articles of all kinds of wood, not specially mentioned, gilded or inlaid or with ornaments of any material except precious metal	Kilo, legal ..
72	156	Articles of all kinds of wood, not specially mentioned, when the weight of each does not exceed 1 kilo	Kilo, legal ..
	157	Barrels, casks, and kegs, of wood, fitted together or not, of more than 15 litres capacity	
	158	Cases of common wood for packing purposes, fitted together or not ..	

Furniture.

73	159	Furniture, of common wood, without upholstery, inlaid work, ornaments of metal or cloth, containing silk	Kilo, legal .
73	160	Furniture of common wood, upholstered, without inlaid work, ornaments of metal or cloth containing silk	Kilo, legal .
73	161	Furniture of fine or common wood, veneered with fine wood, without ornaments of metal, inlaid work, upholstery, or cloth containing silk	Kilo, legal .
73	162	Furniture, of fine or common wood, veneered with fine wood, upholstered, without ornaments of metal, inlaid work, or cloth containing silk	Kilo, legal .

Notes.	Tariff No.	CLASSIFICATION.	Unit of quantity.	Rate of duty. Pesos.
73	163	Furniture, of wood of all kinds, gilt, or with inlaid work or ornaments other than of precious metal, or with cloth containing silk ....Kilo, legal		.70
		Articles of various vegetable materials.		
	164	Sandals of cloth, with soles of esparto or hemp, up to 20 centimetres in length ....Pair		.16
	165	Sandals of cloth, with soles of esparto or hemp, of more than 20 centimetres in length ....Pair		.25
	166	Articles of straw, cane, or rushes, not specially mentioned ....Kilo, legal		.45
	167	Articles of amber, not specially mentioned ....Kilo, legal		2.00
	168	Cordage, of cotton, aloe, hemp, and other similar fibres, measuring 3 centimetres or more in diameter .Kilo, gross		.09
134	169	Sacks made of jute, pita, ixtle, henequen, or hemp, enumerated in No. 382 ....Kilo, gross		.22
134	169A	Same, enumerated in No. 382a ...Kilo, bonto		0.18
134	169B	Same, enumerated in No. 382b ....Kilo, bonto		0.13
134	169C	Same, enumerated in No. 382c .... Will pay the rate on the weight of the cloth, as in Nos. 169, 169a, and 169b, plus 20 %		
	170	Straw wrappers for bottles ....Kilo, gross		.03
	171	Brooms and brushes of heather or millet .. ..Kilo, legal		.22
	172	Mats of esparto or palm ....Square metre		.30
74	173	Rope and cordage up to 1 centimetre in diameter ....Kilo, legal		.14
74	174	Rope and cordage of more than 1 and less than 3 centimetres in diameter .... Kilo, gross		.09
	175	Cotton wicks for lamps ....Kilo, legal		.33
	176	Tobacco, in cakes, for chewing ....Kilo, legal		1.10
	177	Tobacco, sifted or cut in shreds, for cigarettes ....Kilo, legal		1.70
	178	Tobacco in powder or snuff ....Kilo, legal		3.30
	179	Cigarettes of tobacco ....Kilo, legal		2.20

52

Notes.	Tariff No.	CLASSIFICATION.	Unit of quantity.	Rate of duty. Pesos.
	180	Cigars ....Kilo, net		7.70
	180A	Braids of straw for making 1ats ..Kilo, legal		.20

Art. 1138.   MINERALS.

I.— METALS.

GOLD, SILVER, AND PLATINUM.

Ores and metals.

75	181	Gold, silver, and platinum ores, **or** in ingots or dust		Free.

Manufactured articles.

76	182	Wire, purl, and other wire-drawn articles of silver, gilded or not ..Kilo, net		11.00
	183	Jewelry, and all kinds of articles of gold or platinum, or of both metals, combined, with pearls or precious stones ....Kilo, net		100.00
	184	Jewelry, and all kinds of articles of gold or platinum, or of both metals, combined, without pearls or precious stones ....Kilo, net		55.00
	185	Jewelry, and all kinds of articles of silver or of silver and gold, combined, with pearls or precious stones ....Kilo, net		60.00
	186	Jewelry, and all kinds of articles of silver, or of silver and gold, combined, without pearls or precious stones ....Kilo, net		12.00
	187	Crucibles of platinum	—	Free.
	188	Diamonds, emeralds, rubies, sapphires, and other precious stones, with or without settings of any material other than of precious metal ....Kilo, net		100.00
77	189	Galloons and tissues of silver up to 15 centimetres in width ....Kilo, net		15 00
77	190	Galloons and tissues of gilt silver up to 15 centimetres in width ...Kilo, net		18.00
	191	Foreign gold or silver currency ...	—	Free.
	192	Mexican silver coin, in pieces **of 1** peso, when imported in amounts exceeding 5 pesos .. ..Kilo, gross		15.00

Notes.	Tariff No.	CLASSIFICATION.	Unit of quantity.	Rate of duty. Pesos.
	193	Gold beaten into leaves, for gilding	Kilo, legal	18.00
	194	Silver beaten into leaves, for silvering	Kilo, legal	2.50

COPPER AND ITS ALLOYS.

Ores and metals.

	195	Bronze, brass, and white metal, in pigs or granulated	Kilo, gross	.05
	196	Copper, in pigs or granulated, copper ores in natural state, and copper matte		Free.
78	197	Copper, brass, bronze, and white metal, in bars	Kilo, gross	.13
79	198	Copper, brass, bronze, and white metal, in plates, sheets, or tubes	Kilo, gross	.17

Manufactured articles.

	199	Wire of copper, brass, bronze, or white metal, covered with any material	Kilo, gross	.10
80				
	200	Wire of copper, brass, bronze, or white metal, not covered with any material, up to 2 millimetres in diameter	Kilo, gross	.10
	201	Wire of copper, brass, bronze, or white metal, not covered with any material, of more than 2 millimetres in diameter	Kilo, gross	.06
	202	Wire, spangles, thread, and tinsel of common metal, gilt or silvered	Kilo, legal	1.10
	203	Articles of copper, brass, bronze, or white metal, not specially mentioned	Kilo, legal	.50
	204	Articles of copper, brass, bronze, and white metal, not specially mentioned, when the weight of each article exceeds 10 kilos	Kilo, legal	.22
	205	Articles of copper, brass, bronze. or of any other common metal, gilt or silvered, when the weight of each article does not exceed 10 kilogrammes	Kilo, legal	1.80
	206	Articles of copper, brass, bronze, or		

Notes.	Tariff No.	CLASSIFICATION.	Unit of quantity.	Rate of duty. *Pesos.*
		of any other common metal, gilt or silvered, when the weight of each article exceeds 10 kilogrammes ....Kilo, legal		.50
	207	Cable, without sheath, of brass, bronze, or white metal, covered with any material, and cable uncovered, cylindrical or flat, of the same metals and of different diameters ....Kilo, gross		.06
81	208	Cables with metallic sheaths and covered with any insulating substance		Free.
	209	Purl, tinsel, and other drawn products, not specially mentioned, of common metal, not gilt or silvered ....Kilo, legal		1.00
	210	Purl, tinsel, and other drawn products, not specially mentioned, of common metal, gilt or silvered . Kilo, legal		2.20
82	211	Galloons and gauze of common metal, not gilt or silvered, up to 15 centimetres in width ....Kilo, legal		3.00
82	212	Galloons and gauze of common metal, gilt or silvered, up to 15 centimetres in width ....Kilo, legal		4.00
83	213	Jewelery or jewels of any common metal, not gilt or silvered ......Kilo, legal		.80
83	214	Jewelery or jewels of any common metal, gilt or silvered ....Kilo, legal		2.00
84	215	Tinsel and enamel, in leaves or cut ....Kilo, legal		1.10
85	216	Bronzing powder .. ..Kilo, legal		.60

TIN, LEAD, AND ZINC.

Ores and metals.

Notes.	Tariff No.	CLASSIFICATION.	Unit of quantity.	Rate of duty.
	217	Tin in bars and granulated ......Kilo, legal		.10
86	218	Ingots of alloys of lead and antimony, for casting printing type .		Free.
	219	Tin. lead. or zinc ores	—	Free.
	220	Lead in bars, pigs, or ingots .... Kilo, gross		.04
	221	Zinc in ingots, filings, grains, and wire		Free.

Notes.	Tariff No.	CLASSIFICATION.	Unit of quantity.	Rate of duty. Pesos.
		Manufactured articles.		
87	222	Articles of tin, zinc, and of zinc, lead, and tin alloys, not specially mentioned ....Kilo, legal		0.30
	223	Articles of lead, not specially mentioned ....Kilo, legal		.10
	224	Lead in sheets, in tubes or piping, and lead used by glaziers ......Kilo, gross		.06
	225	Zinc in sheets of 1 metre in width by 2.25 in length and 1 millimetre in thickness, when imported in such conditions that it can only be used for treating ores		Free.
	226	Zinc in sheets, not specially mentioned ....Kilo, gross		.08

IRON AND STEEL.

Ores.

	227	Iron ores		Free.

Construction and mining materials.

	228	Steel in bars, round, square, flat, channel, in an octagonal or hexagonal section, or cruciform ....100 kilos, gross ..		5.50
88	229	Iron or steel wire of more than 1 millimetre in diameter ....100 kilos, gross ..		5.50
88	230	Iron or steel wire 1 millimetre in diameter or less ....Kilo, gross		.09
89	231	Iron wire for fences, and hoops of iron with their rivets, for packing purposes ....100 kilos, gross ..		2.50
90	232	Ploughs and loose parts or pieces thereof, spades, scythes, and other agricultural and grading tools ..100 kilos, gross ..		1.65
	233	Iron barrels, empty ....100 kilos, gross ..		3.30
	234	Iron or steel wire cables ....100 kilos, gross ..		1.10
	235	Iron piping up to 15 centimetres interior diameter, even tinned ..100 kilos, gross ..		2.50
	236	Iron tubing of more than 15 centimetres interior diameter, even tinned ....Kilo, gross		.01
	237	Iron piping coated with bronze, brass, copper, or white metal ...Kilo, gross		.06

Notes.	Tariff No.	CLASSIFICATION.	Unit of quantity.	Rate of duty. Pesos.
91	238	Ferro-manganese, containing 25 per cent. or more of manganese	100 kilos, gross ..	1.50
92	239	Iron in ingots of first fusion or in filings or scrap	Kilo, gross	.02
92	240	Iron, roughly wrought (bar) in ingots, and steel in ingots	100 kilos, gross ..	2.50
93	241	Iron, round, square, flat, channel, angle, and T shaped	Kilo, gross	.06
93	242	Hoop iron	Kilo, gross	.08
	243	Iron or steel in sheets, plain, not specially mentioned, also corrugated and in tiles for roofs, even when painted or galvanized	100 kilos, gross ..	6.60
	244	Tin plate, neither painted nor stamped, in sheets up to 55 centimetres in length by 40 in width	100 kilos, gross ..	1.10
	245	Tin plate in sheets, not specially mentioned, stamped, painted or varnished	Kilo, gross	.08
	246	Steel springs for cars and carriages	Kilo, gross	.11
	247	Posts, crossbars, and pegs of iron or steel for overhead electrical conductors	Kilo, gross	.03
	248	Rails of iron or steel for railroads, weighing more than 10 kilos per linear metre	Kilo, gross	.02
	249	Rails of iron or steel for railroads when the weight per linear metre does not exceed 10 kilogrammes, needles, discs, sleepers, frogs, bolts, and attachments for fixing rails	Kilo, gross	.01
94	250	Beams and joists of iron or steel, when not specially perforated or slotted	Kilo, gross	.03
94	251	Beams, joists, and columns of iron or steel, when specially perforated or slotted; frames, brackets, base plates for columns, butt or connecting plates, braces or tie beams, with or without nuts, and other parts, not specially mentioned, of iron or steel, for construction purposes	Kilo, gross	.04

Notes.	Tariff No.	CLASSIFICATION.	Unit of quantity.	Rate of duty. Pesos.
		Articles of iron or steel.		
	252	Iron or steel wire covered with cotton, linen, wool, silk, or paper...	Kilo, legal	.14
	d253	Articles, not specially mentioned, of iron or steel, tin plate, of iron tinned, nickelled, covered with copper or brass, painted or galvanized with zinc, wholly or in part, when the weight of each article exceeds 10 kilogrammes ...	Kilo, legal	.12
	d254	Articles, not specially mentioned, of iron or steel, tin plate, of iron tinned, nickelled, covered with copper or brass, painted or galvanized with zinc, wholly or in part, when the weight of each article does not exceed 10 kilogrammes	Kilo, legal	.22
	255	Articles of iron, enamelled, not specially mentioned	Kilo, legal	.30
95	256	Chains of iron, when the thickness of the links is not less than No. 5 Birmingham gauge	Kilo, legal	.11
96	257	Nails, tacks, screws, bolts, nuts, and rivets of iron or steel, not specially mentioned	Kilo, legal	.12
	258	Stoves of iron for cooking or heating purposes, not specially mentioned	Kilo, gross	.08
97	259	Iron or steel rods covered	Kilo, legal	.22
		Other metals.		
	260	Aluminium, in powder or bars....	Kilo, legal	.60
	261	Antimony, arsenic, cadmium, magnesium, and nickel	Kilo, legal	.30
	262	Mercury	—	Free.
	263	Metals not specially mentioned ...	Kilo, legal	1.00

II.— STONES AND EARTHS.

98	264	Asbestos in fibres or powder, emery in powder or lumps, marble or alabaster, rough or in powder, pumice stone and lava, unwrought, gypsum and stucco	Kilo, gross	.01

Notes.	Tariff No.	CLASSIFICATION.	Unit of quantity.	Rate of duty. Pesos.
99	265	Clay, sand or moulding sand, fire-clay, rotten stone, and tripoli ..	—	Free.
100	266	Jet, unwrought	Kilo, legal	.25
101	267	Sulphur	—	Free.
102	268	Common and hydraulic lime, Roman or Portland cement, and carbonate of lime, or Spanish white....	100 kilos, gross ..	.55
	269	Coal	—	Free.
102	270	Carbonates of magnesia, of barytes, of strontia, and peroxide of manganese	100 kilos, gross ..	3.30
103	271	Spar	Kilo, gross	.10
	272	Marble and alabaster, sawn in slabs, not polished	Kilo, gross	0.05
	273	Mineral stone of all kinds	—	Free.
104	274	Black plumbago	Kilo, gross	.06
105	275	Talc	Kilo, legal	.04

Mineral products.

Notes.	Tariff No.	CLASSIFICATION.	Unit of quantity.	Rate of duty. Pesos.
106	276	Mineral oil, not refined	100 kilos, net	3.30
107	277	Mineral oil, refined, benzine, mineral wax, and parafine	Kilo, legal	.09
108	278	Coal tar and asphalt	Kilo, gross	.04
	279	Coke	—	Free.
109	280	Vaseline	Kilo, gross	.11

Manufactured articles.

Notes.	Tariff No.	CLASSIFICATION.	Unit of quantity.	Rate of duty. Pesos.
110	281	Paving stones and slabs	—	Free.
	282	Articles of alabaster or marble, not specially mentioned, when the weight of each does not exceed 50 kilos	Kilo, gross	.30
	283	Articles of alabaster or marble, not specially mentioned, when the weight of each exceeds 50 kilos..	Kilo, gross	.18
	284	Articles of clay, cement, and lava, not specially mentioned	Kilo, gross	.05
	285	Articles of gypsum or stucco, not specially mentioned	Kilo, gross	.15
	286	Articles of agate, jet, and meerschaum, not specified	Kilo, legal	2.00
111	287	Ceramic tiles (Dutch tiles), with mouldings	Kilo, gross	.06
111	288	Ceramic tiles (Dutch tiles), not specially mentioned	Per 1.000	8.00

Notes.	Tariff No.	CLASSIFICATION.	Unit of quantity.	Rate of duty. Pesos.
	289	Paraffin candles ....Kilo, gross		.20
	290	Crayons and chalk .... Kilo, legal		.15
112	291	Bricks, slabs, tiles, ridge tiles, ventilators, and tubes of clay ......Per 1,000		2.75
	292	Pencils of all kinds .... Kilo, legal		.15
	293	Sand or emery, on paper or cloth ..Kilo, legal		.08
	294	Slabs of cement, or artificial stone, even with coloured designs ......Kilo, gross		.01
	295	Marble slabs for floors ....100 kilos, gross		1.60
	296	Marble slabs for furniture, and slabs with polished or moulded edges ....Kilo, gross		.15
113	297	Mosaics of artificial stone for flooring ....Kilo, gross		.02
	298	Millstones .... —		Free.
	299	Slates in slabs, polished on both surfaces ....Kilo, gross		.17
	300	Slates for roofing ....Kilo, gross		.01
	301	Slates for schools, even though framed and with slate pencils ..Kilo, gross		.10

Art. 1139. CRYSTALS, GLASS, CROCKERY, AND PORCELAIN.

Notes.	Tariff No.	CLASSIFICATION.	Unit of quantity.	Rate of duty. Pesos.
	302	Insulators of glass, china, and porcelain ....Kilo, gross		.01
114	303	Bottles of common glass, without stoppers of the same material, used generally for bottling wines, brandies, liqueurs, and beers .. 100 kilos, gross		2.20
114	304	Bottles or flasks of common glass, without stoppers of the same material, for bottling special liquids, provided that the glass be indelibly stamped with some distinctive mark indicative of the exclusive use of the receptacle ....Kilo, gross		.06
	305	Demijohns or carboys .... Kilo, gross		.04
	306	Mirrors with frames of brass, zinc, tin plate, white metal, wood, or pasteboard, the glass part of which in its greatest visible length measures up to 75 centimetres . ...Kilo, gross		.22

Notes.	Tariff No.	CLASSIFICATION.	Unit of quantity.	Rate of duty. Pesos.
	307	Mirrors with frames of celluloid, gutta-percha, or covered with cloth not combined with silk, the glass part of which in its greatest visible length measures up to 75 centimetres ....Kilo, gross		.30
	308	Mirrors with frames of crystals, or covered with leather or cloth combined with silk, and those ornamented with artificial flowers or feathers, the glass part of which in its greatest visible length measures up to 75 centimetres . Kilo, gross		.45
	309	Mirrors with frames of any material, except precious metal, the glass part of which in its greatest visible length measures more than 75 centimetres ....Kilo, gross		.60
	310	Mirrors without frames, up to 75 centimeters in their greatest length ....Kilo, gross		.22
	311	Mirrors without frames, the greatest length of which exceeds 75 centimetres ....Kilo, gross		.40
	312	Flasks, jars, and vessels of common clay, for bottling industrial products ....Kilo, gross		.01
	313	Flasks of glass, covered with leather, cane, cloth, gutta-percha, or common metal ....Kilo, legal		.60
	314	Spectacles of all kinds, with handles or frames other than precious metal ....Kilo, legal		1.00
	315	Faïence and porcelain in articles not specially mentioned ....Kilo, gross		.24
115	316	Glass and crystal in wares not specially mentioned ....Kilo, gross		.22
115	317	Glass and crystal in wares, cut or engraved, not specially mentioned .... Kilo, gross		.30
115	318	Glass and crystal in wares, not specially mentioned, with gold, silver, or coloured ornaments .... Kilo, gross		.40
	319	Glass, crystal, china ware, and por-		

Notes.	Tariff No.	CLASSIFICATION.	Unit of quantity.	Rate of duty. Pesos.
		celain, figured, in articles not specially mentioned, with mountings or settings of common metal, not gilt or silvered ....Kilo, gross		.45
	320	Glass, crystal, china ware, and porcelain, figured, in articles not specially mentioned, with mountings or settings of common metal, gilt or silvered ....Kilo, gross		1.25
116	321	Glass and crystals in smooth sheets, not specially mentioned ....Kilo, gross		.07
116	322	Glass and crystal in smooth sheets, bevelled, engraved, or ornamented, or with mountings of common metal for joining them to form windows .... Kilo, gross		.20
116	323	Glass tiles, for flooring, of at least 1 centimetre in thickness ... . Kilo, gross		.04
117	324	Glasses for spectacles and watches .Kilo, legal		1.00

Art. 1140. TEXTILES AND MANUFACTURES THEREOF.

I.— COTTON. (Note 118.)

Yarns.

119	325	Cotton cord, not exceeding 10 millimetres in diameter .. . .Kilo, legal		1.32
	326	Cotton cord, exceeding 10 millimetres in diameter ... . Kilo, legal		.18
120	327	Cotton yarn ....Kilo, legal		.50
	328	Cotton thread in balls, and skeins .Kilo, net		1.40
	328A	Cotton thread in spools ....1,000 metres		.07
121	329	Cotton wicks ....Kilo, legal		.22

Textiles.

	330	Cotton lace and point lace of all kinds, and manufactures thereof .Kilo, legal		6.00
	331	Handkerchiefs, of cotton fabric, neither cut nor hemmed .... —		(d)
	332	Handkerchiefs, of cotton fabric, cut or hemmed .... —		(e)
122	333	Cotton fabrics, bleached or un-		

(d) Duty on the material of which they are made.

(e) Duty on the material of which they are made, plus a surtax of 25 per cent.

Notes.	Tariff No.	CLASSIFICATION.	Unit of quantity.	Rate of duty. Pesos.
		bleached, of smooth texture, not exceeding 130 centimetres in width, and having not to exceed 20 threads, warp and woof, in a square of 5 millimetres side	Square metre	.08
122	333A	Cotton fabrics, bleached or unbleached, of smooth texture, not exceeding 130 centimetres in width, having over 20 but not exceeding 30 threads, warp and woof, in a square 5 millimetres side	Square metre	.10
122	333B	Cotton fabrics, bleached or unbleached, of smooth texture, not exceeding 130 centimetres in width, and having over 30 threads, warp and woof, in a square of 5 millimetres side	Square metre	.12
122	334	Cotton fabrics, bleached or unbleached, of smooth texture, exceeding 130 centimetres in width, and having not to exceed 20 threads, warp and woof, in a square of 5 millimetres side	Square metre	.09
122	334A	Cotton fabrics, bleached or unbleached, of smooth texture, exceeding 130 centimetres in width, and having over 20 but not to exceed 30 threads, warp and woof, in a square of 5 millimetres side	Square metre	.11
122	334B	Cotton fabrics, bleached or unbleached, of smooth texture, exceeding 130 centimetres in width, and having over 30 threads, warp and woof, in a square of 5 millimetres side	Square metre	.14
122	335	Cotton fabrics, colored, printed, or dyed, of smooth texture not exceeding 20 threads, warp and woof, in a square of 5 millimetres side	Square metre	.11
	335A	Same as 335, except having from 20 to 30 threads per mm.	Square metre	.14

Notes.	Tariff No.	CLASSIFICATION.	Unit of quantity.	Rate of duty. *Pesos.*
122	336	Cotton fabrics, colored, printed, or dyed, of smooth texture, exceeding 30 threads, warp and woof, in a square of 5 millimetres side ....Square metre		0.17
	337	Cotton fabrics, bleached or unbleached, or coloured, of a texture which is not smooth ....Square metre		.20
123	338	Cotton fabrics of all kinds, embroidered with wool ....Square metre		.28
124	339	Cotton fabrics of all kinds, with admixture of base metal in the form of showers, or with woven or embroidered designs or patterns ...Kilo, legal		2.20
124	340	Cotton fabrics of all kinds, with admixture of precious metal in the form of drops or threads ....Kilo, legal		3.30
125	341	Cotton fabrics of all kinds, with admixture of precious metal, in woven or embroidered designs or patterns ....Kilo, legal		5.50

Manufactured articles.

Notes.	Tariff No.	CLASSIFICATION.	Unit of quantity.	Rate of duty.
126	342	Carpets and rugs of uncut cotton velvet or shag, with a basis of any vegetable fibre ....Square metre		.28
127	343	Cotton tassels, even with core of any other material ....Kilo, legal		.70
128	344	Cotton tassels, with cords of the same material ....Kilo, legal		1.80
139	345	Cotton hosiery, even when containing ornaments of other material than precious metal or silk .....Kilo, legal		2.50
139	346	Cotton hosiery, with silk ornaments .... Kilo, legal		3.00
129	347	Cotton drawers, undershirts, and shirts for men and boys ....Kilo, legal		2.50
129	348	Cotton undershirts and shirts for men and boys, with ornaments of wool or silk, or with fronts, collars, and cuffs of linen ....Kilo, legal		3.00
139	349	Cotton undershirts, drawers, corset covers, and other articles of cotton network, not specially mentioned, even with ornaments of other material than precious metal or silk ....Kilo. legal		3.00

Notes.	Tarilt No.	CLASSIFICATION.	Unit of quantity.	Rate of duty. Pesos.
139	350	Undershirts, drawers, corset covers, and other articles of cotton network, not specially mentioned, with ornaments of silk ....Kilo, legal		3.50
	351	Bed covers, blankets, quilts, curtains, table covers, shawls, furniture covers, and pillow cases, of cotton fabric, without embroidery ....Kilo, legal		1.10
	352	Bed covers, blankets, quilts, curtains, table covers, shawls, furniture covers, and pillow cases, of		
	352A	Cotton cravattes .... Kilo, legal		2.30
		cotton fabric, embroidered ......Kilo, legal		1.70
	353	Cotton corsets, even with ribbons and small ornaments, other than of precious metal ....Kilo, legal		3.00
130	354	Dress patterns of cotton fabrics, even with embroidered ornaments or trimmed with cotton or linen lace, for ladies and girls ....Kilo, legal		1.60
130	355	Dress patterns of cotton fabrics, with ornaments of fabrics containing silk, with skirts or overskirts of lace or guipure of cotton ....Kilo, legal		2.50
131	356	Rufflings, fringes, galloons, lace trimmings, lace edging, ribbons, and cotton nettings ....Kilo, legal		2.30
131	357	Rufflings, fringes, galloons, lace trimmings, lace edging, ribbons, and cotton nettings, combined with glass beads, common metal, or paste ....Kilo, legal		1.15
	358	Garters and suspenders, of cotton Kilo, legal		1.20
	359	Cotton handkerchiefs with cotton or linen lace trimming ....Each		.22
	360	Cotton umbrellas, parasols, and sunshades ....Each		.66
	361	Shirt fronts, collars, and cuffs, of cotton fabrics, neither embroidered nor open worked ....Kilo, legal		1.70
	362	Shirt fronts, collars and cuffs, of cotton fabrics, embroidered or open worked .. .. Kilo, legal		2.20

Notes.	Tariff No.	Classification.	Unit of quantity.	Rate of duty. Pesos.
	363	Shawls of cotton, up to 26 threads in warp and woof, in a square of 5 millimetres side	Square metre	1.30
	364	Shawls of cotton, of more than 26 and up to 38 threads in warp and woof, in a square of 5 millimetres side	Square metre	2.40
	365	Shawls of cotton, of more than 38 threads in warp and woof, in a square of 5 millimetres side	Square metre	5.50
	366	Elastic webbing of cotton and rubber, exceeding 4 centimetres in width	Kilo, legal	.66
	367	Elastic webbing of cotton and rubber, not exceeding 4 centimetres in width	Kilo, legal	1.00
132	368	Ready-made clothing, not specially mentioned and separate parts thereof, when sewn, of cotton fabrics of all kinds and textures, even ornamented with lace or embroidery, of cotton or linen, silk ribbons, or common metal, for adults and children	Kilo, legal	2.75
132	369	Ready-made clothing, not specially mentioned and separate parts thereof, when sewn, of cotton fabrics of all kinds and textures, when ornamented with silk ribbons, pure or mixed silk fabrics, with skirts or overskirts of lace or point of cotton, for adults and children	Kilo, legal	3.30
133	370	Cotton insertions, open worked or embroidered with cotton, wool, or linen	Kilo, legal	2.20
133	371	Cotton insertions, open worked or embroidered with cotton, wool or linen, with beads of glass, common metal, or paste	Kilo, legal	1.40

Notes.	Tariff No.	CLASSIFICATION.	Unit of quantity.	Rate of duty. Pesos.
		II.— FLAX, HEMP, AND OTHER SIM-ILAR VEGETABLE FIBRES. (Note 136.)		
		Yarn.		
	372	Cord of linen or hemp not exceed-ing 10 millimetres in diameter ..	Kilo, legal	1.65
	373	Cord of linen or hemp exceeding 10 millimetres in diameter	Kilo, legal	.18
120	374	Linen or hemp yarns, and other similar fibres, not specially men-tioned	Kilo, legal	.18
120	375	Yarn of henequen, ixtle, New Zea-land fibre (Piormium tenax), crotalaria, or sunn hemp (Cro-talaria juncea), or an admixture of these materials not exceeding 403 metres per kilogramme; and yarn of abacá or manila hemp not exceeding 437 metres per kilo-gramme	Per 100 kilos, gross	.70
	376	Thread of linen or hemp, in balls, spools, or skeins	Kilo, legal	.25
	377	Linen or hemp thread, in spools...	Kilo, legal	1.10
	378	Pressed linen thread for shawls ..	Kilo, legal	1.50
		Fabrics.		
	379	Linen lace and points of all kinds and manufactures thereof	Kilo, legal	7.00
	380	Linen handkerchiefs, neither cut nor hemmed	—	(c)
	381	Linen handkerchiefs, cut or hemmed		(d)
134	382	Coarse tissues of jute, abacá, pita, ixtle, henequen, New Zealand fibre (Piormium tenax), or hemp, un-bleached, of all textures, up to 32 threads of warp and woof, in a square of 2 centimetres side, and weighing up to 400 grammes per square metre	Kilo, gross	.22
134	382A	Idem, weighing from 450 to 650 grammes per square meter	Kilo, gross	.18

(c) Duty on the material of which they are made.

(d) Duty on the material of which they are made, plus a surtax of 25 per cent.

Notes.	Tariff No.	CLASSIFICATION.	Unit of quantity.	Rate of duty. *Pesos.*
134	382B	Idem, weighing over 650 grammes per square meter	Kilo, gross	.13
134	382C	Idem, white, brownish or colored ..	Will pay the above rates, according to weights, plus sur- tax of 20%.	
134	383	Coarse tissues of jute, abacá, pita, ixtle, henequen, New Zealand fibre (Phormium tenax), or hemp, white, brownish, or coloured, of all textures, up to 32 threads of warp and woof, in a square of 2 centimetres side, and gummed, prepared or adhered to paper, for wall-papering	Kilo, gross	.40
122	384	Tissues of jute, abacá, pita, ixtle, henequen, New Zealand fibre (Phormium tenax), or hemp, white, brownish, or coloured, of smooth texture, not included in the five preceding numbers, and having up to 12 threads in warp and woof in a square of 5 milli- metres side	Square metre	.15
122	385	Fabrics of flax, or of other similar fibres, not included in Nos. 382, 383, and 384, white, brownish, or coloured, of smooth texture, hav- ing up to 12 threads in warp and woof in a square of 5 millimetres side	Square metre	.15
122	386	Fabrics of flax, hemp, and other similar fibres, white, brownish, or coloured, of a smooth texture hav- ing more than 12 threads in warp and woof in a square of 5 millimetres side	Square metre	.22
122	387	Fabrics of flax, hemp, and other similar fibres, white, brownish, or coloured, not of a smooth tex- ture	Square metre	.25
123	388	Fabrics of flax, hemp, and other similar fibres, white, brownish, or coloured, embroidered with wool .	Square metre	.40

53

Notes.	Tariff No.	CLASSIFICATION.	Unit of quantity.	Rate of duty. *Pesos.*
124	389	Fabrics of flax, hemp, and other similar fibres, white, brownish, or coloured, with admixture of tinsel in figures or designs, woven or embroidered	Kilo, legal	2.20
124	390	Fabrics of flax, hemp, and other similar fibres, white, brownish, or coloured, with admixture of precions metal, in showers or threads	Kilo, legal	3.30
125	391	Fabrics of flax, hemp, and other similar fibres, white, brownish, or coloured, with admixture of precions metal, in figures or designs, woven or embroidered	Kilo, legal	5.50

Manufactured articles.

Notes.	Tariff No.	CLASSIFICATION.	Unit of quantity.	Rate of duty.
126	392	Carpets and rugs of pure hemp, jute, or any other similar vegetable fibre, of a smooth texture, twilled, figured, with uncut pile (*rizo*)	Square metre	.28
126	393	Carpets and rugs of pure hemp, jute, or any other similar vegetable fibre, with cut pile (*tripe*)	Square metre	.40
126	394	Carpets and rugs of pure hemp, jute, or any other similar vegetable fibre, with fringes or selvage of wool	Square metre	.45
127	395	Tassels of flax or hemp, jute, or any other similar vegetable fibre, even with cores of other material	Kilo, legal	.70
128	396	Tassels of flax or hemp, jute, or any other similar vegetable fibre, when provided with cords of the same material	Kilo, legal	1.80
139	397	Linen hosiery, even when containing ornaments of other material than precious metal or silk	Kilo, legal	3.00
139	398	Linen hosiery having ornaments of silk	Kilo, legal	3.30
135	399	Linen drawers and shirts for men and boys	Kilo, legal	3.80

Notes.	Tariff No.	CLASSIFICATION.	Unit of quantity.	Rate of duty. *Pesos.*
139	400	Shirts, drawers, corset covers, and other articles of linen network, not specially mentioned, when trimmed with silk	Kilo, legal	4.00
139	401	Undershirts, drawers, corset covers, and other articles of linen network, not specially mentioned, even with trimmings of other material than precious metal or silk	Kilo, legal	3.50
	401A	Linen cravattes	Kilo, legal	2.50
	402	Linen or hemp corsets, even with ribbons and small trimmings other than precious metal	Kilo, legal	3.50
130	403	Linen dress patterns, even with embroidered trimmings or of cotton or linen lace, for ladies and girls	Kilo, legal	2.00
130	404	Linen dress patterns, with trimmings of a tissue containing silk or with skirts or overskirts of cotton or linen lace or point	Kilo, legal	3.00
	405	Curtains, quilts, bedspreads, table covers, furniture covers, and pillow cases of linen or hemp fabric, not embroidered	Kilo, legal	1.40
	406	Curtains, quilts, bedspreads, table covers, furniture covers, and pillow cases of linen or hemp fabric, embroidered	Kilo, legal	2.00
131	407	Rufflings, fringes, galloons, lace trimmings, lace edging, ribbons, and nettings of linen	Kilo, legal	2.50
131	408	Rufflings, fringes, galloons, lace trimmings, lace edging, ribbons, and nettings of linen combined with glass beads, common metal, or paste	Kilo, legal	1.25
	409	Garters and suspenders of linen or hemp, of all kinds, with or without fittings	Kilo, legal	1.50
	410	Linen handkerchiefs, with trimmings of cotton or linen lace	Each	.45
	411	Linen parasols, umbrellas, and sunshades	Each	.66

Notes.	Tariff No.	CLASSIFICATION.	Unit of quantity.	Rate of duty. Pesos.
	412	Linen shirt fronts, collars and cuffs, neither embroidered nor open-worked .... Kilo, legal		2.20
	413	Linen shirt fronts, collars and cuffs, embroidered or open-worked .. Kilo, legal		3.30
	414	Linen shawls up to 26 threads, in warp and woof, in a square of 5 millimetres, side .... Square metre		2.20
	415	Linen shawls exceeding 26 and up to 38 threads, in warp and woof, in a square of 5 millimetres, side . Square metre		3.30
	416	Linen shawls exceeding 38 threads, in warp and woof, in a square of 5 millimetres, side .... Square metre		6.60
	417	Linen or hemp elastic webbings, combined with rubber, of more than 4 centimetres in width.... Kilo, legal		.66
	418	Linen or hemp elastic webbings, combined with rubber, not exceeding 4 centimetres in width ..Kilo, legal		1.00
132	419	Ready-made clothing, not specially mentioned, and separate parts thereof, when sewn, of linen fabrics of all kinds and textures, even when trimmed with lace, embroidery, or common metal, for adults and children .... Kilo, legal		3.30
132	420	Ready-made clothing, not specially mentioned, and separate parts thereof, when sewn, of linen fabrics of all kinds and textures, when trimmed with ribbon or any fabric containing silk, or skirts or over-skirts of cotton or linen lace or point .... Kilo, legal		4.30
133	421	Insertions of linen, open-worked or embroidered with cotton, wool, or linen .... Kilo, legal		2.75
133	422	Insertions of linen, open-worked or embroidered with cotton, wool, or linen, when trimmed with beads of glass, common metal or paste . Kilo, legal		1.70

Notes.	Tariff No.	CLASSIFICATION.	Unit of quantity.	Rate of duty. Pesos.

WOOL. (Note 137.)

Yarn.

	423	Cord of wool not exceeding 10 millimetres in diameter ... .Kilo, legal		2.75
	424	Cord of wool exceeding 10 millimetres in diameter ....Kilo, legal		1.10
	425	Cord of cotton or hemp, covered with wool, not exceeding 10 millimetres in diameter ....Kilo, legal		1.70
	426	Cord of cotton or hemp, covered with wool, exceeding 10 millimetres in diameter ....Kilo, legal		.55
138	427	Worsted or woollen thread, even with admixture of metal thread		
-		and woollen yarn ....Kilo, legal		2.00

Fabrics.

	428	Woollen lace or point of all kinds, and manufacture thereof [1] ...... Kilo, legal		9.00
123 124	430	Woollen fabrics of all textures, even embroidered with wool, cotton, or linen, or interwoven with silk or metal thread, weighing up to 150 grammes per square metre ......Kilo, net	Kilo, net	3.00 3.00
123 124	431	Woollen fabrics of all textures, even embroidered with wool, cotton, or linen, or interwoven with silk or metal thread, weighing more than 150 and up to 450 grammes per square metre ....Kilo, net		4.75
123	432	Woollen fabrics of all textures, even embroidered with wool, cotton, or linen, or interwoven with silk or metal thread, weighing more than 450 grammes per square metre ..Kilo, net		3.20

Manufactured articles.

126	433	Carpets of coarse frieze, plain or twilled, or of fulled wool ......Square metre		.85
126	434	Carpets and rugs of wool, with uncut pile (*rizo*) with warp of hemp or any other material ....Square metre		1.00
126	435	Carpets and rugs of wool, with cut pile (*tripe*), with warp of hemp or any other material ....Square metre		1.70

[1] (Repealed 11 Dec., '08.)

Notes.	Tariff No.	CLASSIFICATION.	Unit of quantity.	Rate of duty. *Pesos.*
126	436	Carpets of corded wool, with warp of hemp or any other material .	Square metre	1.00
129	437	Hosiery or knitted goods of wool or worsted, not specially mentioned, even when trimmed with other material than precious metal or silk	Kilo, legal	3.00
127	438	Tassels of wool, even with core of other material	Kilo, legal	1.10
128	439	Tassels of wool, with cords of the same material	Kilo, legal	2.20
129	440	Undershirts or shirts and drawers of woollen fabric, even with small trimmings of silk	Kilo, legal	3.25
	440A	Woollen cravattes	Kilo, legal	2.50
	441	Woollen corsets, even with ribbons and small trimmings other than of precious metal	Kilo, legal	3.00
130	442	Dress patterns of wool of all kinds, even embroidered with cotton, linen, or wool, or even with trimmings of cotton, linen, wool, silk ribbons, or beads of glass, metal. or paste, for ladies and girls	Kilo, legal	3.50
130	443	Dress patterns of woollen stuffs, mixed with silk in the texture or in the embroidery, even with trimmings of silk or beads of glass, common metal, or paste, for ladies and girls	Kilo, legal	5.00
	444	Woollen curtains ready for use, or with cotton, linen, or woollen lining, even containing embroidery, trimmings, or fittings of other material than precious metal or silk	Kilo, legal	3.50
	445	Ruffling of woollen stuffs, even with woollen lace and small ornaments of silk or of metal thread and fringes, galloons, lace, trimmings, edging, ribbons. and woollen nettings	Kilo, legal	3.30
140	446	Woollen felt. weighing up to 350 grammes per square metre	Kilo, legal	1.10

Notes.	Tariff No.	CLASSIFICATION.	Unit of quantity.	Rate of duty. Pesos.
140	447	Woollen felt, weighing more than 350 grammes per square metre	Kilo, legal	.30
	448	Woollen felt, in endless bands, for machinery, whether imported with the corresponding machinery or not	Kilo, gross	.06
	449	Fringes, galloons, lace trimmings, edgings, ribbons, and woollen nettings, with beads of glass, common metal, or paste	Kilo, legal	2.00
	450	Woollen gloves, neither knitted nor lined	Kilo, legal	3.30
	451	Woollen gloves, not knitted and lined	Kilo, legal	1.70
141	452	Chenille, woollen, even when combined with tinsel	Kilo, legal	2.75
	453	Gaiters and braces of wool, of all kinds, with or without fittings	Kilo, legal	2.00
	454	Woollen umbrellas, parasols and sunshades	Each	1.10
	455	Woollen shawls up to 26 threads in warp and woof, in a square of 5 millimetres, side	Square metre	1.70
	456	Woollen shawls exceeding 26 threads in warp and woof, in a square of 5 millimetres, side	Square metre	2.75
	457	Elastic webbings of wool and rubber exceeding 4 centimetres in width	Kilo, legal	.90
	458	Elastic webbings of wool and rubber not exceeding 4 centimetres in width	Kilo, legal	1.60
132	459	Ready-made clothing, not specially mentioned, and separate parts thereof, sewn, of woollen fabrics of all kinds of texture, even trimmed with materials other than precious metal or silk	Kilo, legal	6.50
132	460	Ready-made clothing, not specially mentioned, and separate parts thereof, when sewn, of woollen fabrics mixed with silk in the texture, in embroidery or trimmings, even with other trimmings than precious metal	Kilo, legal	7.50

Notes.	Tariff No.	CLASSIFICATION.	Unit of quantity.	Rate of duty. Pesos.
	461	Woollen shawls for men (sarapes), imitating those of Saltillo, figured or printed ....Square metre		8.00
133	462	Insertions of woollen fabric, open-worked or embroidered, with cotton, wool, or linen ....Kilo, legal		3.30
133	463	Insertions of woollen fabric, when trimmed with beads of glass, common metal, or paste ....Kilo, legal		2.20

IV.— SILK.

Yarns.

	464	Silk cord ....Kilo, net		17.50
	465	Spun silk, twisted or not, of all kinds, in skeins, balls, or spools .Kilo, net		6.60

Silk fabrics.

	466	Blondes, lace and point, of silk ..Kilo, net		17.50
	467	Silk fabrics of all kinds of texture .Kilo, net		17.50
237	468	Silk bolting cloth ....Kilo, net		5.00

Manufactured articles.

	469	Articles and manufactures not specially mentioned, of knitted or other silk fabric ....Kilo, net		17.50
130	470	Dress patterns of silk fabric, even trimmed with beads of glass, common metal, or paste ....Kilo, net		17.50
	471	Silk umbrellas, parasols, and sunshades .. ..Each		2.50
	472	Shawls of silk up to 26 threads in warp and woof, in a square of 5 millimetres, side ....Kilo, net		18.00
	473	Shawls of silk exceeding 26 and up to 38 threads in warp and woof, in a square of 5 millimetres, side ....Kilo, net		25.00
	474	Shawls of silk. exceeding 38 threads in warp and woof, in a square of 5 millimetres, side ....Kilo, net		34.00
132	475	Silk ready-made clothing, and separate parts thereof, even trimmed with beads of glass, common metal, or paste ....Kilo, net		17.50

Notes.	Tariff No.	CLASSIFICATION.	Unit of quantity.	Rate of duty. Pesos.

V.— SILK WITH ADMIXTURE OF OTHER MATERIALS.

Yarn.

| | 476 | Yarn of silk and wool, even combined with tinsel ....Kilo, net .... | | 3.30 |

Fabrics.

	477	Blondes, lace and point, of silk, trimmed with beads of glass, common metal or paste ....Kilo, net		13.20
	478	Ribbons and insertions of cotton, wool, or linen, embroidered with silk ....Kilo, net		4.00
	479	Ribbons and insertions of cotton, wool, or linen, embroidered with silk, trimmed with beads of glass, common metal, or paste ....Kilo, net		2.75
142	480	Fabrics with warp and woof of cotton, linen, or wool, when having an admixture of silk only in the warp or woof ....Kilo, net		4.75
142	481	Fabrics with warp of silk and woof of cotton, linen, or wool, or vice-versa ....Kilo, net		8.25
142	482	Fabrics with warp of silk and woof of cotton, wool, or linen, with admixture of silk, or vice-versa ....Kilo, net		5.50
	483	Fabrics of cotton, linen, or wool, with admixture of silk, both in the warp and woof, when the silk does not predominate on the surface of the fabric ....Kilo, net		5.50
	484	Fabrics of cotton, linen, or wool, with admixture of silk both in the warp and woof, when the silk predominates on the surface of the fabric ....Kilo, net		8.25
124	485	Silk fabrics combined with cotton, wool, or linen and admixture of tinsel ....Kilo, net		6.00
124	486	Silk fabrics with admixture of tinsel .. ..Kilo, net		7.20
125	487	Silk fabrics combined with cotton,		

Notes.	Tariff No.	CLASSIFICATION.	Unit of quantity.	Rate of duty. *Pesos.*
		wool, or linen and admixture of tinsel .... Kilo, net		11.00
125	488	Silk fabrics with admixture of precions metal .... Kilo, net		17.50

Manufactured articles.

Notes.	Tariff No.	CLASSIFICATION.	Unit of quantity.	Rate of duty.
	489	Articles of silk with admixture of cotton, linen, or wool, not specially mentioned, even embroidered or trimmed with other than precious metal or beads .... Kilo, net		10.00
	490	Articles of silk with admixture of cotton, linen, or wool, not specially mentioned, when trimmed with beads of glass, common metal, or paste .... Kilo, net		9.00
	491	Articles of silk, of all textures, not specially mentioned, trimmed with beads of glass, common metal, or paste .... Kilo, net		13.20
139	492	Manufactured articles of cotton, knitted, with trimmings of silk, not specially mentioned .... Kilo, legal		3.50
139	493	Manufactured articles of linen, wool, or worsted, knitted, with trimmings of silk, not specially mentioned .. .. Kilo, legal		4.00
139	494	Manufactured articles of cotton, linen, or wool, knitted, with admixture of silk in the texture, not specially mentioned, provided the first-mentioned fibres predominate on the surface of the fabric .... Kilo, net		4.50
139	495	Manufactured articles of silk, knitted, with admixture of cotton, linen, or wool in the texture, not specially mentioned, provided the last-mentioned fibres do not predominate on the surface of the fabric .... Kilo, net		8.00
127	496	Silk tassels, even with core of other materials .... Kilo, net		4.50
128	497	Silk tassels, with cords of the same material .... Kilo, net		6.60

Notes.	Tariff No.	CLASSIFICATION.	Unit of quantity.	Rate of duty. Pesos.
	498	Silk tassels, with admixture of cotton, linen, or wool, even with core of any other material and with cords of the same mixed materials	Kilo, net	3.10
	499	Hemp cord, covered with silk	Kilo, net	4.50
	500	Hemp cord, covered with silk, mixed with cotton, linen, or wool.	Kilo, net	3.10
	501	Corsets of silk with an admixture of cotton, linen, or wool	Kilo, net	5.00
130	502	Dress patterns of silk fabrics, mixed with cotton, linen, or wool, even with embroidery or trimmings other than precious metal, or beads of glass, common metal, or paste	Kilo, net	10.00
	503	Sacerdotal ornaments in silk fabrics, in patterns or made up, mixed with cotton, linen, or wool, even embroidered or with galloons of tinsel or admixture of tinsel in the texture	Kilo, legal	10.00
	504	Sacerdotal ornaments in silk fabrics, in patterns or made up, mixed with cotton, linen, or wool, with embroidery or galloons of silver, gilt silver, or an admixture of silver or gilt silver in the texture	Kilo, legal	15.00
	505	Sacerdotal ornaments in silk fabrics, in patterns or made up, even with embroidery or galloons of silver or gilt silver, or an admixture of silver or gilt silver in the texture	Kilo, legal	25.00
	506	Umbrellas, parasols, and sunshades of silk, mixed with cotton, linen, or wool	Each	2.00
	507	Shawls of silk with admixture of cotton, linen, or wool, up to 26 threads in warp and woof, in a square of 5 millimetres to the side	Kilo, net	10.00
	508	Shawls of silk mixed with cotton, linen, or wool, exceeding 26 and		

Notes.	Tariff No.	CLASSIFICATION.	Unit of quantity.	Rate of duty. *Pesos.*
		up to 38 threads in warp and woof, in a square of 5 millimetres to the side .... Kilo, net		15.00
	509	Shawls of silk mixed with cotton, linen, or wool, exceeding 38 threads in warp and woof, in a square of 5 millimetres to the side .... Kilo, net		25.00
	510	Elastic webbings of rubber and pure silk or mixed with cotton, linen, or wool, exceeding 4 centimetres in width .... Kilo, legal		1.50
	511	Elastic webbings of rubber and pure silk or mixed with cotton, linen, or wool, not exceeding 4 centimetres in width .... Kilo, legal		3.50
132	512	Ready-made clothing, not specially mentioned, and parts thereof, of silk, with admixture of cotton, linen, or wool, in the texture or in embroideries even when trimmed with beads of glass, common metal or paste .... Kilo, net		10.00
	513	Shawls for men (sarapes), imitating those of Saltillo figured or painted, of silk with admixture of cotton, wool, or linen .... Kilo, net		15.00
		Artificial or vegetable silk.		
149	514	Yarns, fabrics, and manufactured articles exclusively of vegetable silk or mixed with other vegetable fibres	—	(c)

Art. 1141.   CHEMICAL AND PHARMACEUTICAL PRODUCTS.

143	515	Aniline oil, alizarine, natural or artificial, and anthracene .... . Kilo, gross		.08
144	516	Acetates of alumina, ammonia, lime, copper, chrome, iron, lead, and soda .... Kilo, legal		.06
145	517	Arsenious acid .... Kilo, legal		.02

(c) Duty on similar yarns, fabrics, and manufactured articles of linen, plus a surtax of 20 per cent.

Notes.	Tariff No.	CLASSIFICATION.	Unit of quantity.	Rate of duty.
				Pesos.
146	518	Sulphuric acid	—	Free.
146	519	Hydrochloric and sulphurous acids	100 kilos, gross ..	1.50
147	520	Acetic, boric, citric, chromic, nitric, oxalic, pyroligneous, and tartaric acids ....Kilo, legal		.04
148	521	Liquid acids, not specially mentioned ....Kilo, legal		.10
	522	Acids in crystals or in powder, not specially mentioned ....Kilo, legal		.20
150	523	Size for fabrics, liquid soaps, alkaline sulpho-oleates, and sulporicinates ....Kilo, gross		.04
151	524	Aromatic waters, distilled, not containing alcohol ....Kilo, legal		.55
152	525	Alcohol or spirits of wine ....Kilo, net	.. .	.80
153	526	Amylic, methylic, and methylated alcohol ....Kilo, legal		.10
154	527	Aseptic and antiseptic cotton and gauze ....Kilo, legal		.25
155	528	Ammonia ....Kilo, gross		.01
156	529	Milk sugar ....Kilo, legal		.25
157	530	Varnishes, white and coloured, and blacking and polish, in paste or liquid .... Kilo, legal		.22
160	531	Bicarbonate of potash and of soda.. Kilo, legal		.09
158	532	Medicine chests .. ..Kilo, legal		1.00
159	533	Cases with chemical reagents	—	Free.
160	534	Carbonate of potash or of soda ...Kilo, gross		.02
179	535	Carbide of calcium ....Kilo, gross		.04
161	536	Alkaline cyanides	—	Free.
164	537	Chloral ....Kilo, legal		1.00
165	538	Chlorate of potash or of soda .....Kilo, legal		.07
166	539	Chloroform .... Kilo, legal		1.00
167	540	Chloride or hypochlorite of calcium, soda, or potash, chloride of zinc, and protochloride of tin ....Kilo, gross		.01
	541	Chlorides of gold and platinum ....Kilo, legal		4.00
162	542	Collodion ....Kilo, legal		.50
163	543	Colours, in powder or crystals ....Kilo, gross		.08
163	544	Prepared colours . ...Kilo, gross		.15
168	545	Cream of Tartar ....Kilo, legal		.11
169	546	Creoline, and all kinds of disinfectants, not specially mentioned ..Kilo, legal		.03
170	547	Medicinal drugs and chemical and		

Notes.	Tariff No.	CLASSIFICATION.	Unit of quantity.	Rate of duty. *Pesos.*
		piarmaceutical products, not specially mentioned	Kilo, legal	1.00
171	548	Drugs and preparations of all kinds for veterinary uses	Kilo, legal	.05
172	549	Ether of all kinds	Kilo, legal	.40
173	550	Extracts of dyewoods	Kilo, gross	.08
174	551	Piosphorus, white or red	Kilo, legal	.35
175	552	Wood and wax matches of all kinds	Kilo, legal	1.70
176	553	Hyposulphite of soda	—	Free.
177	554	Medicinal soaps	Kilo, legal	1.00
178	555	Yeast of all kinds	Kilo, legal	.09
180	556	Piotographic dry plates	Kilo, legal	.40
	557	Salt, common or table	Kilo, gross	.02
181	558	Salts and oxides of all substances, not specially mentioned	Kilo, legal	.18
182	559	Saltpetre or nitrate of potasi or soda		Free.
183	560	Silicates of alumina, potasi, or soda	Kilo, gross	.03
184	561	Caustic soda and potash .	Kilo, gross	.01
185	562	Sulpate of copper	—	Free.
185	563	Sulpate of iron and ammonia	Kilo, gross	.01
186	564	Sulpate of alumina, magnesia, potash, and of soda	100 kilos, gross ..	4.50
187	565	Sulpite, bisulpite, and trisulphite of lime, of potasi, and of soda	100 kilos, gross ..	1.50
188	566	Sulpide, bisulpide and tetrachloride of carbon	—	Free.
	566A	Sulpide of calcium	Kilo, legal	.10
	567	Writing ink	Kilo, gross	.12
189	568	Medicinal wines and elixirs	Kilo, net	.45

Art. 1142. SPIRITUOUS, FERMENTED, AND NATURAL BEVERAGES.

190	569	Spirits in earthen or glass vessels	Litre	.75
190	570	Spirits in wooden vessels	Litre	.55
	571	Mineral waters, natural or artificial	Kilo, legal .	.02
191	572	Beer, cider, and refreshing beverages in bottles	Kilo, net . .	.25
191	573	Beer and cider in barrels	Kilo, gross ...	.10
192	574	Bitters of all kinds	Kilo, net .	.45

Notes.	Tariff No.	CLASSIFICATION.	Unit of quantity.	Rate of duty. Pesos.
193	575	Liqueurs ....Kilo, net		.45
	576	Vinegar in wooden vessels ....100 kilos, gross ..		5.50
	577	Vinegar in glass vessels .. ..Kilo, net		.11
194	578	Wines in wooden vessels .... Kilo, gross . . .		.13
194	579	Wine in glass vessels . ... Kilo, net		.25
	580	Sparkling wines . . ..Kilo, net		.65

Art. 1143. PAPER AND PAPER PRODUCTS.

I.— WASTES AND PULP FOR THE MANUFACTURE OF PAPER.

195	581	Refuse and waste of paper and pulp of vegetable fibre in sheets for the manufacture of paper, not dyed, perforated at spaces not exceeding 10 centimetres	—	Free.

II.— PAPER AND CARDBOARD.

196	582	Paper of all kinds weighing up to 50 grammes per square metre ..Kilo, legal		.16
196	583	White paper containing more than 40 per cent. of mechanical wood pulp and weighing more than 50 and not more than 150 grammes per square metre ....100 kilos, legal ..		7.50
196	584	White paper containing up to 40 per cent. of mechanical wood pulp and weighing more than 50 and not more than 150 grammes per square metre ....Kilo, legal		.20
196	585	Paper of dyed pulp, and all paper not specially mentioned, weighing more than 50 and not more than 150 grammes per square metre .... Kilo, legal		.20
196	586	Paper of the natural colour of the pulp, weighing more than 50 and not more than 150 grammes per square metre ....Kilo, legal		.09
196	587	Paper and cardboard of the natural colour of the pulp, weighing more than 150 grammes per square metre ....Kilo, legal		.06

Notes.	Tariff No.	CLASSIFICATION.	Unit of quantity.	Rate of duty. *Pesos.*
196	588	White paper and cardboard weighing more than 150 grammes per square metre .. ..Kilo, legal		.15
196	589	Paper and cardboard of dyed pulp, weighing more than 150 grammes per square metre ....Kilo, legal		.12

III.— MANUFACTURED PAPERS.

Notes.	Tariff No.	CLASSIFICATION.	Unit of quantity.	Rate of duty. *Pesos.*
197	590	Advertisements, printed, engraved, or lithographed on paper or cardboard, unframed ....Kilo, legal		.22
198	591	Paper cut in strips not exceeding 5 centimetres in width ....Kilo, legal		.22
199	592	Paper cut in sheets, of less than 45 centimetres on any of its sides, ruled paper, and water-marked paper ....Kilo, legal		.33
200	593	Paper with monogram, letter heads printed, engraved, or lithographed ....Kilo, legal		1.10
201	594	Paper, mottled, coloured, embossed, and glazed, not bronzed, gilt, or silvered ....Kilo, legal		.15
201	595	Paper, mottled, coloured, embossed and glazed, when bronzed, gilt, or silvered in whole or in part ..Kilo, legal		.30
201	596	Paper, mottled, coloured, embossed, and glazed, combined with cloth of silk, or any other material not specially mentioned ....Kilo, legal		.55

IV.— MANUFACTURED ARTICLES.

Notes.	Tariff No.	CLASSIFICATION.	Unit of quantity.	Rate of duty. *Pesos.*
202	597	Manufactured articles of paper, not specially mentioned ....Kilo, legal		.45
203	598	Geographical, topographical, and nautical charts, wall pictures, not framed. for schools. drawing and copying books, with samples, for primary schools, books, periodicals of all kinds, and printed music, unbound	—	Free.
204	599	Pictures, printed, engraved, or lithographed, oleographs, and		

Notes.	Tariff No.	CLASSIFICATION.	Unit of quantity.	Rate of duty. Pesos.
		paintings, on paper or card-board ....Kilo, legal	......	.90
	600	Blank or ruled books, with card-board, leather, or cloth binding, even with metal corners and clasps other than of gold, silver, and platinum ....Kilo, legal	......	1.40
	601	Books, printed or blank, bound in velvet, shell, ivory, tortoise shell, gutta-percha wood, celluloid, or other than precious metal ......Kilo, legal	......	2.00
	602	Books and music, printed or manu-script, bound in cardboard, leather, or cloth ....Kilo, gross	......	.05
	603	Playing cards ....Kilo, legal	......	3.00
238	604	Paper bags, for packing, even with labels and names, not specially mentioned ....Kilo, legal	......	.25
	604A	Paper bags, imprinted ....Kilo, legal	......	.45
	605	Common envelopes not specified ..Kilo, legal	......	.45
	605A	Paper envelopes, with monogram, name-card, or other impression, although an advertisement .....Kilo, legal	......	1.10
		Return-notice if not delivered is not considered as such printing.		

Art. 1144.   MACHINERY AND APPARATUS.

Notes.	Tariff No.	CLASSIFICATION.	Unit of quantity.	Rate of duty.
205	606	Fire-extinguishing apparatus, with not more than six extra charges .	—	Free.
206	607	Manifolding appliances ....Kilo, gross	......	.06
	608	Bulbs for the manufacture of lamps for incandescent electric lighting, switches, light extin-guishers, contacts and their pins, fuses, circuit closers, rings, and safety switches ....Kilo, gross	......	.11
207	609	Scientific instruments and appara-tus		Free.
208	610	Automatic toys operated by string, steam, or electricity ....Kilo, legal	......	.80
209	611	Electric arc lamps ....Kilo, gross	......	.06
	611A	Incandescent electric lamps ......Kilo, gross	......	.22
210	612	Machinery of all kinds for mann-facturing industries, agriculture,		

54

Notes.	Tariff No.	CLASSIFICATION.	Unit of quantity.	Rate of duty. Pesos.
		mining, and the arts, not specially mentioned, and separate parts thereof, and extra pieces	100 kilos, gross	1.65
		(The several pieces which form one installation of machinery, in whole or part, may be imported in separate lots, at the above rate, where so permitted by the Department of Hacienda in view of the circumstances of each case, upon complying with the requisites established by the Department.)		
	613	Movements for clocks of all kinds	Kilo, legal	.70
	614	Movements for repeating watches	Each	6.00
	615	Movements for watches other than repeating	Each	1.25
	616	Clocks for towers and public buildings	Kilo, gross	.02
	617	Table or wall clocks of all kinds	Kilo, legal	1.00
211	618	Repeating watches of gold, or gold filled, even containing precious stones	Each	16.00
211	619	Watches, other than repeating, of gold or gold filled, even containing precious stones	Each	8.00
	620	Repeating watches of silver or other material, except gold, when containing incrustations or parts of gold or gold filled	Each	6.50
212	621	Watches, not repeating, of silver or other materials, except gold	Each	1.25
	622	Watches, not repeating, of silver, common metal, or other material, containing incrustations of gold or parts of gold or gold filled	Each	2.50

Art. 1145.   VEHICLES.

| 213 | 623 | Carts, cars, wagons, and all kinds of vehicles, not specially mentioned, for commerce, agriculture, and the transportation of merchandise, when the weight of each does not exceed 200 kilos | Kilo, net | .22 |

Notes.	Tariff No.	CLASSIFICATION.	Unit of quantity.	Rate of duty Pesos.
213	624	Carts, cars, wagons, and all kinds of vehicles, not specially mentioned, for commerce, agriculture, and the transportation of merchandise, when the weight of each exceeds 200 kilos ......100 kilos, net		5.50
		(The duty on the first 200 kilos of each vehicle is $0.22 per kilo, and each additional kilo pays its corresponding rate.)		
214	625	Wheelbarrows of one or more wheels, separate parts thereof, and extra pieces, when not fit for other purposes ....100 kilos, gross ..		1.65
215	626	Railroad cars and coaches of all kinds, and extra pieces thereof, when not fit for any other purpose		Free.
216	627	Carriages and automobiles of all kinds, not specially mentioned, used for the exclusive transportation of persons, weighing not more than 250 kilos . .. .Kilo, net		.66
216	628	Carriages and automobiles of all kinds, not specially mentioned, used for the exclusive transportation of persons, weighing more than 250 and not exceeding 750 kilos ....Kilo, net		.55
		(The duty on the first 250 kilos of each vehicle is $0.66 per kilo, and each additional kilo, up to the limit of the weight specified, shall pay $0.55.)		
216	629	Carriages and automobiles of all kinds, not specially mentioned, used for the exclusive transportation of persons, weighing more than 750 kilos . . ..Kilo, net		.45
		(The duty on the first 250 kilos of each vehicle is 0 66 peso per kilo, and each of the 500 kilos following shall pay 0 55 peso, and each additional kilo shall pay 0.45 peso.)		

Notes.	Tariff No.	CLASSIFICATION.	Unit of quantity.	Rate of duty. *Pesos.*
217	630	Carriages, skeleton, not upholstered or painted, weighing up to 250 kilos ....Kilo, net		.33
217	631	Carriages, skeleton, not uphol- stered or painted, weighing more than 250 kilos and not exceeding 750 kilos .... Kilo, net		.22
		(The duty on each of the first 250 each vehicle shall be 0.33 peso per kilo, and each additional kilo, up to the limit specified, shall pay 0.22 peso.)		
217	632	Carriages, skeleton, not uphol- stered or painted, weighing more than 750 kilos ....Kilo, net		.11
		(The duty on each of the first 250 kilos of each vehicle shall be 0.33 peso per kilo, each of the following 500 kilos shall pay 0.22 peso, and each additional kilo shall pay 0.11 peso.)		
	633	Craft of all kinds	—	Free.
	634	Shafts or front running gear, and separate wheels for wagons or carriages ....Kilo, net		.30
	634A	Ruber tires for vehicles, although some parts are of leather .....Kilo, net		0.66
	635	Tricycles without rubber tires ... Kilo, net		.30
	636	Velocipedes of all kinds, not spe- cially mentioned, and separate and extra parts thereof ....Kilo. net		1.10

Art. 1146.   ARMS AND EXPLOSIVES.

	637	Side arms of all kinds and detached blades thereof . ... Kilo, legal		.90
	638	Firearms, repeating or breech-load- ing, of all kinds, and extra parts thereof ....Kilo, legal		2.00
	639	Firearms, other than repeating or breech-loading, of all kinds, and extra parts thereof .. . .. Kilo, legal		.60
	640	Loaded and unloaded cartridges and percussion caps for firearms Kilo, gross		.60
	641	Primers of all kinds for explosives Kilo, gross		.06

Notes.	Tariff No.	CLASSIFICATION.	Unit of quantity.	Rate of duty. Pesos.
218	642	Dynamite, blasting powder, pyroxylin, or gun-cotton, and other explosives, not specially mentioned .	100 kilos, gross ..	3.30
	643	Fireworks	Kilo, gross	.40
	644	Slow matches and quick matches for mines	100 kilos, gross ..	3.30
218	645	Powder, other than blasting	Kilo, gross	.60

Art. 1147. MISCELLANEOUS ARTICLES.

	646	Fans with ribs of wood	Kilo, legal	1.40
219	647	Lubricating oils	Kilo, gross	.06
	648	Hat frames of all kinds	Each	.30
	649	Articles .of tortoise shell, ivory, or mother-of-pearl, with ornaments of skins or cloth containing silk, not specially mentioned	Kilo, legal	2.50
	650	Articles of all materials, not specially mentioned, ornamented with skins or cloth containing silk	Kilo, legal	.75
	651	Articles of all kinds of materials, not specially mentioned, with ornaments or attachments of gold, silver, or platinum	Kilo, legal	6.00
220	652	Articles not specially mentioned, of gutta-percha and of celluloid, oiled and varnished cloths	Kilo, legal	.45
221	653	Articles, not specially mentioned. for artificial flowers	Kilo, legal	1.70
	654	Rubber belts for machinery, whether they are imported with the corresponding machinery or not	Kilo, gross	.11
	655	Walking sticks and whips. not specially mentioned, without ornaments of precious metal	Kilo, legal	1.40
	656	Buttons covered or woven with silk or with fabrics mixed with silk	Kilo, legal	1.50
	657	Buttons covered with fabric not mixed with silk	Kilo, legal	.50
	658	Caps of all kinds and materials with or without visors	Each	.55
	659	Paint boxes of all kinds	Kilo, legal	.30

Notes.	Tariff No.	CLASSIFICATION.	Unit of quantity.	Rate of duty. Pesos.
	660	Travelling baskets with table accessories ....Kilo, legal		1.00
	661	Rubber hose, even combined with cloth ....Kilo, legal		.12
	662	Masks of all kinds ....Each		.30
	663	Sieves and strainers of silk, horsehair, leather, or wire ....Kilo, legal		.30
	664	Belts, not specially mentioned, not containing precious metal ......Kilo, legal		.75
	665	Cushions, mattresses, and pillows, filled with feathers, when the lining does not contain silk ....Kilo, legal		1.25
	666	Cushions, mattresses, and pillows, filled with feathers, when the lining contains silk .. ..Kilo, net		4.50
	667	Cushions, mattresses, and pillows, filled with any material, not specially mentioned, when the lining does not contain silk .... .Kilo, legal		.80
	668	Cushions, mattresses, and pillows, filled with any material, not specially mentioned, when the lining contains silk ....Kilo, net		3.00
222	669	Collections of all kinds for educational purposes .... —		Free.
	670	Numismatical, geological, or zoological collections for museums, &c.		Free.
	671	Patterns (uppers) of slippers, shoes, gaiters, of cloth not containing silk ... .Kilo, legal		1.00
	672	Patterns (uppers) of slippers, shoes, gaiters, of cloth containing silk .... Kilo, net		9.00
	673	Transparent curtains of coloured cloth .... .Kilo, legal		.55
223	674	Strings for musical instruments . Kilo, legal		1.00
	675	Artificial teeth of all substances .Kilo, legal		4.00
	676	Designs, moulds, patterns, or models for artistic and industrial purposes .. .. —		Free.
	677	Packing of all kinds and materials for machinery ....Kilo, legal		.04
	678	Frames for parasols and umbrellas,		

Notes.	Tariff No.	CLASSIFICATION.	Unit of quantity.	Rate of duty. Pesos.
		with handles other than of precious metal ....Kilo, legal		1.00
	679	Artificial flowers of cloth not containing silk ....Kilo, legal		4.00
	680	Artificial flowers and feathers of silk or cloth containing silk ....Kilo, legal		9.00
226	681	Linings of all kinds for hats .....Kilo, net		2.25
	682	Hand bellows and feather dusters..Kilo, legal		.50
227	683	Sheaths of all kinds for umbrellas and parasols, not containing silk ....Kilo, legal		.60
	684	Mucilage for offices, rubber erasers, sealing wax, and wafers ....Kilo, legal		.50
	685	Tools of all kinds ....100 kilos, legal		5.50
	686	Ice	—	Free.
	687	Rubber footwear, even containing cloth ....Kilo, legal		1.00
	688	Rubber in sheets, combined with cloth ....Kilo, legal		.10
	689	Caoutchouc prepared for dentists .Kilo, legal		3.00
224	690	Sanitary water-closets and urinals, and separate and extra parts thereof, when not fit for any other purpose ....Kilo, gross		.10
	691	Musical instruments ....Kilo, legal		.55
	692	Soap, perfumed ....Kilo, legal		1.00
	693	Soap, not perfumed ....Kilo, legal		0.25
228	694	Sheets of asbestos, cardboard, and tarred tow, for roofing ....Kilo, gross		.04
229	695	Miners' lamps	—	Free.
	696	Pencil-holders and penholders, not specially mentioned, not containing precious metals ....Kilo, legal		.50
230	697	Type, rulers, chases, dashes, rollers, moulds, galleys, composing sticks, and other appliances for printing and lithographing ....100 kilos, gross		1.50
	698	Memorandum books of real or imitation slate ....Kilo, legal		.70
231	699	Billiard tables of any material, not including cloth and attachments .Kilo, gross		.40
225	700	Toilet and sewing cases, of all kinds, not specially mentioned, with fittings ....Kilo, legal		2.00

Notes.	Tariff No.	CLASSIFICATION.	Unit of quantity.	Rate of duty. Pesos.
	701	Tapestry, unfinished or finished, on canvas, felt, or cloth, not containing silk, not specially mentioned ....Kilo, legal		1.00
232	702	Perfumery ....Kilo, legal		1.25
233	703	Artificial plants ....Kilo, legal		1.25
234	704	Ready-made clothing, of oilcloth ..Kilo, legal		2.50
	705	Game bags ....Kilo, legal		.90
	706	Felt hats, unfinished, without fittings or trimmings ....Each		.75
	707	Hats of esparto, shavings, prepared cotton texture, or paper pulp, unfinished ....Each		0.25
	707A	Hats of esparto, shavings, prepared cotton texture or paper pulp, unfinished or with fittings or trimmings other than feather, silk, or articles containing silk ....Each		.50
	708	Hats of all kinds, not specially mentioned, and hats known as "jipijapa" or Panama hats, or imitation thereof, with or without fittings or trimmings ......Each		1.50
	709	Hats, not specially mentioned, unfinished, without fittings or trimmings ....Each		.50
	710	Hats or caps for miners or firemen .	—	Free.
235	711	Oilcloth of all kinds .. ..Kilo, gross		.33
236	712	Tents of all kinds, not including the poles for setting same ......Kilo, gross		.22
	713	Black ink for printing purposes ..	—	Free.

BOOK XXIII.

CORPORATE BOND LAW.[1]

(Law of 29 November, 1897, as amended.)

CHAPTER 1.

THE TEXT OF THE LAW.

Art. 1147A. THE PRESIDENT OF THE REPUBLIC has been pleased to address to me the following decree:

PORFIRIO DÍAZ, Constitutional President of the United States of Mexico, to the inhabitants thereof — Know ye: That the Congress of the Union has seen fit to address to me the following decree: The Congress of the United States of Mexico decrees:

ARTICLE 1.— Railroad, mining and public works companies, as well as all other joint stock companies, will be allowed to issue, subject to this law, obligations or bonds with or without special guarantees.

These bonds or obligations will be considered for all legal purposes as personal property, even when guaranteed by mortgage; they will confer equal rights on their holders without any preference whatever, and they will simply represent the individual share of each bondholder in the debt constituted by the contract which gives rise to the issue, which will nevertheless preserve the judicial character given to it by the laws.

ARTICLE 2.— The obligations may be issued either in a specific name or to bearer, and they will be subject to all the

[1] This Bond Law, borrowed from the " Mexican Year Book," of 1909, is rendered in full, in the form in which it was enacted, with the amendment to Art. 18. and the added Articles 19 and 20, translated by the author.

provisions relating to the shares of joint stock companies which are contained in the three first sections of Article **180** and in Articles 181 and 182 of the Commercial Code of **the** 15th of September, 1889.[1]

ARTICLE 3.— No agreement will be allowed for the obligations to be redeemed by drawings at any price above that of the issue at par, or with any premium or bonus, unless they comply with the following requisites: —

    (1) That the interest payable to all the bondholders shall not be less than 4 per cent. per annum.

    (2) That the sum which according to the contract is to be from time to time devoted to the redemption of the obligations and payment of interest, shall be the same during the whole period stipulated for such redemptions.

        Any bondholder will have authority to demand the cancellation of the whole issue that may be made contrary to the provisions of this article.

ARTICLE 4.— The obligations may be issued by public subscription or in accordance with special contracts, which must always be recorded in a public deed (*escritura pública*).

When the obligations are issued by public subscription it must be preceded by the publication in the official periodical, and any other in the place of residence of the company, of a notice which will set forth: —

    (1) The name, object and residence of the company, with date of the constitution thereof, citing the deed of association or the records of the general meeting by which it was organised.

    (2) The date of the general meeting of shareholders in which the issue was decided on, or else a reference to the deed of association that authorises such issue without the necessity of a resolution by the general meeting.

[1] See Arts. 631-632.

(3) The amount of the obligations previously issued, with an indication of their principal conditions respecting guarantees, interest and dates of redemption.

(4) The conditions of the subscription, one of which must be that the subscribers at once pay into some bank or commercial house at least 10 per cent. of the amount under subscription.

(5) The number and nominal value of the obligations, the interest payable thereon and dates for such payment, as well as the dates, conditions and methods under which the redemption of the obligation is to be carried out.

(6) The purpose to which the proceeds of the issue are to be devoted whenever it is intended to present it as a guarantee or security for the debt.

(7) The special guarantees that are offered to the bondholders.

(8) A balance-sheet of the company specially prepared in view of the issue of obligations.

(9) The amount that will annually be placed by the company at the disposal of the representative of the bondholders for the payment of his own remuneration and the expenses incurred in the execution of his office.

This notice will be inserted in the subscription lists and in the event of any of the above requisites being omitted from said notice, the tribunal will have power to declare the issue null and void on petition of any of the bondholders.

ARTICLE 5.— No issue of bonds shall be made for any sum larger than the assets shown in the last approved balance-sheet; but, nevertheless, companies will be allowed to issue bonds even in excess of such assets when they represent the value or price of the property or securities whose purchase is contracted for and is the cause of the issue.

ARTICLE 6.— The debtor company will convene the bond-holders to a general meeting within the thirty days following the date on which the subscription to the bonds is closed.

The call for such meeting must be published in the official periodical and in another one in the residence of the company for at least eight days before the day on which the meeting is to be held, and it will specify the day, hour and place of the meeting.

The meeting will be held as legally opened with an attendance of bondholders who represent more than the half of the amount subscribed; but in the event of the non-attendance of a sufficient number of subscribers to obtain this representation, the call will be repeated under the same conditions as the first, and the meeting will be held, whatever may be the number of bondholders present or the amount represented.

The president or vice-president of the company which makes the issue will preside over the meeting, and, with the approval of the same, he will appoint a secretary and two tellers from among the bondholders present.

Each bondholder will have a vote in the meeting for each bond that he may have subscribed for and the resolutions will be passed by a majority of the bonds represented.

ARTICLE 7.— The objects of the meeting referred to in the preceding article will be as follows: —

(1) To prove that the entire amount of the bonds has been subscribed for, and at least 10 per cent. of their value has been paid into some bank or mercantile house.

(2) To decide by a unanimous vote of the subscribers, and in the event of the whole of the bonds not being subscribed for, whether the issue shall be reduced to the amount already subscribed, always provided that the company making the issue accepts such resolution.

(3) To elect a general representative for the bondholders, who may be one of themselves or an outside person, or else to appoint a committee who shall represent the whole of the bondholders.

(4) To approve the regulations to which the general representative or committee are to be subject, specifying the time that they are to continue in office, the remuneration, in the case of its being allowed, the way in which the temporary absence of the general representative or member of the committee is to be covered, and the regulations for the calling and opening of the general meeting as well as the functions that are to be exercised by such meetings, and, generally, everything that relates to the joint interests of the bondholders.

The offices of general representative or member of the committee, notwithstanding any stipulation to the contrary, are revocable.

ARTICLE 8.— The general representative or committee of the bondholders will have the following powers: —

(1) To execute in the name of the bondholders the contract in which their rights are set forth, always taking care that it is done by public instrument and registered in accordance with law.

(2) To execute all other contracts and cancellations that may be necessary in accordance with the stipulations and condition of the issue, taking care that they are registered whenever so required by law.

(3) The provisions of this article shall not deprive the bondholders of the right of proceeding individually and by executive summary suit for obtaining the payment of the coupons that may become due or of the principal due to each one by

redemption, and the summary suit may be entered after proving the authenticity of the respective document by comparison with its original; but this requisite will not be exacted if on demanding payment from the proper person such document is not impugned as being false.

(4) To call the general meetings in accordance with the forms and conditions provided in the regulations.

(5) To attend the general meeting of the shareholders of the debtor company with the right to take part in the discussion but not to vote, and likewise to inspect all the books and documents that are placed at the disposal of said shareholders. For this purpose he must be cited to the general meeting in the same form as the shareholders.

(6) To represent the bondholders, judicially, either in person or by attorney, in all matters that refer to the exercise of their joint right.

The powers conferred by this Article on the general representative or the committee of bondholders exclusively pertain to them and cannot be exercised directly by the bondholders, except in the cases foreseen under Articles 3 and 4 of this law.

ARTICLE 9.— In the absence of any special provision in the regulations referred to in Section 4 of Article 7, the bondholders representing at least a fourth part of the bonds subscribed for, will have authority to take judicial proceedings for the purpose of obliging the general representative or committee to comply with their duty and demand that a general meeting be called. This having been solicited, notice of the meeting and of the order of the day will be issued at least three days after the petition, so that it can be held within the thirty days following.

ARTICLE 10.— In the event of the permanent absence of the general representative or of any member of the committee, his place will be filled in accordance with the provisions of the regulation referred to in Section 4 of Article 7, and if for any reason it should be found impossible to proceed in that form, any one of the bondholders may apply to the judicial authority in order that it may appoint a temporary representative, who shall without delay call a general meeting of the bondholders, which will proceed to the election of a new representative.

ARTICLE 11.— The debtor company shall have no power to dispose, either. wholly or in part, of the funds proceeding from the issue of obligations until the general meeting referred to in Article 6 has been held and the instrument under which the rights of the bondholders are secured, has been signed and registered by the general representative or committee of the bondholders.

The bank or mercantile house with which the funds have been deposited will satisfy itself of the fulfilment of this provision under its own responsibility, and in case of doubt, it may, before delivering such funds, demand the explicit consent of the general representative or committee of bondholders.

ARTICLE 12.— Whenever the obligations have been issued under special contracts, they will comply with the requisites referred to in Sections 1, 2, 3, 5, 6, 7, 8 and 9 of Article 4, and the regulation referred to in Section 4 of Article 7 must be prepared and set forth in a public instrument before the obligations are issued.

When the obligations are to be issued in favour of a company, both the aforesaid regulations as well as the appointments that are to be made, will be valid and binding on all the shareholders, always provided that they are approved by the majority of these, unless otherwise provided by the by-laws of said company.

ARTICLE 13.— The wording of the bonds will succinctly set forth the data that are required for the notices referred to in Sections 1, 5 and 7 of Article 4, as well as the date and place in which the contract is executed authorising the issue, the date and place of registry of such contract and the minutes of the first general meeting of shareholders. The bonds will be signed by the legal representative of the debtor company and countersigned by the representative of the bondholders.

ARTICLE 14.— Every contract authorising the issue of obligations and the minutes of the first general meeting of the holders thereof, if the issue be made by public subscription, will be inscribed in the Commercial Registry of the place in which the debtor company has its residence.

ARTICLE 15.— Articles 173, 203, 204, 205, 210 and 211 of the Commercial Code of the 15th of September, 1889, will apply to the general meetings of the bondholders as far as they are not contrary to this law and to the regulations that must be issued in accordance with Section 4, Article 7.

ARTICLE 16.— In the event of the bankruptcy of a company that has issued obligations of the class provided for in Article 3, they shall only appear amongst the liabilities for the amounts due and unpaid, and for the sum that they may amount to, after deducting from their present value the instalments not yet due. This deduction will be made at the nominal rate of interest stipulated with respect to such obligations.

ARTICLE 17.— In the event of the bankruptcy of the debtor company, the bondholders cannot be compelled to pay instalments on the obligations that may be due at the date of bankruptcy.

The holders of bonds already issued, or whose issue may have been contracted for in the Republic before the date of the present law, will enjoy the benefits thereof as far as it is not contrary to the legally executed agreements with the debtor companies, and always provided that they previously appoint their general representative or committee.

ARTICLE 18.— Obligations issued in foreign countries by corporations or companies (*empresas*) established in the Republic shall be given effect therein, if they possess the following requisites:

I. That the laws of the country in which they are executed have been observed in regard to the external form or solemnities of the contract which authorized their issuance;

II. That their issuance was made in accordance with laws of the country in which they were issued;

III. That the two foregoing circumstances are proven by a certificate that the contract was executed and the issue was made in accordance with the laws of the respective country, issued by the Mexican Minister in said country, or in the absence of a diplomatic representative, by the Mexican Consul;

IV. That the contract which authorizes the issue shall be protocolized in the Republic, and inscribed in the Public Register of Commerce in accordance with the provisions of paragraph 14 of Art. 21 of the Code of Commerce (see Art. 954);

V. That if said obligations are secured by a mortgage, the latter shall be registered in accordance with the laws then in force in the State, Federal District, or Territory in which the property is located. (Amendment of 4 June, 1902.)

ARTICLE 19.— The rights and obligations arising from the contract shall be governed by the laws of the place where it was executed, provided that the same are not contrary to prohibitive Mexican laws or to the public order, although the

55

Republic, unless it is expressly stipulated in the contract that it shall be governed by the Mexican Law. Obligations secured by the mortgage of real estate located in the Republic shall be governed by the Mexican laws in respect to everything concerning the mortgage guarantee. (Amendment of 4 June, 1902.)

ARTICLE 20.— The Mexican tribunals shall in all cases be competent and have jurisdiction over controversies which may arise in respect to obligations contracted in accordance with this law. (Amendment of 4 June, 1902.)

BOOK XXIV.

BOOK OF DOCUMENTS AND FORMS.

CHAPTER 1.

LEGAL FORMS IN SPANISH AND ENGLISH.

Art. 1148. Remarks on Mexican Legal Forms.— The legal instruments reproduced in the following pages are those in most general use in Mexico, and in all instances contain and illustrate the requisites of such instruments under Mexican law. Several forms of promissory notes, with their respective endorsements, are shown, together with a draft and a bill of exchange, and are in the form commonly in use in civil and commercial transactions. The forms of petitions for patents, trademarks, etc., are taken from the Regulations of the respective laws; naturally they are but outlines, and require in each instance of practical use to be completed by a competent expert. The same is true of the other forms, such as powers of attorney, deed of conveyance, etc., which because of the manifold variety of clauses they may contain under variant circumstances, cannot serve except as models to be followed in general. But they all conform with the requirements of the Mexican Law, in respect of all " external and internal solemnities," conformity with which is a requisite of validity. Naturally it will require a lawyer or some one quite familiar with the Spanish language and with the legal formalities of Mexican documents, to adapt the forms to particular instances and concrete cases, where special clauses are required. Reference to the Index under " Special Powers," will indicate all instances in the codes and laws where special clauses are required for certain acts in Powers of Attorney; and the Index will also give ready reference to all places in the text where the legal requisites of all kinds of instruments are defined. Where the lawyer reader is yet unable to satisfy himself as to the proper language to use in any case, recourse must be had to a specialist in the matter. But it is believed that a careful study of the translations accompanying each instrument will enable the intelligent reader to select his own form and adapt it to all practical purposes. As stated in the Preface, the Author will be pleased to be of any service to those using this Book who may wish such assistance.

Art. 1149. No. 1. PAGARÉ — PROMISSORY NOTE, AND ENDORSEMENT.[1]

Pagaré á la órden del Señor Juan Tenorio en México el dia 16 de Septiembre de 1910, la cantidad de Mil Pesos, en moneda fuerte del cuño corriente, valor recibido (*or* en cuenta, etc.).

México, á 2 de Abril de 1910.

Manuel Perezoso.

ENDORSEMENT.

Páguese á la órden del Sr. Quién Sabe, valor recibido en efectivo. México, 5 de Mayo de 1910.

Juan Tenorio.

Art. 1150. No. 1. TRANSLATION.

I will pay to the order of Mr. Juan Tenorio, in Mexico on the 16th day of September, 1910, the sum of One Thousand Pesos, in current silver money, for value received (or on account, etc.).

Mexico, April 2, 1910.

(Signed) Manuel Perezoso.

---

[1] Both a note and its endorsements must recite the consideration given, or transaction out of which it arose, unless executed by one merchant in favor of another merchant; such recital may be briefly: "for value received," "on account," "value understood," or other statement of the origin of the debt. Both must be dated.

Pay to the order of Mr. Quién Sabe, for value received in cash. Mexico, May 5th, 1910.

Art. 1151. No. 2. PAGARÉ — NOTE, WITH INTEREST FROM MATURITY, AND WAIVER OF PRESCRIPTION.

Pagaré á la órder del Sr. Fulano de Tal, en esta Ciudad y el día 16 de Septiembre de 1910, la suma de Mil Pesos, por valor recibido en efectivo á mi entera satisfacción, en calidad de préstamo mercantil.

Si no fuere puntualmente cubierta á su vencimiento la suma que este documento expresa, pagaré además de ella el interés que corresponda desde la fecha del vencimiento hasta que sea totalmente cubierta, á razón de seis por ciento anual, haciendo formal renuncia de la prescripción y de la fracción I del Art. 1044 del Código de Comercio que la establece.

México, á 2 de Abril de 1910.   Mengano de Otrosí.

Art. 1152.   No. 2. TRANSLATION.

I will pay to the order of Mr. Fulano de Tal, in this City on the 16th day of September, 1910, the sum of One Thousand Pesos, for value received in cash to my entire satisfaction, by way of mercantile loan.   If the amount which this instrument expresses shall not be punctually paid at its maturity, I will further pay interest accruing from the date of maturity until it is fully paid, at the rate of six per cent. per annum, and making formal waiver of prescription and of clause I of Art. 1044 of the Commercial Code which establishes it.

Mexico, April 2, 1910.   (Signature.)

Art. 1153. No. 3. NOTE, PAYABLE IN INSTALLMENTS, WITH COLLATERAL SECURITY.

*PAGAREMOS de mancomún é insólidum á la órden del Sr   .
    la cantidad de   que en efectivo
á nuestra entera satisfacción hemos recibido de él para pagárselos*

en moneda de plata corriente, en abonos ....de á........
...............que pondremos en casa del acreedor, comenzando
............de la fecha: si faltásemos á........abonos, se dará por
vencido todo el plazo y haremos el pago en una sola partida de lo
que resultemos deber, causando desde la fecha en que se falte al primer
abono, el interés..........mensual, hasta la completa solución; si
faltásemos al pago en los términos estipulados, pagaremos al Sr.
...................como perjuicios ó pena convencional............
á cuyo efecto renunciamos los artículos 1313, 1314, 1316 y 1317 del
Código Civil, consintiendo en ser requeridos por suerte principal y
pena, conforme á lo dispuesto en el artículo 1022, fracción 2ª del
Código de Procedimientos, del que renunciamos expresamente la frac-
ción 4ª del mismo artículo del citado Código. Consentimos en ser
compelidos por la vía ejecutiva, si así conviniere al acreedor, á cuyo
efecto renunciamos el artículo 325 del citado Código de Procedimientos.

Para garantía del pago, el Sr. ....afecta al pago
las existencias, útiles y enseres de...................cuyo comercio
es de su absoluta propiedad, libre de todo gravamen, y así lo con-
servará hasta la solución de este adeudo, sujetándose á lo prevenido
en los artículos 414 y 416 del Código Penal, si apareciere no ser dueño
legítimo de dicha propiedad, la negare ó afectare en manera alguna.

Hacemos presente que en caso de litigio no tendremos otra excep-
ción que exponer que la de pago, justificándola con los recibos firmados
precisamente por el Sr............... y de no presentarlos al ser
requeridos de pago, no se nos admitirá ninguna otra prueba, á cuyo
fin renunciamos los artículos 361, 362, 363, 1048 y 1049 del mencionado
Código de Procedimientos.

Renunciamos la excepción de dinero no entregado, pues declaramos
haberlo recibido á nuestra entera satisfacción.

Y para sus efectos firmamos el presente en..........á.............
de.......... de 19..

Art. 1154. No. 3. TRANSLATION.

We will pay, jointly and severally, to the order of Mr.
————, the sum of ——— Pesos, which we have received
from him in cash to our entire satisfaction, and which we
will pay to him in current silver money in ——— installments of ——— Pesos, which we will deliver in the house of
the creditor, beginning ——— after the date; if we should
fail to make ——— installments, the entire term will be
taken as matured, and we will pay the balance which may
be due in a single payment, together with interest at the
rate of ——— per cent. a month from the date of default

on the first installment until the entire payment is made; if we should fail to make payment within the stipulated terms, we will pay to Mr. ———, as damages or conventional penalty ——— Dollars, and to this effect we renounce Articles 1313, 1314, 1316 and 1317 of the Civil Code, and agree that we may be sued for the principal debt and penalty in accordance with the provisions of Article 1022, fraction 2, of the Code of Procedure, and we expressly waive fraction 4 of the said Article of said Code. We consent to be compelled by executive suit, if the creditor so elects, for which purpose we renounce Article 324 of the said Code of Procedure.

As a guaranty of the payment, Mr. ——— subjects to the payment all of the stock, tools and implements of ———, which is his absolute property free from all encumbrance; and he will so keep it until the payment of this debt, subjecting himself to the provisions of Articles 414 and 416 of the Penal Code, if it should appear that he is not the lawful owner of said property or should deny or encumber it in any way. We declare that in the event of suit we will interpose no other defense than that of payment, evidenced by receipts signed by Mr. ———, and if we should not produce the same upon being sued for payment, no other proof· can be offered by us, to which end we renounce Articles 361, 362, 363, 1048 and 1049 of the said Code of Procedure. We renounce the defense of money not delivered, as we declare that we have received it to our entire satisfaction.

For the foregoing purposes we sign these presents in ——— on the ——— day of ———, 19—.

(Signatures.)

Art. 1155. No. 4.   LETRA DE CAMBIO—BILL OF EXCHANGE.

$1000.00
México, á 2 de Abril de 1910.

A la vista (*or* á ——— días vista) se servirá Vd. mandar pagar por ésta única (*or* segunda, terza, etc.) de Cambio, en la ciudad de Guadalajara, á la órden del Sr. Juan Tenorio, la cantidad de Mil Pesos; valor recibido en efectivo (*or* en cuenta, etc.), que sentará Vd. en cuenta que tenemos según aviso (*or* sin aviso) de

S. S. S.

(Signed) Quién Sabe.

Al Sr. Adalberto Calabazas.

Guadalajara, 5a Degollado 23.

ACCEPTANCE.

Guadalajara, 3 de Abril de 1910.   Acepto.

(Signed) Adalberto Calabazas.

Art.-1156.   ·No. 4.   TRANSLATION.

$1000.00

Mexico, 2 April, 1910.

At sight (or ———— days' sight) please pay on this first (or second, third, etc.) of Exchange, in the City of Guadalajara, to the order of Mr. Juan Tenorio the sum of One Thousand Pesos, value received in cash (or on account, etc.), which you will please charge according to advice (or without advice) to the account of, the undersigned.

(Signed) Quién Sabe.

To Mr. Adalberto Calabazas,

Guadalajara, 5th Degollado St. 23.

ACCEPTANCE.

Guadalajara, 3 April, 1910.   I accept.

(Signed) Adalberto Calabazas.

Art. 1157.   No. 5.   PODER — POWER OF ATTORNEY BY CORPORATION.

En la ciudad de ———— Condado de ———— Estado de ———— Estados Unidos de América, el dia ———— del mes de ———— 19—, ante mi ———— Notario Público en dicho Condado y Estado, y testigos que á continuación se expresan, comparecieron personalmente ———— y ———— en su carác-

ter de representantes legales de ———— una sociedad **anónima**
debidamente organizada conforme á las leyes del Estado de
———— siendo el primero de ———— años de edad, con residencia en ———— Estado de ———— y siendo el segundo de
———— años de edad, con residencia en ———— Estado de
———— y dijeron : que necesitando persona á quien **confiar en**
la República Mexicana los negocios de la compañía, á **fin**
de que esa persona pueda representarla ante los tribunales y
autoridades, por el presente instrumento y en ejercicio de las
facultades que tienen conferidas, en nombre de la compañía,
otorgan : que confieren poder amplio á los Señores ————,
para que ejercitándolo conjunta ó separadamente, representen á dicha compañía en todos los asuntos administrativos y judiciales, ya fueren civiles ó criminales, **que**
tuviere pendientes ó en lo sucesivo le ocurrieren en la República Mexicana, otorgando al efecto, á dichos abogados,
todas y cada una de las facultades que las leyes mexicanas
otorgan á los mandatarios, y especialmente las siguientes :
para que representen á la compañía en los denuncios de minas,
que actualmente tenga ó en lo sucesivo tuviere, en las concesiones de tierras, aguas, ferrocarriles, navegación, pesque-
rias, industrias nuevas con los privilegios inherentes ; para
que soliciten patentes de invención, y registren marcas de
fábrica y avisos y nombres comerciales, así como también,
para que persigan ante las autoridades respectivas, las in-
fracciones y falsificaciones cometidas en contravención de
esos privilegios ; para que soliciten del Ejecutivo el permiso
necesario para adquirir bienes raices ó minas dentro de la
zona prohibida á los extranjeros, para que cobren, demanden
judicialmente y reciban de quien corresponda cualquiera cantidad de dinero, bienes ó mercancías que se adeudaren á
la compañía, y otorguen los recibos y cancelaciones correspondientes ; para que comparezcan en juicio demandando
ó defendiendo en nombre de la compañía, para lo cual se
les faculta expresamente para articular y absolver posiciones,
para reconocer firmas, para desistirse, para transigir, judicial

ó extrajudicialmente, para comprometer en árbitros, otorgando al efecto en nombre de la compañia los instrumentos necesarios; para recusar jueces, magistrados y otros funcionarios que por la ley lo fueren; para otorgar y firmar todos los instrumentos privados ó públicos que el ejercicio del presente mandato requiera; para substituir este poder en su totalidad ó en parte, para revocar las substituciones que hicieren y otorgar otras nuevas, y para que otorguen poderes y cartas-poder. Otorgado en presencia de los testigos Señores ———— y ———— siendo el primero de ———— años de edad, y el segundo de ———— años de edad, ambos vecinos de este lugar, á quienes doy fe conocer personalmente. Yo el notario, certifico: haber leido la escritura constitutiva de dicha compañía, debidamente autorizada por el Secretario de Estado del Estado de ———— los Estatutos y actas de la misma debidamente autorizados por el Secretario de dicha compañía, y por la presente, doy fé de que en ellos se autoriza á los comparecientes para otorgar poderes en nombre de la compañía; y de que en los mismos consta que son representantes legales de ella, debidamente electos y habilitados. Habiendo leido este instrumento á los comparecientes y enterados de su valor y fuerza legal, lo firmaron en unión de los testigos y del subscrito Notario que da fé.

Art. 1158. No. 5. TRANSLATION — POWER OF ATTORNEY BY CORPORATION.

In the City of ———— County of ———— State of ———— United States of America, on the ———— day of ———— 19—, before me, ———— a Notary Public in and for said County and State, and the witnesses, who will be hereinafter named, personally appeared ———— and ———— as legal representatives of ———— a corporation duly organized under the laws of the State of ———— the first being ———— years of age, residing in ———— State of ———— and the second ———— years of age, residing in ————

State of ———— and said: that needing some one to whom the
business of the corporation may be confided in the Republic of
Mexico, in order that such person may represent the corporation before the Courts and Authorities, by these Presents, and
in exercise of the powers conferred upon them, in the name of
said corporation, they hereby constitute and appoint ————
and ———— to be the true and lawful attorneys for said corporation in the Republic of Mexico, exercising this power either
separately or together, giving and granting unto said attorneys
full power to represent said corporation in all matters, administrative and judicial, either civil or criminal, which the said
corporation may have now pending, or which, in the future,
may arise in the Republic of Mexico, giving and granting to
our said attorneys all and every faculty which the laws of
Mexico concede to mandataries, and especially the following:
to represent the corporation in the denouncement of mining
claims, which it may have pending, or which it may desire to
file; in the concessions for lands, water rights, railways, navigation rights, fishery privileges, new industries with the privileges attached; to solicit patents, trademarks, and the registry
of commercial names and advertisements, as well as to prosecute infringements and falsifications of the same before the
proper authorities; also to solicit from the executive the necessary permit to acquire real estate or mines within the zone
forbidden to foreigners; to collect, sue for, and receive from
the parties who may be indebted to the corporation, monies,
goods or chattels, giving the proper receipts and cancellations
therefor; to appear before the Courts either as plaintiff or
defendant, in the name of the corporation, for which purpose
they are especially empowered to recognize signatures, to
desist, to settle, either out of or in court; to name arbitrators,
executing, in the name of the company, the necessary legal
instruments; to recuse judges, magistrates and other officials
who, by law, may be recused; to execute and sign all private
or public documents which the exercise of this power may
require; to substitute this power of attorney in whole or **in**

part, to revoke such substitutions and make others; also to grant powers and letters of attorney. Executed in presence of the witnesses Messrs. ———— and ———— the first being ———— years of age, and the second ———— years of age, both residents of this place, to me personally known. I, the Notary, certify: to have read the Articles of Incorporation of said company, duly authorized by the Secretary of State of the State of ———— the by-laws and minutes of the same duly authenticated by the Secretary of said company, and I hereby certify that the same authorize the persons executing this instrument to give and grant powers of attorney in the name of the corporation, and that they are duly elected and qualified officers of said corporation. Having read and thoroughly understood the clauses and the force of this instrument, the grantors signed same, with the witnesses, and the subscribed Notary.

Art. 1159. No. 6. CORPORATE POWER OF ATTORNEY — AMPLER FORM, TO GENERAL MANAGER OF COMPANY.

En la Ciudad de St. Louis, Estado de Missouri, Estados Unidos de América, á Veintiocho de Julio de 1902, ante mí JOSEPH WHELESS, Notario Público de dicho Estado, con residencia en la Ciudad de St. Louis, y testigos que al fin se expresarán, comparecieron personalmente los Sres. Thomas Taggart y Samuel E. Morss, mayores de edad, comerciantes y vecinos de la Ciudad de Indianapolis, Condado de Marion, Estado de Indiana, Estados Unidos de América, en su calidad de Presidente y Secretario, respectivamente, de la Sociedad denominada INDIANA-SONORA COPPER & MINING CO., Sociedad debidamente organizada de acuerdo con las leyes del Estado de West Virginia, uno de los Estados Unidos de América, cuyo asiento de operaciones está en esta Ciudad, en la cual tiene establecidas oficinas, con la capacidad legal necesaria, á quienes doy fé conocer y cuya personalidad queda comprobada con el acta de la sesión celebrada por el Consejo de Administración de dicha Sociedad en la ciudad de Indianapolis, de la cual aparece que los comparecientes fueron elegidos respectivamente Presidente y Secretario, de lo que doy fé por haber tenido á la vista el libro de actas respectivo, y protestando los comparecientes estar en el ejercicio de su encargo, dijeron:

Que el Consejo de Administracion de dicha Compania por resolución aprobada en la sesión que tuvo verificativo el dia • veintidos de Julio de 1902, que yo el Notario doy fé haber tenido á la vista en el libro de actas respectivo, acordó nombrar apoderado de la Compañía al Sr. F. A. Provot, de Bisbee, Territorio de Arizona.

Que en cumplimiento de lo acordado los comparecientes, con la personalidad que tienen acreditada, dan y confieren poder amplio, bastante y cuanto en derecho se requiera á dicho Señor F. A. Provot, para que en nombre y representacion de la INDIANA-SONORA COPPER & MINING CO., rija y administre los bienes que la Compañía posee en la Republica Mexicana y los que en lo sucesivo en ella adquiera, sean de la clase y naturaleza que fueran; para que investido con la representacion de la Compañía gestione y defienda ya sea ante el Gobierno Federal de la República Mexicana ó ya sea ante el del Estado Libre y Soberano de Sonora ó cualesquiera otras autoridades de los Estados ó locales, los derechos de la Empresa que actualmente tuviere en virtud de contratos ó concesiones celebrados con las mencionadas autoridades ó los que en lo sucesivo adquiera ú obtenga por cualquier título legal, y para que promueva cuanto fuere necesario ó util para la existencia y desarrollo de los intereses de la Compañía; debata todo género de diferencias y celebre nuevos contratos ya sea con el Ejecutivo Federal ó cualesquiera otras autoridades administrativas de la República Mexicana, ya sea que se relacionen con contratos y concesiones actualmente existentes ó que tengan por objeto adquirir nuevas concesiones, promoviendo cuanto fuere necesario para su validéz y cumplimiento y obtenga las exenciones, franquicias y privilegios que fueren conducentes para asegu-

rar el éxito de las concesiones actuales ó de las que en lo
sucesivo se obtuvieran, y modifique tanto los contratos existentes cuanto los que el mismo apoderado celebrare; para
que celebre todos los contratos que crea oportuno, sean de la
clase y naturaleza que fueran, con particulares, corporaciones
ó Bancos, y que la Compañía puede celebrar con arreglo al
acta constitutiva y Estatutos de la misma; para que pueda
exijir el cumplimiento de todos los compromisos prometi-
dos ó contraidos con la Compañía, consentir en las esperas ó
quitas que á su juicio fueren necesarias para asegurar alguna
parte de los créditos, y en general practicar ó determinar que
se practiquen por los empleados de la Compañía todas las ges-
tiones que conduzcan á obtener la percepción de lo que se
adeudare ó la ejecución de todas las obligaciones que á favor
de la compañía hayan sido contraidas. Para que pida y
tome posesión de los bienes que por cualquier titulo pertenezcan á la Compañía; para que dé y tome cuentas á todas personas á quienes la Compañía deba darlas y tomarlas, hacién-
doles cargos, recibiendo sus descargos justos, competentes y á
derecho conformes, nombrando contadores, partidores y personas inteligentes para su revisión y exámen y un tercero para
el caso de discordia. Para que transija, componga y ajuste
judicialmente ó extrajudicialmente todos los pleitos, causas
y negocios que al presente tenga ó en lo sucesivo se le ofrezcan á la Compañía, en las cantidades y bajo los requisitos y
condiciones que le parezcan convenientes, pudiendo, compro-
meterlos á la decisión de árbitros juris ó arbitradores amiga-
bles componedores, con pena convencional ó sin ella. Para
que fomalice ó acepte sobre todos y cada uno de los particulares asentados y los que se ofrezcan, las escrituras y documentos correspondientes, con las cláusulas, renuncias de leyes
y recursos que crea convenientes ó necesarios y con los demás
requisitos que conduzcan á su estabilidad. Para que presente
para su registro ante el funcionario que corresponda las escrituras, contratos y documentos que deban ser registrados
conforme á las leyes de la República Mexicana. Para que

comparezca ante todas las oficinas administrativas, y así
mismo ante todos los Juzgados y Tribunales competentes de
la expresada República, como actor, demandado ó tercer o-
positor, y ante ellas ponga demandas civiles y criminales, con-
teste las de contrario ó las niegue, haga toda clase de pedi-
mentos, requerimientos, citaciones, alegaciones, protestas,
súplicas, desistimientos, embargo, desembargo de bienes, venta
y remate de ellos, de que pida y tome posesiones, adjudicación
y amparo y lanzamiento, pida pruebas, permisos, su restitu-
ción ó los renuncie, saque y haga compulsar toda clase de documentos de donde se hallen, con citación contraria, ó sin ella,
asista á juntas, audiencias, almonedas y otras diligencias, ar-
ticule y absuelva posiciones, recuse Jueces, Secretarios, Magistrados y demas funcionarios con causa ó con la simple protesta de la ley, pida reconocimiento de firmas y reconozca las
de los legítimos representantes de la Compañía, pida provi-
dencias precautorias, haga sumisión expresa, decline jurisdicción de los Jueces incompetentes, interponiendo la inhibitoria
ó declinatoria correspondientes, oiga autos y sentencias interlocutorias y definitivas, consienta lo favorable y de lo adverso
apele y suplique, siga su grado ó se desista, ejecute las sentencias que recayeren, y en general para que haga y practique
todos cuantos actos, agencias y diligencias sean conducentes
al mejor desempeño de este poder que se le confiere con facultad expresa de interponer toda clase de recursos ordinarios
y extraordinarios, inclusos los de amparo, casación y responsabilidad de funcionarios públicos y con la de substitu-
irlo en todo ó en parte por poderes especiales, cartas-poder,
revocar substitutos y apoderados especiales, y nombrar otros
de nuevo, pues á todos los releva en forma la Compania.
Leido que les fué este instrumento á los senores comparecientes lo ratificaron y firmaron en union de los testigos que lo
fueron los Sres.   Fulano de Tal y Mengano, vecinos de esta
Ciudad, con la capacidad legal necesaria.   Doy Fe.

Art. 1160. No. 6. TRANSLATION.

In the City of St. Louis, State of Missouri, United States of America, on the 28th day of July, 1902, before me, Joseph Wheless, a Notary Public of said State resident in the City of St. Louis, and the witnesses hereinafter named, personally appear Messrs. Thomas Taggert and Samuel E. Morss, of lawful age, merchants, residents of the City of Indianapolis, Marion County, State of Indiana, United States of America, in their capacity as president and secretary respectively of the corporation known as " Indiana-Sonora Copper & Mining Company," a corporation duly organized in accordance with the laws of the State of West Virginia, one of the United States of America, and having its principal place of business in this City, where it has established offices, and who have the necessary legal capacity, and with whom I am personally acquainted, and whose personality is proven by the minutes of the meeting held by the board of directors of said corporation in the City of Indianapolis, whereby it appears that said parties were elected respectively President and Secretary, which I certify through having before me the said minute book, and making oath that they are in the exercise of their offices, they said:

That the Board of Directors of said Company by a resolution adopted at the meeting held on the 22nd day of July, 1902, and which I the Notary certify from having seen the said record in the minute book, resolved to appoint Mr. F. A. Provot, of Bisbee, Territory of Arizona, as the attorney-in-fact of the said Company.

That in compliance with said resolution, the above-named parties, in their capacity proven as aforesaid, give and confer ample and sufficient power as in law may be required, upon said Mr. F. A. Provot, for the purposes that in the name and as the representative of the Indiana-Sonora Copper & Mining Company, he may manage and administer

56

the properties which the Company owns in the Mexican Republic, and such as it may hereafter acquire there of whatever kind and nature they may be; that as the representative of the Company, he may promote and defend before the Federal Government of the Mexican Republic, or before the government of the free and sovereign State of Sonora, or any other authorities, State or local, the rights which the Company at present has, or may hereafter acquire, by virtue of contracts or concessions made with said authorities or which it may acquire by any lawful title; and that he may do everything which may be necessary or useful for the existence and development of the interests of the Company; that he may settle all kinds of differences and make new contracts with the Federal Government or any other administrative authorities of the Mexican Republic, whether in regard to existing contracts or concessions, or having for their object the acquisition of new concessions, doing every thing which may be necessary for their validity and performance; and may obtain such exemptions, franchises and privileges as may tend to assure the success of the present and any future concessions which may be obtained, and may modify existing contracts, and any others which the said attorney may make; that he may enter into such contracts as he deems proper, of whatever kind or nature they may be, with individuals, corporations or banks, which the company is authorized to execute in conformity with its charter and by-laws; that he may enforce performance of all the obligations promised or contracted with the company, consent to the delays or acquittances which in his judgment may be necessary in order to secure some part of the debts, and in general may take, or determine that the employés of the company shall take all steps which may tend to obtain the collection of all that may be due or the performance of all the obligations which may have been contracted in favor of the Company; that he may demand and take possession of the property which by any title belongs to the company;

that he may render accounts to and demand accounting from all persons to whom the Company should render them or from whom it should receive them, making all just and lawful charges and credits and pointing accountants and intelligent persons to revise and examine the same, and a third person in case of disagreement. That he may compromise, compose, and adjust judicially or extra-judicially all law suits, causes and affairs, which the Company has now or in the future may have, for such amounts and upon such terms and conditions as he may deem proper, being empowered to submit the same to the decision of legal arbitrators or friendly adjusters, with or without conventional penalty. That he may execute or accept, in respect to the foregoing matters, and others which may arise, such instruments and documents as may be proper, with such clauses, renouncements of laws and recourses as he may deem proper or necessary, and with such requisites as may tend to their efficiency. That he may present for registration before the proper officials such instruments, contracts and documents as require to be registered according to the laws of the Mexican Republic. That he may appear before all the administrative officers, as well as before all the competent courts of the said Republic, as plaintiff, defendant or intervenor, and may institute before them civil and criminal suits, answer or deny those brought against him, make all kinds of petitions, requisitions, citations, pleadings, protests, requests, withdrawals, embargos and releases of embargos of property, sale and auction of the same, of which he may demand and take possession, adjudication, amparo and levy. Demand proofs, permits, and making restitution or renouncement of the same; that he may make and have made copies of all kinds of documents wherever they may be, with or without citation to the opposite party; that he may attend meetings, hearings, auction sales and other proceedings, propound and answer interrogatories, challenge judges, secretaries, magistrates, and other officials for cause or by simple legal protest; demand the acknowledgment of signatures and acknowledge those of the lawful representatives of the company; demand precautionary measures, make express submissions, and decline the jurisdiction of incompetent judges, interposing the corresponding legal procedure; hear interlocutory and definitive *autos* and judgments, consent to those which are favorable and appeal from those which are adverse, and prosecute or dismiss the same, execute the judgments which may be rendered, and in general that he may do and practice all such acts, agencies and proceedings as may tend to the best performance of this power which is conferred upon him, with the express authorization to interpose all kinds of ordinary and extraordinary recourses, including those of amparo, cassation and responsibility of public officials, and with the power of substitution in whole or in part by special powers of attorney and letters of attorney, to revoke substitutes and special powers of attorney, and to appoint others anew, as the company formally relieves them all. This instrument being read to the said appearing parties they ratify and sign it, together with the witnesses, who were Messrs. ———— and ————, residents of this city, with the necessary legal capacity.

I attest.

(Signatures of President, Secretary, Notary and Witnesses.)

Trt. 1161. No. 7. CARTA-PODER—LETTER OF ATTORNEY.

México, á ...... de ...... de 19—.

Sr ....

Por la presente confiero á Ud. poder ámplio, cumplido y bastante para que me represente en ....

así como para contestar las demandas y reconvenciones que á propósito de este negocio se entablen en mi contra; para que en mi propia representación promueva é intervenga en las tercerías y cualesquiera otros incidentes que, con motivo del mismo asunto, se susciten; para oponer excepciones perentorias ó dilatorias, reconocer firmas, presentar, reconocer y pedir que se reconozcan documentos y redargüir de falsos los que para su reconocimiento le fueren presentados; para articular y absolver posiciones y rendir las demás pruebas autorizadas por la Ley, pudiendo, para ese objeto, pedir términos, ya sean ordinarios ó extraordinarios y prórroga de los mismos; para repreguntar y tachar testigos, nombrar y recusar peritos, asistir á toda clase de diligencias judiciales, inclusos los remates, embargos y almonedas y representarme en los que en mi contra se decreten; para constituir y recibir en mi nombre depósitos judiciales ó extrajudiciales, pudiendo Ud. otorgar y recabar los documentos con que todos estos actos se acrediten; para oir resoluciones judiciales interlocutorias ó definitivas, consentirlas ó interponer contra ellas los recursos que estime procedentes, incluso los de casación y amparo de garantías; para intentar y proseguir las acciones del órden penal que, con motivo de este negocio, procedan; para recusar con ó sin causa jueces superiores ó inferiores; para desistir del juicio; transigir judicial ó extrajudicialmente y comprometer en árbitros; para substituir el presente mandato en favor de la persona ó personas que crea convenientes; para revocar dichas substituciones y hacer otras nuevas, y en fin, para todos los demás actos á que se refiere la Ley.

Tendré por firme y valedero y ratifico desde hoy cuanto Ud. haga en el negocio cuya procuración le encomiendo por medio de la presente.

Soy de Ud. Afmo. S. S.

Art. 1162. No. 7. TRANSLATION.

\exico, ⸺ day of ⸺, 19—.

Mr. ⸺.

I hereby confer upon you ample, complete and sufficient power to represent me in ....
....;
also to answer all demands and claims which may be presented against me in regard to the said business; that as my representative you may institute and intervene in all interventions and other incidents which may arise in the course of said business; to interpose peremptory or dilatory exceptions, acknowledge and demand the acknowledgment of documents, and impeach as false those which may be presented to you for acknowledgment; to propound and answer interrogatories and produce other proofs authorized by law, and for such purpose, you may request ordinary and extraordinary terms and extension of the same; to cross-examine and impeach witnesses, appoint and challenge experts, be present at all kinds of judicial proceedings, including judicial sales, embargos and auctions, and to represent me in those which may be ordered against me; to make and receive in my name judicial or extra-judicial deposits, executing and requiring the execution of the documents evidencing all such acts; to hear interlocutory or definitive judicial decisions, and to consent to them or to interpose against them such recourses as you may deem proper, including those of cassation and amparo; to institute and prosecute any penal actions which may arise in regard to this business; to challenge superior or inferior judges with or without cause; to dismiss the suit; to compromise judicially or extra-judicially and to submit to arbitration; to substitute this power of attorney in favor of such person or persons as you may deem proper, and to revoke such substitutions and make new ones, and finally, for all other acts permitted by law.

I hereby ratify and will hold as valid and binding from this day whatever you may do in the business which is hereby intrusted to you in which to represent me.

Yours very truly.

Art. 1163. No. 8. CARTA-PODER — LETTER OF ATTORNEY BEFORE PATENT AND TRADEMARK OFFICE.

—— de 190—

Sr. ———

Presente.

Muy Señor mio:

Por la presente doy á Ud. mi poder amplio, cumplido y bastante para que á mi nombre y representación solicite de la Oficina de Patentes y Marcas de la República..........

....

....

así como para contestar ante los Tribunales las demandas en mi contra, pedir revocación de resoluciones administrativas, rendir toda clase de pruebas, articular y absolver posiciones, recusar lo recusable, oir autos y sentencias, consentir los favorables, y pedir revocación, apele, suplique ó interponga el recurso de casación ó amparo de los adversos, trance ó desista, perciba documentos y valores y otorgue recibos y cartas de pago, presentar, corregir, aclarar ó retirar solicitudes, dibujos, descripciones ó reivindicaciones, pedir exámenes ó reposiciones de títulos ó documentos, ó registro de traspasos de derechos, abonar pagos, recibir notificaciones y avisos, substituir en todo ó en parte la presente, revocar substituciones y nombrar de nuevo, ratificando desde hoy todo lo que Ud. haga en este particular.

De Ud. afmo. S. S.

Art. 1164. No. 8. TRANSLATION.

Mexico, ——— day of ———, 19—.

My Dear Sir:

I hereby confer upon you, ample, complete and sufficient power, for me and in my name to solicit from the Patent and Trademark Office of the Republic (here insert name and character of the invention, trademark, etc., stating fully what the attorney is to do); also to answer before the Tribunals any suits brought against me; to request the revocation of administrative decisions; to render all kinds of proofs; to propound and answer interrogatories, to make challenges wherever proper; to hear autos and judgments, and to consent to those which are favorable, and ask the revocation, and to appeal or interpose the recourse of cassation or amparo against those which are adverse, and to settle or dismiss the same; to receive documents and valuable securities and to execute receipts and acknowledgment of payments; to present, correct, explain or withdraw petitions, drawings, descriptions or claims; to request examinations or the replacing of titles or documents, or the registry of assignments of rights; to make or accept payments on account; to receive notifications and notices; to substitute this power in whole or in part, and revoke substitutions and make new appointments; and I ratify from this day all that you may do in the premises.

Yours very truly.

Art. 1165.   No. 9.   PETITION FOR COPYRIGHT.

(50ct. Stamp).

C. Secretario de Instrucción Pública y Bellas Artes:

El subscripto, Joseph Wheless, con domicilio en el Hotel Iturbide en esta Capital, ante Usted con el debido respeto expone:

Que con fundamento del Artículo 1234 del Código Civil, se reserva los derechos de la propiedad literaria que le corresponde respecto de la obra intitulada "Compendium of Mexican Law," de la cual es autor, y á Usted pide se sirva hacer la declaración de ley, á cuyo efecto acompaño los dos ejemplares de la mencionada obra, protestando á Usted mi respeto.

JOSEPH WHELESS.

México, 25 de Julio de 1910.

Art. 1166.   No. 9.   TRANSLATION.

Hon. Secretary of Public Instruction and Fine Arts:

The undersigned, Joseph Wheless, domiciled in the Hotel Iturbide in this capital, before you with due respect declare:

In accordance with Article 1234 of the Civil Code, I reserve the rights of literary property to which I am entitled in respect of the work entitled "Compendium of Mexican Law," of which I am the author, and I request that you will please make the declaration required by law for which purpose I send herewith the two copies of the said work, assuring you of my respect.

(Signed) JOSEPH WHELESS.

Mexico, ——— day of ———, 19—.

Art. 1167.   No. 10.   APPLICATION FOR PATENT OF INVENTION.

Patente número ———.

(50ct. Stamp).

Expediente número ———.

Señor Director de la Oficina de Patentes y Marcas:

Deseando obtener una patente de invención por lo que en seguida se refiere, acompaño á esta solicitud, por triplicado, los documentos que previene la ley vigente en su Articulo 9, debidamente autorizados con mi firma.

Objeto de la invención ———.

Nombre y profesión de ——— inventor ———.

Domicilio de ——— inventor ———.

Nombre del apoderado ———.

Domicilio del apoderado ———.

Lugar para recibir las notificaciones ———.

México, ——— de ——— de 19—.

(Firma del Inventor) ———.

NOTE.— The foregoing should be entirely typewritten.

Art. 1168. No. 10. TRANSLATION.

Patent number ———.
Application number ———.
Director of the Office of Patents and Trademarks:

Desiring to obtain a patent of invention for the device hereinafter referred to I send you herewith in triplicate the documents required under Article 9 of the law now in force, which are duly executed by me.

Object of the invention ———.
Name and profession of the inventor ———.
Residence of the inventor ———.
Name of the attorney in fact ———.
Residence of the attorney in fact ———.
Place where notices may be sent ———.

Mexico, ——— of ———, 19—.

(Signature of Inventor).

Art. 1169. No. 11. APPLICATION FOR PATENT FOR MODEL OR INDUSTRIAL DRAWING.

Same as No. 10, except: Descando obtener una patente por Modelo ó Dibujo industrial, por lo que abajo se refiere, acompaño á esta solicitud por triplicado, una descripción y reivindicación completa y demás documentos que previene la ley.

Art. 1170. No. 11. TRANSLATION.

Same as No. 10, except: Wishing to obtain a patent for an industrial model or drawing for the object below mentioned, I remit with this petition, in triplicate, a complete description and claim, and the other documents required by law.

NOTE.— It is idle to give examples of descriptions and claims, as each must be in the technical language required by the nature of the invention, and must of course be the work of an expert.

Art. 1171. No. 12. APPLICATION FOR REGISTRY OF TRADEMARK.

Marco número ———.

(50ct. Stamp).

Expediente número ———.

Señor Director de la Oficina de Patentes y Marcas:

Deseando obtener el registro de la marca cuyo facsimile va adjunto, acompaño á esta solicitud los documentos y cliché á que se refiere el Art. 3 de la Ley.

Nombre del propietario de la marca ———.

Domicilio del mismo ———.

Ubicación de la fábrica ó establecimiento comercial ———.

Nombre de la misma ———.

Articulos á que se aplica la nueva marca ———.

Nombre del apoderado ———.

Domicilio del mismo ———.

Lugar para recibir notificaciones ———.

México, ——— de ——— de 19—.

(Signature of applicant or his attorney.)

Art. 1172. No. 12. TRANSLATION.

Mark No. ———.

Application number ———.

Director of the Office of Patents and Trademarks:

Wishing to obtain the registry of the Trademark, a facsimile of which is hereto attached, I remit with this petition the documents and cliché required by Article 3 of the Law.

Name of the owner of Trademark ———.

Domicile of the same ———.

Location of the factory or commercial establishment ———.

Name of the same ———.

Articles to which the new trademark is to be applied

Name of the attorney in fact ————.
Domicile of the same ————.
Place at which to receive notifications ————.
  Mexico, ———— day of ————, 19—.

Art. 1173. No. 13. APPLICATION FOR REGISTRY OF ASSIGNED TRADEMARK.

Marca número ————.
Expediente número ————.

(50ct. Stamp).

Señor Director de la Oficina de Patentes y Marcas:
  Estimaré á Vd. que se sirva registrar que la marca cuyo ejemplar acompaño, ha sido adquirida desde el ———— de ———— de 19— por ————, á cuyo fin acompaño el documento original y su copia.
Número de registro de la marca ————.
Titulo de la marca ————.
Nombre del antiguo poseedor ————.
Productos que ampara ————.

  Méxieo, ———— de ———— de 19—.
    (Signature of applicant or his attorney.)

Art. 1174. No. 13. TRANSLATION.

Trademark No. ————.
Application No. ————.
Director of the Office of Patents and Trademarks:
  You will please register the trademark a copy of which is hereto attached, which was acquired on the ———— day of ————, 19—, by ————, for which purpose I remit the original document and a copy of the same.
  Register number of the trademark ————.
  Title of the trademark ————.

Name of the former owner ———.
Articles protected by the trademark ———.
Ɛexico, ——— day of ———, 19—.

Art. 1175. No. 14. APPLICATION FOR DUPLICATE.

Marca número ———.
Aviso número ———.

(50ct. Stamp).

Expediente número ———.

Señor Director de la Oficina de Patentes y Marcas:
    Deseando obtener
el duplicado del certificado número ——— del registro de
la marca (ó aviso) de la (casa comercial, fábrica, etc.) que
gira bajo la razón social ———, he de merecer á Vd. se
sirva dictar sus superiores órdenes para que, de conformidad
con el Art. 13 del Reglamento respectivo, se me extienda el
duplicado de dicho titulo, por haberse extraviado el original
(ó la causa que motiva la solicitud).
Titulo de la marca ———.
Nombre del propietario ———.
Domicilio del mismo ———.
Ubicación de la fábrica, etc. ———.
Articulos que ampara la marca ———.
    Ɛéxico, ——— de ——— de 19—.
    (Name and rubric of the applicant or his attorney.)

Art. 1176. No. 14. TRANSLATION.

Trademark No. ———.
Advertisement No. ———.
Application No. ———.
Director of the Office of Patents and Trademarks:
    Wishing
to obtain the duplicate of the certificate No. ——— of the

registry of the trademark (or advertisement) of the (commercial house, factory, etc.) known under the firm name of ———, will you please order a duplicate of said title to be issued to me, in accordance with Art. 13 of the Regulations, for the reason that the original of said document has been lost (or other legal reason of the petition).

Title of the Trademark ———.

Name of the owner ———.

Domicile of the owner ———.

Location of the factory, etc., ———.

Articles protected by the trademark ———.

Mexico, ——— day of ———, 19—.

Art. 1177. No. 15. APPLICATION FOR EXTENSION OF TRADEMARK.

Marca número ———

Expediente número ———.

(50ct. Stamp.)

Señor Director de la Oficina de Patentes y Marcas:

El día ——— de ——— de 19— se vence el plazo de viente años de la marca número ———, y como se desea seguir usándola con arreglo á la ley de la materia, suplico á Vd. que se prorrogue el plazo por otros veinte años, á cuyo efecto acompaño un ejemplar de la marca.

Nombre del propietario de la marca ———.

Domicilio del mismo ———.

Titulo de la marca ———.

Ubicación de la fábrica ó establecimiento comercial ———.

Nombre de la misma ———.

Articulos á que se aplica la marca ———.

Nombre del apoderado ———

Domicilio del mismo ———.

Dirección para recibir notificaciones ———.

Méxizo, ——— de ——— de 19—.

(Signature of applicant or his attorney.)

Art. 1178. No. 15. TRANSLATION.

Trademark No. ————.

Application No. ————.

Director of the Office of Patents and Trademarks:

On the ———— day of ————, 19—, the twenty-year term of the trademark No. ———— will expire, and as it is desired to continue using the trademark, in accordance with the law on the subject, I request you to extend the term for another period of twenty years, for which purpose I herewith remit the copy of the trademark.

Name of the owner of the trademark ————.

Domicile of the owner ————.

Title of the trademark ————.

Location of the factory or commercial establishment ————.

Name of the same ————.

Articles to which the trademark is applied ————.

Name of the attorney in fact ————.

Domicile of the same ————.

Address for receiving notifications ————.

Mexico, ———— day of ————, 19—.

Art. 1179. No. 16. APPLICATION FOR REGISTRY OF ADVERTISEMENT.

(50ct. Stamp.)

Aviso número ————.

Expediente número ————.

Señor Director de la Oficina de Patentes y Marcas:

Sírvase Vd. mandar registrar el aviso comercial que acompaño, y que se destina á anunciar ————, á cuyo efecto remito el cliché y documentos á que se refiere el Artículo respectivo del reglamento de la ley.

Nombre del propietario ————.
Domicilio del mismo ————.
Nombre del apoderado ————.
Domicilio del mismo ————.
Dirección para recibir notificaciones ————.
   México, ———— de ———— de 19—.
               (Signature of applicant or his attorney.)

Art. 1180.   No. 16.   TRANSLATION.

Advertisement No. ————.
Application No. ————.
Director of the Office of Patents and Trademarks:
                             You will
please order the registration of the accompanying commercial advertisement, which is intended to advertise (state the article), for which purpose I remit the "cut" **and documents** required by the regulations of the law.
Name of the owner ————.
Domicile of the same ————.
Name of the attorney in fact ————.
Domicile of the same ————.
Address for receiving notices ————.
   México, ———— day of ————, 19—.

Art. 1181.   No. 17.   APPLICATION **FOR EXTEN-**
SION OF ADVERTISEMENT.

Aviso número ————.
Expediente número ————.
                         (50ct. Stamp).

Señor Director de la Oficina de Patentes y Marcas:
                           Debiendo vencerse el
———— de ———— de 19— el plazo por el que se registró el
aviso comercial, cuyo número está arriba, suplico á Vd. que se

renueve el registro para que pueda seguirse usando por otros ——— años.

Objeto ó negociación que anunciará el aviso ———.

Nombre del propietario ———.

Domicilio del mismo ———.

Nombre del apoderado ———.

Domicilio del mismo ———.

Dirección para recibir notificaciones ———.

México, ——— de ——— de 19—.

(Signature of applicant or his attorney.)

Art. 1182. No. 17. TRANSLATION.

Advertisement No. ———.

Application No. ———.

Director of the Office of Patents and Trademarks:

As the term for which the commercial advertisement under the above number was registered will expire on the ——— day of ———, 19—, I request you to renew the registration in order that the use of it may be continued for another period of ——— years.

Object or business advertised by the advertisement ———.

Name of the owner ———.

Domicile of the same ———.

Name of the attorney in fact ———.

Domicile of the same ———.

Address for receiving notifications ———.

México, ——— day of ———, 19—.

Art. 1183. No. 18. COMPRA-VENTA — DEED OF SALE, BY ATTORNEY, WITH DEFERRED PAYMENTS.

En la ciudad de San Louis, Mo., U. S. A., á los diez y seis dias del mes de febrero del año de mil novecientos siete, NOSOTROS: Carolina Bloke de Doe, representada por su esposo don Juan Doe, por la primera parte, quién

57

también concurre á este acto para prestarle su consentimiento, domiciliado en Autlán, Jalisco, México, y por otra parte el señor John Dill, de esta ciudad, con oficina en el número 411 Olive St., el primero minero, comerciante el segundo y ambos con capacidad legal, hemos convenido en celebrar un contrato de compraventa de ciertas propiedades mineras, á cuyo efecto el señor Juan Doe expuso: que el veintiuno de enero del presente año y conforme al artículo ochenta y cinco de la ley del Notariado, la señora Carolina Bloke de Doe, su legitima esposa, le otorgó ante el Notario licenciado Alejandro Yáñez su poder general, sin limitación alguna facultándolo expresamente para que celebre todo género de contratos, bien sean estos de venta, permuta, etc., y para que otorgue los documentos públicos ó privados que demande el ejercicio de sus facultades; que este mandato, cuyo testimonio exhibe en el presente acto, no ha sido revocado, ni limitado por acto posterior de su citada poderdante y por tanto, haciendo legitimo uso de sus facultades, vende, cede y traspasa en nombre de la señora Carolina Bloke de Doe, y en favor de don Juan Dill, todo dominio, posesión y usufructo que su poderdante tiene en las siguientes propiedades mineras: (Here follows description).

Las seis últimas propiedades mineras arriba expecificadas, es decir, exceptuando Volcancillos, fueron tituladas por el Ciudadano Presidente de la República de México, en las fechas y bajo los números indicados, en favor del señor Juan Mann, quién las traspasó al señor David P. Richardson, según consta de la escritura pública extendida, en la ciudad de Autlán, Estado de Jalisco, México, bajo el número cincuenta y tres, el diez y ocho de noviembre de mil novecientos cinco, por ante el señor Notario don Zeferino Reyes Ramirez. A su vez el señor David P. Richardson, según escritura pública pasada bajo la autoridad del Notario Alejandro Yáñez, el dia once de septiembre de mil novecientos seis, enajenó á favor del señor Juan P. Delaney, dichas propiedades mineras, siendo este último el causa-habiente de los derechos de propiedad de la señora Carolina Bloke de Doe, según se comprueba con el testimonio de la escritura pública otorgada bajo el número ciento cuarenta ·y siete, en la ciudad de Autlán, Estado de Jalisco, México, el once de septiembre de mil novecientos seis, ante el Notario don Alejandro Yáñez, debidamente registrada bajo las inscripciones números ciento veintiuno á la ciento veintiseis inclusive, cuyos respectivos documentos exhibió en este acto el señor Juan Doe. Continuó diciendo este mismo señor que obrando de entera conformidad con las instrucciones que tiene de su poderdante la señora Carolina Bloke de Deo, y dando también en su propio nombre su expreso consentimiento, como legítimo esposo de la contratante, vende las minas descriptas al señor Juan Dill bajo las condiciones siguientes: Primera. El precio de la venta es la suma de doce mil quinientos dollars moneda americana por la mina denominada " Volcancillos " y el de ocho mil quinientos dollars, tambien moneda americana, por el conjunto de las otras seis minas restantes, denunciadas por Juan Mann. Segunda. Dichas dos cantidades serán cubiertas separadamente dentro del término de tres años contados desde hoy, en la forma siguiente: Con referencia al lote de veinticinco mil dollars, con la suma de cien dollars mensuales durante los tres años dichos que se entregarán en esta ciudad al Banco que elija la vendedora Doña Carolina Bloke de Doe el dia preciso de su vencimiento y además al cumplirse el primer año el veinte por ciento de la cantidad restante; al finalizar el segundo año otro veinte por ciento de lo que entonces se adeude; y al vencerse el último plazo ó sea el tercer año lo que falte para completar los veinticinco, digo, los doce mil quinientos dollars oro americano. Igual forma de pago se observará con los ocho mil quinientos dollars que corresponden al precio de las otras minas, con la única diferencia de que los pagos, tanto mensuales como anuales, deberán hacerse en esta ciudad en el Banco que elija el señor Juan Mann, á cuyo efecto la señora Carolina Bloke

de Doe renuncia en este acto dicha suma transfiriendo todos
sus derechos á dicho señor Juan Mann, cuyo actual domicilio
es el Estado de Jalisco, México. Tercera. Si el comprador Mr. John Dill al vencer alguna de las anualidades,
no pudiere verificar el pago, lo hará sin responsabilidad
alguna al año siguiente, pero sin que por ningún motivo deje
de pagar las mensualidades de dos cientos pesos, pues sobre
este punto han convenido en que si se dejan de pagar tres
mensualidades consecutivas, por este solo hecho se dará por
rescindido el presente contrato, perdiendo el señor John Dill
las cantidades que hasta entonces tuviere entregadas. '
Cuarta. En virtud de este contrato el señor John Dill
entra desde luego en posesión de las minas y por lo mismo
puede explotarlas, vender los metales y hacer con ellas cuanto
estime conveniente, advirtiendo que aun en el caso de que
el presente contrato no se llevare adelante, el señor John
Dill dispondría de los metales extraidos hasta entónces, sin
obligación de rendir cuentas. Quinta. En caso de que
el señor don John Dill enajenare las minas antes de haber
consolidado la propiedad por pago total de los precios estipulados, pasarán al comprador las mismas obligaciones y
derechos que contiene este contrato. Sexta. Los precios
aqui estipulados son los justos y legítimos de las minas ven-
didas, que no valen mas; pero para el caso de que mas
valieren, la señora Bloke de Doe hace donación del exceso
en favor del comprador y al efecto renuncia el derecho que
podría tener para rescindir este contrato por lesión ú otro
motivo y lo dispuesto en los articulos mil seis cientos cincuenta y ocho, mil seis cientos sesenta y dos y dos mil
ochocientos noventa del Código Civil Mexicano. Que las
relacionadas minas están libres de todo gravámen y al
corriente en el pago de sus contribuciones y que el vendedor
obliga sus bienes presentes y futuros á la evicción y saneamiento del presente contrato. Además está convenido que
cualquier defecto ó nulidad en todos ó cada uno de los títulos
de dichas propiedades mineras, materia de este contrato,

dará derecho al señor John Dill ó sus causa-habientes para la rescisión de todas las obligaciones contenidas en este contrato, quedando completamente relevado él ó sus representantes de todo pago por virtud de este convenio. En caso de que el señor John Dill, ó sus representantes, den exacto y fiel cumplimiento á este contrato, haciendo todos los pagos en él prevenidos, la señora Carolina Bloke de Doe se obliga á extender en favor del señor John Dill ó sus representantes, el mas cumplido finiquito, que será considerado como el mas absoluto é irrevocable titulo de dichas propiedades mineras, cumpliendo en este acto con todas y cada una de las condiciones exigidas por la ley de los Estados Unidos de México, sin gravámenes ó sobrecargos de ninguna clase. También es especialmente convenido entre los contratantes, en el caso de pérdida de los derechos de propiedad de estas minas, por culpa, motivo, omisión ó cualquiera otra causa de la señora Carolina Bloke de Doe referidas en este contrato, la segunda parte ó sea John Dill ó quien su derecho represente quedará completa y definitivamente relevado de toda obligación nacida en este convenio. En testimonio de lo cual las partes contratantes firmaron de su puño y letra el presente contrato, siendo las once de la mañana del dia, mes y año mencionados en la ciudad de San Louis, Mo. U. S. A. Se hace constar que el Banco elegido por el apoderado de la señora Carolina Bloke de Doe, es el "St. Louis Unión Trust Company, cuya oficina está en Fourth and Locust Streets de esta ciudad de San Louis Missouri.= El vendedor.= John Doe.= El comprador,= John Dill.= Attorney in fact for Carolina Bloke de Doe.= Testigos.= F. Robleda. T. P. de Montfort.

Art. 1184.   No. 18.   TRANSLATION.

In the City of St. Louis, Mo., U. S. A., on the 16th day of the month of February of the year 1907, we, Carolina Bloke de Doe, represented by her husband John Doe, for the first party, who also concurs in this act in order to grant her his consent, domiciled in Autlán, Jalisco, Mexico, and for the other party Mr. John Dill, of this City, with office at No. 411 Olive St., the first a miner, and the second a merchant, and both with legal capacity, have agreed to execute a contract of purchase and sale of certain mining properties, to which effect Mr. John Doe declared: that on the 21st of January of the present year, and according to Article 85 of the Notarial Law, Mrs. Carolina Bloke de Doe, his legitimate wife, executed to him before the Notary Alejandro Yáñez her general power of attorney without any limitation, expressly empowering him to execute all kinds of contracts, whether of sale, exchange, etc., and to execute such public and private documents as the exercise of these powers may require; that this power of attorney, a certified copy of which he exhibits in the present act, has not been revoked nor limited by any subsequent act of his grantor aforesaid, and therefore, making legitimate use of his powers, he sells, grants and conveys in the name of Mrs. Carolina Bloke de Doe, and in favor of Mr. John Dill, all dominion, possession and usufruct which his grantor has in the following mining properties: (Here follows description).

The six properties last above specified, towit, excepting " Volcancillos," were granted by the C. President of the Republic of Mexico, on the dates and under the numbers indicated, in favor of Mr. John Mann, who conveyed them to Mr. David P. Richardson, as appears by the public deed of writing executed in the city of Autlán, State of Jaliseo, Mexico, on the 18th day of November, 1905, before the Notary Zeferino Reyes Ramirez. Thereafter Mr. David P. Richardson, by public deed executed before the Notary Alejandro Yáñez, on September 11th, 1906, conveyed said mining properties in favor of Mr. John P. Delaney, the latter being the *causa-habiente* of the rights of property of said Mrs. Carolina Bloke de Doe, as is proved by the certified copy of the public deed executed under the number 147, in the city of Autlán, State of Jalisco, Mexico, on the 11th of November, 1906, before the Notary Alejandro Yáñez, duly registered under the inscriptions numbers 121 to 126, inclusive, which respective documents the said Mr. John Doe exhibited in this act.

And said Mr. John Doe further declared: that proceeding in full conformity with the instructions which he has from his principal, said Mrs. Carolina Bloke de Doe, and giving in his own name his express consent as the legitimate husband of the contracting party, he sells the above-described mines to Mr. John Dill under the following conditions:

First: The price of the sale is the sum of twelve thousand five hundred dollars, American money, for the mine known as " Volcancillos," and that of eight thousand five hundred dollars, also American money, for the group of the other six mines remaining, denounced by John Mann.

Second: Said two amounts shall be paid separately within the term of three years counted from to-day, in the following manner: with reference to the sum of twenty-five thousand dollars, by the sum of $100.00 monthly during the said three years, which shall be delivered in this city to the bank which the seller, Mrs. Carolina Bloke de Doe, may select, on the exact day on which it becomes due, and moreover at the expiration of the first year twenty per cent. of the amount remaining due; at the end of the second year another twenty per cent. of what is then owing, and at the end of the term of the third year, what yet remains to complete the twenty-five thousand, that is, the twelve thousand five hundred in American gold. A like method of payment shall be observed with the eight thousand five hundred dollars representing the price of the other mines, with the only difference that the payments, both monthly and annual, shall be made in this city to the bank which may be selected by Mr. John Mann, to which effect Mrs. Carolina Bloke de Doe renounces in this act the said sum, transferring all her rights to said Mr. John Mann, whose present domicile is the State of Jalisco, Mexico.

Third: If the purchaser, Mr. John Dill, cannot make any of the annual payments as they become due, he may make it without any responsibility the following year, but under no circumstances shall he fail to pay the monthly payments of two hundred pesos, for upon this point they have agreed that if three consecutive monthly payments shall not be made, by that fact alone the present contract shall be rescinded, said Mr. John Dill losing the amounts which until then he may have paid.

Fourth: By virtue of this contract Mr. John Dill enters at once into possession of the mines and thereupon may exploit them, sell the ores and do with them whatever he deems proper, it being provided that even in the event that the present contract should not be carried out, the said John Dill may dispose of the ores extracted up to that time, without rendering accounts.

Fifth: In the event that said Mr. John Dill should transfer the foregoing mines before having fully acquired the property by the total payment of the stipulated prices, the same obligations and rights which this contract contains shall pass to the purchaser.

Sixth: The prices herein stipulated are the just and legitimate prices of the mines sold, which are not worth more; but in the event that they should be worth more, said Mrs. Carolina Bloke de Doe makes a donation of the excess in favor of the purchaser and to that effect she renounces the right which she would have to rescind this contract on account of lesión or other grounds and the provisions of articles 1658, 1662 and 2890 of the Mexican Civil Code.

That the aforesaid mines are free of all encumbrance and all taxes up to date are paid, and that the seller obligates her present and future property to the warranty (evicción y saneamiento) of the present contract. Moreover it is agreed that any defect or nullity of all or any one of the titles of said mining properties, shall give the right to said Mr. John Dill or his privies of estate for the rescission of all the obligations contained in this contract, he or his representatives remaining completely relieved of all payment by virtue of this agreement. In the event that said Mr. John Dill or his representatives shall make exact and faithful compliance with this contract, making all the payments in it provided, the said Mrs. Carolina Bloke de Doe obligates herself to execute in favor of said Mr. John Dill or his representatives, the fullest receipt and acquittance, which shall be considered as the most absolute and irrevocable title of said mining properties, said act complying with all and every the conditions required by the laws of the United States of Mexico, without charges or expenses of any kind.

It is also especially agreed between the contracting parties, in the case of loss of the rights of property of these mines, by reason of the fault, motive, omission, or whatever other cause of said Mrs. Carolina Bloke de Doe, the second party, John Dill, or whoever represents his right, shall be completely and definitely relieved of every obligation arising out of this contract.

In testimony whereof, the contracting parties signed with their proper hands this present contract, at 11 o'c A. M. of the day, month and year mentioned, in the City of St. Louis, Mo., U. S. A.

It is indicated that the Bank chosen by the Attorney in Fact of Mrs. Carolina Bloke de Doe, is the St. Louis Union Trust Co., whose office is on Fourth and Locust Streets in this City of St. Louis, Mo.

(Signed) JOHN DOE — The Vendor,
Attorney in Fact for Carolina Bloke de Doe.
JOHN DILL — The Purchaser.

Witnesses:
F. Robleda,
T. P. Montfort.

(Here follow: Notarial Certificates of the acknowledgments of John Dill and John Doe, dated February 18/07, before a Notary Public; and Consular Certificate of the exican Consulate, of the same date.)

Art. 1185. No. 19. PETITION FOR UTILIZATION OF WATER POWER.

(50ct. Stamp).

Señor Secretario de Fomento,
    éxico, D. F.

 iguel Ahumada, Jr., soltero, agente de negocios, ciudadano mexicano; Fernando Castaños, abogado, casado, también ciudadano mexicano, y Ricardo Ivey, inglés, industrial y soltero, todos mayores de edad y residentes en esta ciudad de Guadalajara, calle de Benito Juárez número noventa y uno y medio, ante usted con el debido respeto:

Deseamos utilizar para fuerza hidráulica las aguas del río de Santiago, que corren en este Estado de Jalisco, en una extensión de siete kilómetros que mide aproximadamente el lindero Sur de los terrenos de la "Hacienda de la Soledad" con aquel rio; y en aquella extensión se elegirá el punto más á propósito para hacer la presa y boca-toma del canal que deba construirse para producir la fuerza solicitada; y estando facultado el Ejecutivo de la Unión, por la ley de 6 de junio de 1894, para otorgar concesiones á particulares ó compañías para el aprovechamiento de las aguas de la Federación, con fundamento en el artículo I de dicha ley, pedimos á usted que, previos los trámites legales, se sirva:

Primero. Autorizarnos para aprovechar como fuerza hidráulica las aguas del mencionado río, tomándolas en cualquier punto comprendido en la extensión de siete kilómetros que al principio indicamos, y volviéndolas al propio río, bajo el concepto de que la cantidad de agua de que necesitamos disponer, será hasta veinticinco mil litros por segundo; y á fin de precisar con toda claridad los nombres de los lugares en que tomarémos y devolverémos las aguas solicitadas, tenemos la honra de acompañarle un plano del lindero Sur de la hacienda de La Soledad con el rio Grande de Santiago, manifestándole que ese lindero comienza en el punto llamado " Arroyo del Sabino Gordo " y concluye en el llamado " Arroyo Verde "; que tomarémos el agua en el punto " Piedras Chinas," del lado de La Soledad, cerca de la Cueva del Hostio, y la devolverémos en el punto Arroyo Verde, que está quinientos metros aproximadamente al Oeste del Arroyo del Sabino Grande.

Segunda. Concedernos dos meses de plazo para la presentación de planos, perfiles y memorias descriptivas.

Tercero. Eximir por cinco años de todo impuesto federal, con excepción del Timbre, á los capitales empleados en el trazo, construcción y reparación de las obras que defina la concesión respectiva.

Cuarto. Permitirnos la introducción libre de derechos de importación, por una sola vez, de las máquinas, instrumentos científicos y aparatos necesarios para el trazo, construcción y explotación de las mismas obras.

Quinto. Permitirnos ocupar gratuitamente los terrenos baldios y nacionales para el paso de canales, etc.

Sexto. Concedernos el derecho de expropiar á particulares con arreglo á la ley.

" La Soledad " está 40 kilómetros al Norte de aquí.

Hacemos esta solicitud para nosotros ó para la Compañía que al efecto proyectamos organizar.

Queda ya indicado nuestro domicilio en esta ciudad.

Guadalajara, octubre diez y seis de mil novecientos nueve.

Art. 1186. No. 19. TRANSLATION.

Hon. Secretary of Fomento,
Mexico, D. F.

Miguel Ahumada, Jr., unmarried, business agent, Mexican citizen; Fernando Castaños, lawyer, married, also Mexican citizen, and Richard Ivey, Englishman, engaged in industrial pursuits, all of lawful age, and residents in this city

of Guadalajara, Benito Juárez street, No. 91½, before you
with due respect:

We wish to utilize for hydraulic power the waters of the
Santiago River, which flow in this State of Jalisco, for an
extension of seven kilometers approximately along the southern border of the "Hacienda de La Soledad" upon said
river, and within which extension the most appropriate site
will be chosen for the construction of the dam and boca-toma
of the canal which will be constructed to produce the solicited power; and inasmuch as the Executive of the Union
is empowered, by the law of 6 June, 1894, to grant concessions to individuals or companies for utilizing the waters
of the Federation, we request of you, in conformity with Art.
I of said law, and after the proper legal procedure:

First. To authorize us to make use of the waters of said
river for hydraulic power, taking the water from some point
within the aforesaid extension of seven kilometers and returning them to the said river, it being declared that the
quantity of water which we will need will amount to 25,000
liters per second; and in order to specify with all accuracy
the names of the places where we will take and return the
said waters, we have the honor to remit herewith a plan
of the southern boundary of the Hacienda de La Soledad
with the Rio Grande de Santiago, explaining that the said
boundary begins at a point called "Arroyo del Sabino
Gordo" and ends at a point known as "Piedras Chinas";
that we will take the water at the point "Piedras Chinas"
on the side of La Soledad near the Cave del Hostio, and
that we will return it at the point Arroyo Verde, which is
about 500 meters west of the Arroyo del Sabino Grande.

Second. To grant us two months' time in which to present
plans, profiles and descriptive reports.

Third. To exempt the capital employed in the laying out,
construction and repair of the works described in the concession, for five years, from all federal taxes except the Stamp
Tax.

Fourth. To permit us to import for one time only free of duty, the machinery, scientific instruments and apparatus necessary for the survey, construction and exploitation of the said works.

Fifth. To permit us to occupy gratuitously baldios and national lands for the passage of canals, etc.

Sixth. To grant us the right to expropriate private lands in accordance with the law.

"La Soledad" is 40 kilometers north of here.

We make this petition for ourselves or for the Company which we intend to organize for the purpose.

Our domicile in this city is above stated.

Guadalajara, 16 October, 1909.

Art. 1187. No. 20. ЛINING DENOUNCEMENT.

(50 ct. Stamp.)

C. Agente de Fomento, en el Ramo de Лineria:

Tirante al Blanco, vecino de .... ante Ud. con el debido respeto digo: que en el Distrito de .... y terrenos del pueblo de .... existe una veta de (oro, plata ó metal que alli se encuentre) que llamaré (aqui el nombre con que se le designe) cuya veta corre en un lugar circunscripto dentro de los puntos ó linderos siguientes: al Norte .... al Sur .... al Oriente .... al Poniente.

Sobre esta veta deseo adquirir .... pertenencias mineras y para este efecto presento por duplicado esta mi solicitud, con el objeto de que, tramitado en la forma legal el expediente respectivo, se me adjudiquen dichas pertenencias y se me expida el titulo respectivo.

Designo como perito que se encargará de la medición y plano correspondiente al Sr. Ingeniero Don ...., residente en .... para que se sirva nombrarlo el Ciudadano Agente y comunicarle su nombramiento.

Dichas pertenencias se situarán y medirán á hilo de veta (ó sobre la longitud de la misma). Por lo tanto á Ud.

suplico se sirva registrar esta solicitud para todos los efectos de la ley de la materia y proveer á esta mi solicitud en los términos que prescribe la misma ley.

México ——— de ———, de 1910.

Art. 1188.   No. 20.   TRANSLATION.

Agent of Fomento:

Tirante al Blanco, residing in ...., represents to you with all due respect that in the District of .... and on the lands of the town of .... there exists a vein of (gold, silver or any metal which is found there) which I will call (here insert the name which the mine is to bear), which vein occurs in ground located within the following points or boundaries: on the north .... on the south .... on the east .... on the west ....

I desire to acquire .... mining *pertenencias* upon this vein and therefore present in duplicate this my petition to the end that upon due legal investigation and procedure said *pertenencias* may be adjudicated to me and the legal title issued to me.

I designate as expert to take charge of the measurement and preparation of the map, the Engineer ...., residing at ...., in order that he may be duly appointed by the Agent and notification of such appointment given him.

Said *pertenencias* will be located and measured along the length of the vein. Therefore I pray you record this application in compliance with the law on the subject and dispose of this my petition in the manner provided by the same law.

(Signature.)

México, ——— day of ———, 1910.

Art. 1189. No. 21. DEED OF SALE, BY ATTOR-
NEY-IN-FACT.

NUMERO CIENTO CUARENTA Y SIETE. En Au-
tlán, á los once dias del mes de septiembre de mil novecientos seis, ante mi Alejandro Yáñez, Notario supernumerario
de este municipio y de los testigos que al fin mencionaré,
comparecieron de una parte, el señor Juan Doe, casado, como
apoderado del señor D. P. Richardson, según consta del documento que exhibe, el cual doy fé tener á la vista y al fin se
insertará en lo conducente, y de la otra el señor Juan P. Delaney, soltero, siendo ambos mineros, mayores de edad, y de
esta vecindad, capaces para contratar y obligarse, á quienes
doy fé conocer, y el primero dijo: que según consta de la
escritura que presenta extendida en esta ciudad bajo el
número cincuenta y tres el diez y ocho de noviembre de
mil novecientos cinco por ante el señor Notario don Zeferino
Reyes Ramirez, y cuya escritura doy fé tener á la vista, su
representado es dueño por compra que hizo á don Juan Mann
de las minas siguientes, á saber: Continuó diciendo el señor
Doe que las seis minas antes expresadas se las vende al señor
Juan P. Delaney, en cien pesos que tiene recibidos á su entera satisfacción, advirtiendo que dicha cantidad es el justo
y legitimo precio de las mismas: que no valen más; pero
para el caso de que más valieren, del exceso le hace donación
al señor Delaney y al efecto renuncia el derecho que podría
tener para rescindir este contrato por lesión ó por cualquier
otro motivo y lo dispuesto en los articulos mil seis cientos
cincuenta y ocho, mil seis cientos sesenta, y dos mil ocho
cientos noventa del Código Civil; que las relacionadas minas
están libres de todo gravámen y se obliga á la evicción y
saneamiento.   En seguida el señor Delaney manifestó que
acepta en todas sus partes lo expuesto por el señor Doe.   El
poder presentado por este señor y que he dado fé tener á la
vista en lo conducente dice: " Número ciento cuatro.   En
Autlán, á los veinticuatro dias del mes de junio de mil novecientos cinco, ante mi Alejandro Yáñez, Notario supernu-

merario de este municipio y de los testigos que **al fín se**
mencionarán, compareció el señor D. P. Richardson, casado,
minero, mayor de edad, originario de los Estados Unidos
de América en la ciudad de San Luis Missouri, y **acciden-**
talmente en esta ciudad, capaz para contratar y obligarse, á
quien doy fé conocer y dijo: que para todos los asuntos judiciales y extrajudiciales que en la actualidad tiene pendientes y para cuantos en lo sucesivo se le ofrezcan sean de la
naturaleza que fueren, le confiere poder general sin limitación alguna, conforme al articulo ochenta y cinco de la ley del
Notariado al señor Juan Doe, vecino de esta ciudad, **facul-**
tándolo además . . . para que celebre todo género de
contratos, bien sean estos de venta, permuta, hipoteca, ó de
cualquiera otra naturaleza: para que otorgue los **instrumen-**
tos públicos ó privados que demande el ejercicio de las **fa-**
cultades que anteceden." Concuerdan los anteriores inser-
tos con sus originales á que me refiero. Se dió lectura por
mi de la presente escritura á **los** señores contratantes y **con-**
formes con su contenido firman, así como el Notario y **los**
testigos que lo fueron los señores Cándido Pelayo y **Alejan-**
dro Córtes, ambos casados, mayores de edad, conocidos mios
y de esta vecindad.— Juan Doe.— John Delaney.— Cándido
Pelayo.— A. F. Córtes.— Alejandro Yáñez.— El sello con
que autorizo.

Art. 1190. No. 21. TRANSLATION OF DEED OF SALE.

NUMBER 147. In Autlán, on the 11th day of the month
of September, 1906, before me Alejandro Yáñez, Notary
supernumerary of this Municipality, and the witnesses whom
at the end I will mention, appeared on the one part **Mr.**
John Doe, married, as the attorney in fact of **Mr. D. P.**
Richardson, as appears by the document which he exhibits,
which I certify I have before me, and which I will insert
in its material parts, and on the other part **Mr. John P. De-**
laney, unmarried, both being miners, of lawful age, and **res-**
ident here, capable of contracting and obligating themselves,

whom I certify that I know, and the first said: that as appears from the instrument which he exhibits, executed in this City under the number 53 on the 18th day of November, 1905, before the Notary Don Zeferino Reyes Ramirez, and which instrument I certify to have before me, his principal is the owner by purchase which he made from Mr. John Mann of the following mines, to-wit: — (Here are named, with their descriptions as taken from the Mining Titles, the mines "Ampliacion de Anexas de Buenavista," "Socabon," "Anexas de Buenavista," "Anexas de la Purisima," "Anexas de la Purisima, No. 2," and "La Junta"). Mr. Doe continued saying: That the six mines above mentioned he sells to. Mr. John P. Delaney for one hundred pesos which he has received to his entire satisfaction, declaring that said amount is the just and lawful price of the same; that they are not worth more; but that in the event that they should be worth more, he makes a donation of the excess to Mr. Delaney, and to that end renounces the right which he would have to rescind this contract on account of "lesión" or for any other reason, and renounces the provisions of Articles 1658, 1670 and 2890 of the Civil Code; that the said mines are free from encumbrance and he binds. himself to warrant them. Thereupon Mr. Delaney declared that he accepts in all its parts what had been declared by Mr. Doe. The power of attorney presented by the latter and which I have certified I have before me, in its material part says: "No. 104. In Autlán on the 24th day of the month of June, 1905, before me Alejandro Yáñez, Notary supernumerary of this municipality and the witnesses who at the end will be mentioned, appeared Mr. D. P. Richardson, married, a miner, of lawful age, and resident of the United States of America in the City of St. Louis, Missouri, and temporarily in this City, capable of contracting and binding himself, whom I certify that I know, and he said: "That for all matters judicial and extrajudicial which he now has pending and for all such as may hereafter be offered, of

58

whatever nature they may be, he confers general power without any limitation, according to Article 85 of the Notarial Law, on Mr. John Doe, resident of this city, empowering him moreover . . . to execute all kinds of contracts, whether of sale, exchange, mortgage, or of whatever other nature; and to execute the public and private instruments required in the exercise of the foregoing powers." The foregoing extracts agree with their originals to which I refer. The present writing was read by me to the contracting parties, and agreeable to its contents they sign, as also the Notary and the witnesses, who were Cándido Pelayo and Alejandro Córtes, both married, of lawful age, my acquaintances, and residents here.

(Signed.)

(Seal.)

Art. 1191. No. 22. ESCRITURA DE SOCIEDAD — ARTICLES OF INCORPORATION.

NUMERO CATORCE.— En la ciudad de Hermosillo, Sonora, México, á los diez y seis dias del mes de Diciembre del año de mil novecientos ocho, ante mi Alberto Flores, Notario Público Número dos y los testigos Señores Ignacio M. Robles, casado y Benjamin Landgrave, soltero, ambos mayores de edad, empleados, de este domicilio y sin tacha legal, comparecieron los Señores JOSEPH WHELESS, casado, abogado, vecino de San Louis, Missouri, E. U. A.; ROBERT D. WOOD, casado, minero, del mismo domicilio que el anterior, y JAMES PENMAN, célibe, minero, con domicilio en esta ciudad, todos hábiles para obligarse, mayores de edad, conocidos del infrascrito Notario, y por no poseer el idioma español el Señor Wood, le sirve de intérprete, bajo la protesta de ley, que en este acto rinde ante mi, el Señor L. T. Bristol, mayor de edad, soltero, empleado, de este domicilio y de mi personal conocimiento. Exponen los comparecientes que celebran el contrato de sociedad consignado en las cláusulas siguientes: — *PRIMERA.* La sociedad se denominará " Hermosillo Copper Company, S. A.," se constituye en la forma privada á que se contrae la segunda parte del articulo ciento sesenta y séis del Código de Comercio, y tendrá su domicilio en esta ciudad.— *SEGUNDA.* El objeto de la sociedad es adquirir toda clase de propiedades mineras para explorarlas, explotarlas, venderlas, rentarlas ó de cualquiera otra manera disfrutarlas, haciendo dichas adquisiciones por denuncio, ó por cualquier otro titulo legal. Adquirir terrenos adyacentes, maderas, aguajes y establecer casas de comercio, instalaciones de todos géneros y cualesquiera industrias necesarias para el aprovechamiento de las minas.— *TERCERA.* La duración de la sociedad será de veinticinco años contados desde hoy, pero podrá disolverse anticipadamente por acuerdo de la Asamblea General de Accionistas, aprobado cuando menos por los votos que representen las tres cuartas partes de las acciones emitidas.— *CUARTA.* La sociedad se constituye con un capital de VEINTICINCO MIL PESOS, PLATA, representado por veinticinco mil acciones libradas del valor de un peso cada una y de las cuales acciones veinticuatro mil novecientos noventa y ocho corresponden al Señor Joseph Wheless, y una á cada uno de los otros socios. Dichas acciones son pagadas en la forma siguiente: Los Señores Wood y Penman exhiben en efectivo el valor que representan sus acciones, según recibo que para su resguardo les expide el Tesorero del Consejo de Administración que en lo de adelante se mencionará, y el Señor Wheless declara: que en el Juzgado segundo de primera Instancia de este Distrito, sigue un juicio ejecutivo mercantil sobre pago de setenta y cinco mil ciento cincuenta y nueve pesos noventa y dos centavos oro americano, con más los intereses al tipo pactado, contra la " Verde Grande Copper Company, S. A." teniendo en la actualidad embargadas las siguientes propiedades: Minas " La Verde," " La Cobriza," " Verde Grande " y " San Luis," con la maquinaria, casas, herramienta, implementos, etcétera, especificados en el acta respectiva; y que el dia de ayer recayó una senteueia cuya parte resolutiva literalmente dice: —"*Primero.* El actor probó plenamente su acción en el presente juicio; en consecuencia ha lugar á hacer trance y remate de los bienes embargados á la Compañía 'Verde Grande Copper Company' para hacer pago al acreedor de la cantidad de ciento cincuenta mil trescientos diez y nueve pesos, ochenta y cuatro centavos, más los interses legales á razón de doce porciento anual en moneda. del cuño mexicano á contar desde la fecha del otorgamiento de las obligaciones hasta que se verifique su pago.— *Segundo.* Serán á cargo de la Compañia demandada las costas legales del presente juicio.— *Tercero.* Notifíquese. Así definitivamente juzgando lo sentenció y firmó el Juez segundo de primera Instancia. Ricardo Searcy.— A.— M. Gómez.— A.— Joaquin L. Pérez." Concuerda con su original que obra en los autos de referencia, los que se han tenido á la vista en el precitado Juzgado, de lo que doy fé. Agrega el Señor Wheless que en pago de sus veinticuatro mil novecientas noventa y ocho acciones, sin reserva de ningún género, traspasa á la Compañía incorporada en este instrumento, todo el crédito, cuya acción deduce en el juicio de referencia, con todos sus privilegios, incidencias y prerrogativas, á fin de que la "Hermosillo Copper Company, S. A." pueda con el carácter de única dueña hacer ejecutar la sentencia de que se acaba de hacer mérito y adjudicarse los bienes rematados.— *QUINTA.* Las acciones serán nominativas é indivisibles, sé expedirán á favor de las personas á quienes pertenecen y sus dueños podrán enajenarlas libremente en los términos del articulo ciento ochenta y uno del Código de Comercio, declarándolo y firmándolo en el Registro de Acciones de la Compañia.— *SEXTA.* Las acciones se extenderán en la forma establecida por el Código de Comercio y deberán ser firmadas por todo el personal del Consejo de Administración.— *SÉPTIMA.* El dueño de una ó más acciones queda obligado de pleno derecho y de una manera absoluta á las estipulaciones de esta escritura y á las resoluciones de la Asamblea General, así como á todo lo prac-

ticado en los negocios sociales.— *OCTAVA.* Si por ex-
travio, robo ó destrucción de cualquier titulo de acción, se
solicitare un duplicado, el Consejo de Administración pub-
licará la solicitud en los periódicos durante un mes, y si no se
presentare oposición en ese tiempo, se expedirá el duplicado
del titulo, á costa del interesado.— *NOVENA.* Cada acción dá derecho en la división del capital social, cuando ter-
mine la sociedad y en el reparto de las ganancias, á una suma
proporcional á la cantidad total de las acciones emitidas.—
DÉCIMA. Los socios fundadores no tendrán derecho á ninguna suma adicional en las utilidades por el sólo hecho de
ser fundadores.— *UNDÉCIMA.* El Consejo de Administración se compondrá de un Presidente que hasta la primera
Asamblea General lo será el Señor Joseph Wheless, un Vice-
presidente que lo será el Señor Robert D. Wood, por el mismo
término, y un Secretario y Tesorero que lo será el Señor
James Penman por igual tiempo.— *DUODÉCIMA.* El
Consejo de Administración se nombrará el quince de Diciembre de cada año, en Asamblea General y las personas que
fueren nombradas, y que pueden ser reelectas indefinidamente,
comenzarán á ejercer su encargo el primero de Enero siguiente. Si por alguna circumstancia no se reuniere la asamblea, seguirán ejerciendo sus funciones los Consejeros cesan-
tes hasta que se hiciere la elección.— *DÉCIMA TERCERA.*
El Consejo de Administración se reunirá cuando los negocios
lo exijan y será convocado por el Presidente para informarse
de la marcha de la negociación y dictar las disposiciones
pertinentes.— *DÉCIMA CUARTA.* Las decisiones del
Consejo de Administración se adoptarán por unanimidad ó
por mayoria absoluta de votos de los miembros presentes y
en caso de empate, resolverá el voto del Presidente.— *DÉC-
IMA QUINTA.* Las asambleas generales se formarán de
todos los accionistas que concurran por sí ó por medio de sus
representantes, los cuales pueden ser acreditados ó por poder
jurídico ó por carta-poder.— *DÉCIMA SEXTA.* Sólo se
considerarán accionistas las personas anotadas en el Registro

de la Compañia como dueñas de una ó más acciones.—
DÉCIMA SEPTIMA. Las asambleas generales serán or-
dinarias ó extraordinarias, debiendo celebrarse las primeras
el quince de Diciembre de cada año y las segundas cuando las
convoque el Consejo de Administración ó lo pidan por escrito
por lo menos tres accionistas que en conjunto representen la
tercera part ó más de las acciones emitidas, expresando el
objeto para que lo solicitan. Las votaciones se computarán
por acciones y no por personas.— *DÉCIMA OCTAVA.* El
Consejo de Administración y sus miembros tendrán las facultades y ejercerán las funciones siguientes: I. El Consejo
dispondrá los trabajos generales que han de emprenderse en
las minas y resolverá sobre la compra, gravámen, venta ó
cualquiera otro contrato para realizar el objeto de la Compañía. II. El Presidente regirá las sesiones del Consejo, lo
convocará á juntas y acuerdos, llevará la firma de la sociedad
en todas las escrituras y documentos que se otorguen, órdenes
que se expidan y en cuantos actos sean necesarios para la administración de los negocios, y cuidará del cumplimiento de
esta escritura. III. El mismo Presidente tendrá facultades
para contratar toda clase de obras acordadas por el Consejo,
nombrar empleados y factores de cualquiera categoria, seña-
lándoles sus sueldos. Para comprar maquinaria, herramienta,
materias fungibles y efectos de todos géneros indispensables
para el laboreo y explotación de las minas; y para ejercer
los demás actos administrativos que requiera el objeto de la
sociedad. IV. Igualmente tendrá facultades para compa-
recer ante las autoridades federales, del Estado ó Municipales
á fin de ejercer todos los derechos y cumplir las obligaciones de
la Compañía; promoviendo negocios civiles ó criminales, de
jurisdicción voluntaria ó mixta, expedientes gubernativos y
demás en que tenga interés la sociedad, así demandando como
defendiendo; para presentar demandas, contestaciones, es-
critos, recusaciones, testigos, documentos y pruebas de todo
género: para pedir requerimientos, secuestros, embargos, ventas de bienes, subastas y adjudicaciones; para articular y

absolver posiciones por personales que fueren; para oir autos
y sentencias é interponer los recursos de revocación, apelación
y sus denegados, así como los de nulidad y amparo y seguir
los pleitos hasta su conclusión, pudiendo nombrar apoderados y delegarles las facultades que sean necesarias; revocar
poderes y conferir á los mandatarios autorización para revocar
y sustitiur. V. El mismo Presidente ordenará los gastos
que deban hacerse con motivo de los trabajos de las minas y
de los demás asuntos sociales y expedirá las órdenes de pago
á cargo del Tesorero; debiendo presentar una cuenta general
informada en la primera asamblea que se verifique, rindiendo
al propio tiempo informe sobre el estado de todos los trabajos
y negocios de la Compañia. VI. El Secretario llevará el
libro de registro de acciones, así como el de actas, acuerdos
y los demás que fueren necesarios y cuidará de la correspon-
dencia y documentos de la Compañía. VII. El Tesorero recibirá y cuidará los fondos de la Compañia, otorgando recibos; pagará las órdenes que expida el Presidente y llevará
en debida forma la contabilidad.— *DÉCIMA NOVENA.*
Por falta ó ausencia del Director ó Presidente, cualquiera
que sea la causa de que proceda, ejercerá sus funciones el
Vice-Presidente con las mismas facultades que á aquel se le
han concedido en esta cláusula.— *VIGÉSIMA.* La vigi-
lancia de la sociedad se confiará á un Comisario nombrado
anualmente en Asamblea General. Mientras ésta se reune,
se concede tal nombramiento al Señor James D. Fresh, con
todas las facultades que la ley le confiere, y para dar principio á sus funciones tanto él como los demás miembros del
Consejo depositarán, cuando ménos, una acción en la Tesore-
ria de la Compañía.— *VIGÉSIMA PRIMERA.* Cuando
los negocies de la sociedad produzcan utilidades, se separará
anualmente el cinco por ciento de su importe para formar el
fondo de reserva, hasta que éste haya alcanzado el veinte por
ciento del capital social.— *VIGÉSIMA SEGUNDA.* Sep-
arado el fondo de reserva, el resto de las utilidades que re-
sulten en el año, se distribuirá entre los accionistas en pro-

porción de las acciones que cada uno tenga. Para hacer esta distribución, el Consejo citará á los accionistas á fin de que presenten sus acciones y'reciban el dividendo que les toque. — *VIGÉSIMA TERCERA.* Cuando haya de disolverse la sociedad, la Asamblea General nombrará los liquidadores que formen la liquidación general, con la cual se dará cuenta á una nueva Asamblea para su aprobación ó para que se le hagan las . observaciones que procedan.— *VIGÉSIMA CUARTA.* El Consejo de Administración cuidará de que los liquidadores cumplan debidamente con su encargo hasta que la liquidación sea aprobada por la Asamblea General.— *VIGÉSIMA QUINTA.* Aprobada la liquidación, el capital social existente se dividirá y distribuirá entre los accionistas proporcionalmente á su representación. Si entre el capital social existen valores que no sean numerario y no se pusieren de acuerdo los accionistas sobre la manera de distribuirlos, se rematarán al mejor postor para repartir su producto en dinero.— *VIGÉSIMA SEXTA.* En la Asamblea General en que se aprueben las cuentas y liquidación, se nombrarán los socios á cuyo cargo quedará hacer la distribución final del capital.— *VIGÉSIMA SEPTIMA.* En los casos no previstos en esta escritura, se procederá conforme lo acuerde la mayoria de votos en Asamblea General, calculada por acciones y no por personas. LEIDO que fué este instrumento á los Señores otorgantes, con el que se manifestaron conformes y advertidos de la obligación de registrarlo, lo ratificaron y firman. Doy fé. Joseph Wheless.— R. D. Wood. — James Penman.— L. T. Bristol.— B. Landgrave.— I. M. Robles.— A. Flores.— Rúbricas.— Sello Oficial. . . . .

NOTA.

Bajo el número catorce se firmó hoy en la Notaria de mí cargo una escritura de constitución de la sociedad denominada " Hermosillo Copper Company," S. A., con capital de vienticinco mil pesos.— Otorgantes: Joseph Wheless, Robert D. Wood y James Penman.— En mi concepto causa la ·

cuota de veinticinco pesos con arreglo al articulo 14, fracción 96, inciso I, letra A de la Ley del Timbre.— Libertad y Constitución.— Hermosillo, Diciembre 16 de 1908.— A. Flores.— Rúbrica.— Al. C. Admor. Pral. del Timbre.— Presente.— Estampillas por valor de veinticinco pesos debidamente canceladas y una certificación que dice; —" El Administrador Principal del Timbre en este lugar, Certifica: que hoy pagó el Lic. A. Flores la suma de veinticinco pesos en estampillas que se fijaron y cancelaron en esta nota, según liquidación formada bajo la responsabilidad del Notario que la suscribe.— Hermosillo, Diciembre 16 de 1908.— El A. P. — J. R. Delahanty.— Rúbrica. " Testado — Nueve — Séptima — no vale — Entre lineas — Cuatro — Sexta — Vale,

— ES PRIMER TESTIMONIO SACADO PARA USO DE LA " HERMOSILLO COPPER COMPANY S. A."; VA EN TRES FOJAS CON LOS TIMBRES DE LEY Y CONCUERDA CON SU ORIGINAL. DOY FE. HERMOSILLO. DICIEMBRE DIEZ Y SIETE DE MIL NOVECIENTOS OCHO.

TRANSLATION.[1]

Art. 1192. No. 22. CORPORATE CHARTER.

Numero 14. In the City of Hermosillo, Sonora, Mexico, on the sixteenth day of the month of December, 1908, before me Alberto Flores, Public Notary No. 2, and the witnesses Mess. Ignacio M. Robles, married, and Benjamin Landgrave, Bachelor, both of full age, public employés, residents of this City and without legal disqualifications; appeared Mess. Joseph Wheless, married, lawyer, resident of Saint Louis, Missouri, U. S. A.; Robert D. Wood, married, miner, of the same residence as the former, and James Pen-

[1] The following translation was made by the official "*perito*," and is not at times the choicest English, but is substantially correct after being pruned in some respects.

man, Bachelor, miner, residing in this City, all legally capable to enter into obligations and of full age, known to the undersigned Notary, and because Mr. Wood does not understand the Spanish language, he was assisted by Mr. L. T. Bristol as interpreter, who in my presence made the necessary legal protestations, of full age, bachelor, employé, resident of this City and personally known to me: The exponents declare, that they have celebrated the contract of incorporation set forth in the following clauses:

FIRST: The Company will be called " Hermosillo Copper Co. S. A.," and constituted under the private form referred to in the second part of Article 166 of the Commercial Code and will have its domicile in this City.

SECOND: The object of the Company is to acquire all classes of mining properties in order to work, develop, sell, rent or in any other manner profit by them, making said acquisitions by denouncement or in whatever other legal method; acquire adjoining lands, woods and waters of all classes, and whatever industries may be necessary for the service of the mine.

THIRD: The duration of the Company will be for twenty-five years counted from to-day, but it may be dissolved previously by agreement of the General Meeting of shareholders, with the approval of not less than three-fourths of the votes representing the shares issued.

FOURTH: The Company is constituted with a capital of twenty-five thousand dollars silver, represented by twenty-five thousand fully paid and non-assessable shares of the value of one dollar each, and of which shares twenty-four thousand nine hundred and ninety-eight belong to Mr. Wheless, and one to each of the partners. Said shares are paid for in the following manner: Mess. Wood and Penman pay in cash the amount of value represented by their shares in accordance with the receipt issued for their security by the Treasurer of the Board of Administration which will be mentioned further on, and Mr. Wheless declares: that in the Second Court of the First Instance of this District, legal proceedings have been instituted for the payment of seventy-five thousand, one hundred and fifty-nine dollars, ninety-two cents American Gold and in addition the interest agreed upon, against the " Verde Grande Copper Co. S. A.," the following properties having actually been attached: The mines " La Verde," " La Cobriza," " Verde Grande " and " San Luis," together with the machinery, houses, tools, implements, etc., specified in the respective suit, and that yesterday a sentence was given, part of which rendered literally is as follows: " First. — The prosecutor fully proved his case in the present suit, in consequence of which, cause has been shown for the sale by auction of the goods of the Verde Grande Copper Co. in order to make payment to the creditor of the sum of one hundred and fifty thousand, three hundred and nineteen pesos and eighty-four cents and in addition the legal interest at the rate of twelve per cent. annually, in Mexican Silver, to count from the date of contracting the obligations until payment is made. Second.— The costs of the present legal proceedings will be paid by the defendant Company. Third — Notify: That the second Judge of the first Instance definitely passes the sentence and signs.— Ricardo Searcy. Witnesses: M. Gómez.— Joaquín L. Pérez." The copy agrees with its original which will be found in the proceedings referred to, which we have had before us in the afore-cited Court to which I certify.— Mr. Wheless adds that in payment of his twenty-four thousand, nine hundred and ninety-eight shares, he transfers to the Company incorporated in this deed, without reserve of any nature, all the credit (assets) derived from the suit referred to, with all its privileges, appurtenances and prerogatives with the object that the " Hermosillo Copper Co. S. A." may with the character of sole owner carry into effect the execution of the sentence which has been pronounced and have adjudicated to it the property to be sold.

FIFTH: The shares will be nominative and indivisible, and will be issued in favor of the person to whom they belong and their owners may freely transfer them in the terms of Article 181 of the Commercial Code, declaring and signing in the Share Register of the Company.

SIXTH: The shares will be issued in the form established by the Commercial Code and must be signed by all the members of the Board of Administration.

SEVENTH: The owner of one or more shares is absolutely bound by the stipulations of this deed and the resolutions passed at the General Meetings, as also to all that is done in the business of the Company.

EIGHTH: If any share certificate should be mislaid, stolen or destroyed and a duplicate is solicited, the Board of Administration will publish the applications in two Newspapers for a period of one month and if no opposition is presented during that time the duplicate of the certificates will be issued at the expense of the applicant.

NINTH: Each share will have a right in the division of the capital of the Company at its termination, and in the partition of the profits, in an amount proportionate to the total number of shares issued.

TENTH: The founders of the Company will have no right to any additional profits for the mere fact of being founders (incorporators).

ELEVENTH: The Board of Administration will be composed of a President, who until the first General Meeting will be Mr. Joseph Wheless, a Vice-President who will be Mr. Robt. D. Wood, for the same term, and a Secretary and Treasurer who will be Mr. James Penman for an equal term.

TWELFTH: The Board of Administration will be nominated on the 15th of December each year, at the general meeting, and the persons who may be nominated, can be re-elected indefinitely, and will begin to exercise their duties on the first of the following January: If for any circumstance the general meeting is not held, the officers then holding their positions will continue to do so until such election is held.

THIRTEENTH: The Board of Direction will meet whenever the business of the Company requires it, and will be called by the President in order to give information as to the progress of the business, and to adopt all proper resolutions.

FOURTEENTH: The decisions of the Board of Administration will be adopted by an absolute majority of votes of the members present and in case of tie the President will have the casting vote.

FIFTEENTH: The general meetings will be formed of all the shareholders who attend in person or by means of their representatives, who may be accredited (authorized) by a legal power of Attorney or by letter of proxy.

SIXTEENTH: Only those persons will be considered shareholders, whose names appear on the share Register of the Company as the owners of one or more shares.

SEVENTEENTH: The general meetings will be Ordinary or Extraordinary and the first must be held on the 15th of December each year, and the second when called by the Board of Administration or when requested in writing by not less than three shareholders who jointly represent the third part or more of the shares issued, stating the object of their call. The votes will be computed by the number of shares and not by persons (shareholders).

EIGHTEENTH: The Board of Administration and its members will have the faculties and exercise the following duties:

I. The Board will direct the general works to be carried on in the mine and decide upon the purchase, mortgaging, sale or any other contract for carrying out the objects of the Company.

II. The President will preside over the Board Meetings, he will summon meetings and consultations, will use the signature of the Company on all the documents and deeds executed, orders issued, and in such acts as may be necessary for the administration of the business, and will take care that the conditions of this deed are complied with.

III.   The said President will have the faculties to contract for all class of work decided upon by the Board, engage employés and workmen of whatever nature and determine their salaries: Purchase machinery, tools, the necessary materials and effects of all classes necessary for the working and development of the mines; and to carry out the rest of the administrative acts required by the objects of the Company.

IV.   He will also have the faculties to appear before the Federal, State and Municipal Authorities, with the object of exercising all the rights, and complying with the obligations of the Company, promoting all the proceedings, civil, criminal and of voluntary jurisdiction, administrative proceedings and all the rest that the Company has interest in, as plaintiff, also as defendant: To present claims, pleas, deeds, injunctions, sequestrations, attachments, sales of goods, auctions and adjudications: To interrogate witnesses and answer interrogatories, and generally to prosecute all such proceedings until their completion: He can nominate Attorneys in fact and delegate to them such powers as may be necessary; revoke such powers and confer upon said Attorneys authority of revocation and substitution.

V.   The said President will order the expenses that may be necessary in the working and development of the mines and in the rest of the business of the Company and issue the corresponding orders for payment against the Treasurer: He must present a general statement of accounts duly audited, rendering at the same time a report upon all the workings of the mines, and the rest of the business of the Company.

VI.   The Secretary will keep the Share Register and the Minute book of the meetings and assemblies and the rest of the books which may be necessary and will take care of the correspondence and other documents of the Company.

VII.   The Treasurer will receive and take care of the funds of the Company, executing the corresponding receipts, paying the orders issued by the President and keep in due form the books of accounts of the Company.

NINETEENTH: In the absence of the Director or President from any cause whatever his duties will be fulfilled by the Vice-President, who will have the same powers to those conceded in this clause.

TWENTIETH: The supervision of the Company will be exercised by a Comisario, nominated annually at the General Meeting, until this takes place this nomination will be conferred upon Mr. James D. Fresh with all the faculties conceded by the law, and in order to commence his duties, he in common with the rest of the Board of Direction will deposit at least one share in the Treasury of the Company.

TWENTY-FIRST: When the business of the Company produces profits five per cent. of their import will be set aside annually as a reserve fund until this amounts to a sum equal to twenty per cent. of the share capital.

TWENTY-SECOND: When the reserve fund is set aside, the rest of the profits made in the year will be distributed among the shareholders in proportion to the number of shares held by each: In order to make this distribution the Board of Direction will cite the shareholders, in order to present their shares, that they may be paid the dividends corresponding thereto.

TWENTY-THIRD: When it is necessary to dissolve the Company the General Meeting will appoint the liquidators who will make the general liquidation of the business, of which they will render an account to a fresh general meeting for approbation or that they may make such observations as they deem necessary.

TWENTY-FOURTH: The Board of Direction will take care that the liquidators duly comply with their duties until the liquidation is approved of by the general meeting.

TWENTY-FIFTH: The liquidation being approved of, the capital of the Company (assets) existing will be divided and distributed among the shareholders in proportion to their representation. If among the assets there exist values, that are not in cash and the shareholders cannot agree as to the method of distribution, they will be sold by auction to the highest bidder and the proceeds divided in money.

TWENTY-SIXTH: At the general meeting at which the accounts of the liquidation are approved of, the shareholders will be nominated, in whose charge will be given the final distribution of the assets.

TWENTY-SEVENTH: In the cases not provided for in this, proceedings will be adopted in conformity with the deliberations of the majority of votes in a General Assembly, counted by the number of shares and not by persons.

This deed was thus read to the executing parties who manifested their conformity and being advised of the obligation of registering, they ratified and signed same: To which I attest.

Signed:

Nota.

Under the number fourteen was signed to-day in the Notarial Office in my charge a deed of incorporation of the Company called " Hermosillo Copper Company S. A." with a capital of twenty-five thousand dollars: Executing parties, Joseph Wheless, Robert D. Wood, and James Penman: In my opinion this called for the payment of twenty-five dollars, in conformity with Article 14, fraction 96, clause I, letter A. of the Stamp Law. Liberty and Constitution. Hermosillo, December 16, 1908.— Alberto Flores (Seal). To the Principal Administrator of Revenue: Presente: Stamps for value of twenty-five dollars, duly cancelled and a certificate stating: The Principal Administrator of Revenue in this place, Attests: That to-day Counsellor at Law A. Flores, paid the sum of twenty-five dollars in stamps which are fixed and cancelled on this note, in conformity with the liquidation made under the responsibility of the attesting Notary.

Hermosillo, Decr. 16th, 1908. The Principal Administrator: J. R. Delahanty. (Seal.)

This is the first certified copy made for the use of the

"Hermosillo Copper Company S. A." and carries upon its pages the stamps required by law and agrees with its original; To which I give faith: Hermosillo, Deer. 17th., 1908. — A Flores, Official Seal.

Hermosillo, December 17th, 1908.

CERTIFICATE OF REGISTRY.

To-day being at four in the evening and under the number 265 the present deed remains recorded in folios from one hundred and eighty-one to one hundred and eighty-three of the Book Number five, special section of Minería. Which I authorize and sign in conjunction with my assistants. To which I give faith.

Art. 1193. No. 23. MORTGAGE SECURING ISSUE OF CORPORATE BONDS.

(COURTESY OF ROBERT J. KERR, ESQ., OF CHICAGO, AUTHOR OF THE "HANDBOOK OF MEXICAN LAW.")

No. 3603.— En la Ciudad de Mexico, á las ocho de la mañana del dia primero de Mayo de mil novecientos diéz, ante mí, Rafael Carpio, Notario número treinta y siete, asistido de los testigos Don Florencio Fernández Villarreal, de sesenta y un años y vive en la calle del Montón número uno, y Don Juan B. Nuño, de veintisiete años y vive en el Cuadrante de Santa Catarina número once, solteros, empleados, aptos legalmente y vecinos de esta Capital, los Señores C y Licenciados D, E y F, en representación de la "A B. Company," Sociedad Anónima, de una parte, y el Señor R, como Representante Común de los tenedores de bonos de la misma Compañia, otorgan el contrato que detallan las siguientes cláusulas y declaraciones previas:

DECLARACIONES:

I. Para los efectos legales correspondientes, el suscrito Notario da fé de haber tenido á la vista el certificado del

59

tenor siguiente, el cual queda protocolizado bajo la letra **A.**: " Como Encargado del Registro Público de la Propiedad del Partido Judicial de Tequila, Certifico: Que he registrado los libros del Registro que es á mi cargo, para averiguar los gravámenes que reporten los bienes pertenecientes á la Sociedad denominada " A. B. Company, S. A." y no encontré ningún gravamen ni limitación de dominio constituído sobre dichos bienes, habiendo hecho el registro con vista de los títulos y de las inscripciones de veintiseis de Abril de mil ochocientos noventa á la fecha. Extiendo el presente certificado . . . á los veintiseis dias del mes de Abril de mil novecientos diez. A. M. Topete." . . . II. **Por** escritura pública otorgada en esta Capital por ante el suscrito Notario, el veinticuatro de Febrero de mil novecientos nueve, fué constituida la sociedad anónima A. B. Company, Sociedad Anónima, con el objeto expresado en dicha escritura . . . cuyo objeto es. . . . III. Con el objeto, entre otros, de determinar el modo de allegarse recursos para explotar y desarrollar los negocios de la Compañía, fueron reunidos en una asamblea general extraordinaria conforme á los estatutos de la Compañía, todos los accionistas de la misma, verificándose esta asamblea el dia treinta de Marzo de este año en los términos que expresa el acta respectiva que obra á fojas veintiseis y siguientes del libro de actas de la sociedad y que doy fé haber tenido á la vista y es como sigue: " **En** la Ciudad de México, á treinta de Marzo de mil novecientos diéz, á las tres de la tarde, en la casa número ocho de la Avenida San Francisco, se reunieron los Señores C, Licenciados D, E y F, accionistas de la " A. B. Company," Sociedad Anónima. Formada la lista de presencia, resultaron **según** ella representadas diez mil acciones de las que los concurrentes representan el siguiente número de acciones respectivamente: C, cuatro mil novecientas cincuenta acciones: Licenciado D, cuatro mil novecientas cincuenta acciones, Licenciado F, noventa acciones y Licenciado E diez acciones, total diez mil acciones. Resultando presentes la totalidad de las acciones de la Compañía, representando todo el capital social de la misma, el Presidente declaró constituída legalmente la asamblea. Se dio lectura á la órden del dia como sigue: I. Discusión y aprobación de las actas de asambleas generales anteriores, cuyas actas no hayan sido aprobadas. II. Enmendaciones y adiciones á los estatutos de la Compañía. III. Elección de los cinco Directores y del socio Comisario de la Compañía para el año fiscal. IV. Determinación del modo de allegarse recursos para explotar y desarrollar los negocios de la Compañia. So dió lectura al acta de la asamblea general de los accionistas de la Compañia, verificada á los veintiocho dias del mes de Enero de mil novecientos diéz, cuya acta obra á fojas diéz y seis á veinticinco, ambos inclusives, del libro de actas de la Compañía y sin discusión fué aprobada dicha acta. . . . El Señor C expresó que para llevar á efecto los negocios de la Compañía habrá necesidad de emitir bonos de la Compañia, en la suma de cién mil dólares oro americano, y que para conseguir la venta de dichos bones habrá necesidad de asegurar dichas emisiones y garantizar el debido pago de dichos bonos con una hipoteca en primer lugar sobre todos sus bienes, no solamente los que ahora tiene sino también los que en lo futuro adquirirá la Compañía y que este asunto se ha incluído en la convocatoria de la presente asamblea general para que los accionistas resuelvan lo que estimen conveniente. La junta de accionistas, teniendo en consideración las razones expresadas por el Señor C, acordó lo siguiente: Se autoriza ampliamente al Consejo de Administración para negociar un préstamo ó préstamos de cien mil dólares oro americano, en moneda de oro de los Estados Unidos de América y que se autoriza al Consejo para negociar dichos préstamos en las mejores condiciones que sea posible, pactando el plazo, los réditos y demás condiciones de los contratos respectivos con garantia de los bienes inmuebles y muebles de la Compañia ó bien con cualquiera otra garantía que estime oportuna, en una ó diversas operaciones, sin más limitación que la del préstamo en su totalidad no excederá

la suma de cien mil dólares de moneda de oro de los Estados Unidos de América ni el interés de las cantidades que se reciban del diez por ciento anual. El Consejo de Administración podrá, si lo estima oportuno, negociar el empréstito por medio de la emisión de bonos hipotecarios y podrá otorgar todos los instrumentos públicos y privados que sean consecuencia de las facultades que se le conceden. No habiendo más asuntos de que tratar se suspendió la sesión levantándose de ella la presente acta, que para constancia fué firmada por todos los presentes. C. Presidente. D—E—F. Secretario."
IV. En ejercicio de las facultades concedidas por la asamblea general de accionistas, el Consejo de Administración de la Compañía resolvió emitir bonos hipotecarios de la Compañía, como aparece del acta de una junta de dicho Consejo que se verificó el mismo dia treinta de Marzo de este año, cuya acta obra á fojas treinta y siguientes del libro de actas de la Compañía y que doy fé haber tenido á la vista y es como sigue: "En la Ciudad de México, á los treinta dias del mes de Marzo de mil novecientos diez á las cinco de la tarde, en la casa número ocho de la Avenida San Francisco de esta Capital, que es el domicilio de la A. B. Company, S. A., se reunió el Consejo de Administración de dicha Compañía, presentes los Directores C, Lies. D, E y F, ausente Señor G. El Señor Director C. presentó la siguiente resolución que después de una discusión fué adoptada por el voto unánime de todos los Directores presentes: Se acuerda que la mayoría del Consejo de Administración de A. B. Company, Sociedad Anónima, es decir, tres de los cinco Directores, sean y están por esta resolución autorizados á emitir bones hipotecarios de la Compañia montando á la suma de cien mil dólares en moneda de oro de los Estados Unidos de América cuyos bones se emitirán en tales condiciones respecto al plazo, á los réditos y demás estipulaciones que dicha mayoria estime conveniente, y además á otorgar una escritura en que se determinarán todas las condiciones de dichas emisiones y que garantizará dichas emisiones con hipoteca sobre los bienes

muebles é inmuebles de la Compañia, dándoles á los tres Directores las más amplias facultades para determinar todas las cláusulas y condiciones de dicha escritura y de los otros documentos que sean necesarios para dar efecto á esta resolución. No habiendo más asuntos de que tratar se suspendió la sesión del Consejo de Administración, levantándose de ella la presente acta, que para constancia fué firmada por todos los Directores presentes. En virtud de la autoridad á ellos conferida por las resoluciones de los accionistas y del Consejo de Administración que preceden, los comparecientes Señores C y D, E y F, en representación de A. B. Company, Sociedad Anónima, y el Señor R como representante común de los tenedores-de los boños referidos, otorgan las siguientes.

CLÁUSULAS:

Primera. La A. B. Company Sociedad Anónima declara: que con fecha primero de Mayo del año mil novecientos diez emitió cien bonos hipotecarios de á mil dólares oro americano, cada uno, haciendo un total de cien mil dólares en moneda de oro de los Estados Unidos de América, cada bono siendo del tenor siguiente: " A. B. Company, Sociedad Anónima. Número ——. $1000.00 oro E. U. A. Bono de primera hipoteca de seis por ciento pagadero en oro de los Estados Unidos de América. A. B. Company, Sociedad Anónima, constituida conforme á la escritura de veinticuatro de Febrero del año mil novecientos nueve, otorgada ante el Notario Público Rafael Carpio en la Ciudad de México, Distrito Federal, reconoce que debe, y por valor recibido promete pagar al portador un mil dólares en moneda de oro de los Estados Unidos de América, el dia primero de Mayo del año mil novecientos cincuenta y promete además pagar durante el plazo del vencimiento y entretanto el capital del bono no sea pagado, desde la expresada fecha y también en moneda de oro de los Estados Unidos de América, el rédito á razón de seis por ciento al año, pagadero semi-anualmente en primero de Noviembre y primero de Mayo de cada año,

mediante la presentación y entrega de los cupones anexos de
réditos á medida que cada uno llegue á su vencimiento.
Tanto la suma capital como los réditos de este bono serán
pagaderos en moneda de oro de los Estados Unidos de América del actual talón de peso y ley ó su equivalente en pesos
del cuño mexicano en el Banco Central Mexicano en esta
Ciudad de México. Este bono es uno de la serie de cien
bonos de primera hipoteca, emitidos por dicha sociedad anónima en la misma fecha que el presente con el mismo valor,
tenor y vencimiento haciendo en conjunto una cantidad de
cien mil dólares en moneda de oro de los Estados Unidos de
América y teniendo los números de uno á cien, ambos inclusive, quedando todos los referidos bonos igualmente garanti-
zados por dicha hipoteca, otorgada á favor del Representante
Común de los tenedores de bonos el dia primero de
Mayo del año de mil novecientos diez ante el Notario Público
Rafael Carpio en esta Ciudad de México, en cuyo instrumento se hipotecan los bienes muebles é inmuebles de dicha
A. B. Company, Sociedad Anónima. Este bono podrá ser
pagado y cancelado después de cinco años contados desde esta
fecha, bajo las condiciones prescritas en dicha hipoteca.
Este bono no será obligatorio si no contiene en el reverso el
certificado de su autenticidad, firmado por el Representante
Común ó sus sucesores en la representación. En testimonio
de lo cual A. B. Company, Sociedad Anónima, ha acordado
que este bono sea firmado por su Presidente y Secretario y
que su sello oficial sea fijado y que los cupones de réditos
anexos sean firmados con la firma litografiada de su Tesorero,
hoy primero de Mayo de mil novecientos diez. A. B. Company, Sociedad Anónima. . . . Presidente . . .
Legalizado. . . . Secretario." Forma de cupón: " No.
. . . Dls. 30.00. El dia primero de Noviembre Mayo
de 19. . . . A. B. Company, Sociedad Anónima, promete
pagar al portador treinta dólares en moneda de oro de los
Estados Unidos de América ó su equivalente en pesos mexicanos en el Banco Central Mexicano, México, D. F. por

rédito semestral que se vence en aquella fecha sobre su bono número . . . de primera hipoteca al seis por ciento pagadero en oro de los Estados Unidos de América y fechado en primero de Mayo de mil novecientos diez. H. Tesorero." En su reverso los bonos tienen lo siguiente: " Certificado del Representante Común. Este certifica que este bono es uno de los de primera hipoteca emitidos conforme á la escritura de primero de Mayo de mil novecientos diez otorgada por A. B. Company, Sociedad Anónima, en la Ciudad de México, Distrito Federal, ante el Notario Público Rafael Carpio. México, D. F. . . . de Mayo de 1910. . . . Representante Común." Nota del Registro de la hipoteca. " La escritura de hipoteca referida en este bono fué debidamente registrada en Tequila, Estado de Jalisco el dia . . . de Mayo de 1910 y además fué debidamente registrada en el Registro de Comercio de México, D. F., el dia . . . de Mayo de 1910." Segunda. La misma Compañía dándose por recibida en préstamo de la suma de cien mil dólares en moneda de oro de los Estados Unidos de América, valor de los cien bonos referidos en la cláusula anterior, declara que es deudora de la mencionada suma en los términos y bajo las condiciones de esta escritura á favor de los tenedores de dichos bonos, en la inteligencia de que este préstamo tiene el carácter de mercantil, supuesto que su objeto es el desarrollo, fomento y giro de los negocios de la misma Compañía. Tercera. El capital de cien mil dólares en moneda de oro de los Estados Unidos de América ó su equivalente en pesos mexicanos del corriente cuño, será pagado por la Compañia en el término de cuarenta años contados desde el dia primero de Mayo de mil novecientos diez y terminando el dia primero de Mayo del año de mil novecientos cincuenta. Cuarta. Durante este plazo de cuarenta años y todo el más que transcurra sin que el expresado capital esté integramente cubierto, la Compañía pagará el rédito de seis por ciento anual por semestres vencidos que se cumplirán los dias primeros de los meses de Noviembre y Mayo de cada año. Quinta. Transcurridos cinco años después de la fecha de los bonos la Compañia tendrá el derecho de aplicar á la amortización parcial de dichos bonos la suma de cinco mil dólares de moneda de oro de los Estados Unidos de América ó cualquier múltiple de dicha suma, aun pagando la totalidad de los cien bonos emitidos, sujetándose á las siguientes condiciones: I. El pago de la amortización parcial ó total solo podrá hacerse en los dias de vencimiento de los intereses semestrales. II. En caso de la amortización parcial de dichos bones se pagarán en el primer lugar los que tienen los números de órden más altos. III. En el caso que no estén presentados para su pago todos los bonos que la Compañia propone pagar en cualquier caso, á la fecha del pago advertida, la Compañía tendrá que depositar con Banco Central Mexicano una suma de dinero suficiente para cubrir á la par con un premio de cinco por ciento de la par y también con los intereses vencidos y no pagados, los bonos no presentados. El dueño ó los dueños de dichos bonos podrán presentarlos á dicho Banco Central Mexicano dentro de cinco años y recibir el pago de la suma correspondiente á sus bonos respectivos, pero si no reclaman dicho dinero ó cualquiera parte de ello dentro de cinco años después de la fecha de dicho depósito, el Banco Central Mexicano pagará á la Compañía la parte de dicha suma no reclamada. IV. Además del capital é intereses vencidos la Compañía tendrá que pagar un premio de cinco por ciento de la par de los bones amortizados antes de su vencimiento. V. Una vez pagados los bonos se inutilizarán y se cancelarán por el Representante Común ó por la Compañia, levantándose una acta en el libro de actas de la Compañia en la que se expresará los números de órden de los bonos y el hecho de haber sido cubiertos y cancelados y esta acta será firmada por el Representante Común y por el Presidente y Tesorero de la Compañia. Sexta. Tanto el capital como los intereses de los bonos se pagarán en esta Ciudad de México en el Banco Central Mexicano, y el pago se hará al portador y á la presentación de los bonos ó de los cupones respectivamente. El pago se hará en moneda de oro de los Estados Unidos de América ó su equivalente en pesos mexicanos del cuño corriente con exclusión de otra moneda ó de papel creada ó por crear, para cuyo efecto la Compañía adopta las disposiciones que contienen los articulos veinte, veintiuno, veintidós y veintitrés de la Ley de Reforma Monetaria del veinticinco de Marzo de mil novecientos cinco. Séptima. Este pago tanto del capital como de los intereses se hará por la Compañía libre para los tenedores de bonos de toda clase de contribuciones ó impuestos creados ó por crear, sean cuales fueren su origen, naturaleza ú objeto y la autoridad legitima ó ilegitima que las decrete, obligándose la Compañía en el caso de que se imponga alguna contribución ó impuesto, á pagarlo por su cuenta ó á libertar á los tenedores de los bonons de hacer el pago aun cuando la ley disponga y prevenga que el impuesto ó la contribución deben ser cubiertos por los acreedores ó los tenedores de bones. Octava. La Compañía, para garantizar el fiel y exacto cumplimiento de todas las estipulaciones y pactos de este contrato y además de dejar obligados todos sus bienes, presentes y futuros, hipoteca especial y expresamente en favor del Representante Común de los tenedores de dichos bonos, todos sus bienes y propiedades, inmuebles y muebles, ya poseidos ó que fueren en el futuro adquiridos por la Compañia, con todas sus entradas y salidas, usos y servidumbres y con todas las contrucciones y mejoras, incluyendo . . . y también todo y cada uno de los otros bienes, acciones, derechos, intereses, privilegios, concesiones, franquicias, propiedades y cosas que la Compañia ahora tiene, posee ó reclama y que en lo futuro tuviere, poseyere ó adquiriere en cualquier lugar. Novena. Mientras que la Compañia hace todos los pagos de la suma principal y de los réditos, de acuerdo con el tenor y el efecto de los bonos y mientras que se cumplen todas las condiciones de esta escritura, la Compañía quedará en la posesión de dichos bienes hipotecados y de sus rendimientos y utilidades, y podrá vender todos los productos salvo las prescripciones aqui consigna-

das; pero la Compañia se compromete á cubrir todas las
contribuciones é impuestos que fueren legalmente causados
sobre los bienes aqui gravados, de manera que la prelación
de los bonos quedará en todo tiempo debidamente conservada.
Y la Compañía conviene en que conservará todos los derechos
que actualmente se le han conferido por las leyes de la República Mexicana. Décima. Todos los bonos aqui garanti-
zados y montantes á la cantidad de cien mil dólares de
moneda de oro de los Estados Unidos de América, serán
otorgados inmediatamente después del otorgamiento de este
instrumento y serán entregados al Representante Común
Señor R y en seguida serán certificados por dicho Representante Común y por él entregados al Presidente de la Compañia ó á la persona que él por escrito designare. Ningún
bono será obligatorio hasta que haya sido otorgado el certificado que sobre él se endose y suscrito por el mismo Representante Común. Undécima. La Compañía se compromete
á pagar y cancelar los cupones anexos á los bonos aquí gar-
antizados á medida que lleguen á su vencimiento respectivo y
además á cancelar todos los bonos cuando sean pagados respectivamente. Duodécima. Esta hipoteca constituida á
favor del Señor R con el carácter de Representante Común
de todos los tenedores de bonos por la cantidad de cien mil
dólares en moneda de oro de los Estados Unidos de América,
ocupará el primer lugar en el registro de obligaciones de la
Compañia, pues se hace constar muy expresamente que la
Compañía no ha emitido anteriormente ningunas otras obligaciones. Décima Tercera. Ninguno de los bonos ó de los
tenedores de bonos tendrán prioridad ó preferencia con respecto á los demás ó sobre ninguno de ellos, quedando por
el contrario expresamente constituida la hipoteca para la
utilidad, beneficio y garantia de todas y de cada una de las
personas, sociedades ó asociaciones que en cualquier tiempo
sean tenedoras de alguno ó algunos de dichos bonos, con entera igualdad y á prorrata entre todos los pendientes de pago.
Queda convenido que ningún tenedor ó tenedores de cual-

quier de dichos bonos ó cupones, tendrá derecho de iniciar diligencias judiciales de cualquiera clase para hacer efectiva esta escritura ó cualquiera de sus cláusulas ó condiciones, sin previa notificación por escrito al Representante Cómún de la comisión de alguna falta y á menos que los tenedores de la mayoria de los bones entonces en circulación hayan notificado y requerido por escrito á dicho Representante Común como antes se dice, y se le haya dado un plazo razonable después de la fecha de la notificación y requisitoria para que inicie diligencias y ejerza las facultades aqui contenidas en su nombre, como Representante Cómún y también sin haber ofrecido al Representante Común una garantia adecuada contra las costas, gastós y responsabilidades que resultaren al Representante Común; y tal notificación, requisitoria y oferta de indemnización pueden ser requeridas por el Representante Común como previa condición á la ejecución de las facultades de esta escritura. Décima Cuarta. No se libertará á la Compañía de la obligación de pagar el capital y los réditos ni aun en el caso de que transcurra el término fijado en la ley para la prescripción de uno y otro, y para este efecto, la misma Compañía renuncia las disposiciones que contienen los articulos mil noventa y uno y mil ochocientos cuarenta y ocho y sus correlativos del Código Civil del Distrito Federal, y también el articulo mil ochocientos cincuenta del mismo Código. En cualquier caso los bienes hipotecados quedarán afectados por el gravamen de esta hipoteca hasta el pago del importe total del capital y de los réditos correspondientes hasta lá fecha en que se verifique dicho pago. Décima Quinta. En caso de que se dejaren de pagar puntualmente en todo ó en parte los intereses sobre los bonos y que esta falta continuase durante los seis meses posteriores al vencimiento el tenedor ó los tenedores de los bonos pendientes de pago, tendrán el derecho de dar por vencido el capital representado por dichos bonos, y desde entonces el expresado capital deberá pagarse inmediatamente con el mismo efecto y con igual obligación que si hubiere transcurrido todo

el término de cuarenta años fijado en la cláusula tercera.
Décima Sexta. En caso de que esté vencido y sea exigible
el pago del capital representado por los bonos ya sea porque
se haya cumplido el plazo señalado para el pago, ya sea
porque se hubiere dejado de pagar los intereses y esta falta
continuase durante los seis meses posteriores al vencimiento,
declarándose vencido el capital en los términos que expresa
la cláusula décima quinta de esta escritura ó sea en algun
otro de los casos establecidos por las leyes, el Representante
Común, siempre que sea requerido por un tenedor ó tenedores
que en la totalidad representen la mayoria de los bonos
pendientes de page, procederá por cualquiera de los medios
siguientes con sujeción á los que el expresado tenedor ó tenedores hubieren decidido: I. Nombrar uno ó mas depositarios
que entren en posesión de los bienes hipotecados. II. Nombrar uno ó mas interventores que funcionen en respecto á
dichos bienes. III. Tomar posesión de los bienes hipotecados. IV. Proceder á la venta de dichos bienes. El ejercicio de una ó mas de las facultades concedidas en esta
cláusula, no impide que el Representante Común pueda en
todo tiempo ejercer las demás que le competan. Décima
Séptima. Todo depositario nombrado por el Representante
Común en virtud de lo establecido en la cláusula anterior,
deberá exigir y recibir en nombre de la Compañía y del
Representante Común el pago de todos los productos de los
bienes hipotecados y está facultado para otorgar recibos por
dichos productos. Tendrá también facultad para examinar
los documentos, libros y papeles de la Compañía y para
tomar conocimiento de todos los actos y operaciones de la
misma. Dicho depositario tendrá también el derecho de administrar los negocios de la Compañia, manejando sus propiedades y plantas y haciendo todos los negocios de la misma
en todos sus ramos con todas las facultades de un administrador general de la Compañía. En el caso de que el depositario tomare dicha posesión, se le entregarán los libros, documentos y papeles necesarios para el manejo y administración

de los negocios de la Compañia. Décima Octava. Todo interventor ó interventores nombrados por el Representante Común, tendrán las mismas facultades que el depositario y además la Compañia después del nombramiento no hará ningun nuevo contrato ni pago sin el consentimiento escrito del interventor ó interventores y éste ó estos pueden concurrir á todas las sesiones de la Compañía ó del Consejo de Administración á cuyo fin se les dará el correspondiente aviso de la hora en que las sesiones han de tener lugar y por último tienen la facultad de que se les dé conocimiento de todos los actos y contratos que hicieren los empleados ó agentes de la Compañía. Décima Novena. En caso de que el Representante Común tomare posesión de los bienes hipotecados de la Compañia, se le entregarán los libres, documentos y papeles necesarios para el manejo y administración de los negocios de la Compañía, quedando encargado de dichos negocios con exclusión de cualquiera otra persona y con todas las facultades de la Compañía y en consecuencia dicho Representante está autorizado para administrar los bienes hipotecados, hacer los contratos que requiera la administración, pero con la obligación de informar mensualmente á la Compañía de todas las operaciones, acompañando en cada mes copia de las que hubiere efectuado así como de la cuenta de ingresos y egresos. Vigésima. Si se decidiere ejecutar esta hipoteca vendiendo los bienes hipotecados se procederá en los términos siguientes: I. Ambas partes convienen en que la venta de los bienes hipotecados se haga sin que preceda juicio ni sentencia, sino solo en virtud de esta escritura y en almoneda pública judicial. II. Durante el procedimiento para la venta el Representante Común tendrá el derecho de tomar la posesión de los bienes hipotecados, pero en todo tiempo podrá suspender el ejercicio de su derecho y designar el depositario ó interventor que se haga cargo de la posesión entretanto el Representante Común tenga en suspenso la facultad en cuanto á la posesion. Quedan en consecuencia renunciadas las disposiciones de los articulos mil trescientos noventa y dos del

Código de Comercio y el novecientos noventa y seis del Código de Procedimientos Civiles del Distrito Federal. III. El Representante Común tiene libertad para fijar á los bienes hipotecados el precio que ha de servir de base para el remate, pero de manera que no sea menor del valor á la par de todos los bonos emitidos y pendientes de pago ó su equivalente en moneda mexicana. En el caso de que no hubiere postura legal en el primer remate se prorrogará el remate como se previene el articulo ochocientos cuarenta y siete del Código de Procedimientos Civiles del Distrito Federal y el Representante Común tendrá el derecho de fijar otro precio que servirá de base para el segundo remate, pero de manera que no sea menor de la mitad del valor á la par de todos los bonos emitidos y pendientes de pago ó su equivalente en moneda mexicana. En el caso que habría necesidad de prorrogar el segundo remate se observarán las disposiciones del mismo articulo ochocientos cuarenta y siete respecto al precio tomando el último precio fijado por el Representante Común como base y las del artículo ochocientos cuarenta y ocho del mismo Código se observarán respecto de los otros términos y condiciones, hasta que sea realizado legalmente el remate. Las partes adoptan las disposiciones del articulo ochocientos cincuenta y cinco del mismo Código para dar efecto á esta cláusula. IV. Para la venta se publicarán edictos una vez por semana durante dos consecutivas en dos periódicos de la Ciudad de México: la primera publicación tiene que ser á lo menos diez dias antes de la fecha del remate. En este edicto se expresarán el lugar, dia y hora de la almoneda y los bienes que se han de vender. Quedan por lo mismo renunciadas las disposiciones del articulo mil cuatrocientos once del Código de Comercio y de los articulos setecientos cincuenta y dos y setecientos cincuenta y cuatro del Código de Procedimientos Civiles vigente en el Distrito Federal. V. En toda venta se recibirán los bonos hipotecarios y sus cupones é intereses vencidos en pago del precio de compra con un valor que no exceda de la par: pero se disminuirá en la

proporción que corresponda si el precio de compra no bastare para pagar todos los bonos pendientes de pago, los cupones vencidos, los otros intereses y los gastos. En este caso, el precio de la compra, deducidos los gastos, se distribuirá pro- **porcionalmente** entre todos los bonos y cupones é intereses vencidos, y tanto unos como otros serán admitidos en pago de aquel precio en la parte que de éste se le deba aplicar. VI. El Representante Común por sí y en beneficio de los tenedores de bonos hará postura á los bienes que se han de vender ó pedirá su adjudicación conforme á los articulos ochocientos cuarenta y nueve y ochocientos treinta y uno del citado Código de Procedimientos siempre que sea requerido por el tenedor ó tenedores de una mayoria de los bonos pen- dientes de pago. En el caso de que el Representante Común compre en el remate, los tenedores de bonos deberán con- tribuir al pago de los expresados gastos en proporción de los bonos que les pertenezcan. VII. El Representante Común está autorizado para otorgar al comprador ó compradores de los bienes la escritura de enajenación y esta escritura de ena- jenación tendrá la misma fuerza y validez que si se hubiere otorgado por la Compañia, pero si dicho Representante no usare de esta facultad, la misma escritura será autorizada por el juez. VIII. El Representante Común recibirá el precio que se pague por el comprador de los bienes. Vigé- sima Primera. Para la más fácil ejecución de la hipoteca se conviene lo siguiente: I. Los depositarios ó interventores que nombre el Representante Común no necesitan tener bienes raices ni otorgar fianza, renunciándose en conse- cuencia, las disposiciones del articulo ochocientos nueve del citado Código de Procedimientos; pero el Representante Común puede, si lo cree conveniente, exgirles una garantia de su manejo. II. El mismo Representante tendrá en todo tiempo el derecho de remover libremente á los depositarios é interventores que hubiere nombrado aunque su nombramiento haya sido confirmado judicialmente. III. Los depositarios ó interventores, agentes ó abogados nombrados por el Repre-

sentante Común serán nombrados bajo la responsabilidad sub-
sidiaria de la Compañía, quedando renunciada la disposición
del articulo ochocientos doce del repetido Código de Procedimientos. IV. En todos los casos en que los depositarios
ó interventores cesen en su encargo, el Representante Común
tendrá derecho de nombrar á nuevos depositarios ó interventores, quedando renunciadas las disposiciones del articulo
ochocientos once del citado Código de Procedimientos. V.
Ni el Representante Común ni los tenedores de bonos tendrán la obligación de acudir á los tribunales para ejercer algunos de los derechos ó de las facultades contenidas en esta
escritura excepto en cuanto á la venta que ha de hacerse en
almoneda judicial conforme al párrafo primero de la cláusula
vigésima; pero tanto uno como los otros puedan, si así lo
desean, acudir á dichos tribunales para obtener su ayuda en
los expresados derechos y facultades salvo las excepciones
contenidas en la clausula décima tercera. VI. En caso de
seguirse el procedimiento judicial, las sentencias ó resoluciones que se pronuncien, cuando sean apelables, solo lo serán
en el efecto devolutivo, quedando renunciadas las disposiciones del articulo mil trescientos treinta y nueve del Código
de Comercio. Admitida la apelación, si ella fuere favorable
á los tenedores de bonos, el Representante Común no estará
obligado á otorgar la fianza que ordena el articulo seiscientos
cincuenta y seis del Código de Procedimientos antes citado,
y en consecuencia la resolución ó sentencia favorable á los
tenedores de bonos se ejecutará sin que sea necesario el otorgamiento de la fianza, quedando por lo mismo renunicadas
las disposiciones del articulo último citado. VII. Ni el
Representante Común ni los postores que admita la Compañía ó el Representante Común ni la Compañía misma en
caso de hacer posturas estarán obligados á abonar sus posturas
y pujas quedando de consiguiente renunciadas las disposiciones del articulo ochocientos nueve del citado Código de
Procedimientos Civiles. VIII. Siempre que el Representante Común ó los tenedores de bonos ocurran á los tribunales

con el fin de ejercitar alguno de los derechos ó de las facultades que respectivamente se les conceden en esta escritura, no tendrán obligación de presentar los bonos á que se refiere la cláusula primera, siendo suficiente en todos los casos que exhiban este instrumento ó los suplementarios ó confirmatorios si se otorgasen ó una copia certificada de ellos; los tenedores de bonos además presentarán documentos otorgados ante un Notario Público en el que se haga constar el número de órden y monto de los bonos, certificando el Notario que los bonos le fueron presentados originales por, quien y lo que á cada uno pertenece. Vigésima Segunda. De todas las sumas y productos que recibiere el Representante Común ya sea en virtud de las cláusulas décima novena ya con motivo de la venta conforme á la cláusula décima sexta, se deducirán primeramente todos los gastos de administración, de conservación, ejecución de la hipoteca, los honorarios del Representante Común ó Representantes Comunes, si estos fueren varies, los depositarios ó interventores, apoderados y abogados, y el remanente se aplicará primero al pago de los intereses vencidos y después al de los bonos á prorrata, es decir sin preferencia de un bono respecto á otro y si resultará algún sobrante se entregará á la A. B. Company, Sociedad Anonima, debiendo ser el Representante Común él que haga estas distribuciones. Vigésima Tercera. Además de las facultades que en la cláusula que precede se conceden al Representante Común tendrá las siguientes: I. Tendrá todas las facultades de los apoderados inclusas las que mencionan el articulo dos mil trescientos ochenta y siete del Código Civil del Distrito Federal y los articulos ciento cincuenta y siete, cuatrocientos seis, cuatrocientos cuarenta y nueve, seiscientos veinticuatro fracción primera y mil doscientos setenta y seis del Código de Procedimientos Civiles del Distrito Federal, así como cualquiera otra que conforme á las leyes requiera cláusula ó poder especial, sin excepción alguna. II. Podrá nombrar apoderado ó apoderados, agente ó agentes generales ó especiales para dentro de la República ó fuera de ella, con

60

ó sin la facultad de substituir y revocar las substituciones, revocar el nombramiento de estos apoderados ó agentes y conferir á estos todas y caulesquiera de las facultades que él tiene derecho á ejercer. III. Nombrar abogados y empleados. IV. Convenir, señalar y arreglar los sueldos, honorarios y compensaciones que hayan de pagarse á los apoderados, agentes, abogados, depositarios, interventores, empleados y en general á cualquiera persona que preste sus servicios á la Compañía así como fijar y arreglar todos los demás gastos que requiera el ejercicio de sus facultades. V. Cancelar la hipoteca y otorgar los instrumentos de cancelación cuando la Compañia pague el capital que recibe en préstamo ó cuando los bienes hipotecados hayan sido vendidos. Vigésima Cuarta. El Representante Común no responde personalmente de las deudas que contraiga en nombre de la Sociedad ni tampoco es responsable de los actos de los depositarios, interventores, apoderados, agentes ó abogados excepto cuando en el nombramiento haya procedido por negligencia culpable, y por último tampoco es responsable por sus propios actos sino en el caso de dolo ó mala fé, renunciándose en consecuancia á la disposición de los articulos mil cuatrocientos noventa y dos, dos mil trescientos sesenta, dos mil trescientos sesenta y dos mil trescientos setenta y tres del Código Civil del Distrito Federal. Vigésima Quinta. Queda expresamente convenido que cualquiera falta que cometiere la Compañia podrá ser excusada por los tenedores de la mayoria de los bonos emitidos y pendientes de pago y que el Representante Común hará tales cosas y seguirá el curso que dirigieren los tenedores de la mayoria de los bonos emitidos y pendientes de pago de cuando en cuando. Vigésima Sexta. La Compañia tendrá que depositar con el Representante Común la suma de quinientos pesos en cada año mientras que no estén pagados los bonos con los réditos y gastos, cuya suma debe ser aplicada por dicho Representante en el pago de su remuneración y los gastos hechos en el desempeño de su cargo. ·El Representante Común tiene derecho á una remuneración fijada de acuerdo con la Compañia y á falta de este acuerdo la señalará un tribunal competente. Dicho Representante entregará á la Compañia al fin de cada año la parte de la suma de quinientos pesos que no haya empleado para los usos aqui expuestos. Vigésima Séptima. El Señor R ejercerá el cargo de Representante Común de los tenedores de bonos mientras dure insoluta cualquiera parte de la deuda y se cumplan todas las estipulaciones de este contrato; pero dicho Señor ó quien le suceda en el mismo cargo podrá dejar de ejercer sus derechos como Representante por cualquiera de las causas siguientes: I. Por renuncia del mismo Señor ó de su sucesor. II. Por la decisión del tenedor ó de los tenedores de la mayoria de los bonos pendientes de pago. Vigésima Octava. En el caso de la muerte, renuncia ó remoción del Representante Común, los tenedores de la mayoria de los bonos emitidos y penidentes de pago tendrán el derecho de nombrar nuevo Representante Común, otorgando un documento público ante cualquier Notario Público en México ó en los Estados Unidos de América, cuyo documento una vez aceptado por el nuevo Representante Común y protocolizado en México y registrado en el Registro de Comercio de la Ciudad de México, Distrito Federal, tendrá el efecto de constituir la persona nombrada en ello el Representante Común de todos los tenedores de bonos emitidos bajo los términos de esta escritura y después dicho Representante Común tendrá todos los derechos y facultades indicados en este instrumento ó en el de su nombramiento. Vigésima Novena. Las partes contratantes se entenderán domiciliadas para todos los efectos legales de este contrato en esta Ciudad de México y en consecuencia, todas las cuestiones que se puedan presentar y ofrecer acera de su interpretación y cumplimiento serán decididas conforme á los Códigos vigentes en el Distrito Federal y los jueces y tribunales del mismo son los únicos competentes para conocer de ellas y decidirlas. Trigésima. Los gastos todos á que dé lugar el presente contrato, timbres, renta del Timbre, testimonios y registro, serán cubiertos por la Compañía, así como todos los á que dé lugar cualquiera otro instrumento que extienda, confirme ó ratifique el presente contrato. Trigésima Primera. El Señor R. acepta el cargo de Representante Común que se le confiere por medio de la presente escritura y se obliga á desempeñarlo leal y fielmente en los términos que el mismo instrumento expresa. Trigésima Segunda. Ambas partes contratantes convienen en que los bonos emitidos por esta escritura van á ser vendidos por el Presidente de la Compañia de tiempo en tiempo cuando haya necesidad y por esto renuncian las disposiciones de los articulos seis y siete de la ley de veintinueve de Noviembre de mil ochocientos noventa y siete con respecto á la junta de los tenedores de bonos y además convienen en que todas las cosas que deban ser decididas y hechas por dicha junta están fijadas é incluidas en esta escritura. Trigésima Tercera. El balance de la Compañia á que se refiere el articulo cuarto de dicha ley de veintinueve de Noviembre de mil ochocientos noventa y siete es como sigue:

(Aqui se inserta el balance.)

Bajo cuyos términos los denominados comparecientes declaran dejar celebrado este contrato que se obligan á cumplir conforme á derecho.

Art. 1194. No. 23. TRANSLATION.[1]

The formal beginning is the same as that already given in the form of Deed of Sale. If the mortgage is executed in Mexico the notary is required to insert before any of the other clauses of the document the certificate of the Recorder showing what if any liens there are on the property, which certificate must cover a period of twenty years prior to its date. If the mortgage is executed in a foreign country this certificate is not required.

[1] This is not an actual translation of the foregoing mortgage in Spanish securing corporate Bonds, but of a similar one, and serves the purpose of exemplifying the form and requisites. It is reproduced, by the courtesy of R. J. Kern, Esq., from his "Handbook of Mexican Law."

Other preliminary recitals show the organization of the corporation, the notary certifying that he has seen the authentic record of incorporation, the resolutions of the Board of Directors and the Stockholders authorizing the issue of bonds and the giving of security therefor, the naming of someone to act as Trustee, or as he is called under the Mexican law, *Representante Común* or Common Representative of the bondholders, and are followed by the clauses of the instrument itself as follows:

First: In accordance with the foregoing resolutions the A. B. Company has issued its bonds to the amount of.... ....dollars, which bonds are in the words and figures following, to-wit: (Here the bond is copied in full.)

Second: The A. B. Company acknowledges having received as a loan the sum of.....................dollars represented by the above described bonds and acknowledges itself indebted to the holders of said bonds in said amount, recognizing the loan as a mercantile transaction under the terms of the Commercial Code of the Republic of Mexico and it hereby agrees to pay the principal of said bonds together with interest thereon at the rate of......per cent per annum in accordance with the tenor and effect of said bonds, further agreeing to cancel all coupons and bonds as the several installments of interest and principal are paid. The company shall not be relieved from the obligation of paying said principal and interest by the lapse of time provided for the prescription of said principal and interest respectively and therefore the company hereby renounces the provisions of Articles one thousand and ninety-one, one thousand eight hundred and forty-eight and one thousand eight hundred and fifty of the Civil Code of the Federal District of the Republic of Mexico to the end that in any event the property hereinafter subjected to a mortgage lien shall remain subject to such lien until the full and complete payment of the principal and interest of the obligation represented by said bonds.

Third: Both the principal and interest of said bonds shall

be payable in the City of..............and the payment
shall be made to the bearer of said bonds or coupons, upon
presentation of the same, in gold money of the United States
of America or its equivalent in Mexican money of the current coinage to the exclusion of any other money created or
to be created. To give effect to this clause the company
adopts the provisions contained in Articles twenty, twenty-
one, twenty-two and twenty-three of the law of monetary reform of the twenty-fifth of March, one thousand nine hundred and five.[2]

Fourth: In consideration of the premises and in order to
secure due and punctual pro rata payment of said several
bonds and interest thereon the company has given, granted,
bargained, sold, transferred, mortgaged, warranted and conveyed and by these presents does give, grant, bargain, sell,
transfer, mortgage, warrant and convey[3] to the trustee hereinafter named all the following described property, to-wit:
(Here insert full description of the property, giving all the
facts as indicated in the Deed of Sale, page 911. ·

Fifth: The mortgage herein constituted is for the equal
pro rata benefit and security of the holders of the bonds above
described which may be issued hereunder, at whatever date
the same may be so issued, without any preference, priority
or distinction of one bond over another. The company
agrees to pay all taxes, assessments and levies that shall from
time to time be legally imposed, assessed or levied upon the
property and franchises hereby conveyed so that the priority
of this mortgage as a first lien upon the property hereby
conveyed shall at all times be duly maintained and preserved,
and the company further covenants and agrees to pay all
taxes, general or special, that may be levied or assessed

[2] That part of this clause referring to the payment of the obligation in gold money of the United States is only to be used when the
bonds provide for payment in that way.

[3] If the deed is executed originally in Mexico a simple statement
that the company mortgages its property in favor of the *Representante
Común* is sufficient, in lieu of the form of conveyance given in the
text.

against the mortgage interest or estate created by this document, to the end that the said principal and the stipulated interest shall be paid to the legal holders of said bonds and coupons without any reduction or rebate whatever.

Sixth: So long as the company shall make all the payments of principal and interest in accordance with the tenor and effect of said bonds and shall fulfill all the conditions of this instrument it shall remain in possession of said mortgaged property and may sell the products thereof subject to the conditions of this instrument.

Seventh: All the bonds guaranteed hereby shall be exccuted immediately upon the execution of this document and shall-be delivered to the trustee, by whom they shall be duly certified and thereafter delivered to the president of the company or to the person designated by him. No bond shall be valid or binding until the certificate endorsed on the back thereof shall have been duly signed by the trustee. All parties to this instrument agree that the bonds issued hereunder are to be sold by the president of the company from time to time as necessity arises and they therefore renounce the provisions of articles six and seven of the law of the twenty-ninth of November, one thousand eight hundred and ninety-seven, with respect to the meeting of the holders of bonds and further agree that all matters and things which are provided in and by said law to be decided at such meeting are fixed and determined by the terms of this instrument.

Eighth: In the event of a default by the company in the payment of the principal or interest of said bonds in strict accordance with the terms and conditions thereof, or in the event of the failure of the company to perform any of the covenants and conditions of this instrument, and in the further event that such default or failure shall continue for the term of sixty days, the holders of a majority of the bonds then outstanding and unpaid may thereupon declare due and payable the entire principal of all said bonds.

Ninth: In the event that the principal of said bonds becomes due either by the maturity thereof under their terms
or by determination of a majority of the holders thereof as
herein provided, the trustee, upon the request of the holder
or holders representing a majority of the bonds outstanding
and unpaid shall have the right to:

1. Name one or more receivers who shall take possession
of the mortgaged property and operate the same.

2. Take possession of the mortgaged property in his own
name and operate the same.

3. Procure a public judicial sale of the mortgaged property.

The trustee may exercise simultaneously any one or more
of the powers herein given him and the exercise of any such
powers shall not prevent the trustee from adopting any other
remedies provided by law for enforcing the payment of the
obligation secured by this mortgage.

Tenth: The trustee or any receiver or receivers appointed
by him hereunder shall have power to take possession of the
mortgaged premises and of all the books, papers and documents of the company and may thereafter carry on the business of the company as theretofore conducted upon said
mortgaged premises. After possession has been so taken by
the trustee or the receiver appointed by him as herein provided, the company shall not make any contract or any payment affecting the business theretofore conducted by it upon
the mortgaged premises. The receiver or receivers appointed
by the trustee under the terms of this instrument shall not
be required to give the bond provided for in article eight hundred and nine of the Code of Civil Procedure of the Federal
District of the Republic of Mexico and to that end the parties
hereto hereby renounce the provisions of said article. But
the trustee may exact from such receivers whatever bond or
other security he thinks proper. No bond shall be required
of the trustee in the event of his taking possession of the
mortgaged premises. The receivers, agents or attorneys

named by the trustee shall be named under the subsidiary responsibility of the company, the provisions of Article eight hundred and twelve of the Code of Civil Procedure aforesaid being hereby renounced. In the event of the resignation or removal by the trustee of a receiver or receivers theretofore appointed, the trustee shall have the right to name a new receiver or receivers, the provisions of article eight hundred and eleven of said Code of Civil Procedure being hereby renounced.

Eleventh: In the event of the foreclosure of this mortgage by public judicial sale as herein provided, notice of the place, day and hour of such sale and of the property to be sold shall be published once each week for three consecutive weeks in two newspapers published in the City of Mexico and no other notice shall be required, the provisions of article one thousand four hundred and eleven of the Commercial Code of the Republic of Mexico and of articles seven hundred and fifty-two to seven hundred fifty-four of the Code of Civil Procedure of the Federal District of the Republic of Mexico being hereby renounced. During the advertisement of such sale the trustee, by himself or through the receiver appointed by him, may retain possession of the mortgaged property, the provisions of articles one thousand three hundred and ninety-two of the Commercial Code and of article nine hundred and ninety-six of the Code of Civil Procedure of the Federal District being hereby renounced. The trustee may fix the amount to serve as a basis for such sale in accordance with the provisions of article eight hundred and fifty-five of the Code of Civil Procedure of the Federal District of the Republic of Mexico.

Twelfth: In the event of a sale neither the trustee nor the company nor any holder of bonds owning bonds to the amount of five thousand dollars shall be required to guarantee any bid he may make at such sale and therefore the parties hereto hereby mutually renounce the provisions of article eight hundred and twenty-nine of said Code of Civil Procedure requiring all bids at judicial sales of real estate to be guaranteed.

Thirteenth: The above-named........................
hereby accepts the nomination of trustee hereunder and
undertakes and agrees to discharge the duties of such trustee
as herein provided, but with the understanding that such acceptance imposes no liability or obligation whatsoever other
than as determined by the provisions of this instrument. In
the event of the death or resignation of the trustee, his successor shall be chosen by a majority of the holders of outstanding bonds.

Fourteenth: All parties to this contract adopt as their respective domiciles for the purposes of this contract the Federal District of the Republic of Mexico in accordance with
article thirty-seven of the Civil Code of the Federal District
of the Republic of Mexico and they further agree that any
questions which may arise concerning the interpretation of
this contract and any actions which may be instituted to enforce any provisions of this contract shall be determined by
the courts of the Federal District of Mexico in accordance
with the laws in force in said Federal District.

Fifteenth: All expenses of this instrument including its
protocolization and registration shall be paid by the company.
The company shall deposit with the trustee the sum of five
hundred dollars each year until the principal and interest of
the within described bonds shall be fully paid, which sum
shall be used by the trustee in the payment of his remuneration and the expenses incurred in the discharge of his obligations hereunder. The remuneration of the trustee shall be
agreed upon between him and the company and in default of
such agreement may be fixed by any competent tribunal.
The trustee shall deliver to the company at the end of each
year such part of the five hundred dollars as may not have
been used for the purposes herein expressed.

Sixteenth: The balance sheet of the company required to
be inserted herein in accordance with the provisions of article

four of the **law** of November twenty-ninth, **one** thousand eight hundred and ninety-seven is as follows:[1]   (Here insert the last balance sheet of the corporation.)

The foregoing clauses may be elaborated to fit any partien-lar case and clauses covering the payment of insurance and the making of repairs as usually incorporated by American lawyers in trust deeds to be used in the United States may also be included.

[4] Unless the mortgage is executed in Ⱶexico the balance sੈeet does not need to be inserted.

BOOK XXV.

APPENDIX.

Chapter 1. Domestic Corporations in Mexico.
   2. Foreign Corporations in Mexico.
   3. Comparison of New and Former Mining Laws.

CHAPTER 1.

DOMESTIC CORPORATIONS IN MEXICO.

THEIR ORGANIZATION, RIGHTS AND DUTIES.

BY LIC. MANUEL CERVANTES RENDÓN

OF THE MEXICO CITY BAR.

INTRODUCTION.

The Mexican Law recognizes as " Moral Persons ": **1,** The Nation, the States and the Municipalities; 2, such associations or corporations, whether temporary or perpetual, as are founded for the purpose of public utility, **or** whose motive is such, or public and private utility jointly; 3, civil and mercantile companies, viz: partnerships and corporations, formed according to law. The moral or legal personality attributed by law to the above-mentioned associations, corporations or establishments produces two effects: 1, It invests them with a legal entity, that is, it gives them a legal and separate existence, distinct and independent from each one of the members composing same; 2, it confers upon them legal capacity for the exercise of all the rights incident to their object.

We may divide the moral persons, above enumerated, into two principal groups: 1, Public Corporations, which include the Nation, the States, Municipalities, and corporations which are founded with a view to public utility, such as hospitals, &c.; these are governed by the Constitution of the Republic, and the respective organic laws emanating thereform; by the State Constitutions and organic laws, by municipal ordinances, and, in general, by the body of laws which constitute the Constitutional and Administrative Law of the Republic; 2, Private Corporations, including: 1, Foundations and associations established by private persons for scientific, artistic, religious, humanitarian, literary or similar purposes, and, in general, those not having in view the gaining of profit; 2, civil and mercantile associations intended for profit.

Civil and Mercantile Partnerships and Corporations. Mercantile partnerships and corporations are governed by the provisions of the Code of Commerce, a general law enacted by the Federal Congress, and in force throughout the Republic, the States not being permitted to legislate in commercial matters. The companies referred to are those which engage in business classed by law as " commercial transactions."

Commercial Transactions. The law considers as commercial transactions: (1) All acquisitions, transfers and bailments made with the object of commercial speculation, of commodities, chattels, movables or merchandise of any kind, whether in their natural state, or after being manufactured or partly wrought. (2) The purchase and sale of real estate, when made with the object of commercial speculation. (3) The purchase and sale of an interest in and of the shares and bonds of commercial companies. (4) Contracts relating to the obligations of a State, or other securities customary in trade. (5) Concerns having for their object the trading in provisions and other supplies. (6) Concerns for contracting public and private works. (7) Building and manufacturing concerns. (8) Transportation of persons or goods by land or water. (9) Establishments for the sale of books, and editorial and printing houses. (10) Concerns for commission and agency business, mercantile commission and agency and establishments for conducting public sales. (11) Enterprises for public amusements. (12) Banking operations. (13) Contracts relating to maritime commerce and navigation. (14) Insurance contracts of all kinds. (15) Commercial deposits, warehouse deposits and the operations made with their certificates. (16) Contracts involving the issuing of checks, letters of credit, bills of exchange, drafts, promissory notes and other negotiable instruments. (17) All obligations of merchants and those between merchants and bankers, unless they are shown to be of an essentially civil nature. (18) Sales by farmers of their products. (19) Mining enterprises. (20) Other analogous acts. When the nature of these is in doubt, it will be fixed by the courts.

Kinds of Commercial Companies. The law recognizes five kinds of commercial companies: (1) Ordinary partnerships, viz: unlimited liability. (2) Partnerships having one or more dormant partners. (3) Limited companies or Corporations. (4) Joint Stock Companies. (5) Co-operative Societies.

Mercantile Associations. These are according to the Commercial Code associations for mercantile transactions, formed without any special legal formality, either for a special transaction or for various ones for a limited time. These associations are unusual.

Companies Under the Civil Law. These companies or partnerships are such as are formed under and subject to the civil codes of the various states, for the purpose of gain and which do not fall within the definition of Commercial Companies.

There are three categories of them, viz: (1) General, including all property of which the partners are possessed; (2) general partnerships limited to all profits derived; (3) special, or, those referring to such property as may be mentioned as forming the object of the association, to its fruits of production, or to the exercise of a stated industry or profession.

These companies may be organized under the provisions of the commercial code, without losing their character as civil societies.

In this chapter we shall only refer to corporations formed with commercial ends in view.

DO\]ESTIC CORPORATIONS.

Who May Organize a Corporation. The organizers of a corporation must be individuals of full age in possession of all their civil rights. Persons under parental control, guardianship or disability by marriage, cannot organize a corporation, with the following exceptions:

\]inors under 21 but over 18 years of age, legally emancipated or licensed by the Court, or legally authorized by their parents or guardians. \]arried women, over 18, duly authorized by their husbands, in a public document, (declaration before a Notary Public); this authorization may be special or general and is subject to be revoked by the husband at pleasure. This authorization is not required in case of legal separation, declared absence, interdiction or privation of civil rights of the husband.

Form of Organization. The law recognizes two ways of organizing a corporation:

First: Two or more parties may appear before a Notary, either in person, or by a duly constituted attorney, and execute articles of incorporation, which must contain the following requisites:

1. The names and residences of the parties.

2. The name of the corporation.

3. The domicile of the same.

4. The object for which it is organized, its duration, and how same is to be computed.

5. The capital stock, specifying the kind, number and value of the shares into which it is divided, and the value and amount subscribed.

6. The manner in which the affairs of the company are to be directed, specifying the powers of the directors or managers.

7. The amount of the reserve fund.

8. The manner and form of dividing profits or losses.

9. The part of the profits reserved as founders' shares and how to be received.

10. In what cases the winding-up of the corporation is to take place before the time fixed for its expiration.

11. The basis for the liquidation and how the liquidators shall be chosen, if they have not been previously appointed.

12. The proof of the value attributed to the securities, goods or chattels, personal or real property, which may have been contributed by one or more of the organizers.

SOME EXPLANATIONS RELATING TO THE FOREGOING REQUISITES.

Name of the Corporation. After the name of the corporation the words, *"Sociedad Anónima"* or the abbreviation, " S. A." (equivalent to " Ltd."), must always be added.

The name or names of the organizers must not figure in the denomination of the corporation, else the organizer or organizers whose name or names so figure, will be held personally and severally liable for the obligations of the company. For example: " Smith-Jones Hardware Co. S. A."; if Smith and Jones are actively interested in the corporation thus denominated, having included their names in the title they are personally and severally responsible for the liabilities of the corporation.

The name of the corporation must be different from that of any existing corporation.

Domicile of the Corporation. The founders may elect the domicile they choose, always provided it be within the limits of the Republic. The domicile may be changed by modifying the articles of incorporation on this point.

Capital Stock. The capital stock must be divided into shares of equal value.

The capital stock must be subscribed in its entirety, when the company is constituted, either by the founders or others.

At least ten per cent. of the cash capital must be paid in. The founders may stipulate a time for the payment of said ten per cent. or for the first assessment that may be agreed upon by them. In case of organization by public subscription, shares on which assessments are not paid at the periods they fall due, will be considered as not having been subscribed.

The whole or any part of the capital stock may consist of goods, chattels, real or personal property, shares or services contributed by one or more of the shareholders, the value of which shall be represented by non-assessable or paid-up shares.

The capital stock may be increased or decreased as may be stipulated in the articles of incorporation or by-laws. If they contain no stipulations in this respect, a general meeting of which three-fourths of the capital stock is represented may decree the increase or decrease by a unanimous vote of shareholders representing one-half of the capital stock. Such modifications as may be made must be reduced to a public instrument, and then registered in the Register of Commerce.

Shares. The articles of incorporation must state the rights, privileges and obligations of the different kinds of shares issued. If no stipulation is expressed in this respect all shares shall have equal standing. The shares or certificates for same must be signed by the number of directors specified in the by-laws and must contain the following requisites: (1) Name and domicile of the company. (2) Date of incorporation. (3) Capital stock, number of shares in which same is divided and the assessments paid. (4) The duration of the company. (5) The rights reserved to shares by the articles of incorporation or by-laws.

For nominative shares a register must be kept which must contain: (1), The names and residences of the shareholders and the number of shares held; (2), the calls paid; (3), the transfers made, with their respective dates, or, when permitted by the by-laws, the change of nominative shares to bearer, with the date the change is effected: the transfer of nominative shares is made by means of a declaration to that effect in said register, signed by both parties to the contract or their respective agents, on the date the transfer is effected; (4), the number of shares deposited as guarantee by the administrators, directors and examiners.

Classes of Shares. They are generally either to bearer or nominative. In case of bankruptcy of a corporation, such nominative shareholders as may not have paid all their assessments may be required by the receiver to contribute to the extent of their liability, if necessary; but this is not the case with shares to bearer. These are transferred by the delivery of the certificate.

Shares are again divided into payable or assessable; paid-up or non-assessable, common and preferred.

Prohibition for Corporations to Buy their own Shares. Corporations are prohibited from purchasing their own shares, except in the following cases: (1) When fully paid-up shares are purchased with the authorization of a general meeting and with profits not belonging to the reserve fund. (2) When the purchase is made by virtue of an authorization already provided in the by-laws. (3) When the purchase is made with the capital of the corporation, complying with all the formalities prescribed for the reduction of the capital stock.

Shares purchased in the first mentioned case have no representation at general meetings, and cannot be computed in making up the majorities referred to in the by-laws. The titles of shares purchased in the last two mentioned cases shall be cancelled.

Purchases made in spite of above prohibition are not *ipso facto* void, unless bad faith is shown on the part of the vendor, but the directors or managers responsible for them will be held liable for any loss or damage resulting to the corporation thereby, and may also be criminally accountable.

Corporations cannot make loans on their own shares.

Administration. The management of corporations is temporary and revocable. Shareholders holding such trust shall be considered as agents.

Managers. The management of corporations is entrusted to a Board of Directors and one or more managers. Corporations may appoint consulting committees outside of their domicile.

Board of Directors. All members of the Board of Directors shall be elected by a general meeting of stockholders; nevertheless, the first time they may be named in the articles of incorporation. They may be reëlected unless otherwise stipulated.

Vacancies in the Board of Directors shall be filled as prescribed in the by-laws of the corporation.

The position of member of the Board of Directors is personal and cannot be delegated.

Deposit of Shares. The members of the Board of Directors must deposit with the corporation, during their term of office, a certain number of shares as security for the performance of their duties. The by-laws shall designate in all cases the number of such shares.

Powers. These should be specified in the articles of incorporation. The law gives the Board ample powers to carry out any and all contracts according to the nature and object of the corporation, unless restricted by the Articles of Incorporation, or by-laws.

Responsibility of the Directors. They cannot be made personally liable as to third parties with reference to any contract made in the name of the company. To the corporation they are responsible as its agents. For any responsibility incurred, however, they can only be called to account through a general meeting or by the person appointed for the purpose by such meeting.

Managers. The management of the affairs of the corporation as well as its representation in everything relative thereto, shall be entrusted to one or more general managers, whose appointment, dismissal and duties shall be prescribed in the by-laws. It is advisable to specially confer upon them the right to represent the company before the courts.

The responsibility of said agents is regulated by the ordinary principles of law.

Consulting Committees. These will have the powers conferred on them by the articles or by-laws. The law does **not** require their appointment.

SUPERVISION.

The supervision over the affairs of corporations shall be entrusted to one or more shareholders, styled examiners (*comisarios*), and who, before entering upon the discharge of their duties, must deposit the number of shares prescribed by the by-laws.

The examiners shall be named in a general meeting; nevertheless, the first time they may be designated in the articles of incorporation. Notwithstanding any stipulation to the contrary, the examiners shall always be eligible for reëlection and their trust revocable.

The vacancies in the office of examiners shall be filled in the manner prescribed by the by-laws, but always by election at a general meeting.

Powers and Duties of the Examiners. The examiners have an unlimited right of supervision over the operation of the corporation. Whenever they may desire, they shall be permitted to examine the books, correspondence, minutes, and, in general, all the documents and papers of the corporation; in consequence, the shareholders cannot exercise these powers independently. The directors shall deliver to them every year the general balance sheet for verification, and the examiners shall present to the meeting the result of their labors with any proposals which they may deem fit, accompanied by the necessary explanations and demonstrations.

Their Responsibility. The responsibility of the exam-

iners is regulated in the same manner as that of the Board
of Directors.

A general meeting of shareholders has the most ample
power to carry into effect and ratify all the acts of the corporation. Such meeting, unless otherwise prescribed, has the
right to amend the by-laws of the corporation.

Meetings are ordinary or extraordinary:

Ordinary Shareholders' Meetings. Ordinary meetings
shall be held annually after the termination of the corpora-
tive year. The following matters shall be in order at the
general ordinary meeting: (1) To discuss, approve, or
modify the general balance sheet, after hearing the report
of the examiners. (2) To elect the members of the Board
of Directors that are to serve. (3) To elect examiners.
(4) To determine the remuneration to be paid to the members of the Board of Directors and the examiners, if not
prescribed in the by-laws. (5) Any other business indicated in the call for the meeting.

Calls. The call for meetings shall be made by the Board
of Directors or by the examiners, by publishing in the Official Journal of the State, District or Territory in which the
company has its domicile, an advertisement to that effect.
This notice must contain the order of the day.

Special Meetings. The call for special meetings is made
as for the ordinary ones, by the Board with at least one
month's notice; also on the petition of shareholders representing not less than one-third of the capital stock, said petition to contain the points to be discussed and voted upon.

Quorum. To constitute a quorum more than one-half
of the capital stock must be represented. If there should
be less, the call will be repeated, and the meeting held no
matter what number of shares may be represented. Unless
the articles of incorporation or the by-laws provide otherwise, the representation of three-fourths of the capital stock,

and the unanimous vote of shareholders representing half
of said capital stock, shall be necessary to pass the following
resolutions:

1. Dissolution of the corporation before the time prescribed, except in case of the loss of the capital stock.

2. To extend its duration.

3. To consolidate with other corporations.

4. To reduce its capital stock.

5. To increase its capital stock.

6. To change the object of the corporation.

7. Any other modification of the articles of incorporation
or of the by-laws.

Minutes. The minutes of the General Meetings shall be
recorded in duplicate and to one of the copies a list of shareholders present with the number of shares and votes represented by each, shall be attached.

Minute Books. In the minute books, which each company shall keep, treating of general meetings, shall be expressed: the date, those present at them, the number of
shares which each one represents, the number of votes which
he may make use of, the resolutions which may be passed,
which must be recorded to the letter; and when the voting
is not by ayes and nays, the number of votes cast, care being
taken to record everything which may conduce to a complete
knowledge of what was resolved. When the minutes refer to
directors' meeting, there shall be entered: the date, the
names of those present, and an account of the resolutions
passed. These shall be signed by the persons designated in
the by-laws.

Votes. The number of votes to which shareholders are
entitled, as well as the manner of computing them, shall be
determined by the by-laws.

The resolutions adopted at general meetings must be passed
by at least an absolute majority of the votes of the shares that
can be computed.

Members of the Board of Directors cannot vote: (1) **To** approve the accounts. (2) **On** resolutions that affect their personal responsibility.

Shareholders, General Rights of. The shareholders cannot examine the books and papers of the company, that being reserved to the examiners. At the general meetings they may be represented by power of attorney (proxy), as the by-laws may provide. The members of the board of directors cannot hold such representation.

Dividends. Corporations cannot distribute to their shareholders more profits than those appearing in the general balance sheet as having been obtained for their benefit; nevertheless it may be stipulated in the by-laws or articles of incorporation that the shares, during a period not to exceed five years, shall draw a rate of interest not exceeding six per cent. per annum. In that case the amount of such interest shall be considered as forming part of the expenses of organization. Shareholders shall never be obliged to return any dividends that they may have received.

Reserve Fund. From the net profits of the corporation there must be set aside yearly a portion, which shall not be less than five per cent. thereof, to constitute the reserve fund, until it aggregates at least one-fifth of the capital stock.

The reserve fund must be re-formed in the same manner whenever it may, through whatever cause, be diminished.

Dissolution of Corporations. Corporations may be dissolved: (1) By the consent of the shareholders, as before explained. (2) By the expiration of the period for which they were established. (3) By reason of the loss of one-half of their capital stock, whenever the dissolution is approved at a general meeting, by a vote of at least a majority of the shareholders representing one-half of said capital stock. (4) By the bankruptcy of the corporation, legally declared.

Liquidation of Corporations. When the dissolution of a corporation is determined upon at a meeting, the appointment of liquidators shall be made, and if that is not done, the judicial authority shall appoint them when requested to do so.

The appointment of liquidators terminates the trust and duties of the directors of the corporation. The latter shall, nevertheless, lend their aid to the liquidators whenever they are requested to do so.

The accounts of the directors, during the period comprised from the date of the last balance sheet approved by a meeting, and the opening of the liquidation, shall be presented to the liquidators for their approval.

When one or more directors are appointed liquidators, the accounts referred to in the foregoing paragraph shall be published in two or more newspapers of the domicile of the corporation, with the final balance sheet of the liquidation; but if the latter comprises a period beyond the corporation year, the accounts mentioned must be annexed to the first balance sheet that the liquidators shall present to a general meeting of shareholders.

If the liquidation lasts one year, the liquidators shall make up the annual balance sheet, in conformity with the prescriptions of the law and of the by-laws.

On the termination of the liquidation, the liquidators must make out the first balance sheet, stating the portion which corresponds to each share in the distribution of the capital stock, and such balance sheet shall be published for thirty consecutive days in one or more newspapers issued at the domicile of the corporation. The shareholders within fifteen days after the last publication thereof, must present their claims to the liquidators which shall be passed upon at a meeting to be called for that purpose, by a majority of votes, each share to have one vote. After the expiration of the time mentioned, whether there have been no claims presented, or whether they have been acted on by the meeting, the final balance sheet shall be considered as approved, the responsibility of the liquidators to remain in force, as to the distribution of the capital stock.

Distribution of Assets. The amounts belonging to the shareholders that are not demanded within two months after the day when the balance sheet is approved, shall be deposited in any banking institution to the credit and in the name of the shareholder, if the share is nominal, or to the number of the share, if to bearer. Said amounts shall be paid by the banking institution wherein the deposit may have been made, to the person named, or to the bearer of the share.

Taxes. When the articles of incorporation are completed, the Notary, for account of the organizers, pays the imposts, which are: (1) Stamp tax on the capital stock, and (2) stamp tax on the protocol and certified copy of the articles of association.

The tax on the capital stock is as follows:

Up to $500,000.00 Mex., on each $1,000.00 or
   fraction thereof.............................$1.00 Mex.
From $500,000.00 to $1,000,000.00, on each
   $1,000 or fraction thereof................ 0.50
Over $1,000,000.00, on each $1,000.00 or fraction thereof.............................. 0.10

The Register in which the Articles of incorporation are preserved is stamped at the rate of $1.00 Mex. per sheet, as also the certified copy issued for registry.

The by-laws, when protocolized, are stamped at the rate of $2.00 Mex. per sheet.

There is no annual tax on the capital stock.

Certified Copy. The imposts being paid, the Notary issues the certified copy above referred to showing that the corporation has been legally constituted.

Registry. The aforesaid certified copy is presented to the commercial section of the Public Registry, at the place where the incorporation was effected. The Registrar inscribes the articles of incorporation in the book designed for

that purpose, and returns the certified copy with the prop
annotation.

The registry involves no expense.   The office is public a
these inscriptions may, therefore, be consulted at all time
for the purpose of obtaining data, regarding any corpor
tion or partnership.

Any change in a company or dissolution must also be i
scribed, as also the naming or removal of the managers of t
company.

Neglect to register, produces the following effects:

First.   The company has no legal standing, and cann
therefore, sue for the fulfillment of its contracts.

Second.   In case of bankruptcy this will be presume
fraudulent, and, unless the administrators are able to pro
the contrary they will be liable to imprisonment and d
barred from exercising commerce.

With the certificate of the Registry Office the legal cons
tution of the company is completed.

By Public Subscription.   *Second Form of Organizatic*
The second manner of organizing a corporation is to form
late a program to be signed by the initiators.   This p
gram must contain in full the projected by-laws of the p
posed corporation, with such explanations as may be deem
expedient; the amount of the capital to be paid in, whi
in no case must be less than 10% ; besides if any porti
of the capital is represented by other values than ca
this must be duly proven by certificates given by exper
This program must be made public.

The next step is to obtain the subscription of the capi
stock, which must be fully subscribed, and the aforemention
10% of the portion to be contributed in cash, paid in, v
deposited in a banking or mercantile house.   If all, or a
portion of the capital stock, is represented by other val
than cash, these shall be represented by fully paid up, i.

copies of the prospectus, and subscribers must indicate their name, surname, firm name and domicile, number of shares subscribed, date of subscription, and an express declaration on the part of the party subscribing that the contents of the proposed by-laws are fully known to him and that he accepts same. This declaration must be attested by two witnesses. The funds deposited by subscribers shall be at the order of the administrators of the company, who may be named by the shareholders at the first general meeting.

At this meeting, to be held as soon as the entire capital stock is subscribed, the following order of business will be observed: (1) The computation of the amounts deposited by the subscribers, as per call of the initiators, and the approval of such call. (2) Discussion of the values attributed to the securities, goods or chattels or real property which may have been contributed by one or more of the members; on this point the parties contributing are excluded from voting. (3) Discussion and approbation of the by-laws. (4) Agreement as to the participation the founders may have reserved to themselves in the profits. (5) Naming of the administrators and examiners who are to hold office for the term fixed in the by-laws.

The minutes of this meeting, signed by all the shareholders present thereat, with a sheet annexed showing the number of shares represented by each, also signed, are then delivered to a Notary for protocolization, together with the respective by-laws.

These latter must contain the requisites already specified in treating of the organization of companies under the first form.

Books and Accounts. Besides the minute books, already mentioned, the corporation, as all merchants, must keep a set of books, consisting of inventory or balance book, Journal and Ledger. In case sales are made a stamped sales book must also be kept, as well as a stamped book for all bills over twenty pesos, with a stub which must show that the

proper stamps have been attached to the respective bills.
(Five cents for each $10.00 or fraction thereof.)

These books must be kept in Spanish and according to
the rules of scientific bookkeeping universally accepted.

The fact of the merchant being a foreigner does not relieve
him of the obligation of keeping his books in that language,
under penalty of $50 to $300 and expenses of translating said
books; but as he need not keep them personally, that is, in
no way, a difficulty.

The aforementioned books must, before opening them, be
presented to the stamp office for authorization. This office
adheres and cancels the necessary stamps on the first page of
each book, the quota being five cents per leaf, except for the
sales-book, which pays one cent per leaf.

CHAPTER 2.

FOREIGN CORPORATIONS IN MEXICO.[1]

THEIR PROTOCOLIZATION AND REGISTRATION.

BY E. DEAN FULLER, ESQ.,

OF THE MEXICO CITY BAR.

Companies legally constituted in foreign countries, which
establish themselves in the Republic of Mexico, or have in it
an agency or branch, MAY ENGAGE IN COMMERCE, but in order
to do so they are subject to the general provisions of the Commercial Code of Mexico (a General Code governing all matters of a commercial nature throughout the Republic), con-

[1] This chapter 2 is particularly instructive in that it contains, besides important data in regard to foreign corporations establishing
themselves in Mexico, the full particulars of the " Protocolization "
of Charters, and all other public instruments, such as deeds, mortgages,
powers of attorney, and all documents coming from a foreign country
and requiring, before being given any legal effect, to be " protocolized "
before a Notary. The *modus operandi* is carefully explained.

cerning the promotion of their establishments within Mexico; their mercantile operations in Mexico; and the jurisdiction of the courts of Mexico in matters arising therefrom.

Just what is meant by the term " engaging in commerce," is clearly defined by the law. To determine whether or not the foreign corporation is subject to the provisions of the Commercial Code when it " establishes itself in Mexico and has in it an agency or branch," it is necessary to ascertain if the corporation will engage, as its ordinary occupation, in any of those branches of business classed as " Commercial Operations." If so, then it is subject to the laws as prescribed by the above Code.

Having ascertained that the foreign corporation is to engage in " Commercial operations " in Mexico as above defined, it must proceed to comply with the requirements of the law before entering and engaging in its intended business.

STEPS TO BE TAKEN: — These requirements are as follows:

FIRST: That the company legally protocolize in Mexico, its statutes, contracts, and other documents referring to its constitution, in the manner hereinafter explained.

SECOND: That the corporations shall present in the office of the Commercial Register where operating the protocolization above referred to, and the invoice or last balance sheet, if the corporation has one.

THIRD: That it shall secure a certificate from the Mexican Minister, Ambassador, or in his absence from a Mexican Consul, to the effect that the corporation has been constituted and authorized in accordance with the laws of the foreign country.

FOURTH: That it shall publish annually a balance sheet stating clearly its assets and liabilities, as well as the names of the persons who have its management and control. Failure to conform to these requirements renders those who contract in the name of the company personally and jointly liable for all the obligations incurred in Mexico.

PROTOCOLIZATION: This is the legal term for the act of legalizing documents executed in a foreign country, or issued by it, in order to prove their validity and give them legal force in Mexico. This, as already stated, is required of foreign corporations entering Mexico to engage in commerce. We shall therefore proceed to explain the requirements for this purpose.

As will clearly appear by what has preceded, all foreign corporations entering Mexico are not required to be protocolized. For example: foreign corporations acquiring lands in Mexico which are not for the purpose of commercial speculation through an agency or branch located in Mexico as recognized by the law, need not be protocolized.

However, even in those cases where the law does not require same to be done, it is generally advisable to protocolize such foreign corporations for the purpose of facilitating its operations in Mexico and to enable the company to establish its legal existence when such proof is made necessary.

Whether such protocolization be of a " commercial company " or a " non-commercial company," the procedure in making such protocolization will be identical, and as follows:.

CERTIFIED COPY OF ARTICLES OF INCORPORATION: — The charter having been issued to the corporation in the United States, or its Articles of Incorporation having been filed, the State or Territorial authority before whom filed will issue a copy of such Articles of Incorporation (and charter, if any), and will certify to same in regular form.

CONSULAR CERTIFICATE: — Such certificate and copies having been issued, in the event of there being a Mexican Consular Officer in such State or Territory, the documents should be presented to him for the purpose of securing from him two certificates: One to the effect that the signature of such State or Territorial Officer is entitled to credit; and the other, that the company has been constituted and authorized in accordance with the law of such State or Territory.

ABSENCE OF MEXICAN CONSUL: — In some American States and Territories, however, there are no Mexican Consular officers. In that event the above document as received from the State or Territorial Officer must be forwarded to Washington, D. C. where the Secretary of State will first affix his certificate to the State authority, and the Mexican Ambassador will then issue his certificate to that of the Secretary of State, and will also issue certificate as required by Mexican laws that the corporation has been legally organized. For the purpose of obviating delays and difficulties at Washington, it is always best to entrust this work to an attorney at that point for attention.

FURTHER DOCUMENTS: — The statutes of the company having been legalized to this extent they are ready for transmission to Mexico City, to be further dealt with there. But other documents are required before the corporation can be given a legal existence in Mexico, as before set forth: —

COPIES OF MINUTES OF COMPANY AND BY-LAWS: — If the officers are not named in the Articles of Incorporation, or where others have later acquired the office of the original officers, these facts must be made to appear in the documents to be registered in Mexico, by copies of the minutes showing their election. Also copies of the By-Laws, and if any, of the Amendments to same, and resolution of their adoption. These will be made to appear by means of copies of such acts and proceedings which the Secretary of the Company must make and certify to.

FORWARD DOCUMENTS TO MEXICO CITY: — When the above documents have been completed in the manner above set forth, they should all be forwarded to Mexico City, to there be presented to the Department of Foreign Relations, which will legalize the certificates of the Mexican Consul or Ambassador attached to same. Upon this being completed the documents are ready for " Protocolization."

PLACE OF PROTOCOLIZATION: — The act of protocoliza-

tion may be performed in any part of the Republic of
Mexico, but American corporations as a rule prefer that
this work be performed in Mexico City, where the best legal
talent can be secured, and the work be despatched with the
least possible delay.

TRANSLATION OF DOCUMENTS INTO SPANISH: — In order
to protocolize a document the law requires that it shall be
presented to the Court in the Language of the Republic,—
Spanish,— and that being in any other language when
presented to the Court, it shall be translated into Spanish
by a person appointed by the Court for such purpose.
This person having accepted his appointment as translator,
next presents his translation and certifies to the correctness thereof. This translation may, however, be made
and certified to by a Mexican Consul or by the Mexican Department of Foreign Relations, and when this is done, the
translation, together with the original documents, are presented to the Court at the same time.

APPLICATION TO COURT FOR PROTOCOLIZATION: — The
documents having been properly and legally presented to
the Court and the questions of Translations settled in one
of the ways above set forth, a judicial examination is
made to ascertain if the Company and the documents presented are in all respects in conformity with the laws of
Mexico, and being so, an order is made by the Court approving same and directing that the documents be delivered to a
designated Notary Public.

RECORDING BY NOTARY PUBLIC; PAYMENT OF TAX: —
Having received the documents from the Court, the Notary Public then proceeds to engross same in his book kept
for such purpose, together with all orders of court, certificates, etc., as the same may appear by the records received by him from the Court. After engrossing such documents as before stated, a copy is made thereof, the original
documents being retained in the archive of the Notary Public. The copy made by him is then submitted to the Revenue

Stamp Department, together with the Notary's statement as to what, in his opinion, are the taxable costs in favor of the Government by reason thereof, which amount he tenders in payment to the Department. The Department then notes its receipt of this tax upon the copy presented; following which the Notary attaches the necessary adhesive Revenue Stamp of $1.00, Mexican Peso per page, on the copy of the documents. Upon payment to the Notary of his fees and disbursements, this certified copy of the protocolized documents, with its attached receipts, is ready for delivery to its rightful owner. These costs must be paid to the Department within thirty (30) days from the date which the protocolization carries; otherwise the documents are valueless, and for this purpose Notaries require deposit from clients of such costs and their fees, in order that they may make payment with the client's money.

The certified copy as above referred to should be carefully preserved as it will be required upon many occasions in evidencing the legal existence of the corporation, and its protocolization in Mexico.`

GOVERNOR'S CERTIFICATE TO NOTARY'S SIGNATURE: — Should it be necessary to use the above documents outside of the State, District or Territory in which protocolized, then it will be required that the certificate of the Governor of such State, District or Territory be secured to that of the Notary Public.

TAX ON ORGANIZATION OF CORPORATION: — In Mexico this tax is much similar to the tax on new corporations in the States of the United States of America, being based upon the authorized capital stock of such corporation when organized or registered under the laws of such States; that is: The law exacts a tax from a corporation, of a fixed sum per thousand dollars of its authorized stock up to a certain sum, and this tax is decreased as the capitalization increases. In some American States this tax must also be paid by corporations under certain conditions when entering another State, being payable to such other State when registered therein.

In Mexico this tax accrues to the Federal Government and entitles the corporation to engage in business in any of the States, Territories or Federal District of Mexico without the payment of an additional **tax for** such privilege.   To both domestic Mexican, **and** foreign corporations this **tax is** alike. The basis thereof is as follows:

One each $1,000, Mexican pesos, up to $500,000

   Mexican pesos .... $1.00 peso.

On each additional $1,000 Mexican pesos or fraction thereof up to $1,000,000 Mexican pesos   .50 peso.

On each additional $1,000 Mexican pesos or fraction thereof, in excess of said $1,000,000

   Mexican pesos .... .10 peso.

In estimating this tax upon American corporations, **the** American Dollar is considered equal to a fraction less than two Mexican Pesos ($1.98 pesos).

This tax must be paid in order to complete the protocolization of the corporation, and unless paid within a period of thirty (30) days from the date of the entry of the protocolization by the Notary Public in his records as heretofore described, a new record will have to be made at a considerable expense.

NOTARIES PUBLIC AND THEIR FEES: — In Mexico this is a profession to itself, although, as a rule, the person selected holds the title of attorney, owing to the necessity of a legal training.   Only a limited number of licenses to the office **are** granted in each locality, and the incumbents are selected with a view to their fitness for the office.

The fees they charge are regulated by the law.   In matters of protocolization of foreign corporations, this **fee is** about $100.00 Mexican Pesos, equal to about $50.00, United States Currency.

EXPENSES OF PROTOCOLIZATION.

The exact sum in connection with each item cannot be given, but in a general way, expenses will arise from the following sources:

Charges of the State or Territorial authority in the United States of America for issuing certified copy of Articles of Incorporation of the Company (and its charter, when issued).

Consular or Ambassador's fees for certificates in which is authenticated the signature of the State or Territorial authority issuing the foregoing documents.

Costs of Certificates of Consul or Ambassador that the Corporation has been constituted and authorized in accordance with the laws of such State or Territory.

Charges of the United States Secretary of State for his Certificate, when required, as hereinbefore set forth under the title of " Absence of Mexican Consul." Also charges of Washington, D. C., attorney, when his services are required for this purpose.

Revenue Stamps on each certificate of Mexico Consul or Ambassador to be affixed by Department of Foreign Relations in Mexico, when presented to that Department for its certificates.

Costs of translation of documents to be protocolized. Revenue stamps on each of the documents in presenting them to the Court for order of protocolization, as also upon pleadings connected therewith.

Mexican Government Stamp Tax on Corporations.

Charges of Notary Public for services in connection with protocolization.

Stamps on Certified Copy of protocolized documents.

Fees of Mexican Governor when his certificate is required as hereinbefore set forth.

Charges of attorney in Mexico in connection with protocolization of corporation.

WHEN PROTOCOLIZATION COMPLETED: — Upon completion of the protocolization, the corporation becomes a "merchant" as recognized by the law, in all its commercial operations in Mexico, and as such must follow the laws of the country in all such operations within it. It is not required to do so in its foreign operations as before stated, nor in corporate affairs with its stockholders or officers, the State of its creation retaining jurisdiction over the latter, stockholders being required to assert their rights in and under the laws of the country where organized.

REGISTRATION IN COMMERCIAL REGISTER: — Having completed the first and the third requisites of the law as first set forth herein for the purpose of engaging in commerce in Mexico, the commercial corporation becomes subject to the requirements of the laws of Mexico in all things relating to its commercial operations within the Republic.

This law, as before set forth, requires that the corporation shall present the documents evidencing its protocolization; its further documents regarding interests or commercial operations in Mexico, and its last invoice, if there be one, to the Commercial Register of the jurisdiction wherein it has its branch or agency. It will be seen that the presenting of an invoice is not obligatory.

In presenting these documents to the Commercial Register of the locality where the corporation is to engage in business, a petition is also presented, in the form required by the law and furnished by such office, in which is set forth the general information required to be kept by this Department, such as the name of officers, agents, etc. This information is exacted for the purpose of information and record, and is open at all times to the public.

COMMERCIAL BOOK-KEEPING: — One of the bases upon which taxation is exacted in the Republic of Mexico being that of the commercial operations of its merchants, the law requires of them the adoption and strict adherence to a set system of book-keeping for the purpose of avoiding frauds upon the Government in this regard.

The books required to be kept are a "book of invoices and balances"; the "general day-book," and "the ledger."

It is further required that these books be "bound, lined, paged and stamped with the proper stamps in the manner provided by law." They must be kept in Spanish.

The forms to be observed as required by the law are many, and as a statement of this law would be of little interest at this time, we will refrain from going into it. However, the law is very exacting, and heavy penalties are attached to those failing to conform thereto. The books are "authorized" and stamped when presented to the Tax Office for notice.

CHAPTER 3.

COMPARISON OF THE NEW AND FORMER MINING LAWS OF MEXICO.

BY FREDERIC R. KELLOGG, ESQ., OF THE NEW YORK BAR.

(By courtesy of The Corporation Trust Co.).

While the mining law of Mexico of the 25th of November, 1909, is not a radical measure, it does, nevertheless, embody a number of changes which are of much importance to lawyers and investors interested in Mexican affairs.

It is my intention to briefly note such of these points as are of principal importance.

I. The substances which belong to the public domain are now defined as being:

"All inorganic substances which, in veins or masses of whatever form, constitute deposits whose composition is distinct from that of the native rock, such as those of gold, plantinum, silver, copper, iron, cobalt, nickel, manganese, lead, mercury, tin, chromium, antimony, zinc and bismuth;

those of sulphur, arsenic and tellurium; those of rocksalt and precious stones.   Also placers of gold and platinum."

It will be observed that this clause is much more sweeping and general than the provision of Article 3 of the old law which simply defines certain specific substances without any general words.

II. A most important modification is that which applies to mining property wherever located, the provisions of the laws of the Federal District, relative to ordinary property, except as otherwise provided in the new law.

Formerly, except in a few particulars, mining property and mining rights were governed by the laws of the respective States in which the property was located, causing much confusion in some instances and making it necessary for mining men to become acquainted with several different systems of jurisprudence in all matters relative to mortgages, etc. This is now done away with, all such matters being governed by one system of law.   The policy adopted is the same wise one which had previously dictated the adoption of the Code of Commerce by which corporation and commercial matters are considered as being of national and not of state concern.

III. Another very important point is found in the clauses which bring under the operation of the national Code of Commerce all contracts which relate to mining properties and mining rights.   All such contracts may now be recorded in the various commercial registries in the States and Territories of the nation and when thus recorded they are made valid against third persons during such time as such contracts fix, not exceeding two years from the date of registration.

Formerly, in view of the fact that escrow deeds are not recognized in Mexican law, it was a matter of difficulty to obtain a valid "bond and lease" upon Mexican mining properties which would be valid against a trustee in bankruptcy of the grantor or against his successors or assigns; and the new law has certainly performed a great service to intending mining investors by permitting notarial documents, containing options, to be recorded and to thus gain validity against the whole world during the time above mentioned.

IV. Certain mining contracts are likewise made less dangerous by the provision that they shall not be rescindable for what is known as " lesion."

Under the former law of the Federal District and of certain other jurisdictions of Mexico a " lesion " was said to exist when a purchaser subsequently discovered that he had been induced to give two times more than the just price or value of the property or when the grantor found that he had received two-thirds less than said just price or value.

This provision, a relic of ancient law wholly inappropriate to modern conditions, and the source of great danger especially in mining grants, has been wisely abrogated.

V. The Federal courts of the Republic are expressly given jurisdiction over certain matters, and it is also expressly provided that in other matters which still remain in the control of the state courts decisions must be rendered in conformity with the provisions of the Code of Commerce of the nation, thus abolishing the divergencies resulting from the application of the varying laws of the different States.

This is likewise in the interest of harmony and simplicity.

VI. Under the old law exploration of national lands was permitted at the free will of any resident of the Republic without previous permission given by any authority. This has now been changed and permission of the local mineral agent is required. He cannot, however, refuse such permission without just reason.

VII. No foreigner, whether an individual or a corporation, may now explore national lands or denounce or hold title to mining property within a zone of eighty kilometres along any line of division between the Republic and foreign countries without obtaining the special permission of the executive of the nation. This embodies with certain changes principles previously established by former laws.

It does not, however, apply to property located within eighty kilometres of the ocean or the gulf of Mexico.

VIII. Another important change is found in the creation of a new easement in favor of mining property and over adjacent property with reference to the transmission of electric power.

This easement permits the installation of subterranean or of overhead lines from the point where the electricity is produced to the mining property in which it is to be utilized, crossing intermediate tracts. It permits passage, not merely for construction and repair of such lines, but also for their protection.

No such provision was found in the old law, which, however, recognized easements of passage, of transmission of water, of drainage and of ventilation.

IX. The right of eminent domain which was formerly recognized by the old law is also amplified, permitting the construction of private railroads for the facilitation of operations; and the method of exercising the right of expropriation in all cases is provided in detail.

X. A clear and full statement as to denouncements and the method of obtaining titles to property denounced is included in the law, which in this respect is a great improvement on the former statute.

It is impossible to allude here to the less important modifications which have been made. In general it may be said that the mining law of Mexico, as the result of this revision, is a well considered and carefully drawn statute which has clarified and simplified the entire subject and opened the way to a safer and wider development of the mineral wealth of the Republic both by native and by foreign capital.

FINIS

GENERAL INDEX

[*References are to Articles, unless page is cited.*]

A

Abandoned property, disposition of, 229–231.

Abandonment: of action, 753; of denouncement of public lands, 855; of mining denouncement, 885; of work under contract, damages, 437.

Abbreviations: use forbidden, in civil status records, 158; in notarial acts, 934; in judicial pleadings, 761.

Abridgement of work, copyright, 1000.

Abrogation of law, how effected, 143.

Absence: as affecting domicile, 149; as affecting citizenship, 822–823; 825.

Absentees and unknown persons. 215–222; administration of property, 218–220; citation to in suits, 758; declaration of absence, 217; notifications to, 764; presumption of death, 221–222; provisional measures, 215; representation of absentee, 217; 757–758.

Absolver de la instancia, abolished, 24.

Absolver posiciones defined, rules, 777; special power required, 427.

Abstract: book, notarial, 933; of sales, to be kept, 1072; of mining record: See Extract.

Abuse of authority, effect on contracts, 314.

Acceptance: of bills of exchange, 672, of contract, 311; of inheritance or legacy, 524, 554; of inheritance, by creditors, 554; of mercantile commissions, 596; of partial deliveries, 437; of powers of attorney, 427.

Accession, right of: nature of right, 239; "fruits," 239, improvements, 240; crops, 240; works on own and other's land, 241; rules of bad faith, 242; liability of owner, 243; riparian accretion, 244; islands, 245; confusion of goods, 246; indemnization, 247; in cases of inheritances, 552.

Accident: as excuse to performance of contract, 342, 347; meaning of in insurance contracts, 1042.

Acclaration of judgment defined, when available, 796.

Accomplice, of bankrupt, when subject to law, 704; who is, 709.

Accounting, prescription of, 288.

Account books what books must be kept, 570; as evidence, 793; stamp tax on, p. 721; Art. 1080.

1000   INDEX.

64

— distribution, 189; final settlement, 190; separation of property, 191–192; how effected — agreements, 191; judgment of separation — effects, 192; antenuptial and postnuptial gifts, 193–194; dowry, 195; cannot sell to each other, 471; property of, in bankruptcy, 712; as witnesses, 785; responsible for acts of wife, when, 1016; prescription, 300; inheritance between, 544; share of inheritance, 549.

I

Ideas, expression of, 6–7.

Idiots: prescription, 299.

Ignorance of law, no excuse, 141; as element of negligence, 1028–1029.

Illegal contract, recovery under, 384; for impossibility, 315.

Illegitimate children; acknowledgment of, 163; civil status records, 161.

Immigrants, certificates required, 837. See Colonists.

Impeachment: of public officials, 103–107.

Impediments: to marriage, 171; dispensation of, 171; revocation of, 171; dispensation not obtainable, 172; denouncement of impediments, proceedings, 174; effect of impediments, 196.

Imports, free for colonists, 839, 845–846; of machinery for water and irrigation, 876. See Tariff.

Impossibility, in contracts, defined, 315.

Imprisonment, for debt, forbidden, 17; for crime, when, 18; bail allowed, when, 18; length of, 19.

Improvements: in case of eviction, 358; by persons in possession, 252; ownership of, 240–241; patents for, 961.

Incidental actions, defined, 753.

Income, stamp tax, p. 732.

Incompetent judge, acts void, 770.

Indemnity, in fire insurance contracts, 1043.

Indemnization of damages, defined, 1010.

Index: of civil register, must be kept daily, 158; of Notarial acts, 933; of private conveyances, 951; of Public Register, contents, 951.

Individual liability of members of company, 730.

Infractions of stamp tax law, 1104–1108.

Infringement: of copyright, 1004–1006; what is, 1004; what is not, 1005; of patents, 964.

Inheritances, stamp tax, p. 732. See Successions; order of, 544.

Injury: intentional, measure of damages, 1012; to property, measure of damages, 1012.

Innkeepers: general rules, 439; liability for damages, 1017–1018.

Insane persons, responsibility for torts, 1025.

Inscriptions: in Commercial Register, necessary, 953; in registers, form and manner, 951; extinction of, 952.

[*References are to Articles, unless page is cited.*]

Inventors, privileges to, 28.

Invoices: of sales by wholesale required, 1070–1071; of goods sold on order, stamp tax, 1073; stamp tax, p. 733.

Irrigation, concessions, 875–876.

Islands: ownership of, 245; colonization of, 844; public lands on, 850.

J

Job and piece work, acceptance and delivery, 434, 437.

Joinder of actions, 752.

Joint: actions, who may maintain, 755; authorship, copyright, 998; insurance contracts, 1042; creditors, 330–335; contract, performance, 330, 336; debts, set-off, rules, 369; debtors, release of one, 330, 335; defendants, answer, 808; liability, how discharged, 333; obligations, prescription, 302; obligations, penalties, 317; action for damages, 1024–1025; owners and debtors, prescription, as to, 287; representative, in law suits, 759; tort feasors, liability, 349.

Joint-interest. See *Mancomunidad;* prescription of, 287.

Joint-stock Company. See Partnership with Silent Partners.

Judges: of Civil Status, 156; as witnesses, 786; challenges and disqualification, 772; execution of instrument by, when party refuses, 798; must decide all questions, 794; responsibility for wrongful acts, 1022; when disqualified, 772.

Judgment: defined, 762; by default, when, 811; execution of, 798–800; final, when executive, 813; foreign, legalization, 800; hearing, notice of, 765; kinds, general rules, 794–795; legal effect, 794; registration of, 950; registry of, 795; when to be rendered, 812.

Judicial liquidation, of bankrupt estate, 744–745.

Judicial mandates, must be by *escritura pública*, 422, 426

Judicial orders: how signed, 762; for protocolization of foreign documents, 936.

Judicial papers, how written, 761.

Judicial power, 90, 108.

Judicial proceedings: lawful days, 761; on mining oppositions, 917; stamp tax, p. 734. See Costs.

Judicial records, as evidence, 791.

Judicial sales: advertisement, 798; basis of bidding, bidders and bidding, 802–803; how held, 802; of mortgaged property, extinguishes mortgages, 420; of personalty, 804; proceeds, 803; incidents of, 473.

Judicial terms: extension of, 766–768; how computed, 766.

Jurisdiction: general rules of, 770; of mining suits, 898; of Federal courts, 97–102; of Supreme Court of Justice, 98–100; of Federal Tribunals, 97, 101–102.

Jurisprudence. *ratio decidendi,* 147; when established, 820.

[*References are to Articles, unless page is cited.*]

Loans: 450–456; definition, incidents, 450; "*Commodatum*," incidents, 451; simple "*Mutuum*," incidents, 452; "*Mutuum*" with interest, 453; mercantile loans, 454–456; defined, repayment, 454; interest, 455; loans on collateral, 456; of money, stamp tax, p. 735; renewal, stamp tax on, 1085.

Location: of mining property, how made, effects, 913; rectification of, 889.

Loss: of freight or baggage, damages, 1036; of baggage check, 1039; of baggage, limit of liability, 1040; of freight, connecting carriers, 1034; of *boleta* for retail sales, 1068; of goods, measure of damages, 1036; of instruments to bearer, 691–694; of Mining Titles, 905; of object of contract, who liable, 340; of patent title papers, 980; of property, measure of damages, 1012; rules, 229–231; by person in possession, 252; of possession, 253; of subject-matter of contract, rules, 328–329, 342–343; of trademark certificate, 990.

Lost: bills of exchange, 675; records, replacing, 761; wills, how established, 506.

Losses and Damages. See *Daños y Perjuicios.*

Losses and repairs, by usufructuary, 260.

Lotteries, stamp tax, p. 736.

M

Magistrates. See Supreme Court of Justice: responsibility for crimes, 103, 107; civil responsibility, 108, 1022; compensation of, 120.

Majority, legal age, 214.

Malpractice, professional, damages for, 429.

Managers of corporation, appointment and functions, 635.

Managing partner, of civil partnership, 661.

Mancommunity. See *Mancomunidad.*

Mancomunidad (joint-interest): 330–335; defined, kinds, 330; between heirs and representatives, 331; presumption of *mancomunidad*, 332; discharge of liability, 333; contribution between debtors, 334; release of one debtor, 335; insurance contracts, 1042.

Mandato, general rules, 421–428. See Powers of Attorney.

Manifests, stamp tax, p. 736.

Manufacture, when considered as sale, 1073.

Marital license: general rules as to requirements, 177; to engage in commerce, 565.

Maritime actions, prescription, 306; zone, defined, 850.

Mark, upon patented articles, 969.

Marriage: contract, defined, 170; requisites, 170; impediments to, 171; dispensation of, in what cases permitted, 171; age of marriage, 171; consent of parents or guardian, 171; revocation of, 171; guardian and ward, 171; foreign and mixed marriages, 172; legal effects of, 172; dispensation for, 172; marriages in imminence of

[*References are to Articles, unless page is cited.*]

ments, 568–569; commissions, 595, 599; pledges, defined, incidents, 609; bookkeeping. See Bookkeeping.

Merciants, 564–569: defined, who are merciants, 564; who are competent, 565; who are not competent, 566; foreigners, commercial rigits, 567; obligations common to all merciants, 568; mercantile announcements, 569; must furnisi statements for stamp tax, 1064, 1073; must procure *boletas* for payment of stamp tax, 1068; registration of, 954. Commission. See Commission Merciants.

Meridian, of mining property, how located, 913.

Merger: of rigits, 373; of title and usufruct under mortgage, 407.

Metric system, of weigits and measures, adopted, 1109.

Mexican law: governs persons and property, 144; governs contracts and real property, 145; governs foreign marriages, 182.

Mexicans: who are, 30, 822; political rigits of, 8–9, 35; political obligations of, 31; preferences to, 32; quality as citizens, 34–37; loss of citizensiip, 37–38.

Military autiority: exercise of, 122; jurisdiction, 122, 125; law, wien applied, 13.

Minerals: contracts for exploitation, 879; encountered in mining work, 892; subject to mining denouncement, 879.

Mines: acquisition by denouncement, 882–887; stamp tax on titles, p. 744. See Mining Law.

Mining agent: appointment and qualifications, 908, 926–930; decisions reviewable by Fomento, 884; duties, 909; filing denouncement, 884; irregularities of, 930; liability for mistakes, 885; to foiward record to Fomento, 885.

Mining Concessions, registration, 950.

Mining Contracts: nature of, 894; registry of, 894; suits regarding, 898.

Mining Easements: 891–893; nature and extent of easements, 891; rules for use of easements, 892; establisiment of easements, 893; petitions for, 922.

Mining Experts: interference witi, 897; liability for mistakes, 885; resisting, 912; rejection of, new appointment, 911; report on survey, 914.

Mining Inspections, 900.

Mining Law: 879–907; scope of, 879; surface, occupation, of, 881; administrative and judicial procedure, election, 886; free land, wiat is, 882; railways, rigit to construct, 881; rigit of expropriation, 881; suspension of proceedings on denouncements, 886; suspension of works by Fomento, 900; water in workings, use of, 881; application of civil law, 879; claims defined, 880; mining rigits, extent of workings, 881; meetings, failure to attend, 885–886; explorations, rules for conducting, 899; denouncement of land released by reduction, 918; dumps, ownersiip, 881; denouncements, witidrawal of, 885; denouncements, requisites of, 910;

[*References are to Articles, unless page is cited.*]

denouncements, reduction of *pertenencias*, 888; procedure in agency, 884; filing in absence of agent, 908; conflicting, 884; by foreigners, void, w1en, 901; conflicting, w1ic1 admitted, 910; filing wit1 agent, 884. See Denouncements.

Mining plans: location of monuments on, 914; requisites of, 911, 913.

Mining Property, defined, 880.

Mining Record, time allowed for completing, 912.

Mining taxes: payment of, by w1om, 902; time for payment, 930e; fixed and annual, 930D; laws not repealed, 907.

Mining Titles: loss of, 905; delivery of, 916; effect of issuance, 885; effect of, as to t1ird persons, 887; how signed, 905; issuance of publication, 916; issuance refused, w1en, 887; registration, under new law, 894, 907; tax on, 930D, p. 744.

Minister. See Consul.

Ministerio Público: established, 96; defined and functions, 821; party in *amparo*, 818; representing absent defendants, 758.

Minors: legal disability of, 209–213; are subject to commercial prescription, 305; domicile of, 149; 1abilitation of, 214; may be merc1ants, w1en, 565; rig1t to *amparo*, 818; power of attorney to, 422, 426; prescription against, 299–300; responsibility for torts, 1025; as witnesses, 786.

Minority: incidents of, 209; effects on property rig1ts, 210.

Mints, assay and smelting services, 1117.

Minuta, of contracts, 939–940.

Minute Book, must be kept, 570; requisites of, 573.

Minutes: of companies, as evidence, 778; of contracts, requirements, 939–940; of b1okers, 581; probative effect of, 582; of corporate meetings, 639; stamp tax, pp. 722, 737; application of stamp tax on, 1062.

Misdemeanor, definition, 1028; w1en punis1able, 1029.

Mistakes: effect on contracts, 312; payment made by, recovery, 365; prescription of action for, 383; by w1om must be pleaded, 383.

Models, for patent, requ11ed, 965.

Mojoneras. See Monuments.

Momentary Associations for profit-s1aring, 610–612, 654–655.

Monastic Orders, proscribed, 5.

Money: gold standard adopted, 1115; coins, weig1t and fineness, 1116; coinage and circulation, 1117; legal currency of mone1, 1118; vit1drawal of coins, 1119; pro1ibition of tokens, 1119; regulatory fund, 1120; value of old coinage, 1120; value of *peso* in foreign moneys, 1121; 1exican and foreign, as medium of payment, 345.

Money Orders, stamp tax, p. 737.

Monopolies, forbidden, 28.

Mont1, defined, 591; year, defined, 591; how counted for presc11ptions, 304.

Monuments, mining: destruction of, 897; failu1e to erect, 907; time

[*References are to Articles, unless page is cited.*]

for erecting, 915, 907; required, 885; certificate of erection, 915; how to be placed, 915; form and requisites, 915; location of, 914.

"Moral Persons:" defined, 154; civil rights of, 155; prescription applies to, 288.

Morosidad. See Default.

Mortgages: application of insurance money, 409; assignment or transfer, 411; assumption of by creditor, 803; cancellation of, 419; cancellation, stamp tax, p. 722; certificate of encumbrances required, 416; conditions, registry, 411; defined, 407; property subject to, 407; foreclosure in case of bankruptcy, 722; second mortgages, rules, 407; stamp tax, p. 737; subsistence and maturity, 411–412; voluntary, incidents, 411; who may make, 410; when and where registered, 415; destruction of mortgaged property, 409; duty to give new mortgage, when, 407; entirety and division, rules, 408; extension and precedence, 411; extinction of, 420; general rules, 407–420; impairment of security, remedy, 409, 414; legal incidents of mortgage, 410; mortgagee cannot acquire property under, 410; must be registered, 410; necessary, when required, 412–413; necessary, failure to give, 414; never implied or general, 410; prescription of foreclosure, 410; property subject to, 410; registry necessary, rules, 415, 418; register of, 948; requisites for registry, 416; security must be increased, when, 409, 414.

Muebles, defined, 226.

Municipalities, civil responsibility for employés, 1017.

Murder, damages for, 1011.

Museum, of patent office, 973.

Music, copyright, 995, 1004.

Mutual consent, to contract, 309–311.

Mutual mistake, in contracts. 312.

Mutuum, defined, 450; simple *mutuum,* 452; *mutuum* with interest, 453.

N

National lands: defined, 848; classification repealed, 867.

Nationality, declaration of intention, 822–823.

Natural and spurious children: civil status records, 163; defined, legitimation, 206.

Naturalization: 822–831; by birth or marriage, 822–824; how affected by absence, 825; who may be naturalized, 826; application for, 826; procedure for naturalization, 827; special naturalization, 828; effects and incidents, 829, 231; of colonists, 830; obtained by fraud. 829; persons incapable of, 829.

Navigable waters. rules governing, 269, 873–874.

Navy. Department of. 139.

Necessary mortgages, by whom and when required, 412–414.

[*References are to Articles, unless page is cited.*]

Preservation: of books of merchants, 577; of corporation, 644.

President: qualifications of, 77; term of office, 78; failure to qualify, 80, 81; resignation of, 82; protest for oath of office, 83; absence from country, 84; approving and vetoing bills, 71; liability for crimes, 103, 107; civil liability, 108; may suspend constitutional guaranties, when, 29; opening speech to congress, 63; powers and duties of, 75–89; election of, 76.

Presumptions: defined, kinds and effect, 789; in favor of carrier as to loss of baggage, 1033; as evidence of fraud from non-registration, 958; of *mancomunidad*, 332; of release, from possession of evidence of debt, 380; weight of, 792; of just title, 292; of good faith, 292; respecting good and bad faith, 250; in respect to possession, 249–254; of fraudulent bankruptcy, 708; of legitimacy, 201; of death, 221; of validity of marriage, 197.

Price: must be fixed, 469; lien for purchase price, 490, 726; rules, in respect to rescission, 476, 479; *lesión* in respect to, 382, 480; of public lands, 872; what constitutes, for stamp tax, 1073.

Principal and Surety: joint action against, 396; rules of prescription, 287, 302. See Sureties.

Priority: of registered documents, 959; of purchasers' rights, 477.

Prisión, defined, 1029n.

Prisoners: extortion from, 18–19; entitled to bail, when, 18; illegal detention of, 19; mistreatment of, 19; guarantied rights of, 20; extradition of, required, 113.

Private documents: defined, 421, 778; as evidence, 782, 791; certified copies of, how taken, 783; production in evidence, 783; index of must be kept, 948, 951.

Private property, taking for public uses, 27; what minerals are, 879.

Privileges, special, prohibited, 13, 28.

Probative force of proofs, 790–793.

Procedure: code of, 751–820; defective, ground for cassation, 797.

Proceeds: of judicial sale, 803; of sale of public lands, 867, XIV.

Pro confesso, no evidence *contra*, 790.

Procurador. See Attorneys; appearance in suit, 757; *de Justicia*, functions, 821; who cannot act as, 426.

Production: of documents, ordered, 769; of object before suit, 774; of books and papers, 576, 783.

Professional services, fees, 429 434–436.

Professions: exercise of, 3; choice of, 4; regulation of, 4.

Promissory notes: definition and requisites, 685. See Negotiable Instruments.

Promise of sale, of mining property, 894; stamp tax, p. 740.

Promulgation of laws, when effective, 142; no retroactive effect, 143.

Proofs: general rules, 776–793; account books, 793; kinds recognized by law, 776; notice of taking, 776; nullity of, 776; of facts and law, 776; of negative, 776; out of time, void, 776; probative

of attorney, 426; of acts in excess of powers, 427.

Ratio decidendi, 147, 794.

Reading: notarial acts to parties, 934; void if omitted, 944.

Real property: defined, 224; governed by Mexican laws, 144; form of contracts concerning, law governing, 145; ineffective unless registered, 948, 958; wiere registered, 948; real rigits and actions, wien prescribed, 291; acquisition of by foreigners, 30, 832; description in notarial acts, 934; form and registry of contract respecting, 472; how delivered, 362; instruments affecting registration, 950, 955; judicial sale of, 802; naturalization by acquisition of, 30, 822; register of conveyances, 948; rigit of corporation and religious orders to 1old, 27; compensation for expropriation, 27; sales of "more or less," 476.

Rebates: by railroads proiibited, penalty, 1029a; to possessors of public lands, 857; to smelters wien, 930a.

Receipts: must be issued, wien, 1088; for retail sales, 1066; stamp tax, p. 741.

Receiver (*interventor*), in bankruptcy, appointment and duties, 735–736; under *sequestro*, 801.

Reciprocal obligations, performance, 342.

Reciprocity: of copyrigit, 1009; international, concerning execution of judgments, 800; rigits of litigants, 810.

Recognition of legitimacy, 204.

Recompenses, for public services, 12–13.

Records: of civil status, required to be kept, 156; records as evidence, 157, 159; certified copies, to be issued, 159; lost or mutilated, 157; of non-resident Mexicans, 159; of mining denouncement, contents, 884; judicial, as evidence, 791; public, as evidence, 778; Commercial Register is public, 960; of birti, See Birti Records; of Deati, See Deati Records; of Marriage, See Marriage Records.

Recourses, after judgment, wiat are, 796–797.

Recovery: of payments made by mistake, 365; of property wrongfully taken, 1010; of property wrongfully transferred, 344.

Rectification, of civil status records, 168; of mining *pertenencias*, 889, 919, 921.

Recursos, wiat are, 796.

Recusación, special power required for, 427.

Redemption, of property under *retroventa*, 485.

Re-drafts, defined, rules, 684.

Reduction of mining denouncements and *pertenencias*, 888, 918–921.

Re-exciange, defined, rules, 684.

Refund: of fees by Mining Agent, 930; of stamp tax, 1092.

Refusal: of legacies, 524; to acknowledge signature, 774; to perform judgment, 798; to sign contract, effects, 939–940.

[*References are to Articles, unless page is cited.*]

Registers: the Public Register, 948–952; as evidence, 778; must contain wiat, 951; of brokers, 581; probative effects of, 582; of civil status: See Civil Status; of mining denouncements, to be kept, 909; of explorations, 909; of stock, corporation must keep, 632; of valuables, by innkeepers, 1018; parochial, as evidence, 791. See Commercial Register.

Register, Grand. See Grand Register of Property, 859–863.

Registration: wiat must be registered, 950, 954; manner of making, 951; correcting record, 961; effects of, 951, 959; effects of failure to register, 948, 958; in Grand Register of Property, 860–861; may be required by wiom, 958; of foreign instruments. wien required, 949; of property, tax on, 863; priorities, 959; requisites of, 948; wien effective, 959; double registry, 955; how made in Commercial Register, 957; of corporation in Commercial Register, 612; 953–954; of contracts of purciase and sale, 472; of foreign companies, 956–957; of marriage settlements, 418; of mining contracts, 894; of mortgages, duties of registrar, 417; of mortgage, wien and wiere registered, 415; of mortgages, requisites of registry, 416–417; of trademarks, 990; costs of, by wiom paid. 469; stamp tax, p. 742. See Public Register; Commercial Register; Mortgages.

Regulation, of railroad rates, 1029a.

Regulatory fund, for circulation, 1120.

Rehabilitation of bankrupt, 720.

Re-incidence, in violation of stamp law, 1108.

Re-insurance, liability, 1054.

Relationsiip: lines and degrees of, 169; computation of impediment to marriage, 171; disqualifies experts, 785; judges. 772; notaries, 932; witnesses, 786.

Release: of debtor, rules, 380; of joint debtor, effects, 335; of surety, 380, 396, 400; stamp tax, p. 742.

Religion: regulation of worsiip, 123.

Religious orders: proscribed, 5; rigit to iold real estate, 27.

Remainder, creation of by will, forbidden, 527.

Remission, of indebtedness, stamp tax, p. 742.

Renewal of debt, effect on commercial prescription, 305.

Renouncements: in notarial acts, 934; of allegiance and protection, 826; of damages for breaci of warranty, 356; of *órden, excusión* and *división*, 395–396; of responsibility for fraud, 347; of rigits. to prejudice of creditors, 380; of laws, 143; of inieritances, 554; of rigits and actions, 755. See Waivers.

Rent: obligation of payment, 492–493; effect of fire or destruction of leased premises, 494; wien prescribed, 296.

Repairs: by usufructuary, 260; duty of lessor to make, 492, 494; lien for, 726.

Reparation of injury, defined, 1010.

S

[References are to Articles, unless page is cited.]

Timber lands, public exploitation of, 851, 869.

Time: for prescription, computation of, 304; for performance of commercial contracts, 590; computation of, 591; and manner, of contesting legitimacy, 202; computation of, under mining law, 903; for exercising certain judicial acts, 766–768; for Judicial acts, how computed, 766; in contracts, computation, 325.

Title papers: delivery of, on sale, 475; requiring exhibition of, in suit, 744.

Titles and diplomas, stamp tax on, p. 744.

Titles: of public lands, validity of, 864; of property, when passes, 341; professional, 3; of nobility, 12; what may be accepted, 37.

Título. See Mining Titles.

Token money, prohibited, 1119.

Torts: civil responsibility for. See Damages; judgment for, not subject to set-off, 368.

Town lands, distribution of, 866.

Trade, restraint of, forbidden, 28.

Trademarks, Names and Advertisements, 981–993c. Industrial and Commercial Trademarks, 981–985: defined, what may be registered, 981; who may obtain, how registered, 982; issuance of trademarks, effects, 983; assignment, effects, 984; nullity, actions, 985. Trade Names and Advertisements, 986–988: trade names, incidents, 986; commercial advertisements, 987; revenue taxes, 988. Regulations of Trademark Law, 989–993; applications, requisites, 989; registry, certificates, 990; transfer, renewals, 991; advertisements, registry, 992; sundry provisions, 993. Regulations for International Trademarks, 993a–993c; requirements for registration, 993a; registry, notices, publications, 993b; changes, nullity, 993c.

Transfer: of property, special power required for, 427; of business, application of stamp tax, 1069, 1073; of business, announcements, 569; of encumbered property, application of stamp tax, 1073; of personal property, application of stamp tax, 1073.

Transient plaintiff, *arraigo*, 810.

Translator as author, 1009.

Translations: copyright, 999; of foreign documents, in evidence, 936; of foreign documents, for protocolization, 936.

Transmission, of actions for damages, 1023; of power, mining easement of, 891.

Transportation: duty of carrier, 1030; insurance of, 1049, 1058; contracts for, prescription, 306.

Traslado, dar or *correr*, meaning, 761.

Travel and residence in Mexico, right of, 11.

Traveling salesmen: general rules, 602; sales by, application of stamp tax, 1073.

Treasure Trove, rules regarding, 238.

Treaties, for extradition, 15; power to make, 72b.

Trees, restrictions on planting, 276; concessions to colonists for planting, 838.

Trials: in criminal cases, 20; number of instances, 24; no second trial, 241; to be public, 769.

Tribunals, special, forbidden, 13.

Trustees, in bankruptcy. See Sindics; See Corporate Bond Law.

Trusts and Trustees, under wills, 527.

Tunnels, in mining properties, 891.

U

Undue influence, effect on contracts, 314; on wills, 510–511.

Unilateral contract, defined, 307.

Use and occupancy, rules, 264–265.

User of patent, rules, 967–968.

Unknown parties, summons to, 764. See Absentees and Unknown Persons.

Units: of weights and measures, 1109–1114; of coinage, 1116.

Universal partnerships, defined, incidents, 658.

Unstamped documents: revalidation, 1097–1099; as evidence, 1099.

Usufruct: definitions, 255; how created, 255; legal incidents of, 256; rights of usufructuary, 257; exercise of rights, 258; obligations of, 259; losses and repairs, 260; taxes and charges, 261; extinction of usufructs, 262; impediments to use, 263; mortgage of, 407; of public lands, when, 871.

V

Validation of unstamped documents: general rules, 1097–1099. See note to Art. 1059; of foreign documents, 1090. See Revalidation.

Validity of contracts: four requisites, 309; cannot be left to discretion of party, 308; of notarial acts, 935, 944.

Valuables, register of by innkeeper, 1018.

Values: actual and estimative, as damages, 1012; of contract, how estimated, 318; rules for assessing, 349; how determined for stamp tax, 1062a, 1088, 1092.

Vara, defined, 1111; equivalents, 1126.

Vendor of real estate, may require mortgage for unpaid purchase price, 413; obligations of delivery and warranty, 475–477.

Ventilation, mining casement of, 891.

Veto power, 71.

Vice-President: liability for crimes, 103–107; civil liability, 108; term of office, 78; election of, 79; is president of senate, 79; succession to presidency, 80; failure to quality, 81; resignation, 82; oath of office, 83; absence from country, 84.

66

INDEX OF THE PRINCIPAL ARTICLES
ENUMERATED IN THE TARIFF.

1043